12/14

GOD WILLS IT

GOD WILLS IT

Presidents and the Political Use of Religion

DAVID O'CONNELL

Transaction Publishers

New Brunswick (U.S.A.) and London (U.K.)

Library of Congress Catalog Number: 2014010853
ISBN: 978-1-4128-5486-3
Printed in the United States of America

Library of Congress Cataloging-in-Publication Data

O'Connell, David.
  God wills it : presidents and the political use of religion / David O'Connell.
       pages cm
  Includes bibliographical references.
  ISBN 978-1-4128-5486-3
  1. Presidents—United States—Religion. I. Title.
  BR516.O43 2014
  973.92092'2—dc23

                                            2014010853

To Mom and Dad

In all toil there is profit, but mere talk leads only to poverty.
—Proverbs 14:23

Contents

List of Illustrations

List of Tables

Preface

How have American presidents used religious rhetoric? Has it helped them achieve their goals? Why or why not? These are the main questions this book tries to answer.

I argue that there are two basic types of presidential religious rhetoric, each of which represents a fundamental property of religion itself. Communitarian religious rhetoric draws on religion's integrative function. By making use of broad, nondescript spiritual language, a president can help bring the American people closer together.

Coalitional religious rhetoric speaks instead to religion's power to divide. It is often sectarian, and is always tied to a strategic goal. When a president embraces coalitional religious rhetoric, he is hoping to persuade just enough people with his words in order to achieve his political objective.

I focus my study on the latter type. I propose a strict set of rules to identify when coalitional religious rhetoric has appeared and to gauge its possible impact. I find that presidents limit their use of such language to those areas where it seems natural—foreign policy, environmental policy, civil rights, and scandals. The case study chapters explore the religious rhetoric presidents have used in each of these areas.

The limited number of cases yields an interesting finding: presidents do not often make religious arguments for their goals. Two presidents, Truman and Nixon, never used a religious rhetorical strategy. It appears that whether due to personal taste or political complications, absent a crisis, almost all presidents are uncomfortable using religious rhetoric.

The main finding of this book is that religious rhetoric is not helpful to a goal-oriented president. Consistently, public opinion does not respond to the president's religious pleas, the media reacts critically to his ideas and his language, and the reception of his proposals in Congress disappoints.

An experimental chapter explores the causal dynamics behind this finding. Treatments were designed to mimic how religious rhetoric has historically been used. The results of the experiment call into question the persuasiveness of religious rhetoric. Exposure to a religious argument has no effect on an individual's opinion.

The religious dimensions of presidential leadership have been a constant throughout history. This book furthers our understanding of an important subject. It displaces the results of an earlier study of presidential religious rhetoric that claimed such language had a powerful strategic force to it. It also builds upon a growing body of research that questions the impact of any type of presidential speech. It is valuable for anyone interested in either the challenges of presidential power or the role that religion plays in contemporary American politics.

I owe debts of gratitude to many individuals who played important roles in the development of this book. I greatly appreciate having had the opportunity to work with Transaction Publishers. Tom Langston was an enthusiastic early supporter. He understood what I was trying to accomplish, and his feedback was immensely helpful as I began to restructure the manuscript. The comments of the anonymous reviewer were most appreciated as well. He or she thankfully pushed me to improve the quality of my writing, in addition to forcing me to take more seriously the theoretical underpinnings of the study.

This project began with my graduate work at Columbia University. As such, special thanks is due to Ira Katznelson. Ira has been a fantastic mentor. I have never once disagreed with any criticism he has made of my work. Not a single one. It is humbling to know that, fifty years from now, I still won't be half the scholar that Ira is. But I do know that I am certainly a better researcher than I ever could have been without his guidance.

A series of other individuals at Columbia deserve to be mentioned. Fred Harris's understanding of religion helped develop my own. Shigeo Hirano first encouraged me to explore the subject of presidential religious rhetoric, and our conversations helped to crystallize the ultimate methods I chose to use in doing so. Bob Shapiro was kind enough to provide some feedback on the questionnaire design, in addition to some broader reactions he had, which, I believe, substantially improved the case studies. Alissa Stollwerk and Stephen Thompson provided much needed assistance with the statistical work found in the experimental chapter.

Four Columbia students—Robyn Silverman, Yael Munishor, Shane Strumwasser, and Jon Weibel—helped by pretesting the questionnaires. Finally, Justin Phillips, Bernard Tamas, and Dorian Warren graciously gave up class time to allow me to administer the experiment. I owe an even further debt of gratitude to Justin for his professional guidance as I began the publication process.

Jamie Druckman was also an important part of the project. Jamie took time out of his many responsibilities to offer detailed and sincere advice to a stranger working halfway across the country. The final design of the experiment is greatly informed by Jamie's input. Jamie represents the ideal of what we mean when we talk about a community of scholars.

On a personal note, I'd like to offer a special word of thanks to my best friend, Charles Wolf. I've talked more with Charles about this project than I have with anyone else. I trust Charles's opinion—on pretty much everything—more than the opinion of anyone else in the world. I couldn't have written this book without his friendship.

My biggest thanks goes to my parents, Dan and Kathy. My parents have taken a sincere interest in the course of my research. They have encouraged me at every step of the way. They understood when I needed to write over vacations and over holidays. The easiest decision I've made about this project was to dedicate it to them.

And, finally, I thank John Miller, who asked why I wanted to go to law school in the first place.

Introduction

By September 20, 2001 the American people had heard from President Bush on a number of occasions since the September 11 terrorist attacks. All of those earlier speeches had aimed to provide comfort, not to outline the Administration's foreign policy response. This evening, in an address before a joint session of Congress, Bush would begin the transition.

While waiting for British Prime Minister Tony Blair to arrive at the White House, Bush took a brief nap. Blair and Bush then met alone in the Blue Room for around twenty minutes as the president reviewed the country's developing military plans. Knowing the importance of the address Bush would shortly deliver, Blair was stunned by his counterpart's preternatural calm. "You don't seem the least bit concerned or nervous. Don't you need some time alone?" Blair asked. Bush answered, "I know exactly what I need to say, and how to say it, and what to do" (Woodward 2002, 107).

Before an audience of over 80 million Americans, on this night, Bush gave one of the best speeches of his presidency (Bush 2001a). He began the heart of his address by identifying the enemy, Al-Qaeda, "a collection of loosely affiliated terrorist organizations" that "practice a fringe form of Islamic extremism that has been rejected by Muslim scholars and the vast majority of Muslim clerics." He demanded that Afghanistan's ruling Taliban regime surrender all Al-Qaeda members living in their country and that the government forcibly close their training camps. He preached tolerance for members of the Muslim faith. He pleaded with Americans to grant him their patience for a prolonged struggle. Yet, it was Bush's closing lines that were most exceptional:

> Great harm has been done to us. We have suffered great loss. And in our grief and anger, we have found our mission and our moment. Freedom and fear are at war. The advance of human freedom, the great achievement of our time and the great hope of every time, now

depends on us. Our Nation—this generation—will lift a dark threat of violence from our people and our future . . .

The course of this conflict is not known, yet its outcome is certain. Freedom and fear, justice and cruelty have always been at war, and we know that God is not neutral between them.

Fellow citizens, we'll meet violence with patient justice, assured of the rightness of our cause and confident of the victories to come. In all that lies before us, may God grant us wisdom, and may He watch over the United States of America.

These last lines, combining overt invocations of God with a more subtly charged religious vocabulary (i.e., "mission," "patient justice"), were not the only spiritual references to be found in the body of the text. Bush claimed that the terrorists' main goal was "to kill Christians and Jews." He explicitly told the public that they should pray because "Prayer has comforted us in sorrow and will help strengthen us for the journey ahead." The president even went to some lengths to integrate the concepts of patriotism and faith, visible in lines such as: "We've seen the unfurling of flags, the lighting of candles, the giving of blood, the saying of prayers in English, Hebrew, and Arabic" (Riswold 2004, 41). Perhaps, it is more than a coincidence that the military operation announced shortly afterward was originally code-named "Infinite Justice," a phrase with strong religious connotations for Christians who believe that God will ultimately judge both the living and the dead (see, for instance, Matthew 25:31–33).

Whether because of its religious tenor or in spite of it, the reaction to Bush's address was overwhelmingly positive. The *New York Times* reported that "tremendous public support for the president was reflected in the warmth of the reception he received on Capitol Hill." The paper admired how "Mr. Bush rose to the occasion, finding at times the eloquence that has eluded him so often in the past" (Apple 2001). In a surreal scene in Philadelphia, fans at a Flyers-Rangers exhibition game demanded that play be stopped so that they could watch the speech on the arena's Jumbotron. The third period was delayed for over thirty-three minutes as players and fans viewed the broadcast from their seats. When the president finished, the teams engaged in an impromptu handshake line and then cancelled the rest of the game, declaring it a tie (Diamos 2001). From a boisterous restaurant in Longmont, Colorado, Cyndi Morris captured the feelings of many of her fellow citizens when she told a newspaper, "I believe God has sent us an ark in Bush. We're all going to get through this together, side by side. I feel a lot better after hearing him" (McFadden 2001).

God is not neutral. Those are stunning words. And yet, it was with this coda that Bush introduced a line of argument he would repeatedly return to over the course of his two terms: God supported America's mission in the world. God is not neutral.

This style of religious rhetoric became more controversial as time passed. Just consider some of the angry reactions Bush's language provoked from writers, scholars, and ordinary citizens alike:

> It is remarkable how closely Bush's discourse coincides with that of the false prophets of the Old Testament. While the true prophets proclaimed the sovereignty of Yahweh, the God of justice and love who judges nations and persons, the false prophets served Baal, who could be manipulated by the power. Karl Marx concluded that religion is "the opium of the people" . . . How paradoxical, and how sad, that the President of the United States, with his heretical manipulation of religious language, insists on proving Karl Marx right. (Juan Stam, *The Nation*, December 22, 2003)

> Many parishioners at my small, inside-the-Beltway church, by contrast, do not view themselves or the nation in such a saintly light . . . And Bush's increasingly religious justification for the war with Iraq is disturbing, even frightening, to many. "It bothers me that he wraps himself in a cloak of Christianity," said Lois Elieff. "It's not my idea of Christianity." To them, Bush's use of religious language sounds shallow and far more self-justifying than that of other recent political leaders—including Bush's father. (Rev. Fritz Ritsch, *Washington Post*, March 2, 2003)

> That a president invokes the Almighty should no longer surprise us. But the danger of invoking God for any political or military purpose is the presumption that he is on our side. The lesson of history is that no individual or nation is exempt from Divine judgment. (Kenneth Woodward, *Newsweek*, March 10, 2003)

> Dubious at the time, the God's-on-our-side rhetoric is looking even less credible now, after more than a year of frequently bad news for the president and his administration. Therein lies a lesson our political leaders would do well to remember the next time they're tempted to invoke God for partisan politics, whether the cause is liberal or conservative, Democratic or Republican. Be careful, lest unfolding events make you and your pious claims look downright foolish. (Tom Krattenmaker, *USA Today*, January 29, 2006)

> When we do look closely at Bush's religious rhetoric, we discern anti-democratic features discouraging deliberation and dissent, as

well as persistent opacity in its religious claims . . . these overlapping objections provide good grounds to conclude that Bush's particular type of religious discourse is ethically dubious in ways that many other forms of public religious expression are not. (Rogers Smith, *Political Theory*, April 2008)

Let me be clear, the inclusion of this commentary is not meant to imply any type condemnation of Bush's rhetoric. I wish to avoid making such normative judgments. What this section is meant to illustrate is the importance of studying presidential religious rhetoric in the first place. All of the individuals above are concerned because they presume that religious rhetoric *matters*, that it has some type of powerful credibility with the public. But that question has not been definitively answered yet.

It is essential to recognize, though, that there was nothing unique about Bush's religious rhetoric or the handwringing that accompanied it. History is littered with presidents who claimed divine sanction for their agendas. In fact, the country's first president, George Washington, voiced sentiments similar to those offered over two centuries later by Bush.

One of Washington's major projects was to construct a virtuous national character. Like many of the prominent thinkers of his time, Washington believed that a good government first required good self-governance. The experience of the states under the Articles of Confederation had convinced him that a political system could be undermined by individual selfishness. No matter how much the structural condition of the country would be improved by the Constitution, Washington believed the need for sound morals remained (Spalding 1999).

One of the ways Washington tried to incubate these values was by the use of religious rhetoric. In his inaugural address, Washington reminded his countrymen that "No people can be bound to acknowledge and adore the Invisible Hand which conducts the affairs of men more than those of the United States. Every step by which they have advanced to the character of an independent nation seems to have been distinguished by some token of providential agency." As such, Washington warned that "we ought to be no less persuaded that the propitious smiles of Heaven can never be expected on a nation that disregards the eternal rules of order and right which Heaven itself has ordained" (Washington 1789).

The first president acted as if he believed this to be true. As Commander-in-Chief, Washington required his soldiers to attend Sunday services and he ordered that ceremonies be held on a variety of days of prayer and thanksgiving. Washington said that, by their proper observances, the army might "incline the Lord and Giver of Victory, to prosper our arms" (Smith 2006, 45). In his farewell address, remembered more for its admonition against entangling foreign alliances, Washington made a final plea for the importance of good behavior to America's future: "Of all the dispositions and habits which lead to political prosperity, religion and morality are indispensable supports. In vain would that man claim the tribute of patriotism who should labor to subvert these great pillars of human happiness—these firmest props of the duties of men and citizens. The mere politician, equally with the pious man, ought to respect and to cherish them" (Washington 1796). The old general was trying to encourage moral responsibility. Religious rhetoric, talk of "the propitious smiles of Heaven" and the "Giver of Victory," was his means of doing so.

Another of America's most revered leaders, Abraham Lincoln, turned to religious rhetoric in support of his civil war goals. The war had not gone well for the Union in 1864. Confederate troops once more threatened Washington in July. Morale sagged to its lowest point in the entire conflict as many influential Northerners began to speak of a settlement, even if it meant the Confederacy remained independent (McPherson 2008, 209–63).

Sherman's capture of Atlanta and Sheridan's victories in the Shenandoah Valley secured the president's re-election, but they did not end the war. Lincoln's second inaugural, the third shortest and most tragically beautiful on record, sought to explain to the public why the war still had to continue—because it was all part of God's plan:

> The Almighty has His own purposes. "Woe unto the world because of offenses; for it must needs be that offenses come, but woe to that man by whom the offense cometh." If we shall suppose that American slavery is one of those offenses which, in the providence of God, must needs come, but which, having continued through His appointed time, He now wills to remove, and that He gives to both North and South this terrible war as the woe due to those by whom the offense came, shall we discern therein any departure from those divine attributes which the believers in a living God always ascribe to Him? Fondly do we hope, fervently do we pray, that this mighty scourge of war may speedily pass away. Yet, if God wills that it continue until

all the wealth piled by the bondsman's two hundred and fifty years of unrequited toil shall be sunk, and until every drop of blood drawn with the lash shall be paid by another drawn with the sword, as was said three thousand years ago, so still it must be said "the judgments of the Lord are true and righteous altogether."

With malice toward none, with charity for all, with firmness in the right as God gives us to see the right, let us strive on to finish the work we are in, to bind up the nation's wounds, to care for him who shall have borne the battle and for his widow and his orphan, to do all which may achieve and cherish a just and lasting peace among ourselves and with all nations. (Lincoln 1865)

Over the course of his address, Lincoln quoted or paraphrased no less than four separate Biblical verses. His rhetoric was well-chosen. The Civil War armies were the most religious armies in all of American history. Many soldiers carried pocket Bibles with them into battle. So many, in fact, that legends grew about soldiers who were saved from an incoming bullet by their well-placed Bible, their "holy shield" of protection (White 2002).

Lincoln's rhetoric was also strategic, though. In-depth research on the development of the Second Inaugural provides ample evidence that political considerations influenced Lincoln's words and actions (Tackach 2002). At heart, the speech was an appeal to the North to practice what they preach and to forgive their Southern brothers. Christian ethics were being used to accomplish a secular end (Morel 2000, 163–210).

It may surprise some that Jefferson also was not above, in the words of Garry Wills (1990, 372), using "religion as a political weapon." Jefferson was a problematic religious spokesman. The third president rejected Christ's divinity, virgin birth, and resurrection. He thought Christ was a good man who had merely been caught up in the enthusiasm that surrounded him. Jefferson wrote in 1787 that Jesus was "a man of illegitimate birth, of a benevolent heart, enthusiastic mind, who set out without pretensions to divinity, ended in believing them, and was punished capitally for sedition" (357). Jefferson drafted his own version of the Bible by excising all the supernatural and prophetic verses, keeping only those he considered the best expressions of Christ's moral teachings. The remainder of the Good Book was filled, Jefferson said, with "gross effects and palpable falsehoods" (Smith 2006, 55–69).

But despite accusations of atheism, Jefferson would from time to time employ religious rhetoric as he advocated for the separation of church and state. In Virginia, Jefferson was known to refer to one Biblical verse, in particular, Matthew 16:18: "And I tell you, you are Peter, and on this rock I will build my church, and the gates of Hades will not prevail against it" (Wills 1990, 368). To those that felt religion would fail without state support, Jefferson responded that Christ had already precluded that possibility.

Washington, Lincoln, and Jefferson are titans of presidential history. Each is considered among the country's most skilled and effective leaders. All of them used religious rhetoric because it served their political needs, whether that meant strengthening the moral character of the American people, encouraging reconciliation between Civil War combatants, or convincing people of the merits of a separation of church and state. The continuity of religious rhetoric in presidential governance, when combined with its inherently controversial nature, makes it imperative that we fully understand the role it plays in US politics.

Franklin Roosevelt once said the presidency was "preeminently a place for moral leadership." And over three decades ago, James David Fairbanks (1981) called upon researchers to consider the implications of the president's "priestly functions" on his leadership possibilities. This call has gone mostly unanswered. I hope to help change that.

What This Book Can Offer

These tales are just the tip of the iceberg. In this book, the reader will encounter countless examples of presidents delivering jeremiads, quoting Scripture, reciting the Golden Rule, creating martyrs for their causes, capitalizing on the proximity of religious holidays, referring to just war theory, calling for days of prayer, and discussing the importance of mercy, forgiveness, brotherhood, and more.

Hence, one of the reasons this book is of interest is for the intrinsic value of being made aware of the myriad ways that presidents have used religious talk for their own gain. Clinton's famous "I Have Sinned" speech takes on a new dimension when one learns that the Psalm Clinton chose to cite fittingly laments King David's affair with the wife of Uriah (2 Samuel 11–12). One gains a greater appreciation for George W. Bush's religious language when one sees the extraordinary discipline that marked his speech. Bush voiced the same two religious themes about the War on Terror until the last day of his presidency. And there's a certain shock to be had when one encounters a president like Ronald Reagan saying "the Scriptures are on our side in this"; or a president such as Lyndon Johnson warning "Believe me, God is not mocked."

But this book offers more than this benefit alone. I also introduce a new framework for understanding presidential religious rhetoric. This framework is based on the simple premise that religion can both unite and divide, it can both integrate and alienate. If religion is capable of producing each type of effect—of bringing people together or drawing them apart—then our understanding of religious rhetoric must reflect this truth.

One form of religious rhetoric I label communitarian. This term is meant to capture those bland, nondescript religious phrases employed by all presidents as a means of binding the American people together.

The other form of religious rhetoric is far more interesting. Coalitional religious rhetoric is used by goal-oriented presidents trying to strategically accomplish their agendas. It is overt and sectarian. Although there are a lot of potential reasons why presidents choose to talk the way they do (Hart 2002), coalitional religious rhetoric is about winning—nothing more, and nothing less. Ultimately, Jimmy Carter did not use religious rhetoric because he taught Sunday school. He used religious rhetoric because his pollster told him that spiritual words would be a persuasive way of selling his energy policies to the country.

Thus, the perspective of this book is that, when a president uses religious language as a means of shaping the discussion about a particular policy, he is making a strategic choice. He has calculated that this particular kind of claim can improve his odds of getting what he wants. When has this choice been made? Has it worked? Why? These are the questions that I attempt to answer.

These are important questions. It seems clear that religious rhetoric is effective as an electoral strategy (Domke and Coe 2008; Chapp 2012). GOP candidates, in particular, have been shown to have success using coded religious language as a way to signal their affiliation with white evangelical voters. These rhetorical cues are meant to go undetected by the wider public, thus allowing Republican politicians to avoid antagonizing other group members. An example would be a reference to a Biblical parable involving a stray lamb (Matthew 18:12–13). This style of communication can influence the political behavior of evangelicals who catch the meaning (Calfano and Djupe 2009).

Nevertheless, I am not interested in the *electoral* role of religious rhetoric. I am interested in the *executive* role of religious rhetoric—how religious rhetoric can help a president carry out his political objectives.

Or not. This is a study of the challenges of presidential power (Neustadt 1960). This may be the more important question, too, given the literature that questions the impact of campaigns on election outcomes (see, i.e., Lazarsfeld, Berelson, and Gaudet 1944; Campbell et al. 1960; Key and Cummings 1966; Fiorina 1981; Finkel 1993).

I use an approach that I contend melds together the positive attributes of the two main schools of research on presidential rhetoric. On the one hand, many scholars have embraced the descriptive tasks involved in explaining the communication strategies different presidents use (i.e., Medhurst 1993, 2006; Kiewe 1994; Peterson 2004; Aune and Rigsby 2005; Chernus 2008).

On the other hand, another side of presidential rhetoric research has been more quantitative and abstract. Such works focus more on assessing the consequences of presidential language (i.e., Cohen 1995, 2010; Hill 1998; Lim 2008).

I try to do both. Thoughtful and insightful dissections of presidential speech are matched with an original experimental test of religious rhetoric. The case list I generate is comprehensive; it includes every use of a religious rhetorical strategy that can be identified in the postwar period. Every case that is included is included for one simple reason—that it met the requirements of a theoretically driven set of criteria that had been spelled out in advance. Likewise, I determine effectiveness on the basis of another set of carefully considered rules. These procedures are spelled out in detail in the following chapter.

Even more than that, the case studies are then used to design the experiment so that it mirrors how religious rhetoric has been employed throughout history. The issues where religious rhetoric is tested are the issues on which presidents have actually made religious appeals. My approach provides greater leverage than either method could on its own.

A final strength of this book is that I pay an unusual amount of attention to what the president says in minor speeches. Most work on presidential rhetoric, whether qualitative or quantitative, concentrates on major speeches. I focus on major speeches, too. But I do not ignore what the president says to smaller audiences. We know that these day-to-day communications have become a fundamental part of every president's leadership strategy (Kernell 1997). Minor speeches merit more attention than they have been given.

By means of the case studies and the experiment, I will document four major findings about presidential religious rhetoric.

Presidents Use Religious Rhetoric Less Than You Might Think

It is likely safe to say that *a priori* most readers would expect Richard Nixon to be one of the foremost practitioners of the strategic use of religious rhetoric. Despite his extensive and even moderately successful efforts at image rehabilitation post presidency, Nixon is still, by and large, viewed as a master of the dark arts of politics.

However, Nixon did not try to divide Americans through the use of religious rhetoric. On the basis of the rules presented in Chapter 1, Nixon undertook eleven major policy initiatives during his six years in office. This is a reasonable amount of domestic activity for a president who admittedly preferred to devote his time to foreign affairs (Small 1999, 156). Yet, on not one of these polices did Nixon ever use what we would classify as a religious rhetorical strategy.

In a different way, Harry Truman is an equal surprise. Truman had a large agenda (eighteen initiatives) and was additionally a Godly man. Yet, he, too, did not make concerted use of coalitional religious rhetoric.

Although every postwar president besides Nixon and Truman has at one time or another adopted a religious rhetorical strategy, no president has done so more than once. By this study's count, the postwar presidents, collectively, had 144 major objectives that they tried to achieve. But religious rhetoric was the chosen means of argument in just nine of these cases. This is a surprisingly small amount of religious talk.

The answer to this puzzle is that most presidents are reluctant to exploit religion. Before an audience of magazine publishers in July 1990, George H. W. Bush admitted his discomfort when it came to religious discussions: "I'll make you a slight confession: I still am trying to find the appropriate way to discuss, using the bully pulpit of the White House, these matters you talk about—talking about religious values, family values, or whatever. I think there is a danger that one can overdo it . . ." (Bush 1990a). Carter denied that he was the country's spiritual leader: "Well, my own religious faith is one that's much more personal . . . I don't consider myself to be the spiritual leader of this country. I'm the political leader" (Carter 1978b). As the first Catholic president in a country that still was marked by substantial anti-Catholic bigotry, John F. Kennedy, too, was better served downplaying his faith. Even other presidents with more comfortable religious identities have had reason to be cautious. A president like Bush, widely recognized and even admired for his faith, had to be careful to not abuse that image.

At the same time, presidents are likely reacting to what Stephen Carter (1993) has called America's "culture of disbelief." American political society treats religion suspiciously. It is acceptable to participate in religious activities as a hobby, but those who turn to religion to guide or justify their behavior are often treated as irrational. Only zealots do such things. So, when a president claims God's support, it is an inherently risky move.

Religious Rhetoric Is a "Hail Mary" Strategy

Not coincidentally, an additional pattern that emerges from the historical case studies is that religious rhetoric is a tool of the desperate. The existence of a crisis appears to be enough to force many a president to overcome his reluctance to use religious rhetorical themes. In a number of the cases, including Carter's campaign for energy legislation and Clinton's appeals to retire the Monica Lewinsky scandal, religious rhetoric marks a change in approach, turned to after other arguments have failed and the president's position has deteriorated. In another group, such as George H. W. Bush's mobilization of the country prior to the Gulf War, religion is embraced only when the president's drive has stalled and his goals are in unexpected jeopardy. In others, such as Gerald Ford's defense of the Nixon pardon and Johnson's campaign for the Civil Rights Act, an untested new president immediately finds himself backed against a wall and turns to religion as a way out of a threatening situation. And, in others, such as Kennedy's turn to a religious frame for civil rights following the violence in Birmingham, scary conditions on the ground added new urgency to the president's agenda. The common thread for all of these cases is crisis. It is when opinion is falling, when a presidency is threatened, when the country's fate seems to rest on the resolution of a problem that we see religious rhetoric appear.

Religious Rhetoric Is Used on a Narrow Set of Issues

Using religious rhetoric to push a tax cut might be misguided. Similarly, how is religion relevant to free trade or education or highway construction? It is conceivable that it is too big a leap for a president to try to make such a connection. So they do not. Another finding of this study is that presidents are not very creative when it comes to constructing religious rationales. In fact, they use religious rhetoric only on objectives that fall in four broad issue areas: foreign policy, environmental policy, civil rights, and presidential scandals.

The linkage between religious rhetoric and foreign policy intuitively makes sense. Americans have long believed that America has a special role in the world. Dating to the Puritans, Americans have thought they are a chosen people with whom God has made a binding covenant, just as he had done with Israel, Noah, or Abraham (Morone 2003, 34–54). These beliefs have not waned over time; in a recent national survey, 58 percent of Americans either "mostly" or "completely" agreed with the statement "God has granted America a special role in human history" (Public Religion Research Institute 2010).

The connection between religion and the environment can also be easily understood. For many, it is common to see the wonders of nature as gifts from God (Fowler 1995).

Religious rhetoric is equally appropriate when it comes to civil rights. A good number of religious tenets deal with how individuals are meant to treat one another. Most famous of all, is the Golden Rule: "In everything do to others as you would have them do to you; for this is the law and the prophets" (Matthew 7:12). It is not much of a stretch when Lyndon Johnson uses this demand as part of his case for civil rights.

Finally, the language of religion, involving themes of sin, forgiveness, and mercy, also seems natural for presidential scandals. Religion can be the ready toolkit for an apology.

Religious Rhetoric Doesn't Work

The most important takeaway from this research is that religious rhetoric does not seem to help a president much, if at all. Opinion does not respond to the president's pleas, the media does not go any easier on him, and the reception of his ideas in Congress disappoints. The experimental chapter will show that exposure to a religious policy argument has no effect on an individual's views. Evidence is also presented that suggests secular rhetoric is a stronger type of argument.

This conclusion might come as a surprise. To date, only one book length treatment of presidential religious rhetoric as a tool of presidential power has been published, Colleen Shogan's (2006) *The Moral Rhetoric of American Presidents*. Shogan argues that under certain circumstances—when the president must quickly rally the public around a cause the nation is conflicted about, when the president is dealing with complex legislation that cannot be easily explained, when the president was elected on a platform that promised moral leadership, and when the president is threatened by the prospect of Congress taking the lead on a given issue—the use of religious and moral rhetoric does enhance a president's authority.

In addition to this academic evidence, the idea that religious rhetoric can be a tool of presidential power seems to represent the conventional wisdom. Indeed, religious rhetoric arguably *should* be persuasive given that America is an unusually religious country. A majority of people claim to read the Bible at least two times every month, 54 percent of Americans pray daily, and 91 percent of Americans say they believe in God (Prothero 2007, 38; Pew Forum on Religion and Public Life 2010; Wald and Calhoun-Brown 2011, 31). The possibility certainly exists that religious rhetoric is of special power because of the unusual importance of the American people's spiritual beliefs.

At the same time, the finding that religious rhetoric has little value for a goal-oriented president should *not* come as surprise. More and more scholars are coming to accept that the power of presidential speech has been overstated, both by the public and the academy.

For instance, we now know that a president cannot push unpopular initiatives. Rather, presidents choose to appeal to the public on issues that are already popular (Canes-Wrone 2006). When they overlook opposition and try to use opinion data to identify themes to persuade the public to come around, like Clinton did for healthcare reform, they tend to stumble into disaster (Jacobs and Shapiro 2000).

We also know that presidential rhetoric is actually more likely to push the public in the opposite direction. Sophisticated statistical analysis shows that conservative rhetoric by a president produces a liberal public mood, and vice versa (Wood 2009).

And we recognize that the president is operating in a constitutional system that is designed to frustrate presidential rhetoric (Tulis 1987). The Constitution was designed in a time when it was not seen as proper for a president to engage the public. The framers believed the experience of the ancient democracies was a testament to the dangerous consequences of an over-reliance on popular opinion. Early presidents avoided discussing policy in their speeches, and addressed any programmatic suggestions to Congress alone.

What has changed since then is our interpretation of the president's role in that system. This creates problems for presidents who are now expected to lead the public in a government that was not created with that type of leadership in mind.

Take Woodrow Wilson's failed rhetorical campaign for the League of Nations as an illustration of this problem. Wilson failed because he had to lobby two different audiences—the Senate, who needed to ratify the treaty, and the public. What would persuade the Senate would not persuade the public, and vice versa. This dilemma forced him to speak in contradictory ways, undermining his credibility in the process.

Perhaps, no scholar has done more to change the perception of the power of presidential rhetoric than George Edwards. *God Wills It* is heavily influenced by Edwards's work in *On Deaf Ears* (2003). Edwards conclusively shows that presidents fail most of the time in their persuasive campaigns. Statistically significant changes in opinion rarely follow televised addresses, a problem compounded by the steady decrease in average audience size. In compelling chapters, Edwards looks at the record of two of the most gifted presidential orators, Ronald Reagan and Bill Clinton. Edwards shows how, on issue after issue, both men were mostly unable to move public opinion in their preferred direction. The president was lucky if a bare majority of the country wound up on his side. Even more troubling for the president, few of those who watch a president speak are able to recall anything he said afterward.

I hope the reader will consider this book the equivalent study of religious rhetoric. The major conclusion being that religious rhetoric is as equally likely to fall "on deaf ears" as any other type of presidential speech, previous research and conventional wisdom to the contrary.

What This Book Is, and What This Book Is Not

What this book *is* is a simple book. I have tried to accomplish two things in writing. First, I have attempted to identify the religious themes that presidents have historically used. Second, I have attempted to assess whether these arguments helped a president achieve his goals or not. I base my answer on my analysis of the available data, as well as on the results of my own experimental test of religious rhetoric. Although I do offer a useful way of thinking about religious rhetoric, that is not my main contribution. My main contributions are these empirical findings. Like most political scientists, I have only chosen to study political communication because of my more general interest in the workings of power in society (Bell, Conners, and Sheckels 2008).

What this book *is not* is rhetorical criticism. One of the defining features of work on political communication is its tendency to cross disciplinary boundaries (Stuckey 1996). It is common in many studies of presidential rhetoric to find concepts borrowed from philosophy and literature. In these essays and books, authors pay close attention to the context of a speech, to the speaker's delivery style, and to the visuals that accompany the message. This is important work, and in the next chapter, I will draw on some of it.

However, ultimately, I share with others the concern that too much of the discussion about presidential rhetoric is done without regard to a practical consideration of its consequence (Edwards 2003, 6). So, I do not examine any individual speech with the attention to detail that is required to consider the types of issues listed above myself. I have conducted a much broader survey of presidential rhetoric. I consider a lot of speeches, but from a further remove. The payoff—a clear answer to a big question—hopefully justifies my decision for the reader.

Overview

In Chapter 1, I further explore the differences between communitarian and coalitional religious rhetoric while also explaining how cases were identified and analyzed.

Chapters 2 and 3 deal with the religious rhetoric of foreign policy. Chapter 2 traces Dwight Eisenhower's four-year push for mutual security funding, as well as Ronald Reagan's religious claims for increased defense spending. Chapter 3 deals with George H. W. Bush's arguments in the run-up to the Persian Gulf War, plus the religious rhetoric Bush's son used to mobilize the country behind the War on Terror.

In Chapter 4, I detail Jimmy Carter's religious rhetoric on energy policy. Chapter 5 covers the religious arguments Presidents Kennedy and Johnson used in their attempts to secure passage of the landmark Civil Rights Act of 1964. Chapter 6, focusing on Gerald Ford and Bill Clinton, discusses the religious rhetoric of scandal.

Chapter 7 is the experimental chapter. Finally, a conclusion reviews the work and addresses its implications.

1

Conceptualizing Presidential Religious Rhetoric

This chapter is broken into two sections. First, I introduce two different types of presidential religious rhetoric and illustrate the differences between them. The second half of the chapter explains the methods I use to identify and evaluate rhetorical strategies based on religion.

Communitarian and Coalitional Religious Rhetoric

Following Kenneth Burke (1989, 188), I define rhetoric as "the use of language as a symbolic means of inducing cooperation in beings that by nature respond to symbols." Language is inherently a catalyst for action. Different words are linked to specific symbols and these symbols can trigger predictable emotional responses (Edelman 1964).

For instance, a doctor who heard John F. Kennedy or Lyndon Johnson use the phrase "compulsory health insurance" in the 1960s would not have reacted to the dictionary definitions of these words. Rather, that doctor would have responded to the economic and social anxieties those words symbolized, given that they were connected to a series of policy ideas that were thought to threaten the privileged position of America's physicians.

According to this logic, rhetoric fundamentally operates through the use of significant symbols. Phrases only become meaningful when words trigger the same response in both the speaker and the individual to whom the speech is addressed. I might ask someone to bring me a chair. If they take too long, I might get the chair myself. Either way, my response and the response of the other person to the vocal gesture is the same—an impulse to pick up a chair (Mead 1934, 47, 67).

Indeed, the connection between words, what they symbolize, and their emotional cues can be so strong that it can discourage thought. When a politician launches into a screed about high taxes and wasteful spending, the audience is unlikely to consider whether these complaints are actually true or not. The disgust and contempt they feel will be a ritualistic response not much different from an appropriately timed "Amen" said during church prayers.

Religious rhetoric has special symbolic potential because of its ability to either intensify or ease the anxiety people feel, knowing that so much of what happens to them is beyond their control (Edelman 1977, 4). One of the basic contentions of this book, however, is that the symbolism of a president's religious words does not always serve the same purpose. In fact, I argue that there are two basic forms of presidential religious rhetoric, and each stems from a fundamental property of religion itself.

Scholars have long debated how best to define a "religion" (Arnal and McCutcheon 2013). And while the structural functionalist interpretation certainly has its critics (see Gellner 1999), there is much to say for the idea that religion can be a glue or cement that binds a community together.

David Émile Durkheim (1971, 47) was one of the first to adopt this perspective, defining a religion as "a unified system of beliefs and practices relative to sacred things, that is to say, things set apart and forbidden—beliefs and practices which united into one single moral community called a Church, all those who adhere to them." Durkheim believed that the creation of community of laymen and priests is at the heart of the difference between religion and magic. Magic surely has its own beliefs and practices, but, as he observed, there is no church of magic.

Durkheim's study of aboriginal religion in Australia revealed that clans were not united by blood, but instead thought of themselves as families owing to their connection to a totem, typically an animal or vegetable. He held that the attachment of tribe members to these totems is what creates their society.

Durkheim paid particular attention to the rite of Intichiuma, a complex ceremony involving stones that was performed to ensure the healthy reproduction of a clan's totem (326–50). His argument was that ceremonies like this help to reinvigorate a community by bringing people together and reminding them of their shared beliefs and ancestors. Religion can be seen as a symbolic expression of the bonds between them.

Perhaps, an example closer to home will help. Consider funeral rites. The death of an individual is a destabilizing event, and it can lead to destructive impulses in those left behind. People may want to run away from their pain, or dispose of everything that reminds them of the deceased. Yet, religion makes the experience of death sacred and, by doing so, counteracts the fear and hopelessness that people feel. Religion re-establishes a group's morale (Malinowski 1948, 52–53).

As the examples above illustrate, religion also confers a sense of identity on its adherents. It answers the questions "who am I?" and "who are we?" When Catholics attend Mass, they can easily understand the difference between those in the pews, and those not in the pews (Wilson 1982, 34).

And so it is that Durkheim (1971, 427) concluded that religion—or something approximating religion—is indispensable to the successful operation of a community: "There can be no society which does not feel the need of upholding and reaffirming at regular intervals the collective sentiments and the collective ideas which make its unity and its personality . . . hence come ceremonies which do not differ from regular religious ceremonies, either in their object, the results which they produce, or the processes employed to attain these results . . . What essential difference is there between an assembly of Christians celebrating the principal dates of the life of Christ . . . and a reunion of citizens commemorating the promulgation of a new moral or legal system or some great event in the national life?"

Of course, it is well known that presidents also play a constitutive role in the creation of the American community (Stuckey 2004; see also Gerstle 2001). Through their rhetorical choices to include or exclude groups as American, they define the boundaries of the nation. The president, more than any other individual, explains who "we" are. When Andrew Jackson depicted Native Americans as outsiders, he thereby justified the country's westward expansion. Tribal lands could be confiscated because Native Americans were not part of "the people."

Given religion's capability to provide social cohesion, and when combined with the ability of presidential rhetoric to define the American nation, it makes sense that one variant of presidential religious rhetoric be labeled as "communitarian." This style of religious language serves the underlying purpose of uniting the American people.

Some might be tempted to call such language civil religious instead. The idea of a civil religion originally dates to Jean-Jacques Rousseau (1893), who recommended cultivating a civil religion as a means of strengthening the state. Rousseau argued that such a religion should be based on simple dogmas, like the belief in a powerful and intelligent God (219). A civil religion would function to the state's advantage by teaching people that to serve the state is to serve God, and to break the state's laws is to be "impious" (211).

This idea was translated into the American context in an influential essay by Robert Bellah (1967, 1992). Bellah was working from a Durkheimian perspective and argued that the American civil religion can be seen as a means of understanding America's historical experience by reference to the common elements of religious belief that almost all Americans share.

At the heart of the US civil religion is a very un-Christian view of God. The God of the US civil religion is concerned with law and order, not salvation, and has a special interest in the fate of America. With this image of God at its center, the civil religion tells the story of American history in a new light. The New World, populated by a communal society of sexually unashamed natives, becomes a second Eden. The founding of the colonies becomes a reprise of Exodus, with America's forefathers leading their people out of the desert of Egypt and into the Promised Land. Most of all, the Civil War becomes a narrative of sin and judgment, where Abraham Lincoln assumes the role of an American Jesus—a civil saint—who died for our sins. Although not as formal as Rousseau's vision of a civil religion, the US variant still finds expression in a number of ritualistic "holydays," such as Memorial Day (Coleman 1970).

The concept of a civil religion, however, is a problematic one. Critics have pointed out the ambiguities behind the idea (Means 1970). Others have countered that empirical data for the existence of civil religious beliefs are often lacking (Thomas and Flippen 1972). Historians objected that what scholars were really describing was only a product of the upsurge in religious belief in 1950s America (Mathisen 1989).

In an ironic twist of fate, Bellah, in many ways, was a prisoner of his own success. Bellah's scholarly expertise was Japan, and at the time of his seminal article, he admittedly had little understanding of either religion or American politics. Owing to the prominence of his ideas, Bellah was forced to delve more deeply into these subjects and, over the course of his subsequent writing, he modified his thinking. In a set of introductory essays to an edited volume in 1980, Bellah was already walking back from his original essay. He called the debate about civil religion "sterile," admitted that civil religion was "marginal" in American life, and openly asked whether civil religion was really just Biblical religion in disguise (Bellah and Hammond 1980). By the late 1980s, Bellah had all but abandoned the term "civil religion," and had moved on to studying other subjects (see the concluding chapter). Until his death, he continued to publicly complain that civil religion was the only idea people associated with him (Bortolini 2012).

It is not my intention to enter this debate. I have no personal attachment to the concept of a civil religion. I only raise the issue because it may help the reader to understand what I am getting at it. I prefer the concept of communitarian religious rhetoric because it avoids the problems associated with the idea of a civil religion. Furthermore, it is a tidier concept, rooted in the purpose behind a president's words. But whatever we call these kinds of words, it cannot be denied that at least some presidential religious rhetoric has an integrative function.

For example, Gerald Ford (1976d) closed his remarks commemorating the nation's bicentennial in Philadelphia on July 4, 1776 by saying: "The American adventure began here with a firm reliance on the protection of Divine Providence. It continues in a common conviction that the source of our blessings is a loving God, in whom we trust."

Similarly, Richard Nixon (1969) concluded his first inaugural by noting, "Only a few short weeks ago we shared the glory of man's first sight of the world as God sees it, as a single sphere reflecting light in the darkness. As the Apollo astronauts flew over the moon's gray surface on Christmas Eve, they spoke to us of the beauty of earth—and in that voice so clear across the lunar distance, we heard them invoke God's blessing on its goodness . . . Our destiny offers not the cup of despair, but the chalice of opportunity. So let us seize it not in fear, but in gladness—and 'riders on the earth together,' let us go forward, firm in our faith, steadfast in our purpose, cautious of the dangers, but sustained by our confidence in the will of God and the promise of man."

Ford and Nixon's words spoke to a common American spiritual experience. They promoted a religious understanding of the country's history—from founding to lunar landing—that linked all Americans together as part of a sacred project. There needs to be a way to set aside this kind of language.

Yet, communitarian religious rhetoric is not my interest. As the quotes above suggest, this style of language is stereotypically bland and content-less. I am more concerned with the other side of the coin. If the symbols of religion can be a unifying force, as Durkheim and others have shown, those symbols can also be equally divisive. Religion can frustrate as much as it can comfort. It can be difficult for some to reconcile the idea of a just and compassionate God with a world filled with school shootings, natural disasters, and wanton terrorist attacks.

One of the books of the Old Testament tells the story of Job, a faithful servant of the Lord, a man who is known by God to be "blameless and upright" (Job 1:8). However, Satan challenges God, and argues that Job praises him only because God has blessed him with plentiful material possessions. To prove the devil wrong, God allows Satan to test Job.

In rapid succession, all of Job's property is destroyed in raids and fires, his children die in a windstorm, and he is afflicted with a terrible skin disease. Job, knowing that he has been a good man, struggles to understand why God allows him and others to suffer so. He wonders why "From the city the dying groan, and the throat of the wounded cries for help; yet God pays no attention to their prayer" (Job 24:12).

By the end of the book, God gives Job his answer. In a series of rhetorical questions, God suggests that no one can truly comprehend his powers or his will. Job admits that God is right, and apologizes for having "uttered what I did not understand, things too wonderful for me, which I did not know" (Job 42:3).

Most people can relate to Job's tribulations. Many question why bad things must happen to good people. And the Bible's guidance, so beautifully phrased in Proverbs 3:5 to "Trust in the Lord with all thine heart; and lean not unto thine own understanding," provides them little solace. These people instead hear more truth in philosopher Søren Kierkegaard's (1964, 104) lament "Who am I? How did I come into the world? Why was I not consulted? . . . And if I am compelled to take part in it, where is the director? I should like to make a remark to him. Is there no director? Whither shall I turn with my complaint?"

Indeed, for the more radical critics, it is religion's potential to help people accept these injustices that is most problematic. Marx famously argued that religion is a pernicious force by which society's oppressors can justify their treatment of the lower classes as just punishment for the people's sins. Religion accustoms people to their poor material surroundings and, as such, is little more than opium for the masses. This opium distracts the people from achieving true happiness, and separates them not only from each other but also from their true selves (McLellan 1977; Raines 2002).

Whether Marx was right or wrong is beside the point. The overall point I'm trying to make is rather simple. It is easy to see how a politician's attempt to explain a national event in religious terms might divide rather than unify. It is easy to see how such words might fracture a community between those can, and those who cannot, uncritically accept God's will.

Even beyond this, religious rhetoric is often inflammatory and offensive. Religious words get under people's skin. A lot of people don't like to be told that same-sex marriage is part of "the devil's strategy to destroy the church, a confrontation between light and darkness." Or that "You cannot be a born-again Christian who takes the Bible seriously and vote for a pro-choice or anti-family candidate." Or that "the pagans and the abortionists, and the feminists, and the gays and lesbians who are actively trying to make that an alternative lifestyle" were responsible for making 9/11 "happen." Yet, all of these are things that major figures on the religious right have said publicly in recent years (Wilcox and Robinson 2011, 4, 12, 14).

Not surprisingly then, Americans have become increasingly uncomfortable with the role of religion in public life. Forty-three percent of the public now says that, when politicians "talk about how religious they are," it makes them feel "uncomfortable" (Pew Forum on Religion and Public Life 2012a).

Now think for a moment about what happens when such emotional words are connected to policy goals. One of the most recognized trends in presidential approval is that a president's support inevitably decays over time (Erikson and Tedin 2011, 119–20). Although different interpretations have been offered to explain this finding, the intuition behind the trend is not complex. A president cannot please everyone. When he acts, he must disappoint people who would have preferred an alternative course. The longer a president remains in office, the more decisions he must make, and thus, the more people he must antagonize (Mueller 1973).

Anytime a president makes a policy appeal he is bound to trigger opposition. Religious rhetoric might exacerbate that process. All of which begs the question as to why a president would even consider using such words, knowing full well the negative consequences that might follow from such language. The answer to that question gets to the heart of this book's conception of presidential religious rhetoric.

Presidents choose their words carefully, especially in the modern era. Their linguistic choices, which are based on polls and the expert advice of their speechwriters and press secretaries, are strategic. Each case study chapter will prove that presidents chose their religious arguments consciously on the basis of internal information about what kind of appeals would be most successful.

When it comes to religious rhetoric, presidents recognize that religious claims, for all their potential drawbacks, *can* compel people to make great sacrifices in the name of policy change. Religious messages provided African Americans with the strength needed to endure unspeakable violence while protesting for their rights (Chappell 2004). And religion gave Northern White preachers the courage needed to stand beside them (Friedland 1998). By using politically motivated religious rhetoric, the president is making a gamble that his language will inspire more than it alienates.

As such, it makes sense to label the second variant of religious rhetoric "coalitional." This term speaks to the political imperative of assembling a minimum winning coalition in any policy contest (Riker 1962). Any time a collection of individuals or groups is involved in a zero-sum decision, it makes sense to gather just enough people on your own side in order to prevail.

For an example of coalitional religious rhetoric, consider the religious rhetoric Jimmy Carter (1979j) was prone to use as he argued for his energy programs: "So, it may be that facing this particular crisis or challenge of energy can go a long way toward healing some of the problems that our Nation has had too long. I think for us to recognize that we've got to save and not waste is really compatible with what the Bible teaches. God doesn't want us to waste what He gives. I think the fact that we have to now share with each other is a very good principle on which to base a family's style of living."

Or consider Ronald Reagan's (1985a) arguments for higher defense budgets: "You might be interested to know that the Scriptures are on our side in this—Luke 14:31, in which Jesus in talking to the disciples spoke about a king who might be contemplating going to war against another king, with his 10,000 men. But he sits down and counsels how good he's going to do against the other fellow's 20,000 and then says he may have to send a delegation to talk peace terms. Well, I don't think we ever want to be in a position of only being half as strong and having to send a delegation to negotiate under those circumstances— peace terms—with the Soviet Union. So, ultimately, our security and our hopes for success at the arms reduction talks hinge on the determination that we show here to continue our program to rebuild and refortify our defenses."

Obviously, it was going to anger (and surprise!) some people to learn that the Bible said America needed to support Carter's energy policies and pass Reagan's defense budgets. Others were going to be intractably opposed to the policies linked to this language to begin with. But as will be documented in later chapters, Carter and Reagan reasoned that these arguments were their best chances to assemble that winning coalition. Whether they were right or not is the main subject motivating this study. No matter what, though, the difference between Carter and Reagan's religious rhetoric—hard-hitting, overt, goal-oriented—and the nondescript spirituality of Ford and Nixon's speech should be obvious.

Martin Marty (1989) might provide a useful parallel for understanding the difference between communitarian and coalitional presidential religious rhetoric. Marty observes that religious speakers can either be priests or they can be prophets. As a priest, a speaker is celebratory and culture-building. But as prophets, speakers are judgmental. As Marty summarizes, "one comforts the afflicted; the other afflicts the comfortable" (82–83).

Any religion must include both its priests and its prophets. My claim throughout this section has been that religion can unify, but it can also divide. The two typologies I have sketched of presidential religious rhetoric reflect both of these characteristics. To adapt Marty's thinking, we could see communitarian religious rhetoric as the rhetoric of the priest, while coalitional religious rhetoric is the rhetoric of the prophet.

Having an understanding of these two variants of religious rhetoric impacts how we must view different forms of presidential communication. Some have argued that certain presidential speeches, such as inaugural addresses and national eulogies, constitute their own distinct genres. It is claimed that these speeches are inherently religious, with the president only on these occasions representing a national priest (Campbell and Jamieson 2008).

The reality is that the religious rhetoric that appears in these types of addresses is more complicated than this line of thinking suggests. Religious words could serve a communitarian purpose, or they could serve a coalitional purpose. It depends on the context.

Thus, we need to look closely at a president's religious references to understand their function. Similarly, we should not make the mistake of thinking the president only acts as a national priest on solemn national events like inaugurals. It is not the case that some types of speeches (i.e., inaugurals) are religious while others (i.e., State of the Unions) are not. This book proves that presidents are just as likely to use religious rhetoric in their inaugurals as they are to use such words before a gathering of businessmen.

Still, we can anticipate when communitarian or coalitional religious rhetoric is more likely to appear by keeping in mind the primary responsibilities of the modern president (Rossiter 1987). First, the president is the Chief of State. He greets visitors to the White House, issues proclamations, awards medals, and hosts state dinners.

Second, the president is the country's Chief Executive. In theory, the president is in charge of the day-to-day operations of the government. It is the president who is ultimately responsible for providing citizens with quality administration.

Third, the president is the Commander-in-Chief. He alone directs the actions of the country's armed forces.

Fourth, the president is America's Chief Diplomat. Although the president shares power over foreign affairs with the Senate, he still tends to dominate the country's foreign policy. The president negotiates treaties, recognizes governments, appoints ambassadors, and communicates with other governments and their leaders.

Finally, the president is the Chief Legislator. The president lobbies Congress for action on domestic policy concerns. When he does not like a bill, he may veto it. He can set the agenda with his State of the Union address. Further authority has been delegated to him for the purpose of proposing various pieces of legislation, such as the budget.

Given that the president must play all these different roles, it also makes sense to allow that he would use different styles of religious rhetoric as he shifts between them.

When a president is inhabiting his role as Chief of State he "is the one-man distillation of the American people just as surely as the Queen is of the British people" (4). Chief of State is a unifying role. The president's grandeur and statesmanship are reminders of what the country shares—its common beliefs, values and experiences. This an opportune time for the use of communitarian religious rhetoric.

The president is more likely to use coalitional religious rhetoric when he is inhabiting his other roles, particularly those of Chief Executive and Chief Legislator. These roles are inherently conflictual. There are tangled lines of authority running between the president and Congress, and there are differences of opinion about what can and should be done.

Ultimately, the type of religious rhetoric that is used is a function of what the president is trying to accomplish.

How I Determined When a Coalitional Religious Rhetorical Strategy Was Used

I restrict my analysis of religious rhetoric to the postwar presidents, excluding Obama. I maintain this is the best choice for a research question about the president's public role, since the expectations for public leadership have changed in the modern era.

Early presidents avoided discussing policy in their speeches, and addressed any programmatic suggestions to Congress alone. The State of the Union was written, not spoken. Anything else was thought to be improper (Tulis 1987). In the modern era, those norms have changed, while various factors have made it more productive for a president to promote himself and his policies through press conferences, televised speeches, White House ceremonies, and the like (Kernell 1997).

Accordingly, the apparatus surrounding the president has changed in such a way that it has afforded these men greater resources when making a rhetorical argument. It was not until Warren Harding's Administration that a president even employed a speechwriter. Today, a writer like Peggy Noonan is able to draft a moving address like Reagan's 1984 D-Day remembrance in Normandy ("These are the boys of Pointe du Hoc. These are the men who took the cliffs.") without ever talking with the president about it (Nelson 2010).

I believe these kinds of developments—the change in the rhetorical role of the president, the rise of public activities, the development of new institutions for public communication—are strong grounds for my decision to limit my study of religious rhetoric to the modern presidency.

Given this condition, my first step involved determining what each postwar president was trying to accomplish. This is easier said than done. To take an extreme example, Lyndon Johnson proposed an eye-popping 1,902 bills during his five plus years in office (Bernstein 1996, 529). Obviously, not all of these initiatives were equally important. Nor would it be worthwhile to study the arguments Johnson made in favor of each of these policies. What was first needed was a way to identify the goals a president was most invested in. These goals would be the ones the president faced the most opposition on, too. If religious rhetoric is helpful on these contested issues, we can assume it would be persuasive on lesser issues as well.

Unfortunately, using an existing list of accomplishments like Mayhew's (1991) well-known dataset of significant laws was not an option because I am as much interested in cases where a religious rhetorical strategy *failed* as those where it succeeded.[1] My fundamental task is to examine the development of a president's rhetorical arguments from when he first introduced a political goal to when it was ultimately abandoned or adopted and then assess what impact those arguments might have had. I, therefore, developed a set of four coding rules that must be met for a goal to be considered a major presidential objective:

1. Can evidence be found indicating that this objective was a priority for the president?
2. Does the Administration attempt to follow through?
3. Is the objective identified as important by the majority of historical accounts of the Administration?
4. Does the president require the cooperation of other actors in order to achieve his objective?

Rules 1 and 2 are included in order to help us distinguish between the legitimate goals of the Administration and others that stood more as public relations maneuvers. Take, for example, the Americans with Disabilities Act (ADA). It was a tremendous social advance, a bill of great historical import, and something that George H. W. Bush spoke of often. However, historians agree that Bush did not expend much effort for the bill (see, i.e., Mervin 1996, 98–101). It originated outside of the Administration, it was a personal cause for many Senators, and it was broadly popular on its own merits. Bush's rhetoric on the ADA seems more like an attempt to claim credit and should be treated differently than other policies he was more invested in.

Rule 3 is included because it ensures that an expert consensus has formed about the importance of each objective. Although some initiatives that have been excluded from my list may be debatable, all those that have been included should be less so on account of this rule.

Finally, Rule 4 is meant to eliminate what has been called "power without persuasion," those things a president can accomplish unilaterally, whether by executive order, a national directive, or by other executive authority (Howell 2003). All presidents have access to these powers regardless of skill, and it is institutional factors (i.e., the ideological makeup of Congress) that determine the ability of any given president to exercise them. This rule will eliminate many important moments from consideration: Truman's order to desegregate the military, Eisenhower's nationalization of the Guard in Little Rock, Carter's failed hostage rescue attempt, etc. Certainly, presidents speak publicly about these kinds of decisions. But these speeches must be treated differently. In these cases, the president has already acted. His remarks work more to provide justification for what he has done, as opposed to convincing people to support what he plans to do.

Table 1.1 is the list of presidential objectives that were identified for all postwar presidents based upon these rules. There are 144 in total, making for an average of 13.09 objectives per president. The early activist Democrats predictably have the highest numbers. Truman, Kennedy, and Johnson each had eighteen major goals. Ford, president for just two years, had the fewest, with eight.

Table 1.1
Major presidential objectives

President Harry Truman

- Increase in the minimum wage
- Full employment legislation
- Universal military training
- Public housing program
- Reorganization of the nation's defense system
- Civil rights program (anti-lynching law, abolition of poll taxes, FEPC, etc.)
- Aid to Greece and Turkey (Truman Doctrine)
- Marshall Plan
- National health insurance
- Repeal of Taft-Hartley
- Federal aid to education
- Brannan Plan (income support for small farmers)
- Ratification of NATO treaty/funding for NATO
- Point IV program (technical assistance to Latin America)
- Korean War
- Expansion of social security
- Funding for public works
- Establishment of an atomic energy commission

President Dwight Eisenhower

- Defeat the Bricker amendment (limited executive authority in foreign affairs)
- Cut defense expenditures/disarmament
- Expand Social Security eligibility
- Immigration reform
- Atoms for Peace
- Health reinsurance (subsidies to purchase private plans)
- Statehood for Hawaii
- St. Lawrence Seaway construction
- Public housing (140,000 new homes)
- Reducing government involvement in agricultural markets (flexible price supports, soil bank, etc.)

- SEATO
- Formosa resolution
- Interstate highway system
- School construction funds
- Open Skies
- Mutual security program of foreign aid
- Eisenhower doctrine
- Balanced budget for fiscal 1958 ("Battle of the Budget")
- Civil rights legislation
- Nuclear test ban
- Labor reform

President John Kennedy

- Peace Corps
- Alliance for Progress
- Creation of a cabinet-level Department of Urban Affairs
- Address chronic unemployment in West Virginia and other hard hit states
- Education bills—federal aid to elementary and secondary schools and college scholarships
- Medicare
- Worker retraining
- Civil defense program
- NASA lunar landing
- Precautionary measures in response to Berlin crisis of 1961 (additional military appropriations, increase in draft quotas, etc.)
- Redress balance of payments
- Force a rollback in steel industry prices
- Tax cut
- Civil rights bill
- Test ban treaty
- Housing legislation
- Minimum wage increase
- Funding for mental retardation programs

President Lyndon Johnson

- Tax cut
- End to discrimination in public accommodations
- War on poverty
- Medicare
- Federal aid to education
- Financial support for college students (scholarships, loans, work study)
- Voting rights legislation
- Elimination of country-based immigration quotas

- Protection of water sources
- Clean air laws
- Beautification (highway landscaping, restrictions on billboards, etc.)
- Gulf of Tonkin resolution
- Tax increase (1967–1968)
- Fair housing
- Foundations for the arts and humanities
- Model Cities
- Anti-crime legislation
- Creation of a Department of Transportation and passage of auto safety laws

President Richard Nixon

- Safeguard anti-ballistic missile system
- Anti-crime legislation (particularly the DC "no knock" crime control bill)
- Family Assistance Plan
- Revenue sharing
- Vietnamization
- Haynesworth and Carswell Supreme Court nominations
- Busing moratorium and its companion inner city educational aid
- SALT I
- Avoiding impeachment due to Watergate-related offenses
- National health insurance program (employer mandate, HMO support)
- Executive branch reorganization (creation of OMB and Domestic Council, reduction in cabinet departments)

President Gerald Ford

- Moving past Watergate (pardon of Richard Nixon)
- Anti-inflation package, in particular a one-year 5 percent surcharge tax increase
- Whip Inflation Now (WIN) volunteer initiative
- Temporary $16 billion stimulus tax cut to combat late 1974 recession
- Aid to South Vietnam in response to Northern Vietnam offensive (two requests)
- Second tax cut package matching a $28 billion permanent reduction with $28 billion in spending cuts
- Obtaining concessions from New York City in return for federal bailout legislation
- Energy program of oil decontrol plus taxes and fee increases

President Jimmy Carter

- Economic stimulus package featuring a $50 tax rebate
- Cut funding from unnecessary water projects
- First energy plan (tax on domestic oil, gas guzzlers, etc.)

- Panama Canal transfer treaties
- Welfare reform (limited new spending, combination of work and income support)
- Tax reform (end to tax shelters and various loopholes)
- Put an end to "Lance Affair" investigation of Office of Management and Budget director and friend Bert Lance
- Second energy plan (decontrol, windfall profits, synfuels, Energy Mobilization Board, etc.)
- SALT II treaty
- Hospital cost containment legislation
- Deregulation of airline and trucking industries
- Civil service reform
- Creation of a Department of Education
- Balanced budget in 1980

President Ronald Reagan

- Cut income taxes
- Cut domestic spending
- Boost defense spending
- 1982 deficit reduction package
- Strategic Defense Initiative missile defense (Star Wars)
- Tax reform (eliminating loopholes, reducing number of brackets, cutting individual rates)
- Bork Supreme Court nomination
- Intermediate-Range Nuclear Forces treaty
- Aid for Nicaraguan Contras and El Salvadorian government
- Surviving Iran-Contra Scandal

President George H. W. Bush

- S&L bailout and restructuring
- Capital gains tax cut
- Deficit reduction package
- Expelling Iraq from Kuwait (Operations Desert Shield and Desert Storm)
- Amendments to the Clean Air Act
- Nomination of John Tower as Secretary of Defense
- Education programs (school and teacher awards, voluntary testing and model schools)
- Anti-drug legislation
- Thomas Supreme Court nomination

President Bill Clinton

- Deficit reduction package
- NAFTA

- Healthcare reform
- Balanced budget in 1995
- Welfare reform
- Avoiding impeachment due to fallout from affair with Monica Lewinsky
- Stimulus package
- Balanced budget in 1997
- Crime bill (assault weapon ban, addition of 100,000 officers, expansion of death penalty, and three strikes law)

President George W. Bush

- 2001 surplus tax cut
- 2003 stimulus tax cut
- No Child Left Behind educational reform
- Funding for combating AIDS in Africa
- Medicare prescription drug benefit
- Social security privatization
- Immigration reform (temporary worker program with increased border controls)
- War on Terror (Afghanistan and Iraq Wars, PATRIOT Act, Department of Homeland Security, etc.)

A shrewd observer of Table 1.1 would immediately object to one inclusion based on my final rule, Ford's pardon of Richard Nixon. True, Ford did act unilaterally. He had the constitutional authority to grant a pardon and he decided to do so with little to no outside consultation. However, I would make the case that the pardon was not the end, but the means. In fact, Ford was conflicted about pardoning Nixon. His first press conference went a long way toward changing his mind. As he explains in his memoirs,

> All this forced me to address the issue squarely for the first time. I had to get the monkey off my back. I was already struggling with the question of who had jurisdiction over the papers and tapes, and that was cutting into my work schedule more and more every day. It intruded into time that I urgently needed to deal with a faltering economy and mounting foreign policy problems all over the world. With these critical issues pressing upon me—and the nation—I simply couldn't listen to lawyers' endless arguments about Nixon's tapes and documents or answer constant questions about his legal status. (Ford 1979, 159)

Ford's first cabinet meeting was devoted to discussing Nixon's fate, his secretaries faced questions about it wherever they went, and

Nixon holdovers like Alexander Haig and Henry Kissinger hounded Ford about the matter (Greene 1995, 45). Ford's goal was to move on from Watergate. Ford's opinions on Nixon were irrelevant. "My fundamental decision to grant a pardon had nothing to do with any sympathy I might feel for Nixon personally or any concern I might have for the state of his health . . . public policy demanded that I put Nixon—and Watergate—behind us as quickly as possible," Ford (1979, 173) wrote. And, as will be shown in Chapter 6, Ford's speech announcing the pardon on September 8, 1974, was in reality the middle, not the end, of the new president's campaign to accomplish this larger objective.

From this list of presidential objectives, my next step consisted of determining which of these goals involved the use of coalitional religious rhetoric. The sequence and logic of this section are easy to understand if the reader keeps the following in mind. First, I had to develop a way to identify a religious *reference*. After that, I had to develop a way to identify a religious *speech*. And finally, I had to develop a way to identify a religious rhetorical *strategy*.

A president made a religious reference if his language met one of two rules:

- Must meet 1 of 2
1. Does the president make an explicit reference to religious figures or texts?
2. Does the president make a reference to well-known religious beliefs or concepts?

The second rule is the trickier of the two. America may be many things, but a nation of religious scholars it is not. Only half of American adults can name one of the four Gospels. Just one-third of people know that it was Jesus who gave the Sermon on the Mount. 10 percent of individuals think Joan of Arc was Noah's wife (Prothero 2007, 38–39).

In an extensive recent survey of religious knowledge, the Pew Forum on Religion and Public Life (2010) found that, in general, people are not even familiar with the most significant principles of their own faiths. Only 55 percent of Catholics were aware that their church teaches that the bread and wine used in Communion actually become the body and blood of Christ. Similarly, only 28 percent of self-identified White evangelicals associated the teaching that salvation comes from faith alone with Protestantism.

None of this is to say that America is not a religious nation. About 60 percent of US adults claim that religion is "very important" in their lives. About 40 percent attend religious services at least once a week. A majority of people claim to read the Bible at least two times every month (Prothero 2007, 38). Fifty-four percent of Americans pray daily (Wald and Calhoun-Brown 2011, 31). Relative to politics, a greater number of citizens identify with a religious denomination than with a political party. That same citizen is more likely to try to evangelize than they are to try to influence another's vote (12). Most impressive of all, 91 percent of Americans say they believe in God (Pew Forum on Religion and Public Life 2010).

Even beyond the commitment to religious practice, religion is an influential part of popular US culture. Christian themes and references are found in the recordings of some of the most iconic musicians of all time, including artists like Prince and Madonna (Hulsether 2005; Till 2010). On TV, long-running shows like *Star Trek* have repeatedly embraced religious storylines (Porter and McLaren 1999). In the movie theaters, religious films perform well. Mel Gibson's brutal *The Passion of the Christ* grossed over $600 million. Other films with overt religious subjects such as *The Chronicles of Narnia* and *The Da Vinci Code* have also been recent blockbusters.

The point is that just about everyone will have listened to a Prince or Madonna song, or watched an episode of *Star Trek*, or bought a ticket to see *Narnia*, and so on. This makes all Americans, regardless of their beliefs, potentially receptive to political ideas that are wrapped in a religious packaging. It is a terminology people are familiar with.

Thus it is reasonable to assume that most Americans would be able to identify concepts such as sin, salvation, brotherhood, and forgiveness, concepts that the second criterion is meant to signify, as ideas with religious foundations. As poor as the results to the knowledge questions seem, there is another side. While the report proves that Americans do not know everything about religion, it also proves that everyone knows something. The average person got half of the thirty-two possible correct answers (Pew Forum on Religion and Public Life 2010).

Still, it is clearly unreasonable to assume that most Americans are picking up on what has been called "dog-whistle" politics, the use of coded religious communication that is only meant to be recognized and understood by a narrow subset of the population (Albertson 2006). The appearance of a phrase like "wonder-working power" in George W. Bush's 2003 State of the Union is a wink few people, myself included, would be liable to catch. The hope is that the second of my two rules helps me to successfully straddle this line.

One other point to note is that, in my analyses, I will often cite passages from the Bible and/or detail religious doctrine. I am not suggesting that the public is always consciously making these connections themselves. Instead, I am including this material because it helps to contextualize the president's message. All that I am suggesting is that Americans recognize that the message is somehow rooted in religion.

The religious references meeting either of these two criteria were identified by means of a search of the public papers of the president, available online courtesy of the University of California, Santa Barbara's American Presidency Project (see http://www.presidency.ucsb.edu). What distinguishes this search from many others (e.g., Domke and Coe 2008) is that I did not begin by searching the database for religious words or concepts, that is, reading all the papers where the word "God" appears. There is no way that anyone could generate a comprehensive list of all the religious words a president might use. Nor could anyone hope to capture in simple search terms the complexity of some religious ideas.

Instead, I began by searching the database for terms related to the objective, for example, "civil rights." I then carefully read the president's discourse on the topic, examining the content of the speeches for religious references that met one of the two standards listed above.

However, a one-shot religious reference would not be enough for me to classify the speech as having made a religious argument. Kennedy once said at a dinner in Philadelphia in 1963, "'Cast me not off in the time of old age,' says the Psalmist in the Bible, and we intend to see to it that in modern times no American is forgotten or ill-treated or cast off by this country in his time of old age" (Kennedy 1963i). Although he was talking about Social Security and other policies intended for the benefit of senior citizens, Kennedy never expanded on this point. This is an example not of a religious *speech* but that of a religious *reference*.

To be considered a religious speech, a speech had to meet an additional set of criteria:

- *If reference meets Rule 1 or 2, the speech containing it must also meet the following rule:*
3. Is the religious language a focus of a full section of the speech or is it recurrently found throughout the address?

Finally, for the president to be considered as having used a religious rhetorical *strategy*, the following two criteria must be met:

4. Is the religious language used in a major presidential address?
5. Is the religious language used in at least three minor addresses?

These rules raise the question as to what qualifies as a "major" address. Ragsdale (2009, 172) defines a major address as a speech that is "delivered to a national audience during evening listening hours." I reject the requirement that the speech be in the evening. For me, the only important factor is that the speech was nationally broadcast.

The rationale for requiring religious language to appear in a major speech ensures that the entire country is exposed to the argument. We cannot well expect religious rhetoric to have an impact if few people hear it. Furthermore, presidents prepare a great deal for their major addresses, and thus, the use of religious language in these speeches is anything but casual.

The rationale for requiring religious language to also appear in three minor speeches is included because, again, what I am trying to conceptualize is a religious rhetorical *strategy*. "Strategy" implies repetition and persistence.

Overall, these rules are sensible. A religious reference must be explicit or well-known. A religious speech must include a full section of religious content or be marked by a recurring religious theme. A religious rhetorical strategy must include at least one major and three minor addresses. In total, exactly nine presidential objectives meet these criteria.

How I Determined Whether a Coalitional Religious Rhetorical Strategy Had Been Successful

The definition that I adopt of a successful religious rhetorical strategy is as follows:

> *A successful use of religious rhetoric will improve the public's opinion of both the president and his objective, improve the president's media coverage, and result in Congress supporting his goals.*

A president has three relationships that he must constantly work to maintain—his relationship with his constituents, his relationship with the press, and his relationship with the membership of Congress. If religious rhetoric "works," it is reasonable to argue that it should strengthen the president's ties to each of these actors. I have developed a set of measures to gauge the effects of religious rhetoric within each of these vectors.

The first set of measures deals with public opinion, both the president's personal approval ratings and questions measuring his performance on the specific objective he is campaigning for. If a religious rhetorical strategy is successful, then both of these metrics should move in the president's favored direction.

One specific element I pay attention to is the change in the president's approval over the course of the campaign. It will not be possible to use this information in every case. Dwight Eisenhower's campaign for mutual security funding shows why. As the reader will learn in the following chapter, Eisenhower tried to mobilize support for foreign aid on and off for his entire second term. Obviously, we cannot learn anything about the effectiveness of religious rhetoric from a four-year time series of approval data. Rather, this tactic will be used only for campaigns of a shorter duration.

In contrast, one use of approval ratings that will be important in every case is a comparison between the last measurement taken before a major religious speech and the first measurement taken after it. This method is equivalent to one of the techniques Edwards (2003, 29–34) uses to see if a president was able to move public opinion. I will keep in mind his standard of judgment as well; a six-point increase is the benchmark for having some confidence that the speech led to a statistically significant improvement in the president's standing.

As for issue opinion, data on the president's handling of a specific problem are sometimes unavailable. However, where possible, I do chart questions on a presidential objective for the duration of a campaign. I only use identically worded questions that have been asked repeatedly since it has been shown that this is the best way to track changes in collective opinion (Page and Shapiro 1992). Unless otherwise noted, all questions were taken from the iPOLL Databank, courtesy of the Roper Center for Public Opinion Research at the University of Connecticut (http://www.ropercenter.uconn.edu/).

The second set of measures explores the president's relationship with the media. I examine the editorial reaction to a major address where the president employed a religious argument. Beat reporters strive for objectivity in their writing and the regular news cycle is too heavily influenced by events to be of use. During the Gulf War, a story on a military setback would reflect poorly on the president, for sure, but that negative coverage would not say much about the reception of the president's religious argument. In contrast, opinion pieces directly respond to a speech and they are likely to comment on both its political and its rhetorical content. We would expect positive reactions toward each if religious rhetoric was successful.

I began by searching the archives of four newspapers—the *Chicago Tribune*, the *Los Angeles Times*, the *New York Times* and the *Washington Post*—for all editorials covering the objective published the week after a major religious speech. The *New York Times* and the *Washington Post* were selected because they are recognized as the nation's two most prestigious papers when it comes to political news. The *New York Times* occupies a uniquely prominent role in the US political system. Because the *Times* is considered authoritative by the other players in the media universe, it is extensively read by the editors, reporters, and pundits who are responsible for producing content for their own outlets. As a consequence, there is a trickle-down effect whereby the material and opinions first found in the pages of the *Times* often wind up reaching a wider audience (Page 1996, 17). The *Los Angeles Times* and *Chicago Tribune* were included for geographic diversity.

Each op-ed was evaluated on a five-point scale. An article would be assigned a score on the basis of how positive or negative it was from the perspective of the president. This method is a standard practice for research that attempts to gauge the tone of media coverage (i.e., Dalton, Beck, and Huckfeldt 1998; Kahn and Kenney 2002; Druckman and Parkin 2005). The scale is as follows:

1 = Completely Negative
2 = Somewhat Negative
3 = Mixed or Neutral
4 = Somewhat Positive
5 = Completely Positive

These scores are then used to produce an average measure of editorial coverage. It also is possible to break down the distribution of articles (i.e., what percent of pieces were negative).

The last set of data concentrates on the president's relationship with Congress. First, I look at the appropriate roll call votes. If a religious rhetorical strategy works, we would expect the votes to be solid victories. A second way of gauging how successful a religious rhetorical strategy was in Congress lies in the final outcome. My hypothesis is that a successful use of a religious strategy will result in a final outcome closely reflecting the president's priorities.

To review, in each of my nine cases, I will be collecting and interpreting the following data:

- Approval change over the course of the campaign
- Approval change before and after a major religious speech
- Issue opinion change over the course of the campaign
- Tone of editorial coverage after a major religious speech
- Congressional roll call results
- The content of the final policy

The following case study chapters reflect the grouping of issues where such rhetoric has appeared. First, I consider the foreign policy cases, then I turn to the environment case, next to civil rights, and finally I finish with presidential scandals. All in all, the conclusions will be the same: religious rhetoric does not work.

Note

1. Indeed, the emphasis on passed laws is a major criticism of Mayhew made by a group of scholars who refute his findings by instead examining legislation that was not adopted (Edwards III, Barrett, and Peake 1997).

2

Aid, Arms, and Armageddon: Dwight Eisenhower, Ronald Reagan, and the Religious Rhetoric of Defense

The idea that America is God's chosen nation has been visible in American culture since the country's inception (Tuveson 1968). On the one hand, being a chosen people means that America must remain separate from the world. America must be the example for the world to follow. On the other hand, American exceptionalism blends into the doctrine of Manifest Destiny and the calling for America to lead (Stephanson 1996). Either way, the belief that America has a providential role to play in foreign affairs is a long-standing part of American history. It is a part of American history that makes religious rhetoric about foreign policy natural.

This chapter considers the religious rhetoric of Presidents Dwight David "Ike" Eisenhower and Ronald Reagan. The two share much in common. They were the most successful Republican presidents of the postwar era. Both men claimed dramatic international accomplishments and ended their time in office extraordinarily popular. Both men were belittled by their critics, but showed tremendous skill in private. And both men were exceptionally strategic when it came to the use of religion. Neither Eisenhower nor Reagan was personally devout. But, together, they spoke about religion as often as any other president.

In the pages that follow, I will explore the religious arguments these men used in support of bigger budgets for foreign aid and defense. In some places, the two overlap. Both drew a contrast between the atheistic Soviets and the faithful Americans as a precursor to their specific policy appeals. Yet, each would make additional religious claims beyond this distinction. Eisenhower often spoke of religious concepts like brotherhood and adopted the language of Jeremiah. Reagan cited specific passages of Scripture and used strong religious adjectives to describe the purposes of his defense budgets.

In the end, there is yet another similarity linking these two leaders: the record will show that their religious rhetoric did each little good.

Dwight Eisenhower and Mutual Security

For years, Eisenhower's political skills were maligned by observers of his administration. A popular idea had it that his de-facto chief of staff, the powerful Sherman Adams, ran the country while Ike spent his days idling around the greens and fairways of various golf courses.

These critics missed the point. Eisenhower's main skill was being able to successfully merge his roles as a symbol of national unity and as a divisive political actor. He did so by operating in a "hidden-hand" style. Thus, Eisenhower's press conferences were vague and inarticulate, but behind closed doors, his language was precise. He claimed to be nonpartisan and refused to "engage in personalities," but his actions demonstrated a refined sense of political motivation.

Sometimes, Eisenhower's machinations failed, like when he clumsily tried to coerce Nixon into leaving the ticket in 1956. But at other times, it is hard to see how any other approach would have produced better results. The way in which he undermined Sen. Joe McCarthy behind the scenes while refusing to joust with him publicly is a case in point (Greenstein 1982).

Eisenhower's use of religious rhetoric syncs with this image of the General's leadership style. Talking in religious terms allowed Eisenhower to maintain his broad popularity while possibly helping him subtly accomplish his goals. In truth, Eisenhower was "a far more complex and devious man than most people realized." It was none other than Richard Nixon who said that (Boyle 2005, 20).

In terms of religious practices, Eisenhower might have been the most outwardly religious president of modern times. Notably, he began his first inaugural with a prayer he had written himself after attending church services on the morning of his installation. The prayer was so well-received that the Republican Party eventually printed and distributed it. Later, M. Robert Rogers, chairman of the President's Committee for Arts and Sciences, would even set the prayer to music (Bergman 2009, 262).

The prayer was nothing unusual; Eisenhower developed a habit of opening each cabinet meeting with one. Likewise, he searched for appointees with strong religious convictions, especially admiring John Foster Dulles, his Secretary of State, and Ezra Taft Benson, his Secretary of Agriculture and a member of the Mormon Church's Council of Twelve and later its president. Eisenhower went a step further by asking a Congregational minister to join his staff as a special assistant responsible for advising the president on religious matters and adding biblical wisdom to Eisenhower's speeches (264).

Eisenhower helped to establish and organize the National Day of Prayer. He helped create an organization called the Foundation for Religious Action, which attempted, albeit mostly without success, to unite people in a spiritual crusade against Communism (Smith 2006, 222, 232). It was also under Eisenhower's lead that the first annual presidential prayer breakfast was held, that the words "under God" were added to the Pledge of Allegiance, and that the phrase "In God We Trust" was made the national motto.

No one should doubt Eisenhower's personal faith. Eisenhower's parents, Ida and David, were well-known Jehovah's Witnesses, then called "Russellites" or "Bible Students." The Eisenhowers had turned to the Witnesses in grief after the death of their eight-month-old son, Paul, in 1895. Ida and David were comforted by the Witness prophesy that Armageddon would occur in 1914, meaning they would soon be reunited with their departed child. Many family members were understandably disillusioned when the world didn't end in 1914.

Still, Ida continued to be involved with the Witnesses until her death in 1946, regularly hosting meetings in their house. Eisenhower grew up in a family where the Bible was read together, where prayers were said before every meal, and where activities like drinking, gambling, and swearing were discouraged. Eisenhower, his father, and his brothers eventually left the Witnesses and renounced many of their teachings. But Eisenhower retained a respect for the values he had learned as a child. Prayer remained an important part of his life. As Eisenhower told a friend at the end of the war, "Do you think I could have fought my way through this war, ordered thousands of fellows to their deaths, if I couldn't have got down on my knees and talked to God and begged him to support me and make me feel that what I was doing was right for myself and the world?" (Smith 2006, 227).

At the same time, it is undeniable that every religious action Eisenhower undertook he did with political purposes in mind. Despite his general spirituality, prior to becoming president, Eisenhower was not involved in organized religion. On his own for the first time as a cadet at West Point, Eisenhower did not participate in any religious activities, whether church services, Sunday school, Bible study, or even the Young Men Christian Association (YMCA). Over the course of his career in the Army, Eisenhower only occasionally attended chapel. Eisenhower's diaries contain just a handful of references to religion (Holmes 2012, 33). As his biographer Stephen Ambrose (1984, 38) writes, "Theology was a subject about which he knew nothing and cared nothing; he never discussed his idea of God with anyone."

Nevertheless, as he began to contemplate a run for the presidency in 1952, Eisenhower and his staff worried that his lack of a church affiliation would cost him votes. Eisenhower resisted the pressure at first, thinking that joining a church at such a late date in his life would be hypocritical. Most accounts say that he was finally convinced otherwise by a conversation with the writer Clare Boothe Luce who reminded Eisenhower that he needed to set a good example for the country. How difficult would it be for parents to get their children out of bed and into their Sunday best, Luce wondered, if the kids could say the president doesn't go to church, so why should they?

Therefore, in February of 1953, Eisenhower was baptized in a private ceremony, joining the National Presbyterian Church in Washington, DC. His wife, Mamie, had been raised as Presbyterian. Eisenhower was sixty-three years old.

One can understand why Luce's argument about setting an example was persuasive. Eisenhower repeatedly talked in public about how the United States had three pillars of strength—military, economic, and moral/spiritual. As president, he felt part of his job description was providing spiritual leadership. As his speechwriter Stanley High admitted, Eisenhower hoped "to inspire a spiritual reawakening in America" (Bergman 2009, 265).

To Eisenhower, America's entire political system was based on religion. He once told a radio and television audience in 1954, "Now I don't think it amiss . . . that we call attention to this fact: that in conception, our Nation had a spiritual foundation, so announced by the men who wrote the Declaration of Independence. You remember what they said? 'We hold that all men are endowed by their Creator with certain rights.' That is very definitely a spiritual conception" (Eisenhower 1954). More famously, perhaps, Eisenhower told a campaign audience in 1952, "Our government makes no sense unless it is founded on a deeply felt religious faith—and I don't care what it is." Eisenhower's feelings on the subject did not go much deeper than that (see Perret 1999, 428).

As part of his role as a spiritual leader, Eisenhower would work to demonize the atheist Soviets. For instance, Eisenhower opened his 1955 State of the Union by presenting his take on the basis for the Cold War. He told the public that the Cold War was at heart a religious struggle, and not a political or economic one:

> It is of the utmost importance, that each of us understand the true nature of the struggle now taking place in the world.
>
> It is not a struggle merely of economic theories, or of forms of government, or of military power. At issue is the true nature of man. Either man is the creature whom the Psalmist described as "a little lower than the angels," crowned with glory and honor, holding "dominion over the works" of his Creator; or man is a soulless, animated machine to be enslaved, used and consumed by the state for its own glorification.
>
> It is, therefore, a struggle which goes to the roots of the human spirit, and its shadow falls across the long sweep of man's destiny. This prize, so precious, so fraught with ultimate meaning, is the true object of the contending forces in the world. (Eisenhower 1955)

In a little plainer language, Eisenhower made this same point in a press conference held in March of 1956: "I have in public talks pointed out that this is, underneath it all, a battle between those people who believe that man is something more than just an educated animal and those who believe he is nothing else. That is exactly what it is. It is atheism against some kind of religion" (Eisenhower 1956a). This opinion was one Eisenhower would often express.

Depicting the Cold War as a battle between atheism and religion allowed Eisenhower to also express confidence in its eventual outcome. One side was on the side of God, while the other was not. The winner was obvious, as Eisenhower told the graduates of Baylor in 1956:

> Communism denies the spiritual premises on which your education has been based. According to that doctrine, there is no God; there is no soul in man; there is no reward beyond the satisfaction of daily needs. Consequently, toward the human being, Communism is cruel, intolerant, materialistic. This doctrine, committed to conquest by lure, by intimidation and by force, seeks to destroy the political concepts and institutions that we hold to be dearer than life itself. Thus Communism poses a threat from which even this mighty nation is not wholly immune.

Yet, my friends, Communism is, in deepest sense, a gigantic failure.

Even in the countries it dominates, hundreds of millions who dwell there still cling to their religious faith; still are moved by aspirations for justice and freedom that cannot be answered merely by more steel or by bigger bombers; still seek a reward that is beyond money or place or power; still dream of the day that they may walk fearlessly in the fullness of human freedom.

The destiny of man is freedom and justice under his Creator. Any ideology that denies this universal faith will ultimately perish or be recast. This is the first great truth that must underlie all our thinking, all our striving in this struggling world. (Eisenhower 1956b)

Eisenhower's religious comments on the Cold War were linked to a specific policy goal. All the negative religious rhetoric aimed at the Soviets set the stage for Eisenhower to extensively use religious themes and arguments to drum up support for his controversial program of foreign assistance. This aid would be going, naturally, to those countries that opposed the Godless communists. Every speech in which Eisenhower criticized the Soviets for their atheism must be seen as helping to create a context in which he could make a faith based argument for helping other countries who *did* share our religious beliefs. Part of Eisenhower's stated rationale for aiding the countries of the Middle East was, as he said, "The Middle East is the birthplace of three great religions—Moslem, Christian and Hebrew. Mecca and Jerusalem are more than places on the map. They symbolize religions which teach that the spirit has supremacy over matter and that the individual has a dignity and rights of which no despotic government can rightfully deprive him. It would be intolerable if the holy places of the Middle East should be subjected to a rule that glorifies atheistic materialism" (Eisenhower 1957a).

US foreign assistance had taken on a different character following the outbreak of the Korean War. In the Mutual Security Act of 1951, Congress abolished the Economic Cooperation Administration (ECA), which had heretofore overseen the country's foreign aid expenditures, and replaced it with the Mutual Security Agency (MSA). The ECA had been intended as a temporary body that would help promote the economic recovery of countries ravaged by World War II. The MSA had a more pronounced bias toward military objectives, and reflected the belief that the US-Soviet tension was likely to be a permanent feature of the postwar landscape.

But the question of whether the United States should allocate any foreign aid at all was increasingly debated. Many political figures felt the Marshall Plan had achieved its goals—Europe was far along the road to economic recovery by the early 1950s—and hence suggested that perhaps the United States should eliminate foreign aid entirely. Eisenhower himself initially thought that foreign growth could best be achieved by the reduction of trade barriers and the creation of incentives for private investment—in other words, "trade not aid" (Kaufman 1982).

By the end of his first term, however, Eisenhower had experienced a change of heart. Events such as the French defeat in Asia and the stirrings of nationalism worldwide made the Administration leery of the possibility of a wave of Communist takeovers. Even more disconcerting was the new Soviet economic aid offensive. After Stalin's death in 1953, the Soviet leadership had embraced policies that sought to expand Soviet influence throughout the Third World. The new Soviet rulers believed that socialist movements could gain power not only through revolutions but also via parliamentary means. Top officials made high-profile visits to countries like Burma and India, where they promised extensive economic assistance.

Eisenhower was not persuaded that the Soviets were acting out of the goodness of their hearts. Rather, he believed that Moscow wanted to undermine US ties to certain governments and to use their "economic penetration to accomplish political domination" (66–67). Eisenhower responded by advocating more generous and comprehensive aid for the underdeveloped world. His total mutual security request for the 1957 fiscal year was $4.67 billion, an increase of almost $2 billion over the funds that had been appropriated for fiscal 1956.

The White House was caught unprepared by the firestorm that ensued. They expected to encounter opposition to some of their requests, but they also believed the package would win easy approval. Instead, they ran into opposition from leaders on both sides of the aisle.

Fiscal conservatives had long seen mutual security as a worthless giveaway. But these conservatives were now joined by liberal Democrats who were increasingly discomfited by the idea that mutual security was becoming a permanent program. Some even thought that the Soviets' increased effort was reason enough to reduce America's aid programs. As a Wisconsin House member remarked, "If we are so foolish as to enter into a competitive economic aid race with the Communists, we will come out second best. We know they can offer a sales program that promises the moon or everything that the people of Asia desire" (69). For others, cutting foreign aid was almost a form of sport. Otto Passman (D-LA) once told a State Department official, "Son, I don't smoke and I don't drink. My only pleasure in life is kicking the shit out of the foreign aid program of the United States of America" (Pach and Richardson 1991, 165).

In the end, Congress reduced the Administration's request by around $1 billion. The 1956 debate over mutual security had raised so many pressing questions that both Congress and the White House had authorized independent reviews of the program. Eisenhower was willing to make changes. He had already been moving in the direction of favoring development over military assistance. His funding request in February 1957 continued that trend as for the first time since the outbreak of the Korean War the White House asked for more money for its economic programs ($2.1 billion) than for military hardware ($1.8 billion).

But even beyond this, at the start of his second term, Eisenhower sought fundamental changes in the way the mutual security program was structured. He proposed a Developmental Loan Fund of $2 billion to be spread over a three-year period to furnish long-term loans to Third World countries. He also called for a $300 million emergency fund that he could use at his discretion.

Eisenhower would battle fiercely for these proposals and for the continued funding of mutual security for the remainder of his time in office. A variety of circumstances troubled him—the rise of nationalist movements, the new Soviet aid policies, the growing domestic opposition. Eisenhower believed that mutual security was an essential US program and that it was under an unjustified assault. In the midst of this crisis atmosphere, Eisenhower decided in 1957 to launch an educational campaign aimed at convincing the public of the validity of his position.

Eisenhower would make a multitude of arguments in favor of foreign aid. The president claimed that loans and grants to foreign countries would increase US security since the country could not possibly confront the Communist threat without help from strong allies. Foreign aid would also save money, Eisenhower held, by helping other countries build up their own defenses, thus reducing the need for America to spend so much on its own. Additionally, foreign aid would provide an economic benefit, too, by boosting the economies of trade partners.

But Eisenhower made another argument repeatedly and it was a patently religious one; that as a Christian nation America had an obligation to help the less fortunate. While discussing a proposed grant to Pakistan in an earlier press conference, Eisenhower admitted as much: "I believe now that we have a moral value involved . . . Now, you say, 'all right, if it is not socialistic, it is based on a purely humanitarian thing'—and I believe George Kennan argues that humanitarian and moralistic values have no place in foreign relations. But after all, we do believe that we are a product and a representative of the Judaic-Christian civilization, and it does teach some concern for your brother. And I believe in that" (Eisenhower 1953b).

We can pinpoint the precise date when Eisenhower began framing mutual security in religious terms—his second inaugural address (Eisenhower 1957b). Eisenhower devoted the speech to theme of the world's interdependence. He summed up the gist of his message in one brief line: "For one truth must rule all we think and all we do. No people can live to itself alone." As in his more well-known first inaugural, Eisenhower opened with a personal prayer:

> Before all else, we seek, upon our common labor as a nation, the blessings of Almighty God. And the hopes in our hearts fashion the deepest prayers of our whole people.
>
> May we pursue the right—without self-righteousness.
>
> May we know unity—without conformity.
>
> May we grow in strength—without pride in self.
>
> May we, in our dealings with all peoples of the earth, ever speak truth and serve justice.
>
> And so shall America—in the sight of all men of good will—prove true to the honorable purposes that bind and rule us as a people in all this time of trial through which we pass.

Although this religious rhetoric seems communitarian, Eisenhower quickly made clear that he was lobbying for a policy goal. Eisenhower indicated that to build a peaceful world would require that the American people be willing to pay specific costs of foreign aid, which he outlined in some detail.

In addition to the prayer, Eisenhower made his plea for aid by using three different types of religious references. First, he used a series of easily identifiable Christian metaphors like "sacrifice calmly borne," an allusion to Christ's crucifixion, and "burdened shoulders," an allusion to Christ's bearing of the cross.

Second, Eisenhower spoke of the importance of the "brotherhood of all." Brotherhood is a significant Christian concept (Achtemeier 1996, 157), and a concept that Eisenhower frequently related to foreign aid. In the Bible, biological brothers are often villains. Cain murdered his brother, Abel, when his offering to God was rejected. The brothers of Joseph sold their father's more favored son into slavery in Egypt. Metaphorical brotherhood is different. It is the most familiar analogy for the family of God. It signifies an egalitarian relationship of love and service. It was something on which Jesus was very direct: "And pointing to his disciples, he said, 'Here are my mother and my brothers! For whoever does the will of my Father in heaven is my brother and sister and mother'" (Matthew 12:49–50).

Finally, the president also made extensive use of light/dark imagery in order to impress upon his listeners the fundamental goodness of America as opposed to the evil designs of the Union of Soviet Socialist Republics (USSR). This is another recognizable Biblical theme (see, i.e., 2 Corinthians 4:6). The Soviets are described as "dark in purpose." The countries under Communist control are living through "the night of their bondage" and are depicted as "darkened lands." In contrast, the United States represents "the light of freedom" that will "flame brightly." This duality is a fairly common feature of much of Eisenhower's Cold War rhetoric.[1]

Eisenhower would expand upon this religious conception of mutual security in a major radio and television address on the program that coming May (Eisenhower 1957c). Again, as aforementioned, Eisenhower would offer many different points of support for his policy proposals. But the religious overtones were still obvious:

> We do seek to help other peoples to become strong and stay free—and learn, through living in freedom, how to conquer poverty, how to know the blessings of peace and progress.
>
> This purpose—I repeat—serves our own national interest.
>
> It also reflects our own national character. We are stirred not only by calculations of self-interest but also by decent regard for the needs and the hopes of all our fellowmen. I am proud of this fact, as you are. None of us would wish it to be otherwise.
>
> This is not mere sentimentality. This is the very nature of America realistically understood and applied.
>
> If ever we were to lose our sense of brotherhood, of kinship with all free men, we would have entered upon our nation's period of decline.

> Without vision—without a quick sense of justice and compassion—no people can claim greatness.

This passage is a direct appeal to the conscience of the American public. Eisenhower claims that the country is obligated to support mutual security because it is in tune with our values of justice and compassion, values that, on numerous other occasions, he has made clear derive from America's religious traditions.

Note that, once more, we see a reference to "brotherhood." This would become a recurring theme for Eisenhower. For instance, before a group of policy leaders sometime later, Eisenhower presented the idea of Christian brotherhood as the *entire* justification for mutual security (Eisenhower 1960b). The president explained, "Only by thinking of ourselves, and truly conducting ourselves, as brothers under God with those who, with us, want to live and grow in freedom, can we hope to solve problems in which failure will mean disaster for much of humanity . . . There, in those few words, is the very heart of mutual security."

Finally, Eisenhower associates mutual security with Godliness in the sense that a goal of the program is to help others "know the blessings of peace and progress." By means of mutual security, Eisenhower is saying America can help spread those gifts throughout the world. Eisenhower explains the goal of mutual security in terms of "blessings" on two other occasions in the text. At the start, "And we must demonstrate and spread the blessings of liberty—to be cherished by those who enjoy these blessings, to be sought by those now denied them." And later, "I know of no more sound or necessary investment that our Nation can make . . . to securing the blessing of liberty."

Interestingly, in his May address, Eisenhower also claimed that the fundamental purpose of the mutual security program was "to help these people to help themselves." This line would have a Biblical ring to it. Although the phrase "God helps those who help themselves" is not found in the Bible, most Americans think that it is. It is the most widely quoted Biblical verse in the United States, even though the words are actually Ben Franklin's (Prothero 2007, 11, 296).

In other speeches, Eisenhower would advance additional religious arguments. Sometimes, he would emphasize the importance of the Golden Rule (see Metzger and Coogan 1993, 257–58), so named because it was seen as essential wisdom from Jesus: "In everything do to others as you would have them do to you; for this is the law and the prophets." (Matthew 7:12). For instance, as he defended mutual security before the National Conference on the Foreign Aspects of National Security in 1958, Eisenhower said, "If anyone, then, wants to judge this entire program only on a 'what's-in-it-for-me' basis, he can find all the justification he needs. But beyond this, if others want to add another element, 'Do unto others as you would have them do unto you,' I see no reason to apologize for acknowledging this kind of motive" (Eisenhower 1958).

At times, Eisenhower was even more explicit about why America's religious beliefs made it incumbent upon the nation to offer generous foreign aid. A notable example was his nationally broadcast speech at the Pageant of Peace Ceremonies in 1959 (Eisenhower 1959b). Here, Eisenhower chose to opportunistically connect the mutual security program to the meaning of Christmas. Having just returned from a trip abroad that took him to eleven different countries, Eisenhower reflected on what he had learned. He reminded his audience that "in the often fierce and even vicious battle for survival—against weather and disease and poverty—some peoples need help." Why America should provide this financial help was shortly made clear:

> Yet America's own best interests—our own hopes for peace—require that we continue our financial investment and aid; and persuade all other free nations to join us—to the limit of their ability—in a long-term program, dependable in its terms and in its duration.

> But more importantly—in the spirit of the Christmas season, that there may be peace on earth, and good will among men—we must as individuals, as corporations, labor unions, professional societies, as communities, multiply our interest, our concern in these peoples. They are now our warm friends. They will be our stout and strong partners for peace and friendship in freedom—if they are given the right sort of help in the right sort of spirit . . .

> Protected by our defensive strength against violent disruption of our peaceful efforts, we are trying to produce a workable, practical program that will make each succeeding Christmas a little closer in spirit and reality to the message of the first Christmas long ago . . .

> Together we should consider all the ways and the forms such help might take. I fervently hope that in this Christmas Season each of you who is listening will give thought to what you can do for another human, identical with you in his divine origin and destiny—however distant in miles or poor in worldly estate.

This was not a traditional Christmas message. Eisenhower chose to connect Christmas to foreign aid because it suited his purposes. It was a choice well in keeping with the type of rhetoric he had already used to define the mutual security program in the past.

The Christmas 1959 speech is also important because it is representative of a last ditch effort Eisenhower mounted in attempt to gain more solid backing for foreign aid expenditures as he entered his last year in office. Eisenhower decided, at the end of 1959, to embark on a good will tour across the globe. The stated goal of the journey was to explain America's positions directly to foreign audiences. There were personal benefits as well, as Eisenhower would get to visit a series of places he had always dreamed of seeing. No meaningful business was conducted, but from a public relations standpoint, the trip was successful as huge crowds greeted the president at each stop.

Eisenhower used the occasion of his departure as an opportunity to re-emphasize the moral and spiritual obligation underlying mutual security (Eisenhower 1959a). Like so many times before, he reminded his listeners of America's religious foundation. "Our country has been unjustly described as one pursuing only materialistic goals; as building a culture whose hallmarks are gadgets and shallow pleasures; as prizing wealth above ideals, machines above spirit, leisure above learning, and war above peace," Eisenhower said. "Actually, as our declaration proclaims, the core of our Nation is belief in a Creator who has endowed all men with inalienable rights, including life, liberty, and the pursuit of happiness. In that belief is our country's true hallmark—a faith that permeates every aspect of our political, social, and family life."

Eisenhower proceeded to question whether America was living up to that standard. He acknowledged that "in some respects, we have fallen short of the high ideals held up for us." But he also offered a solution:

> So I earnestly make this suggestion, as I start this journey tonight—that you, and those close to you, join with me in a renewed dedication to our moral and spiritual convictions, and in that light re-examine our own record, including our shortcomings. May this examination inspire each of us so to think and so to act, as to hasten our progress toward the goals our fathers established, which have made America an instrument for good. In this rededication we shall replenish the true source of America's strength—her faith; and, flowing from it, her love of liberty, her devotion to justice.

> So believing, we look on our Nation's great wealth as more than a hard earned resource to be used only for our own material good.

We believe that it should also serve the common good, abroad as well as at home.

Mutual security was praised for offering "hope" and "encouragement" to "a world sorely troubled by an atheistic imperialism."

Eisenhower's language bears all the hallmarks of a jeremiad. The term is a reference to the seventh—through sixth-century BC Judean prophet Jeremiah. Jeremiah's prophecies are recorded in the book of Jeremiah, a Hebrew text and part of the Old Testament. The organization of the book is difficult to grasp (stylistically, it mixes prose, historical narrative, and biographical material), but the central failing of the Judeans, according to Jeremiah, is that they had broken their covenant with God. Their trespass became visible in the social problems that Jeremiah describes, including gross acts of violence.

Jeremiah calls for the people to repair this breach by warning them of the impending judgment of God. God's wrath is vividly depicted as a scorching wind, as eating bitter food, as drinking poisoned water, as the pain of childbirth. However, Jeremiah also offers a muted message of hope. Though skeptical of human nature, Jeremiah envisions a new, more personal relationship with God in the future.

Bearing many similarities to this original message, the jeremiad became a common form of Puritan sermon. When trying to explain the difficulties confronting their parishioners, whether disease or poor harvests or Indian attacks, preachers turned their sights skyward. They claimed that these misfortunes were signs that God was displeased with his chosen people.

From its origins in early American religion, the jeremiad has had a long history in secular literature, ranging from the muckraking styles of Upton Sinclair and Lincoln Steffens, to more recent treatises against materialism and economic inequality (Altschuler 2003). It has also been a surprisingly prominent form of presidential speech (Smith and Smith 1994a, 133–64). We will encounter the most famous of these jeremiads, Jimmy Carter's "Crisis of Confidence Speech," in a later chapter. But as James Morone (2003, 45) observes, every iteration of the jeremiad has retained the same rhetorical trajectory, "lamentations about decline, warnings of doom, and promises of future glory (if we just get our act together . . ."

Eisenhower may not have been as harsh as some of his Puritan forbears, but all these elements are present in this address. Eisenhower worries that we have "fallen short," the text is peppered with images of impending doom (i.e., "powder kegs of disaster"), and he promises salvation if we can get our act together by simply remembering to share our wealth. Doing so would allow us to "replenish . . . America's strength" and to "hasten our progress toward the goals our fathers established."

Privately, Eisenhower had been shocked by the level of destitution he had encountered abroad. The experience had made him even more convinced that the most fundamental question facing the world was how the rich countries could help the poor (Ambrose 1984, 553). Combined with his concerns about both the movement of Cuba toward the Communist bloc and a perceptible increase in tensions with the Soviets, the trip left Eisenhower more determined than ever to play an active role in securing the foreign aid amounts he thought necessary (Kaufman 1982, 197). The Pageant of Peace speech reflected this renewed concern. As did his 1960 State of the Union address (Eisenhower 1960a).

Mutual security was one of the first subjects that Eisenhower raised in his lengthy talk. He warned Congress of the dangers of not providing adequate assistance: "These peoples, desperately hoping to lift themselves to decent levels of living must not, by our neglect, be forced to seek help from, and finally become virtual satellites of, those who proclaim their hostility to freedom." For a second time in a month, we see Eisenhower taking the stance of a Jeremiah with respect to foreign aid.

> To remain secure and prosperous themselves, wealthy nations must extend the kind of cooperation to the less fortunate members that will inspire hope, confidence and progress. A rich nation can for a time, without noticeable damage to itself, pursue a course of self-indulgence, making its single goal the material ease and comfort of its own citizens—thus repudiating its own spiritual and material stake in a peaceful and prosperous society of nations. But the enmities it will incur, the isolation into which it will descend, and the internal moral and physical softness that will be engendered, will, in the long term, bring it to disaster.
>
> America did not become great through softness and self-indulgence.

Eisenhower's religious rhetorical strategy for the mutual security program was prominent; he made a religious argument in no less than five nationally broadcast addresses. His strategy was multifaceted. He offered repeated distinctions between the atheist Soviets and the

God-fearing American public. He made use of Christian metaphors and light and dark imagery. He spoke in terms of religious concepts like brotherhood. He framed the mutual security program as being representative of the meaning of Christmas. He even adopted the language of a Jeremiah.

None of this would help.

Eisenhower made a high number of major speeches where he talked at length about mutual security in religious terms. But as Table 2.1 shows, in three of the five instances, there was almost no difference in the president's rating before and after the given speech. It should be noted that Eisenhower's December 3, 1959 speech, the speech prior to his good will trip where Eisenhower adopted a jeremiad style, did seem to provide the president with a strong short-term boost. Eisenhower recorded a 67 percent approval rating on the day of the speech, whereas in the next measurement, taken just a week later, Eisenhower clocked in with a ten point improvement in his standing. The acclaim surrounding Eisenhower's trip, rather than the rhetoric, is the probable cause of this movement. Regardless, this effect is offset by the corresponding eleven-point drop in his approval that surrounded Eisenhower's Pageant of Peace speech.

In terms of how the public's thinking evolved on the issue of mutual security itself, there are data limitations. Pollsters at this time did not often ask voters about their feelings on foreign aid; a database search yielded only nine questions between 1957 and 1960. However, over the four years under consideration, the public's views on foreign aid may not have perceptibly changed.

Table 2.1
Opinion change following Eisenhower's mutual security addresses

Date	Opinion Before	Opinion After	Net Change
1/21/1957	73 (1/17)	72 (2/7)	−1
5/21/1957	62 (5/17)	64 (6/6)	+2
12/3/1959	67 (12/3)	77 (12/10)	+10
12/23/1959	77 (12/10)	66 (1/6)	−11
1/7/1960	66 (1/6)	64 (2/4)	−2

Source: Ragsdale (2009, 184, 228–29).

A Roper survey in March 1957 asked whether the level of foreign economic aid should be "increased, or should it be kept the same as it is now, should it be cut down a little, or should it be cut down drastically?" Only 4 percent of people felt it should be increased; collectively 59 percent of people wanted it cut to some extent (Roper Organization 1957).

The next month, another study reported similar results when 37 percent of respondents agreed that the government was spending "too much" on foreign aid, while only 2 percent felt the amount was "not enough" (National Opinion Research Center 1957).

A year later, Gallup asked a nearly identical question. Again, the results were roughly the same. Only 4 percent of respondents wanted "more" money to be spent on foreign aid; 35 percent wanted "less" (Gallup Organization 1958).

And, finally, in a 1959 survey just 6 percent of participants thought the amount of money the United States devoted to foreign aid should be "increased," as opposed to 39 percent who wanted to see that amount "decreased" (Gallup Organization 1959).

Overlooking the differences in question wording, a visible pattern emerges. Few people ever wanted more spending on foreign aid (the results range from 2 to 6 percent support), while around half the country would have liked to have seen less.

A poll on mutual security conducted right after Eisenhower's May 21, 1957 address confirms this conclusion. Taken immediately after they had heard Eisenhower's religious argument for foreign aid, 42 percent of respondents still felt the program should be cut as opposed to the 32 percent of people who would oppose a reduction (Gallup 1957). Although the basis for such an observation is limited, it still appears unlikely that Eisenhower's religious rhetoric on mutual security had any positive public opinion benefit for the president.

The next relationship we must consider when evaluating the effectiveness of Eisenhower's religious rhetoric involves the media. Given that Eisenhower made five major speeches where he used religious arguments, it is possible to get an accurate read on the impact of this type of language. What is apparent from this investigation is that Eisenhower's religious rhetoric did not serve him well.

Eisenhower's first major address containing religious rhetoric was his second inaugural. The US foreign aid program was a key part of a larger discussion that occurred at the start of the second Eisenhower term. Congress was in the midst of debating the Eisenhower Doctrine, first proposed by the president before a joint session on January 5, 1957.

Motivated by Soviet activity in the Mideast following the Suez crisis, Eisenhower requested a resolution that would allow him to use the armed forces to oppose any aggression in the area and to allocate at his discretion around $200 million in aid. There was never any doubt that Congress would support the military aspect of the Doctrine, but the foreign aid request did spark a dispute. Hence, the dialog on foreign aid was wrapped into a larger debate about US policy in the Mideast, and thus, I had to carefully screen editorials for those commentating on the value of foreign aid in general, as opposed to those concerned with the Eisenhower Doctrine in specific.

Table 2.2 contains the results of this process. Ten editorials on foreign aid were printed in the four papers over the course of the week following the inaugural festivities. Seven of these ten pieces were negative in tone.

The *Chicago Tribune* blasted both Eisenhower's foreign aid programs, and the religious rhetoric which he had used to describe them. In their initial reaction to the address, the paper wrote that "The President's rhetoric tends to obscure the commonplace realities of our situation and to make a dangerous and costly course of action seem wise, good, and even inspired." They went on, "In truth, the course of intervention he recommends is the one we have been following for more than a generation and it has brought us nothing more desirable than three wars, the deaths of more than a third of a million young Americans, and a national debt of more than a quarter of a trillion dollars." Eisenhower, they argued, was "obsessed with what he fancies is the duty of the people of this country to make everybody in the world safe, happy, and peaceful at no matter what the cost to the American people and at no matter how heavy a risk of involving our county in war" (*Chicago Tribune* 1957a).

In another editorial, the *Chicago Tribune* (1957b) took Eisenhower's religious arguments head-on. The paper countered that Eisenhower was misunderstanding Christian ethics. "It can be said that this (foreign aid) is the role of a Christian," the board wrote, "yet a Christian can do good unto others only as long as he can sustain himself. And, furthermore, there is a limit to governmental folly and internationalist infatuation, even when it is wrapped in a quasi-religious appeal." Eisenhower's "salvationist mission" would only be an "endless drain upon our energies, our wealth, and our resources," the paper argued.

Eisenhower's second major instance of religious rhetoric came several months later on May 21. The reaction to this speech was better,

Table 2.2
Editorial coverage of Eisenhower's second inaugural

Date	Paper	Author	Title	Score
1/22/1957	*Chicago Tribune*	Staff Editorial	"Inaugural Message"	1
1/22/1957	*Los Angeles Times*	Staff Editorial	"The President's Inaugural Address"	4
1/22/1957	*New York Times*	Staff Editorial	"An Inaugural Prayer"	5
1/22/1957	*Washington Post*	Staff Editorial	"The Price of Peace"	5
1/23/1957	*Chicago Tribune*	Staff Editorial	"First Dividends on Ike's Doctrine'"	1
1/24/1957	*Chicago Tribune*	Staff Editorial	"For Whom the Bell Tolls"	1
1/24/1957	*Washington Post*	Malvina Lindsay	"U.S. Needs Finesse in Rich Man's Role"	2
1/25/1957	*New York Times*	Arthur Krock	"Resemblance to Monroe was Brief"	2
1/27/1957	*New York Times*	James Reston	"A Few Clouds on the Dark Horizon"	2
1/28/1957	*Chicago Tribune*	Staff Editorial	"All in One Year"	1
Dates: 1/22 to 1/28			**Average score**	**2.40**
			Positive articles	3 (30.0%)
			Negative articles	7 (70.0%)
			Mixed/neutral articles	0 (0.0%)

but still mixed. As seen in Table 2.3, out of eleven total editorials, five were negative and five were positive.

In one piece, the *Chicago Tribune* turned Eisenhower's words against him. In some earlier comments made during the 1952 presidential campaign, Eisenhower had suggested that the country's foreign aid

Table 2.3
Editorial coverage of Eisenhower's mutual security address on May 21, 1957

Date	Paper	Author	Title	Score
5/22/1957	*Chicago Tribune*	Staff Editorial	"What Does Foreign Aid Do for Us?"	1
5/22/1957	*Los Angeles Times*	Staff Editorial	"The President Says He Needs It All"	1
5/22/1957	*New York Times*	Staff Editorial	"In Defense of Freedom"	5
5/22/1957	*Washington Post*	Staff Editorial	"The Battle Joined"	5
5/23/1957	*Chicago Tribune*	Staff Editorial	"Lobbyist in the White House"	1
5/24/1957	*New York Times*	Arthur Krock	"Timing of the President's Counter-Attack"	5
5/26/1957	*Chicago Tribune*	Staff Editorial	"Mr. Eisenhower's Friend Tito"	1
5/26/1957	*Chicago Tribune*	Staff Editorial	"The 80 Year Old 'Emergency'"	1
5/26/1957	*Washington Post*	Stewart Alsop	"Ike Fights Back and Moves Ahead"	5
5/26/1957	*Washington Post*	Staff Editorial	"Mr. Nixon's Blessing"	3
5/28/1957	*Washington Post*	Staff Editorial	"Tools of Leadership"	5
Dates: **5/22 to 5/28**			**Average score**	**3.00**
			Positive articles	5 (45.5%)
			Negative articles	5 (45.5%)
			Mixed/neutral articles	1 (9.1%)

packages were counterproductive. By shilling so enthusiastically for them now, the *Tribune* said Eisenhower was little more than a "huckster and lobbyist" (*Chicago Tribune* 1957c).

In another piece, the *Tribune* criticized Eisenhower for providing aid to countries like Yugoslavia—countries that took American dollars and then later cozied up to the enemy Soviets (*Chicago Tribune* 1957d).

In a third editorial, the paper alleged that communism was only a rationalization for foreign aid, merely "a convenient excuse for hand-outs, and if it did not exist" then "the internationalists would invent another one" (*Chicago Tribune* 1957e).

This time, though, the *Tribune* was joined in their opposition by the *Los Angeles Times* (1957). In an editorial dripping with contempt, the West Coast paper wrote that Eisenhower's arguments for mutual security were built on an "unsupported faith achieved mystically through an inward grace." Eisenhower and the other "philosophers of giveaway," as the paper branded them, believed that American money could remake the world in America's own image. The board disagreed with this premise, arguing instead that American aid had heretofore been ineffective, pointing out that the French were "taking the troops we helped to pay for and the equipment we provided to fight a colonial war in Africa." As such, the paper concluded, "An economizing Congress should study this Presidential message very carefully, and . . . very skeptically."

What positive reaction there was this week was not so much in response to Eisenhower's programs nor to his religious rhetoric. Rather, many were simply impressed that Eisenhower was regaining the upper-hand in his tug-of-war with Congress. A common perception at the time was that Eisenhower's influence was rapidly waning and, further, that the president was curiously disengaged from his agenda. His strong speech on May 21 convinced many otherwise (see, i.e., Alsop 1957).

Eisenhower's three other major addresses featuring religious rhetoric all occurred over the course of the month between the end of 1959 and the start of 1960. No speech by itself produced much commentary on foreign aid and, given that they all were delivered in such a short time span, it makes sense to group the results together, as I do in Table 2.4.

Once more, the media was not favorable to Eisenhower. Six out of thirteen articles were negative in tone and the average piece was scored a 2.69, well below the three that would indicate neutrality.

Capitalizing on Eisenhower's Christmas imagery, the *Chicago Tribune* (1959) compared the president to Santa Claus, but they rued "the difference is that when Santa brings gifts, he holds the bag. When Mr. Eisenhower visits the world's hopefuls, the taxpayers hold the bag."

Table 2.4
Editorial coverage of Eisenhower's mutual security speeches between December 1959 and January 1960

Date	Paper	Author	Title	Score
12/4/1959	*Washington Post*	Staff Editorial	"Image of America"	3
12/9/1959	*Chicago Tribune*	Staff Editorial	"Santa's Competitor"	1
12/10/1959	*New York Times*	James Reston	"Foreign-Aid Problems"	2
12/24/1959	*Washington Post*	Staff Editorial	"Mr. Eisenhower's Odyssey"	4
12/25/1959	*New York Times*	Staff Editorial	"The Torch"	5
12/27/1959	*Chicago Tribune*	Staff Editorial	"Executive Secrets"	1
12/28/1959	*Chicago Tribune*	Staff Editorial	"Hang Up Your Stockings"	1
1/8/1960	*Chicago Tribune*	Staff Editorial	"State of the Union"	3
1/8/1960	*Los Angeles Times*	Staff Editorial	"On the State of the Presdency"	3
1/8/1960	*New York Times*	Staff Editorial	"State of the Union"	4
1/8/1960	*Washington Post*	Staff Editorial	"The Union Adrift"	2
1/10/1960	*Chicago Tribune*	Staff Editorial	"Moral Imperatives"	1
1/10/1960	*New York Times*	Staff Editorial	"The State of the Universe"	5
Dates: 12/4 to 12/10			**Average score**	**2.69**
Dates: 12/24 to 12/30			**Positive articles**	**4 (30.8%)**
Dates: 1/8 to 1/14			**Negative articles**	**6 (46.2%)**
			Mixed/neutral articles	**3 (23.1%)**

In a piece responding to Eisenhower's State of the Union religious rhetoric, in particular, the *Chicago Tribune* (1960) said that listening to the speech was "something like being hit over the head with a two-by-four to impress the wisdom of being good." They claimed that Eisenhower was "feeding the nation a diet of homily grits." However, noting that some of the strongest advocates for foreign aid also had personal financial interests at stake in recipient countries, the board chastised those who would claim that mutual security was important solely as a "moral imperative" as hypocrites.

Even the *Washington Post* (1959), typically supportive of foreign assistance, was no longer fully on board at this point. The *Post* praised Eisenhower's religious rhetoric on December 3. "Reiteration of spiritual values in a Nation that is often advertised by its material culture can serve an important purpose," the board acknowledged. Yet, they lamented that "too often the performance belies the fine phrases."

Overall, Eisenhower's religious rhetoric did not generate positive media coverage for his mutual security budgets. Cumulatively, over the course of five speeches, there were more negative op-eds published than positive ones. Further, in what will become a pattern, even outlets who liked the religious rhetoric were capable of criticizing the policies it was linked to.

Last, Eisenhower did not experience any more success in his dealings with Congress. In 1957, Eisenhower's mutual security requests had to overcome obstacles in both the authorization and the appropriations stages of the political process. The Mutual Security Act of 1957, as originally proposed, included both the president's request for funding and the aforementioned structural changes that Eisenhower wished to see made. The final bill that was agreed to in conference was a mixed bag for the Administration. On the one hand, Congress authorized $3.38 billion in foreign aid, not the $3.87 billion that had been requested. Although disappointed in these cuts, Eisenhower still wanted the bill to pass because Congress had agreed to many of the procedural revisions he wanted, including authorizing the Loan Fund, which was Eisenhower's top priority.

It turned out that Eisenhower's fortunes deteriorated as the bill moved on to Appropriations. By a margin of 129-254, on August 15, the president badly lost a House vote on a motion to recommit sponsored by Walter Judd (R-MN), which would have returned the bill with instructions to restore $715 million in funding. At the end of the month, Congress cut a further $598,323,000 from the amount they had just authorized for the mutual security program. Eisenhower was livid, fuming "Some people are still stupid enough to believe in the concept of 'Fortress America'" (Kaufman 1982, 109–10).

The year 1959 also saw another battle between the Administration and Congress over foreign aid. This year, Eisenhower would request $3.93 billion in authorizations. The discussion over this request would be marked by an attempt to increase the emphasis on economic, as opposed to military, aid. In addition to being forced to make some compromises on the design of the program, Eisenhower was pressured into accepting an appropriation that was $704 million under his request. This was a better result than the $1.1 billion cut that he had to swallow in 1957, but still a hollow victory. The package was, however, well-supported in Congress. Despite a nearly two-to-one Democrat to Republican majority, Eisenhower carried the vote on passage of the Mutual Security Act of 1959 easily, 271-142 in the House, and 56-26 in the Senate.

In 1958 and 1960 Congress did debate appropriations for mutual security, though the fights in these two years were somewhat less significant because of previous authorizations. In 1958, $644 million had already been authorized by previous laws. The main points of contention were both the amount to be authorized and appropriated as well as whether the president would be permitted to funnel aid to Communist nations other than the Soviet Union. The latter issue receded when Eisenhower agreed to seek such authority in a separate piece of legislation.

Overall, Eisenhower had better luck with the 1958 bill as opposed to the previous year's edition, but he was still sorely disappointed by the final outcome. Though the cuts were not as deep, Congress continued to provide less money than the president had requested. The final $3.3 billion appropriation was $600 million below Eisenhower's initial recommendation.

In 1960, $2.72 billion had already been authorized for fiscal 1961, an amount equal to over half the amount requested. Ultimately, Congress would agree to appropriate $3.78 billion in total, about $469 million less than the revised White House request. Although the cuts in fiscal 1961 were, percentage-wise, the smallest of his presidency (9 percent), Eisenhower was, nonetheless, discouraged by the outcome. Perhaps in a sign of defeat, Eisenhower did not even issue a signing statement expressing his displeasure with these cuts, something that heretofore had been his custom (Congressional Quarterly 1958a, 1958b, 1960).

In sum, Eisenhower's religious rhetoric on mutual security did not bear much fruit in terms of his relationship with Congress. Congress dictated the outcomes, cutting funds from Eisenhower's foreign aid requests by no less than 9 percent every year.

Ronald Reagan and Defense Spending

Two individuals played formative roles in Ronald Reagan's spiritual upbringing. One was Reagan's mother. Nelle Reagan was baptized into the Disciples of Christ church in 1910. For the remainder of her life, she was an active member of the Disciples parish in Dixon, Illinois, leading Bible study groups, serving as the song director for the choir, and writing for the church's newspaper. Nelle encouraged her son to follow her example and, in his early years, Ron did. As a teenager, he taught Sunday school and led Bible study. When it was time to attend college, Reagan chose Eureka, a small school that was affiliated with the Disciples.

The other individual who influenced Reagan's religious beliefs was Ben Cleaver, the minister of First Christian Church in Dixon and the father of Reagan's high-school sweetheart, Margaret. Reagan's own father was a troubled alcoholic, so Reagan looked to Cleaver for a male role model. In addition to guiding Reagan spiritually, Cleaver taught him how to drive and prepared him for school. Margaret eventually broke things off with Reagan while the two were engaged in college, but Reagan continued to correspond with Cleaver up until the minster's death in 1975 (Vaughn 1995; Smith 2006, 326–38).

Reagan's childhood habits did not last. Reagan was only an infrequent attendee at services over the course of his adult life, including while he was president. Reagan defended his absence on Sundays by arguing that his presence in church could distract or even jeopardize the security of other worshippers. Yet, safety concerns have not stopped other high-ranking officials, including his own vice president, from attending services. Plus, Reagan always had the option of instituting private services in the White House as an alternative, just as Nixon had done.

In terms of personal conduct, although Reagan was faithful to his wife, Nancy, the fact remains that he had remarried. The New Testament prohibits divorce and remarriage (Matthew 5:32). Over the course of American history, members of the evangelical community who divorced faced possible expulsion from their congregations (Balmer 2008, 112–13). As such, failed marriages had hindered the presidential aspirations of previous contenders like Nelson Rockefeller and Adlai Stevenson.

Reagan's marital history was not the only potential black mark in his biography for religious voters. Reagan also had estranged relationships with several of his children. In a wounded memoir published in 1987, Michael Reagan, the president's adopted son from his first marriage to actress Jane Wyman, revealed that his father had never even seen him play football in high school (Schieffer and Gates 1989, 173). Reagan's daughter, Patti, took her mother's maiden name as her own, and later posed for *Playboy* magazine. All of these complications did not square with ideal Christian ethics.

And then there was the astrology (Benze 2005, 113–17). In one of the many unflattering tell-alls about the Reagan Administration, ex-Chief of Staff Don Regan wrote in 1988 that the First Lady had fallen under the spell of an astrologer named Joan Quigley. According to Regan, the scheduling of major presidential events, including summits with Soviet leader Mikhail Gorbachev, depended on the content of the readings Nancy Reagan received from Quigley.

In her own memoirs, Nancy explains how she began to turn to Quigley for comfort after the attempt on her husband's life in 1981. Quigley had shown Mrs. Reagan charts that identified the period around the attempt as a dangerous time for the couple. However, Nancy denied that any political decisions were influenced by her interest in astrology. Christian conservatives were dismayed either way. Broadcasting executive George Otis collected the signatures of over 25,000 Christians urging the Reagans to "just say no" to astrology.

Given his background, it is easy to question the sincerity of Reagan's commitment to the religious right. The reality is Reagan delivered little of importance to Christian conservatives. By the end of his presidency, almost all of the evangelical agenda remained unfulfilled. Abortion was still legal. School prayer was still not. The pornographic film industry flourished.

Reagan did not expend much energy to change any of these things. One insider candidly acknowledged that the Reagan strategy was premised on the wisdom of *The Godfather*: "hold your friends close, hold your enemies closer." Claiming that the Administration would only offer the religious right "symbolism," the aide explained that the goal was "to keep the Moral Majority types so close to us they can't move their arms" (Pierard 1983, 1185).

As an illustration of this approach, Reagan would speak to anti-abortion protesters every year when they rallied in Washington on the anniversary of *Roe v. Wade*. But Reagan would communicate with these activists via telephone, instead of in person, thereby ensuring that he would not be seen at the rally on the evening news.

In another move designed to protect his standing, rather than risk his own political capital on school prayer, Reagan encouraged religious leaders to lobby on his behalf. In Lou Cannon's (1991, 813) informed opinion, anything Reagan said on prayer was "never more than throwaway lines intended to comfort the so-called Religious Right or some other element of the conservative constituency."

In an additional symbolic gesture, Reagan appointed some visible evangelicals like James Watt and C. Everett Koop to important government posts. Watt promised upon his appointment to follow the guidance of Scripture "to occupy the land until He returns" (Wilentz 2008, 140). Koop was a co-author of the anti-abortion screed *Whatever Happened to the Human Race?* Yet Reagan did not consistently back what these men did in office.

In truth, all of this activity operated at the margins. Reagan's actual legislative accomplishments, like the Adolescent Family Life Act, which provided federal funding for abstinence-based sex education, were relatively minor (Ehrman 2005, 171–81; Balmer 2008, 109–24; Williams 2008, 2010, 187–211).

So, if you are a Reagan acolyte, then you probably agree with Attorney General Ed Meese, who claimed, "He had a very strong personal faith, which came up as a natural thing in private conversation. The president was able to talk about religion in a comfortable way, better than almost any person I've ever met. He did not want to parade it before the public . . ." These individuals were more than willing to write off Reagan's lack of personal piety and his half-hearted attempts at policy change.

If you are a Reagan antagonist, however, your perspective probably falls somewhere closer to that of Miguel D'Escoto, a priest and former Nicaraguan foreign minister, who said, "he is not a person who gives a hoot about religion. The religious dimension was not there, and God became someone to manipulate and to use for the advancement of Reagan's purposes. He used God, playing with the hearts of the American people, touching chords that would produce the effect that he was looking for" (Strober and Strober 2003b, 55–56).

The truth probably lies somewhere in the middle. Reagan seemed to genuinely believe that America had a divine mission in the world (Heclo 2003). But Reagan was also capable of being quite shrewd when it came to the political use of religion. The manner in which he navigated the controversies over school prayer and abortion proves as much.

Billy Graham once told Reagan, "I would think that you have talked about God more than any other president since Abraham Lincoln" (Pemberton 1997, 138). Some have questioned how someone so publicly devout could at the same time be so antagonistic toward US adversaries. Nevertheless, Reagan was no warmonger. He regularly told his audiences that he had already seen four wars in his lifetime. As he saw it, a nuclear war could not be won and hence must not be fought.

In private, Reagan was known to fret that a simple misunderstanding might precipitate a nuclear Armageddon—as in the end of the world as foretold by the Bible. Reagan had become hooked on the contents of the Book of Revelation in the late 1960s (Cannon 1991, 288–91). As Reagan understood it, certain events in Revelation, like a plague, could be interpreted as a prophecy of nuclear war. His political strategist Stuart Spencer remembered, "He was absolutely obsessed with the threat from Russia; the whole nuclear picture revolved around that threat. He used to talk about Armageddon. To my mind, Armageddon tied into his concern about the nuclear chaos that he knew about as president, from the information he would get in his national security and other briefings. These were the things he worried about. He had a vision about them; he read about them, thought about them, and talked to a lot of people about them" (Strober and Strober 2003b, 147).

Reagan staffers worried about how the public would react if they knew of this presidential fixation. Reagan was questioned about his beliefs on Armageddon in his second debate with Walter Mondale in 1984, but the issue never materialized. That does not mean that Reagan kept these thoughts to himself, though. On occasion, Reagan did refer to his apocalyptic visions in public, one example being a December 1983 interview he did with *People* magazine (Reagan 1983g).

The reporters asked Reagan about a curious quote that had been attributed to him by the *Jerusalem Post*. In that exchange, Reagan had suggested that the current generation might witness the end of times. Reagan explained his comments to *People* as such:

> I've never done that publicly. I have talked here, and then I wrote people, because some theologians quite some time ago were telling

me, calling attention to the fact that theologians have been studying the ancient prophecies—What would portend the coming of Armageddon?—and have said that never, in the time between the prophecies up until now has there ever been a time in which so many of the prophecies are coming together. There have been times in the past when people thought the end of the world was coming, and so forth, but never anything like this.

And one of them, the first one who ever broached this to me—and I won't use his name; I don't have permission to. He probably would give it, but I'm not going to ask—had held a meeting with the then head of the German Government, years ago when the war was over, and did not know that his hobby was theology. And he asked this theologian what did he think was the next great news event, worldwide. And the theologian, very wisely, said, "Well, I think that you're asking that question in a case that you've had a thought along that line." And he did. It was about the prophecies and so forth.

Despite his concerns about Armageddon, Reagan still passionately believed it was imperative for the United States to upgrade its defenses (Zakheim 1997; Pach 2003). Like so many observers, Reagan concluded that US security had dangerously eroded during the 1970s. By the early part of the decade, the Soviets had reached strategic parity with the United States. The USSR had dramatically enhanced their naval strength and tactical air force and had even gained numerical superiority in certain weapons like intercontinental ballistic missiles.

President Carter had possibly exacerbated these trends. Carter had campaigned in 1976 on a platform that included significant reductions in defense spending. Within a month of his election, he set a goal of cutting the defense budget by 5 to 7 percent. Carter was unable to deliver on that specific promise, but he was still successful in canceling or cutting a variety of weapons systems, including the neutron bomb, the MX missile, the B-1 bomber, and the Trident submarine.

Carter reversed himself following a series of events that destabilized the US position abroad, including the invasion of Afghanistan and the hostage crisis in Iran. In his last budget, Carter proposed a 5.5 percent real increase in defense spending. It was an irrelevant gesture—he had already lost the election two months earlier—but it was vindication all the same for Reagan, who had been warning his radio listeners about the deterioration of the US military since 1975. Reagan would continue to press for increases in defense spending throughout his entire term in office, even as progress with the Soviets seemed to diminish the need for them.

It is another Reagan paradox that a man so concerned about the onset of Armageddon would at the same time be so committed to providing the supplies that might make it happen. Yet, even if Armageddon was imminent, Reagan thought that he had the personal ability to avoid it. "This was one of the intellectual contradictions in Reagan's thinking. He sees himself as a romantic, heroic figure who believes in the power of a hero to overcome even Armageddon," his security advisor Bud McFarlane said. "I think it may come from Hollywood. Wherever it came from, he believes that the power of a person and an idea could change the outcome of something even as terrible as Armageddon. This was the greatest challenge of all . . . He didn't see himself as God, but he saw himself as a heroic figure on earth" (Cannon 1991, 290).

Given the importance of defense spending to the Gipper, it is no surprise that the subject was a frequent one in his public appearances; the word "defense" appears in 1,629 Reagan public documents between 1981 and 1988. For sure, Reagan did not always use religious rhetoric when speaking about defense spending. Instead, he would often emphasize the horror stories of a military in disrepair—the planes that could not fly, the ships that could not leave harbor, the guns that did not have ammo. He might point to a litany of statistics that illustrated how far the Soviets had pulled ahead. At other times, Reagan would compare his defense budgets to John Kennedy's, always noting his were much smaller by comparison. On still other occasions, he would talk about the benefits of negotiating from a position of strength, about the importance of closing the country's "window of vulnerability." And, of course, the Great Communicator had his usual assortment of lively anecdotes to draw on. In one, Reagan joked about a Russian general who supposedly said, "I liked the arms race better when we were the only ones in it."

Still, religious rhetoric would comprise a substantial portion of Reagan's discourse on defense spending. Like Eisenhower, a large amount of Reagan's rhetoric would serve to draw a contrast between the United States and the Soviet Union on spiritual grounds. Reagan began painting the Soviets in these shades in his first press conference.

The new president was asked by Sam Donaldson what he believed the long-term goals of Russia to be. Reagan answered, "I know of no leader of the Soviet Union since the revolution, and including the present leadership, that has not more than once repeated in the various Communist congresses they hold their determination that their goal must be the promotion of world revolution and a one-world Socialist or Communist state, whichever word you want to use. Now, as long as they do that and as long as they, at the same time, have openly and publicly declared that the only morality they recognize is what will further their cause, meaning they reserve unto themselves the right to commit any crime, to lie, to cheat, in order to attain that, and that is moral, not immoral, and we operate on a different set of standards, I think when you do business with them, even at a detente, you keep that in mind" (Reagan 1981a).

These intemperate remarks would cause immediate difficulties for him. The Soviet ambassador, Anatoly Dobrynin, had his first official visit planned for that day. Dobrynin would privately fume, "How is he going to do business with us? What is the purpose of all that? Why should he set such a tone for the new administration from the very beginning?" (Pemberton 1997, 159–60).

But Reagan refused to retreat from this position, even when given an opportunity to do so. About a month later, Walter Cronkite asked Reagan about his press conference answer. Reagan chose to up the ante:

> Well, now, let's recap. I am aware that what I said received a great deal of news attention, and I can't criticize the news media for that. I said it. But the thing that seems to have been ignored—well, two things— one, I did not volunteer that statement. This was not a statement that I went in and called a press conference and said, "Here, I want to say the following." I was asked a question. And the question was, what did I think were Soviet aims? Where did I think the Soviet Union was going? And I had made it clear to them, I said, "I don't have to offer my opinion. They have told us where they're going over and over again. They have told us that their goal is the Marxian philosophy of world revolution and a single, one-world Communist state and that they're dedicated to that."

> And then I said we're naive if we don't recognize in their performance of that, that they also have said that the only morality—remember their ideology is without God, without our idea of morality in the religious sense—their statement about morality is that nothing is im- moral if it furthers their cause, which means they can resort to lying or stealing or cheating or even murder if it furthers their cause, and that is not immoral. Now, if we're going to deal with them, then we have to keep that in mind when we deal with them. (Reagan 1981b)

Reagan had offered a causal explanation for *why* the Soviets lie and cheat and steal—because "their ideology is without God, without our idea of morality in the religious sense." This was a very Eisenhower-ish perspective on the nature of the difference between the two states.

As we have already seen, Eisenhower saw the Cold War as a religious conflict. By framing the nature of the tensions as such, Eisenhower hoped to strengthen his call for aid to countries fighting the Red Menace.

Reagan attempted to do the same. Reagan would make the distinction between a religious "us" and an atheistic "them," thereby hoping to make his appeals for stronger defense more persuasive (see Reagan 1983d). As the president explained in his speech marking Captive Nations Week in 1983: "Two visions of the world remain locked in dispute. The first believes all men are created equal by a loving God who has blessed us with freedom. Abraham Lincoln spoke for us: 'No man,' he said, 'is good enough to govern another without the other's consent.' The second vision believes that religion is opium for the masses. It believes that eternal principles like truth, liberty, and democracy have no meaning beyond the whim of the state. And Lenin spoke for them: 'It is true, that liberty is precious,' he said, 'so precious that it must be rationed.' Well, I'll take Lincoln's version over Lenin's—and so will citizens of the world if they're given free choice" (Reagan 1983f).

Or, as Reagan said to a conference on religious liberty in 1985:

> But as all of you know only too well, there are many political regimes today that completely reject the notion that a man or a woman can have a greater loyalty to God than to the state. Marx's central insight when he was creating his political system was that religious belief would subvert his intentions. Under the Communist system, the ruling party would claim for itself the attributes which religious faith ascribes to God alone, and the state would be final arbiter of . . . truth, I should say, justice and morality . . . Marx declared religion an enemy of the people, a drug, an opiate of the masses. And Lenin said: 'Religion and communism are incompatible in theory as well as in practice . . . We must fight religion.'
>
> All of this illustrates a truth that, I believe, must be understood. Atheism is not an incidental element of communism, not just part of the package; it is the package. (Reagan 1985e)

Sometimes, Reagan would ruminate more extensively about the consequences that resulted from the Soviet denial of God. One instance would be his speech to the Conservative Political Action Conference dinner in March of 1981 (Reagan 1981c).

> We've heard in our century far too much of the sounds of anguish from those who live under totalitarian rule. We've seen too many

monuments made not out of marble or stone but out of barbed wire and terror. But from these terrible places have come survivors, witnesses to the triumph of the human spirit over the mystique of state power, prisoners whose spiritual values made them the rulers of their guards. With their survival, they brought us "the secret of the camps," a lesson for our time and for any age: Evil is powerless if the good are unafraid.

That's why the Marxist vision of man without God must eventually be seen as an empty and a false faith—the second oldest in the world—first proclaimed in the Garden of Eden with whispered words of temptation: "Ye shall be as gods." The crisis of the Western world, Whittaker Chambers reminded us, exists to the degree in which it is indifferent to God. "The Western world does not know it," he said about our struggle, "but it already possesses the answer to this problem—but only provided that its faith in God and the freedom He enjoins is as great as communism's faith in man."

This is the real task before us: to reassert our commitment as a nation to a law higher than our own, to renew our spiritual strength. Only by building a wall of such spiritual resolve can we, as a free people, hope to protect our own heritage and make it someday the birthright of all men.

Reagan does a couple of interesting things in these paragraphs. For one, he articulates his view that the faith of the West will be the ultimate reason why it will triumph in the Cold War. The men and women who escaped the gulags were able to do so, Reagan submits, because of their "spiritual values," which "made them rulers of their guards." Along the same lines, Reagan quotes Whittaker Chambers to argue that the "answer" to the Communist problem is already available—"faith in God and the freedom He enjoins." Finally, Reagan concludes by claiming that it is necessary for the country to "renew" its "spiritual strength." Only by being strong in faith could the United States hope to prevail.

As a second observation, Reagan also makes reference to Genesis 3:5, "Ye shall be as gods." The line is taken from the chapter where the serpent tempts Eve to eat from the tree in the middle of the Garden, against God's wishes. The way Reagan uses this quote serves to link the "Marxist vision" to the serpent. Both offer nothing more than a "false faith."

Third, the Whittaker Chambers quote that appears in the excerpt is of special importance. Chambers was an ex-Communist spy who emerged as a national figure in 1948 when, as an editor at *Time*, he publicly identified Alger Hiss as a member of his old underground operation. A prominent New Dealer, Hiss had worked in the Agricultural Adjustment Administration, the Department of Justice and the State Department. He was an adviser to Roosevelt at Yalta and was chief advisor to the US delegation at the first United Nations (UN) General Assembly meeting.

Hiss fervently denied having spied for the Soviets in testimony before the House Un-American Affairs Committee and its star Congressman, a young Richard Nixon. In fact, Hiss denied ever having met Chambers, though he later was forced to acknowledge past dealings with Chambers under an alias.

The statute of limitations on espionage charges had already expired, but Hiss's perjury trial was an early Cold War litmus test. Hiss's opponents saw him as a representative of a disloyal element within the US society. Hiss's defenders believed that he was a victim of right-wing paranoia. The investigation itself was a public spectacle, with Chambers leading FBI agents to his Maryland farm where he had hidden covert material in a hollowed-out pumpkin.

In the end, Hiss was convicted and sentenced to five years. There appears to be an emerging consensus that Hiss had been a spy after all, particularly after the release of a series of National Security Agency (NSA) declassified intercepts in the mid-1990s (Scott 1996). Regardless of Hiss's ultimate guilt or innocence, however, the case left a great impression on Reagan. Reagan awarded Chambers a posthumous Medal of Freedom in 1984. In 1988, his Administration declared the farm where the "pumpkin papers" were found a national historic landmark. More to the point, Reagan would repeatedly draw from Chambers's life as part of his rhetorical campaign to delegitimize the Soviets owing to their hostility toward organized religion.

Reagan told one anecdote involving Chambers quite often (Reagan 1982b, 1983b, 1984b). It was borrowed from Chambers's biography *Witness*, a book that traces the author's growing disillusionment with Communism. As Reagan (1984a) told it, the breaking point for Chambers came when he gazed upon the ear of his infant daughter and suddenly realized, as the president said to the graduates of his alma mater in 1984, "that such intricacy, such precision could be no accident, no freak of nature." His daughter had to be the work of God. "Chambers' story," Reagan continued to explain, "represents a generation's disenchantment with statism and its return to eternal truths and fundamental values."

Reagan used Chambers as a symbolic character. Chambers stood as a living allegory that attested to the victory of Christianity over Communism (Erickson 1985, 80–82). In other parts of *Witness*, Chambers recalled how he had nearly been persuaded to abort his daughter. But, as he considered this option, Chambers experienced a rebirth, a rebirth that is shared in the story of his child's ear. The story is, therefore, at its heart about the triumph of faith in God over faith in the state, and therein lies its principal relevance. Again, the point of the tale is to emphasize the fact that the primary difference between the United States and the Soviet Union is a religious one.

The Chambers story is a more subtle rhetorical technique than some of the examples that have already been discussed. Reagan was capable of this kind of nuance. One need only to look to his use of the word "crusade" when referring to his foreign policy.

To an Ohio veteran's organization, Reagan said, "As we've rebuilt America's military and strategic strength, we've also adopted a foreign policy that speaks openly and candidly about the failures of totalitarianism, that advocates the moral superiority of Western ideals like personal freedom and representative government—a foreign policy that calls for a global crusade for personal freedom and representative government" (Reagan 1982f).

Or, as he said to the Heritage Foundation, "Our call was for a forward strategy for freedom, a crusade to promote and foster democratic values throughout the world" (Reagan 1986a).

Or as Reagan concluded his meaningful 1982 address to the British parliament, "Let us now begin a major effort to secure the best—a crusade for freedom that will engage the faith and fortitude of the next generation. For the sake of peace and justice, let us move toward a world in which all people are at last free to determine their own destiny" (Reagan 1982d).

Categorizing a foreign policy as a crusade is a choice with substantial religious implications. The Crusades were a series of religious wars launched mainly by Christians against Muslims, though, by the Fourth Crusade, the Christians would be fighting each other. The origin of the word "crusade" derives from the Latin *crux* for cross. By calling his foreign policy a crusade, Reagan implied that the United States was bearing the cross against an infidel.

In all of these ways—the lengthy disquisitions on the consequences of the lack of Soviet religion, the repeated tellings of the Chambers anecdote, the use of terms like "crusade"—did Reagan seek to contrast the United States with the Soviets on spiritual grounds. This made it much easier for him to later call for defense spending.

Speechwriter Peggy Noonan argues that Reagan spoke this way because he felt it was imperative to tell the "truth" about the Soviets. Reagan believed that past US administrations had been overly diplomatic out of fear that they might offend the Communist leadership. Reagan thought his moralistic rhetoric was "uniquely constructive." People had to know what they were up against (Noonan 2001, 200–201). As Ed Meese (1992, 164) put it, Reagan's anti-Soviet rhetoric was part of the "essence" of his Cold War strategy, part of his "game plan." We should not make the mistake of thinking that there was no purpose behind these words.

In truth, Reagan would use much more specifically targeted religious rhetoric to mobilize support for defense spending, often citing different Biblical passages as part of his appeals. One such example can be found in the president's address to the Bundestag during a visit to Germany in the summer of 1982.

> We also seek peace among nations. The Psalmist said, "Seek peace and pursue it." Well, our foreign policies are based on this principle and directed toward this end. The noblest objective of our diplomacy is the patient and difficult task of reconciling our adversaries to peace. And I know we all look forward to the day when the only industry of war will be the research of historians.
>
> But the simple hope for peace is not enough. We must remember something that Friedrich Schiller said: "The most pious man can't stay in peace if it doesn't please his evil neighbor." So, there must be a method to our search, a method that recognizes the dangers and realities of the world . . .
>
> Without a strengthened Atlantic security, the possibility of military coercion will be very great. We must continue to improve our defenses if we're to preserve peace and freedom. (Reagan 1982e)

The Psalm that Reagan refers to is Number 34. The full verse is "Depart from evil, and do good; seek peace, and pursue it" (Psalm 34:14). Reagan's point is easy to see. The Bible tells readers to seek peace. But, because other countries do not want peace, the West can only meet that dictate if it buttresses its defenses. Therefore, spending on defense really is a way of following the Bible.

Further, in the Schiller quote, Reagan adds another religious dimension to the speech well in keeping with the kind of rhetoric he typically used to describe the Soviets. "The most pious man can't stay in peace if it doesn't please his evil neighbor." It is more than obvious that the West is the "pious man" and the Soviets are the "evil neighbor."

Reagan would use another Psalm as part of a call for greater defense spending in some brief remarks he made before the Young Leadership Conference of the United Jewish Appeal in 1984. "Since taking office, our administration has made significant headway in rebuilding our defenses and making America more secure," Reagan said. "Perhaps you remember the 29th Psalm in which King David said, 'The Lord will give strength to His people; the Lord will bless His people with peace.' Well, today America once again recognizes that peace and strength are inseparable. But we've only begun to repair past damage. Make no mistake: If we heed those who would cripple America's rebuilding program, we will undermine our own security and the security of our closest friends, like Israel, and I am not prepared to let that happen" (Reagan 1984c). The essential thrust of Reagan's argument is much the same as the previous example.

Before a meeting of religious broadcasters the next year, Reagan would make an even stronger Scriptural argument for defense spending: "We mean to maintain a strong defense, because only with a strong defense can we preserve the peace we cherish. And I found myself wanting to remind you of what Jesus said in Luke 14:31: 'Oh, what king, when he sets out to meet another king in battle will not first sit down and take counsel whether he is strong enough with 10,000 men to encounter the one coming against him with 20,000. Or else, while the other is still far away, sends a delegation and asks the terms of peace.' I don't think the Lord that blessed this country, as no other country has ever been blessed, intends for us to have to someday negotiate because of our weakness" (Reagan 1985b).

Reagan either misinterpreted theses verses or intentionally misused them (Briggs 1985). On the face of it, it seems unlikely that the Prince of Peace was discussing military strategy. Which, of course, he was not. Rather, Jesus was using a parable. The explicit point of the parable is revealed in the final line of the passage: "So therefore, none of you can become my disciple if you do not give up all your possessions" (Luke 14:33).

Jesus was warning the crowds that were beginning to follow him that they should be aware of the "cost" of doing so (Luke 14:28). He was asking people to determine for themselves whether they had the strength necessary to make the sacrifices he was asking for. He was not giving guidance about foreign policy.

The reference to Luke before an audience of religious broadcasters may be unsurprising. But Reagan had used the same exact passage earlier that morning in a budget speech he gave to a very secular audience of business and trade representatives (Reagan 1985a). In front of these men and women, Reagan had even explicitly said that "the Scriptures are on our side in this." So, clearly, Reagan did not limit his use of the Bible to sectarian gatherings.

In fact, in a national radio address on his missile defense program in 1985, Reagan would once again quote from Luke in drawing a connection between peace and strength. Reagan observed, "It's better to protect lives than to avenge them. But another reason, equally simple and compelling, persuades us to its merit. As the Book of Luke says: 'If a strong man shall keep his court well guarded, he shall live in peace'" (Reagan 1985f).

This quote comes from Luke 11:21. In the lines that precede it, Jesus casts out a demon from a possessed man. The point about keeping one's "court well guarded" harkens back to this event. Jesus was explaining how an initial conversion was not enough. Discipleship requires perseverance (Luke 11:26; see also Gonzalez 2010, 147–48). Hence, Reagan misused this Biblical passage, too. Like before, Luke 11:21 was a metaphor, not a literal statement of fact.

These rhetorical choices were the most controversial ones that Reagan would make. A number of theologians loudly criticized Reagan's application of Scripture (Briggs 1985). The Rev. Richard John Neuhaus, a prominent Christian intellectual, excoriated Reagan, saying, "I think the President would be well-advised to make the argument for his military budget and strategies on the basis of public reasoning rather than invoking dubious biblical authority." David Adams, a professor at Princeton Theological Seminary, seconded Neuhaus: "When the President cites this verse as a prop for Administration policy, he misuses the Bible. It is not an answer book but a record of faith."

Underscoring that point, others pointed to alternative Biblical passages that offered a contradictory message. At a hearing of the Senate Budget Committee, Sen. Charles Grassley (R-IA) read other lines from Luke focusing on questions of cost (*Los Angeles Times* 1985). Some directed the president's attention to Matthew 5:44 and its demand to "Love your enemies and pray for those who persecute you" (*Washington Post* 1985). Political commentators piled on as critical pieces on Reagan's Biblical lessons appeared from Garry Wills (1985) and Colman McCarthy (1985), among others.

Eventually, Reagan would be forced to publicly defend his use of the Bible. At a press conference at the end of February 1985, a reporter asked the president if he thought "it's appropriate to use the Bible in defending a political argument?" Reagan answered, "Well, I don't think I've ever used the Bible to further political ends or not, but I've found that the Bible contains an answer to just about everything and every problem that confronts us, and I wonder sometimes why we don't recognize that one book could solve a lot of problems for us" (Reagan 1985c). It is hard not to conclude that Reagan was being slightly disingenuous.

In addition to his citation of Scripture, another way in which Reagan used religious rhetoric to supplement his call for higher budgets was by describing defense spending in terms with a high spiritual content. Defense spending, according to the president, was "moral." Not spending enough for defense was "immoral" or "wrong," even "unforgivable." Generous defense funding would serve a "sacred" purpose. The central goal of an adequate defense was to protect the "blessings" the country had already received. The number of instances where Reagan used such phrasings is too numerous too fully count. The reader should treat what follows as a selection of the kinds of claims Reagan was prone to making, with emphasis added:

> Now, the defense budgets over the next several years will be especially important. Studies indicate that our relative military imbalance with the Soviet Union will be—believe it or not—at its worst by the mideighties. As President, I can't close my eyes, cross my fingers, and simply hope that the Soviets will behave themselves. Today a major conflict involving the United States could occur without adequate time to upgrade U.S. force readiness. It's *morally important* that we take steps to protect America's safety and preserve the peace. (Reagan 1982a)

> Now, some would have us get at the deficit by reducing defense spending . . . Every penny we spend is for one *sacred purpose*: to prevent that first shot from being fired, to prevent young Americans from dying in battle. Let us ask those who say we're spending too much: "How much would it have been worth to you to avoid World War II? Who would put a price on the lives that were lost on Guadalcanal, Tarawa, Omaha Beach, Anzio, or Bastogne?" For the sake of our children and their children, I consider it my duty, indeed all of our duties as citizens, to make sure that America is strong enough to remain free and at peace. (Reagan 1982c)

63

I have lived through two world wars. I saw the American people rise to meet these crises, and I have faith in their willingness to come to their nation's defense in the future. But it's far better to prevent a crisis than to have to face it unprepared at the last moment. That's why we have an *overriding moral obligation* to invest now, this year, in this budget, in restoring America's strength to keep the peace and preserve our freedom. (Reagan 1983a)

Nor must we gamble, ever again, with the security of this country by neglecting our defense readiness. The day I took office, our Armed Forces were in a shocking state of neglect . . . I believe it's *immoral* to ask the sons and daughters of America to protect this land with second-rate equipment and bargain basement weapons. (Reagan 1983c)

You and I both know that this debate on defense is about more than deficits and rooting out waste, as important as they are. It's about protecting lives and preserving freedom, *because that's the source of all our other blessings.* What occurred during the last decade when the Soviets raced ahead militarily while we stood still was *dreadfully wrong.* We believe it's *immoral* to ask the sons and daughters of America to protect this land with second-rate equipment and weapons that won't work. (Reagan 1983e)

One of the *most sacred duties* of any President is keeping America secure and at peace. And peace and security are not free commodities; they're precious, and like everything of great value, there's a price to pay. (Reagan 1985d)

You know, sometimes I'd like to take some of those people in Washington who are always trying to cut defense spending and bring them here to Parris Island—or to Fort Jackson, Orlando, or Lackland. And I'd tell them these are the soldiers, sailors, airmen, and marines who are putting their lives on the line to keep America free. And if we ever must send our young service people into harm's way, then it is our *moral duty* to give them absolutely the best equipment and support that America can muster. (Reagan 1986b)

What this collection of quotes should prove is that Reagan was, indeed, quite likely to frame defense spending with the aid of a religiously charged vocabulary.

Bible quotes and these quick moral ripostes aside, at times, Reagan would launch into much more extensive disquisitions on the connections between Soviet iniquity and the preeminent importance of a strong defense. The most famous example of such a discussion was certainly Reagan's "Evil Empire" speech to the annual convention of the National Association of Evangelicals in Orlando, Florida on March 8,

1983 (Reagan 1983b). The speech was seen by many as the keynote of Reagan's push to get Congress to approve a 10 percent real increase in defense spending (Smith 1983). And, in many ways, this speech brought together all the rhetorical themes we have been following.

The last half of the address was centered on foreign affairs. Reagan drew the usual contrast between the United States and the Soviets on religious grounds. The president told his listeners, "There is sin and evil in the world, and we're enjoined by Scripture and the Lord Jesus to oppose it with all our might." That sin and evil was mostly due to the influence of the Soviets. Reagan, recalling his first press conference, said, "I think I should point out I was only quoting Lenin, their guiding spirit, who said in 1920 that they repudiate all morality that proceeds from supernatural ideas—that's their name for religion—or ideas that are outside class conceptions. Morality is entirely subordinate to the interests of class war. And everything is moral that is necessary for the annihilation of the old, exploiting social order and for uniting the proletariat."

Given those motivations, Reagan criticized those who would advocate for something like a nuclear freeze. A freeze could only offer the "illusion" of peace. Instead, Reagan made a plea for continuing to rebuild America's forces:

> Yes, let us pray for the salvation of all of those who live in that totalitarian darkness—pray they will discover the joy of knowing God. But until they do, let us be aware that while they preach the supremacy of the state, declare its omnipotence over individual man, and predict its eventual domination of all peoples on the Earth, they are the focus of evil in the modern world.
>
> It was C. S. Lewis who, in his unforgettable "Screwtape Letters," wrote: "The greatest evil is not done now in those sordid 'dens of crime' that Dickens loved to paint. It is not even done in concentration camps and labor camps. In those we see its final result. But it is conceived and ordered (moved, seconded, carried and minuted) in clear, carpeted, warmed, and well-lighted offices, by quiet men with white collars and cut fingernails and smooth-shaven cheeks who do not need to raise their voice."
>
> Well, because these "quiet men" do not "raise their voices," because they sometimes speak in soothing tones of brotherhood and peace, because, like other dictators before them, they're always making "their final territorial demand," some would have us accept them at their word and accommodate ourselves to their aggressive impulses. But if history teaches anything, it teaches that simple-minded appease-

ment or wishful thinking about our adversaries is folly. It means the betrayal of our past, the squandering of our freedom.

So, I urge you to speak out against those who would place the United States in a position of military and moral inferiority. You know, I've always believed that old Screwtape reserved his best efforts for those of you in the church. So, in your discussions of the nuclear freeze proposals, I urge you to beware the temptation of pride—the temptation of blithely declaring yourselves above it all and label both sides equally at fault, to ignore the facts of history and the aggressive impulses of an evil empire, to simply call the arms race a giant misunderstanding and thereby remove yourself from the struggle between right and wrong and good and evil.

In no other speech does Reagan so explicitly link his rhetorical themes of religion versus atheism and the moral necessity of defense spending. It is clear from the excerpt that spending is necessary *because* the Soviets do not acknowledge God. "Until they do," they will continue to remain "the focus of evil in the modern world." Anyone who fails to support steeling the country against the "aggressive impulses of an evil empire" risks putting the United States in a position of "military and moral inferiority." Spending has to be supported, the freeze must be opposed, because, Reagan argues, the arms race is a "struggle between right and wrong and good and evil"—characteristics that he said ultimately derive from the Soviet Union's underlying atheism.

Even the slightest aspects of these lines can be tied back to this overriding conclusion. For instance, Lewis's *Screwtape Letters*, which Reagan quotes when discussing the Soviet leadership, was written from the perspective of Screwtape, a senior demon, who is attempting to instruct his nephew, Wormwood, in the methods of leading Christians astray. It is not hard to guess which country is taking on the role of Screwtape.

Reagan's words triggered an international controversy, causing critical reactions to be published in outlets ranging from *Time* to *Sojourners* to the Soviet press (Erickson 1985, 76; Smith 2006, 353–54). Anthony Lewis (1983) was one who eviscerated Reagan for the speech. Lewis argued that "If there is anything that should be illegitimate in the American system it is such use of sectarian religiosity to sell a political program." He called Reagan's language "outrageous," "primitive," "crude," and "dangerous." "When a politician claims that God favors his programs," Lewis warned, "alarm bells should ring."

The *Chicago Tribune* (1983) agreed with Lewis. "For all its vigor and truculence, the President's fire-and-brimstone speech to the National

Association of Evangelicals last week is the kind of shouting that disturbs many Americans. It is not that what he said was false, but that it was exaggerated and was delivered in language poised near the edge of frenzy."

Ernest Conine (1983) also expressed similar opinions in a piece appearing in the *Los Angeles Times*. Although he agreed with Reagan's analysis of Soviet intentions, Conine pointed out that "Presidents, unlike priests and preachers, can't afford the luxury of unrestrained truth-speaking." Conine worried that Reagan did not understand that his words resonate at home and abroad. He called the speech "a mistake" and a "blunder."

The close reader will notice that the majority of these citations, including the Evil Empire speech, are clustered in late 1982 and early 1983. I argue that presidents are most likely to embrace religious rhetoric in unfavorable, "crisis"-type circumstances. So it was for Reagan.

The period between 1982 and 1983 was one of the two low points of the Reagan presidency. Beginning in August 1981, the United States slipped into a massive recession. Unemployment would peak in January 1983 with about 11.5 million people looking for work. The unemployment rate, averaging 9.7 percent in 1982, was the highest since the Depression. As a byproduct of the downturn, the country's deficit soared. With no other options, Reagan would be forced to accept a series of tax hikes in the Tax Equity and Fiscal Responsibility Act (TEFRA). The president preserved the individual reductions he had achieved in 1981, but his compromise was resented by some of his supporters.

Accordingly, Reagan's popularity dissipated. He fell to just above 40 percent approval at the end of 1982. His party suffered heavy losses in the 1982 midterm elections as the Democrats picked up twenty-six House seats. There was open speculation that either Reagan would not run for re-election or, were he to run, that he would be a one-term failure. Given all these troubles, it is unsurprising that this period witnessed a major address on defense spending that Reagan wrapped with a religious flourish.

Reagan addressed the nation on his defense policies on November 22, 1982 (Reagan 1982g). The connection between a modern military and peace was the basis for his religious conclusion. Like several other presidents, including Lyndon Johnson and George H. W. Bush, Reagan chose to capitalize on an upcoming holiday that has some religious significance.

I began these remarks speaking of our children. I want to close on the same theme. Our children should not grow up frightened. They should not fear the future. We're working to make it peaceful and free. I believe their future can be the brightest, most exciting of any generation. We must reassure them and let them know that their parents and the leaders of this world are seeking, above all else, to keep them safe and at peace. I consider this to be a sacred trust.

My fellow Americans, on this Thanksgiving when we have so much to be grateful for, let us give special thanks for our peace, our freedom, and our good people.

I've always believed that this land was set aside in an uncommon way, that a divine plan placed this great continent between the oceans to be found by a people from every corner of the Earth who had a special love of faith, freedom, and peace.

Let us reaffirm America's destiny of goodness and good will. Let us work for peace and, as we do, let us remember the lines of the famous old hymn: "O God of Love, O King of Peace, make wars throughout the world to cease."

Thank you. Good night, and God bless you.

Collectively, it is now possible to identify the main contours of Reagan's religious rhetoric on defense.

First, Reagan tried to make people aware that the Cold War was more or less a struggle between God and the Godless. He said as much explicitly, but he also advanced this point in more subtle ways, like his frequent re-telling of Whittaker Chambers's conversion story.

Second, Reagan would refer to the Bible as a source that supported military preparedness. He did not hesitate to claim that "Scriptures are on our side in this." He argued that surely it was not the case that "the Lord . . . blessed this country . . . for us to have to someday negotiate because of our weakness." His Biblical interpretations were not always defensible.

Third, Reagan would employ strong moral and religious adjectives in order to describe the purposes of his defense budgets.

This final speech offers evidence of all three themes. It includes an implicit contrast between a religious United States and an atheistic Soviet Union ("I've always believed that this land was set aside in an uncommon way, that a divine plan placed this great continent between the oceans . . ."). It contains a quotation from a religious text (here, an old hymn). Finally, it includes a forceful moral phrase used to describe the purposes of Reagan's policy ("sacred trust").

In terms of the effectiveness of this language, however, the record does not support the claim that Reagan's religious rhetoric helped him. Reagan had almost no success persuading the public to support his cause of higher defense spending. Figures 2.1 and 2.2 track the

Figure 2.1
Gallup on defense spending

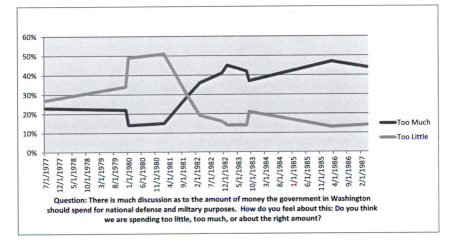

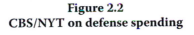

Question: There is much discussion as to the amount of money the government in Washington should spend for national defense and miltary purposes. How do you feel about this: Do you think we are spending too little, too much, or about the right amount?

Figure 2.2
CBS/NYT on defense spending

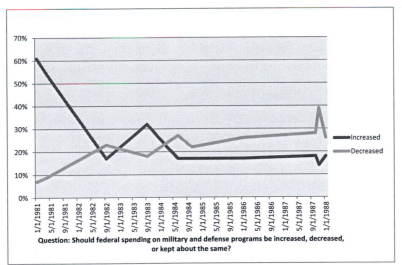

Question: Should federal spending on military and defense programs be increased, decreased, or kept about the same?

preference of the American public for either increases or decreases in defense spending. Each displays the same trend. First, there was a dramatic increase in support for greater defense spending in 1979 and 1980. In the Gallup poll, 27 percent of Americans said the country was spending "too little" on national defense in July of 1977. By the end of January 1980, that figure had soared to 49 percent. In January of 1981, totally 61 percent of respondents told CBS/*New York Times* pollsters that they thought spending on defense should be "increased."

This change was a rational response to world developments. In events also described in Chapter 4, Iranian revolutionaries overran the US embassy in Tehran in November of 1979. A large group of Americans were taken hostage and would remain captive for well over a year. The low point of this embarrassing episode was the disastrous failure of a rescue mission launched in April of 1980. The mission involved a complicated plan where eight helicopters would covertly fly into Iran. The teams would then take unmarked trucks into the city, storm the embassy, and rush the hostages to transport planes that would be waiting nearby at an abandoned airstrip. The plan went awry from the start as a dust storm and hydraulic problems disabled three of the choppers, forcing military planners to abort the operation at the first staging area. But before the forces could turn back, one of the helicopters crashed into a cargo plane, triggering a massive explosion that killed eight soldiers. The smoldering wreckage was broadcast worldwide as a symbol of American ineptitude.

On top of all of this, on Christmas 1979, the Soviet Union invaded Afghanistan. Today, this event is seen as the beginning of the end for the USSR, a desperate move by a crumbling power. At the time, though, the consensus was that the invasion was proof of the growing threat of Soviet militarism. Dating from the fall of Vietnam until the invasion of Afghanistan, the Soviet Empire had absorbed ten different countries, averaging one every six months. It was a startling rate of expansionism that had commentators writing about an "America in retreat" by mid-1979 (Busch 1997, 451). It is logical that the public would be supportive of higher defense spending given these conditions.

The high level of support for defense spending continued throughout Reagan's first year, which culminated in the president winning substantial outlays for the military (see below). However, by 1982, public opinion had reversed—a fact that is visible in both graphs. In the Gallup poll, for the last seven years of the Reagan Administration, around 45 percent of the public felt "too much" was being spent on defense versus the roughly 15 percent who thought the country was spending "too little."

Again, it is easy to understand the change. In 1982, much greater attention began to be paid to the federal deficit. Plus, improvements in relations with the Soviets during Reagan's second term seemed to diminish the need for robust military spending.

The conclusion is obvious: Reagan's religious rhetoric had no impact on the public's opinion on defense spending. Support for higher spending rose before he took office and it fell at almost the same time (1982–1983) that we see the highest concentration of religious statements. Further support for this conclusion is found in the public's reaction to Reagan's major address on November 22, 1982. Reagan's approval on November 19 was 43 percent. By the next reading, on December 10, Reagan was down two points to 41 percent (Ragsdale 2009, 238).

This analysis is hardly controversial (see also Bartels 1994, 488; Edwards 2003, 54–57). Even Reagan knew he was not getting through. Michael Deaver remembers the public being "dead set against the Reagan buildup." Concerned about the polls, Reagan pulled Deaver aside one day and said "Mike, these numbers show you're not doing your job. This is your fault; you gotta get me out of Washington more so I can talk to people about how important this policy is" (Deaver 2001, 153–54). Reagan was talking plenty about defense. The people were just not listening.

Earlier in this chapter, we encountered scattered evidence that suggests Reagan's religious rhetoric was poorly received by the media. This includes his Scripture quotes as well as his "Evil Empire" address. The pattern finds even more support in the response greeting Reagan's major defense speech on November 22. Table 2.5 catalogs the opinion pieces on Reagan's defense policies printed in the four major newspapers the week following his TV appearance. The reaction was unambiguously negative. The average column was scored just a 1.81, and twelve of the sixteen pieces received negative scores of either 1 or 2.

The focus of the opposition centered on Reagan's proposal for the MX missile, a key part of the larger message. There will be more to say on this weapon shortly, but suffice it to say that Reagan's media critics were skeptical of the need for the missile, dubious of the president's plans for basing it, worried that it would abrogate the pre-existing SALT treaty, and concerned that it would increase the chances of a nuclear exchange (i.e., see Beres 1982).

71

Table 2.5
Editorial coverage of Reagan's November 22, 1982 address
on national defense

Date	Paper	Author	Title	Score
11/23/1982	*Chicago Tribune*	Germond and Witcover	"Reagan Meets Political Reality"	1
11/23/1982	*New York Times*	Hedrick Smith	"Arms Impasse Goes On"	3
11/23/1982	*Washington Post*	Michael Getler	"A Rigorous Test of Disarmament Theory"	2
11/23/1982	*Washington Post*	Ernest Hollings	"We Don't Need This Missile"	1
11/24/1982	*Los Angeles Times*	Staff Editorial	"Tempting the Soviets"	1
11/24/1982	*Los Angeles Times*	Staff Editorial	"This Is the Way to Debate"	5
11/24/1982	*New York Times*	James Reston	"Let Us Give Thanks?"	3
11/25/1982	*Chicago Tribune*	Stephen Chapman	"How to Cut the Defense Budget"	1
11/26/1982	*New York Times*	Louis Rene Beres	"Reagan Calls It MX; Actually, It's M-Hex"	1
11/27/1982	*Washington Post*	Ellen Goodman	"The Words Race"	1
11/28/1982	*Los Angeles Times*	William Schneider	"Reagan and the MX: Blindman's Bluff?"	4
11/28/1982	*New York Times*	Tom Wicker	"The Strategic Tango"	1
11/28/1982	*Washington Post*	Harry McPherson	"How Ron and Yuri Cut Defense Spending"	1
11/28/1982	*Washington Post*	James Schlesinger	"Strategic Deterrence—Or Strategic Confusion?"	2
11/28/1982	*Washington Post*	Patrick Leahy	"Reality—Or a Caricature?"	1

(*continued on next page*)

Table 2.5 (*continued*)

Date	Paper	Author	Title	Score
11/29/1982	*New York Times*	Michael Krepon	"Arms Nonpolicy"	1
Dates: 11/23 to 11/29			**Average score**	**1.81**
			Positive articles	**2 (12.5%)**
			Negative articles	**12 (75.0%)**
			Mixed/neutral articles	**2 (12.5%)**

Another point of contention focused on Reagan's analysis of the state of the US military. Some felt Reagan was misleading the country into thinking the United States was less prepared than it actually was. The *Los Angeles Times* (1982) wrote that "the facts that underlie the charts hardly bear out Reagan's suggestion that the United States is now second best in most areas of military weaponry." The paper worried that the Soviets might come to believe what Reagan said, however, and therefore "be tempted to take dangerous gambles that they would otherwise avoid." The board called for Reagan to stop "scaring Congress and the American people with . . . only part of the truth about the U.S.-Soviet military balance" (see also Leahy 1982).

A third objection to Reagan's speech revolved around the implications his defense spending had for the deficit. Jack Germond and Jules Witcover (1982) took Reagan to task for ignoring the meaning of the recent midterm elections, which, according to their interpretation, signaled that the voters expected substantial deficit reduction as a means of improving the long-term prospects of the American economy (see also Chapman 1982).

Finally, Reagan caught some heat for his rhetorical choices. Ellen Goodman (1982) took issue with an important element of Reagan's main stream of religious argumentation, that defense spending served the sacred cause of peace. As she perceptively noted, by speaking this way, Reagan was trying to "justify the military position as being morally correct." For Goodman, this was too much. She proclaimed Reagan the "winner, hands down" of the "1982 George Orwell War-Is-Peace Sweepstakes."

In sum, Reagan's 1982 address on national security, an address that contained a strong religious argument in its final paragraphs, was met with the same reception that welcomed his other usages of religious rhetoric—his ideas were ridiculed and his language offended.

Last, Reagan's defense budgets faced tough sledding in Congress. In 1981, the new Commander-in-Chief proposed a substantial increase over Carter's last defense budget. Reagan initially added $25.8 billion to Carter's fiscal 1982 request, while projecting future increases of about 7 percent annually. In contrast, Carter had planned for around 5 percent annual increases.

While Reagan did ask for more money, in just about every case, he was only accelerating the development of projects that Carter had already committed to. Perhaps, this fact helps to explain why there was little opposition. Even as new data pointing to a worsening deficit forced Reagan to voluntarily cut his own fiscal 1982 request by $2 billion, the president was able to successfully resist any other efforts to trim his proposals.

The situation began to change the following year. With the economy faltering, and with Reagan demanding austerity as a result, the president was unable to forestall heavy cuts. By the end of 1982, Congress had cut over $19 billion from Reagan's $258 billion request for fiscal 1983. The House version of the defense appropriations bill (HR 7355) featured an amount 7.2 percent below Reagan's request. This was the largest Congressional cut to a defense bill in years.

Furthermore, Reagan suffered a humiliating defeat on the MX missile in late December. The MX was a land-based, mobile missile capable of carrying ten independently targeted warheads. It was designed to replace the Minuteman, which was criticized for being vulnerable to a Soviet first strike owing to its storage in hardened silos. The Carter Administration had struggled with how to better base the MX, at one point proposing a plan that would randomly shuttle the missiles back and forth between thousands of underground launch sites in Utah and Nevada.

Reagan also struggled with the basing question, ultimately advocating what was termed "dense pack" siting. Under this plan, MX missiles would be clustered together in armored silos under the theory that incoming Soviet warheads would destroy one another owing to the close proximity of their targets, allowing enough of the MXs to survive unscathed. The problem was that this theory could not be tested owing to restrictions imposed by the Limited Nuclear Test Ban Treaty of 1963.

Fresh off their midterm triumph, emboldened House Democrats capitalized on this uncertainty and voted against the Administration's request to fund the MX by the large margin of 245-176. This was the first time in history that Congress had denied any president's request for funding for a major nuclear weapon.

In 1983, policymakers continued to demand that Reagan scale back his fiscal 1984 request from the previously planned level of around $290 billion. In January, Reagan obliged by asking for $273.4 billion in new appropriations. This gesture did little to placate Congress, especially given that a part of the reduction would be achieved by means of a freeze on military pay. In the end, Congress reduced Reagan's request by an additional $18 billion. Reagan had proposed a fiscal 1984 defense budget that was 10 percent larger than fiscal 1983 in real terms. Congress only allowed for a real increase of about 4 percent.

Reagan did succeed on a number of related issues in 1983. For instance, the Administration abandoned any attempt to make the MX impregnable to attack and agreed to deploy the missile in existing silos. Despite the decision eliminating the rationale for producing the MX in the first place, Congress approved the weapon. Reagan also won support for the B-1 bomber, the Pershing missile, and several cruise missiles.

However, Reagan encountered defeats as well. The House adopted a resolution calling for a freeze on nuclear weapons. The move was political, but it was a resolution that Reagan had opposed. Additionally, the Senate voted by a better than 2-1 margin to eliminate a new version of the neutron bomb artillery shell that was designed to destroy Soviet tank columns. And, the House twice rejected the Administration's request to end the moratorium on chemical weapons.

The year 1984 brought more of the same. Reagan called for a fiscal 1985 defense budget that was 13.3 percent higher than that for the previous year. No one in Congress took this seriously given the demands that the deficit was placing on domestic programs. After a contentious and drawn-out process, Congress finally cut $20 billion from Reagan's request, agreeing to just a 5 percent annual real increase. Reagan also again faced a setback on the MX when Congress deferred a decision on whether or not to continue its production until after the election.

If 1983 and 1984 were the years when Reagan's buildup slowed, beginning in 1985, the tide turned decisively against him. For fiscal 1986, Congress approved a defense budget of $297.6 billion, an amount that was only $3 billion more than the appropriation for the previous fiscal year. Reagan had asked for $322.2 billion. Owing to inflation, Congress would actually have had to spend $302.5 billion just to keep pace. In real terms, the defense budget represented a *decline* of nearly 2 percent. This amount was further diminished by automatic cuts stemming from the Gramm-Rudman-Hollings deficit reduction law. As a consequence, the final budget totaled $286.7 billion, a real decrease from the fiscal 1985 of 5 percent in all.

Moreover, Congress barred Reagan from developing anti-satellite weapons (ASAT). Reagan had protested this move on the grounds that it would shortchange his leverage with the Soviets in scheduled arms control negotiations. The magnitude of these failures detracted from smaller Reagan victories, like Congressional approval of the production of twenty-one more MX missiles.

In 1986, this new trend continued. Congress signed off on a defense budget of under $290 billion, which signaled a cut of over $30 billion from Reagan's request. To produce a zero real growth budget, Congress would have had to authorize $301 billion to meet the cost of inflation. Additionally, in August, the House adopted a series of amendments to the defense bill that served to formally reject several key aspects of Reagan's defense policy. One of these, an amendment that would have banned almost all nuclear testing, was approved by a 3-2 ratio.

Reagan finally acceded to the changed circumstances in 1987. His fiscal 1988 budget tried to increase defense spending by little more than 3 percent in real terms. This was a far cry from Reagan's past proposals that sought double digit percentage increases. Reagan's defense budget totaled $312 billion this year. Yet, he only got $292 billion. This marked the third consecutive year of a real defense decrease. As part of the deal, Reagan also agreed to submit a fiscal 1989 request of $299.5 million, meaning he had accepted in advance another year of real decline (Congressional Quarterly 1982, 1983, 1984, 1985, 1986, 1987, 1988, 1989).

The interpretation of this history is that Reagan experienced initial success increasing military spending during his first year, but his opponents successfully chipped away at that achievement every year thereafter, particularly in 1982, and particularly during his second term when real spending on defense fell every single year. Reagan also suffered a series of more specific losses on issues ranging from the MX to ASAT weapons to chemical agents. Congress does not seem to have been at all persuaded by Reagan's strong religious rhetoric.

None of this is to say that Reagan completely failed. His first term did secure significant increases in defense spending. But the increases were nowhere near as much as Reagan would have liked and they gradually atrophied. As Kenneth L. Adelman, Reagan's Director of the US Arms Control and Disarmament Agency, aptly acknowledges, "The height of the Reagan buildup—this massive, awesome buildup—never got to 7% of GNP. It never got to anywhere near the lower part of the Eisenhower administration. That was before Vietnam. Then Kennedy and Johnson came in and very much jacked up the Eisenhower defense budget, even before becoming involved in Vietnam. So when you look at post-World War II averages, the Reagan buildup at its height was probably at the average, and then the 'dirty little secret' was, of course, that in the last four years—the whole entire second term of the Reagan administration—it went down, down, down" (Schmertz, Datlof, and Ugrinsky 1997, 238).

Conclusion

This chapter opened by alluding to the abundant parallels between Eisenhower and Reagan. Their similar use of religious rhetoric must be added to any such list.

Stephen Ambrose's (1984, 377) shrewd evaluation of the history of mutual security said it best: "Over the next four years, Eisenhower would try every form of persuasion at his command to demonstrate to his countrymen the importance of the Third World to the United States. It was one of the most frustrating experiences of his life. He could not convince the people; he could not convince the Republican Party; he could not even convince his own Secretary of the Treasury." Despite his relentless and varied religious rhetoric, Eisenhower typically did not experience any improvement in his personal standing, the public remained steadfast in its opposition to foreign aid, the media did not respond positively to his five major addresses, and Congress cut his requests every year. Frustrating, indeed.

With respect to Reagan, the president's mantra was "defense is not a budget issue. You spend what you need" (Pach 2003, 90). There can be no conclusion other than Reagan's religious rhetoric did not help him to get the country to spend what he believed it needed. Public opinion responded to larger developments, not Reagan's arguments. The media criticized his ideas and their religious packaging. His last four years in office were marked by real declines in defense spending, not the increases he wanted.

Reagan's religious rhetoric on defense spending may have marked an important departure in the way US presidents had treated the Soviets. Indeed, Reagan's broader confrontational approach may have helped precipitate the changes within the Soviet Union that eventually led to its demise. It just didn't help him get the money he so badly wanted. Like Ambrose, Marlin Fitzwater got it right when he said, "Reagan would go out on the stump, draw huge throngs, and convert no one at all" (Apple 1990).

Note

1. Consider, for example, Eisenhower's "The Chance for Peace" speech in 1953, a speech that is often regarded as his finest (Eisenhower 1953a). At various times, the Soviets are associated with "the shadow of fear," "the cloud of threatening war," and "the black tide of events." In addition, this speech contains one of Eisenhower's starkest Christian metaphors: "humanity hanging from a cross of iron." Chernus (2008, 29–51) has an intelligent discussion of this speech and the story behind it.

3

Holy Warriors: George H. W. Bush, George W. Bush, and the Religious Rhetoric of War

Chapter 3 continues to explore foreign policy rhetoric, focusing on the unique opportunity war presents for the use of religion. Although historians have sometimes seemed less interested in the role that religion has played in American war making, the two have always been closely intertwined. Religion has impacted America's wars through the spiritual convictions of its political leaders, the lobbying of its church-going citizens, and the moral messages of its fearless preachers (Preston 2012).

In the following pages, I trace the religious arguments made by Presidents George H. W. Bush and George W. Bush in support of their decisions to go to war. George H. W. Bush used three key religious arguments for his policy: that the Gulf War was a battle of good and evil, that it would be a just war, and that God was on America's side. George W. Bush would use two religious arguments for his: that the War on Terror was also a battle of good and evil, and that by fighting for freedom America was fighting for God.

Despite the applicability of religious language in times of war, there is little to suggest that the choice of words by either the father or the son made much of a difference.

George H. W. Bush and the Gulf War

George H. W. Bush won a job that required him to constantly give public addresses, yet he was a terrible public speaker. As an aide once acidly observed, Bush "doesn't give speeches. He gives remarks" (Greene 2000, 145).

Regrettably for Bush, his verbal deficiencies were magnified because of his presidency's unfortunate place in political time, following one brilliant orator (Ronald Reagan) and preceding another (Bill Clinton). At least it can be said that Bush was aware of the problem. He once told his speechwriters, "You're all good writers and are all capable of giving me a speech that's a ten. But don't give me a ten because I can't give a ten speech. Give me an eight and maybe I'll make it come out a five" (Barilleaux and Rozell 2004, 67).

Bush also seemed to misunderstand the dynamics of politics in the era of twenty four hour news coverage. He preferred to devote his time to his executive work and he had a distaste for the kind of public relations stunts that Reagan had mastered (47–80). As another aide recounted, "This wasn't going to be like Reagan. We weren't going to be trying to sell the big speeches, we weren't going to be having the prime time speeches or going on TV all of the time" (58). Another made the point that Bush had "a visceral antipathy to public communication . . . he thought poorly of it, he thought it was cheap" (Mervin 1996, 47).

It is not a coincidence, then, that Bush had a distant relationship with his speechwriting office. His speechwriters were underpaid and the best individuals were not always hired. To some extent, Bush did not think such investments of time and money were worthwhile. "I think he saw the rhetorical aspect of the presidency as just one investment of his job . . . He did not consider it as ubiquitous and all-encompassing as Reagan did . . . ," one staffer admitted (Barilleaux and Rozell 2004, 68). Overarching themes for his political goals were never developed.

Bush overcame a lot of these shortcomings and disinclinations as he led the country to war against the regime of Saddam Hussein in 1990 and 1991. Every single word Bush uttered on the conflict was the product of an extensive media strategy that was designed to build grassroots support for the policy (Harlow 2006, 63–64). Within the White House Office of Communications, staff from across the Administration regularly met to coordinate the president's message. By the end of its first two weeks of existence, this working group had already distributed talking points to around 20,000 individuals and groups scattered all across the country. They worked to identify surrogate speakers, they arranged for the placement of supportive editorials in key newspapers, and they planned presidential briefings for important groups like US veterans. This kind of organization was unusual given Bush's habit of downplaying the importance of the public aspects of presidential leadership.

The story of the Persian Gulf War begins in the fall of 1980 when Iraq invaded Iran under Hussein's direction. The eight-year war was costly for both countries. Their collective economic infrastructures were obliterated and Iraq, aside from losing 250,000 men in combat, was left with a foreign debt approaching $80 billion (Wilentz 2008, 297). What made the situation far worse from the perspective of the Iraqis is that the country could not use the profits from their oil exports as debt service because prices were in a tailspin at the end of the decade.

Iraq's neighbor Kuwait compounded these problems. Most Organization of the Petroleum Exporting Countries (OPEC) members had reacted to falling oil prices by pledging to cut back on production. Kuwait refused to follow suit. Saddam also believed that Kuwait was guilty of "slant-drilling," a technique that would allow the country to siphon off oil that was actually found within Iraq's borders. Finally, $10 billion of Iraq's foreign debt was held by the Kuwaitis.

So, it is easy to see why a military offensive began to appeal to Hussein. Still, even as three divisions of the Republican Guard massed along the border in July 1990, few observers believed he would go through with an attack. Kuwait did not even mobilize their forces.

On August 2, 1990, around 140,000 Iraqis stormed into Kuwait. The Kuwaitis, unprepared and overmatched, fell quickly; the capital was in Saddam's possession in under twelve hours. Hussein also moved divisions further south to guard against a counterattack out of Saudi Arabia, a decision that for a while had US commanders convinced that he intended to strike against the Saudis, too. Even if Hussein stood pat, he now controlled 21 percent of the world's oil supply (Wilentz 2008, 297). If he were to capture Saudi Arabia, he would have 40 percent (Greene 2000, 115).

The international community united against Iraq's aggression. Although America took the lead, Britain, France, West Germany, Japan, and seven other nations joined with the United States to freeze Iraqi assets abroad in the immediate aftermath of the attack. Within hours of the invasion, the United Nations (UN) Security Council unanimously passed Resolution 660, which promised sanctions if Iraq failed to immediately withdraw. The Soviets, despite the grumblings of some decaying Cold Warriors, fully backed the world position.

On August 8, 1990, Bush addressed the nation to announce that he was deploying troops for the protection of Saudi Arabia. By the end of the month, 80,000 coalition soldiers were in place as part of operation Desert Shield. For the time being, diplomatic pressure would be given a chance to work.

In the early months of the showdown, Bush made few references to religion. In his August 8 address, the president justified his response to the attack by focusing on points such as "a puppet regime imposed from the outside is unacceptable," and "if history teaches us anything, it is that we must resist aggression or it will destroy our freedoms." Bush emphasized that it was important for America to "stand by her friends" (Bush 1990d).

Bush gave a second major address on September 11 (Bush 1990f). Most of his points were the same as those offered on August 8. Bush did throw a few new rationales for US involvement into the mix. One was an old Bush favorite—America's responsibility to craft a "new world order" out of the wreckage of the end of the Cold War. Bush argued that what was happening in the Gulf offered "a rare opportunity to move toward an historic period of cooperation." This new era would be one where "the nations of the world, East and West, North and South, can prosper and live in harmony."

Bush also specifically made mention of the important role that oil played in America's national interests: "Vital economic interests are at risk as well. Iraq itself controls some 10 percent of the world's proven oil reserves. Iraq plus Kuwait controls twice that. An Iraq permitted to swallow Kuwait would have the economic and military power, as well as the arrogance, to intimidate and coerce its neighbors—neighbors who control the lion's share of the world's remaining oil reserves. We cannot permit a resource so vital to be dominated by one so ruthless," Bush said.

Indeed, initially, oil was very prominent in Bush's comments on the Gulf. In an exchange with reporters on the day of the invasion, Bush acknowledged the role oil would play in motivating a US response: "You've heard me say over and over again, however, that we are dependent for close to 50 percent of our energy requirements on the Middle East. And this is one of the reasons I felt that we have to not let our guard down around the world" (Bush 1990b, 1990c).

However, a conscious decision would be made to instead prioritize the religious dimensions of the standoff as it entered one of its most crucial moments. A quick glance at Figures 3.1 and 3.2 reveals that support for Bush and his handling of the situation in Kuwait steadily declined between August and November.

In Figure 3.1, one can see that Bush's approval was measured at 74 percent on August 9, the first reading following the deployment. By November 15, Bush was down to 54 percent, a precipitous fall of twenty points.

Figure 3.1
Bush July 1990–March 1991 public approval

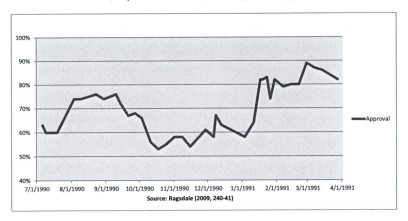

Source: Ragsdale (2009, 240-41)

Figure 3.2
CBS/NYT on Bush's handling of Iraq

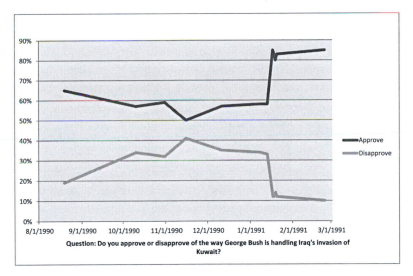

Question: Do you approve or disapprove of the way George Bush is handling Iraq's invasion of Kuwait?

Figure 3.2, on the other hand, provides data for a CBS/*New York Times* poll that surveyed respondents on whether they approved or disapproved of the way the president was handling the invasion. On August 19, Bush's policy was supported by a margin of 65 to 19 percent. On November 15, the data showed that the same margin had closed to just 50 to 41 percent support. Bush's cushion had dropped from 46 percent to only 9 percent in a little over three months.

If Bush needed more evidence that he was starting to lose the country, he needed only to look out in the streets. On October 20, thousands of people marched in sixteen different cities in a coordinated protest against the American military buildup (Nieves 1990).

In truth, the attrition in support was coming at the worst possible time for the Administration. On October 31, Bush approved a doubling of the forces the United States had stationed in Saudi Arabia. Bush understandably wanted to wait to announce the increase until after the midterm elections. It was not until November 8 that the public learned that the number of US troops in the Gulf would surge from 230,000 to more than 500,000. Bush's stated rationale for this tactical change was that he wanted to create an "offensive military option." All told, this represented the largest mobilization of the American military since the Vietnam War.

Congress did not respond well to the troop increase. Bush began to face opposition from anti-war Democrats who were growing increasingly concerned as tensions rose. Sen. Sam Nunn (D-GA), chair of the Senate Armed Services Committee, signaled his intention to hold a series of congressional hearings on the Gulf crisis at the end of November. Nunn worried that the country might be about to repeat its awful experience in Vietnam. "The last thing we need is to have a war over there, a bloody war, and have American boys being sent and brought back in body bags and yet not have the American people behind them," Nunn said. "We've gone that route one time. We don't want to do it again" (Weisskopf 1990).

Yet, Bush could not even count on the support of his own party. Many Republican isolationists saw little strategic purpose in defending Kuwait and, like Nunn, fretted over the possibilities for another Vietnam (Greene 2000, 124).

But at this point, there was no backing down for Bush. No one associated with the Administration believes that Bush ever thought sanctions alone would be enough to force the Iraqis back across their borders. Colin Powell (1995, 469–71) tells a story in his memoirs about a meeting that took place between the president and the country's top military brass on August 15, only a little less than two weeks after the initial invasion. Powell remembers informing Bush that they would have about two months to assess the impact sanctions were having on Hussein's regime. Bush immediately shook his head and replied,

"I don't know if sanctions are going to work in an acceptable time frame."

Bush worried about the difficulties inherent in maintaining international unity against Iraq for a prolonged period of time. Moreover, there was a limited window in which the United States and its allies could launch a counterattack (Bush and Scowcroft 1998, 382). Late February was marked by poor weather in the region, the following month was the Islamic holiday of Ramadan, and after that the oppressive desert heat would preclude many military operations. In the president's mind, the situation needed to be resolved no later than January or February (385).

On several occasions throughout October, Bush's pollster, Robert Teeter, met with the president to discuss the public Gulf campaign. It was Teeter's opinion that the Administration had too many messages percolating in the atmosphere. He urged the president to simplify things and return to the fundamentals (Woodward 1991, 315).

James Baker agreed with this analysis. Baker admitted, "For weeks I'd been frustrated by the administration's collective inability to articulate a single coherent, consistent rationale for the President's policy." In mid-November, Baker believed the Administration was finally "beginning to pay a political price at home as a result of our rhetorical confusion. Public support for Desert Shield was starting to unravel" (Hurst 2004, 384).

Brett Scowcroft, Bush's National Security Advisor, also felt the same. He remembers, "We were also running into increasing difficulty making our point understood about what was at stake. One criticism was that we had failed to explain why our troops were in the Saudi desert, why the United States had to lead the response to Iraq's aggression. Even supporters would tell the President that public backing would be there, but that we had to state our case more clearly. Too much of the reasoning, they argued, seemed abstract" (Bush and Scowcroft 1998, 398).

The president himself was worried. In a November 10 meeting, Bush expressed his confusion over the decline in support and pointedly asked his closest advisors, "What am I doing wrong?" (Mervin 1996, 190).

All of these factors—the attrition in support, the Congressional antagonism, the strategic pressures—worried the Administration, contributed to a pervading sense of crisis, and compelled them to search for new public arguments. One way Bush responded is by moving away from discussing international law and oil in favor of foregrounding issues such as the plight of the hostages Hussein had captured (Hurst 2004). And although Bush had previously made some tentative religious claims (Bush 1990e), henceforth he would also elevate the role of religious themes in his speeches.

Bush grew up Episcopalian in a religious home, attending Sunday services each weekend at Christ Church in Greenwich, Connecticut. Later in Midland, Texas, both he and Barbara taught Sunday school at First Presbyterian Church. He had also been a vestryman at St. Ann's in Kennebunkport, Maine, site of the Bush family summer compound (Lejon 2009, 396–99).

Still, the Jimmy Carter style of religious expression was not the forte of the taciturn Bush. And perhaps as a consequence, Bush was always looked at with some suspicion by the religious right. Early in Bush's term, nasty rumors circulated among evangelicals that they were being systematically excluded from staff positions within the White House (Balmer 2008, 127). Many Christian conservatives felt the moderate Bush offered them only symbolic gestures (Wilcox 1996, 85). Nonetheless, despite his discomfort in doing so, Bush turned to religious rhetoric in the mid-fall of 1990 as his Iraq policy began to face those storm clouds on the horizon.

In particular, Bush made three key religious arguments in support of his Gulf War policy: that this was a battle of good vs. evil, that it would be a just war, and that God was on America's side. I will explore each in turn.

Countless stories in the Bible are tales of good versus evil, including the very first in the Book of Genesis, and the very last in the Book of Revelation (Metzger and Coogan 1993, 208–9). The beginning chapters of Genesis tell the story of creation. As part of his process, God created a paradise, Eden, and in its midst he planted a "tree of the knowledge of good and evil" (Genesis 2:9). God placed the first man, Adam, and the first woman, Eve, in this garden to tend to it, but he warned them against eating from the tree (Genesis 2:17). Succumbing to the temptations of a serpent, the two disobeyed him. For their transgression, the couple was expelled from the garden and doomed to an inevitable death: "you are dust, and to dust you shall return" (Genesis 3:19).

Likewise, the final book of the New Testament, Revelation, forecasts an epic end-of-times battle between the forces of good and evil. The images contained in Revelation are frightening—terrible plagues, locusts with the tails of scorpions, beasts with multiple heads. Revelation prophesies that Christ will reign for a thousand years until Satan launches one final assault on God's people, an assault that will be defeated when a fire from Heaven devours his followers. Interpretations of the book vary and its content is controversial in nature, but its visions have captured the imagination of both Biblical scholars and the wider public for generations (see, e.g., the popular *Left Behind* series of novels).

In addition to the thematic conflict between good and evil, the Bible also repeatedly commands people to choose the former over the latter (Amos 5:14–15; 1 Peter 3:11–12; Psalm 34; Romans 12:9–21). The conflict of good and evil is, thus, a defining feature of Judeo-Christian belief. By calling the United States "good" and Saddam "evil," Bush was creating a narrative with a good deal of religious resonance.

For example, in the brief remarks he gave to the troops stationed at Hickam Air Force Base in Hawaii on October 28, Bush identified the enemy as such: "Well, today in the Persian Gulf, the world is once again faced with the challenge of perfect clarity. Saddam Hussein has given us a whole plateful of clarity, because today, in the Persian Gulf, what we are looking at is good and evil, right and wrong. And day after day, shocking new horrors reveal the true nature of the reign of terror in Kuwait" (Bush 1990g).

Another instance when Bush would make a strong good and evil argument can be found in an open letter he wrote to 460 college newspapers across the country (Bush 1991a). Early in his message, Bush wrote, "The terror Saddam Hussein has imposed upon Kuwait violates every principle of human decency. Listen to what Amnesty International has documented . . . the extrajudicial execution of hundreds of unarmed civilians, including children. Including children—there's no horror that could make this a more obvious conflict of good vs. evil." Bush would write that because of Hussein "a dark evil has descended in another part of the world."

The second theme that Bush used is that of a just war. Just war theory traditionally has two basic components; *jus ad bellum* (the rightness of starting a war) and *jus in bello* (the ethics that govern how the war is fought). Ostensibly, just war theory is a secular device, a way in which a determination can be made about the morality of a war without reference to a higher power. For some scholars, it is treated as such. But historically, just war theory is associated closely with Christianity, and more specifically with Roman Catholicism.

Although meaningful contributions were made by early Greco-Roman thinkers like Aristotle and Cicero, Christian philosopher St. Augustine had a singular impact on the development of just war theory. Augustine argued that a just war was one fought with the right intentions. Cruelty, a love of violence, a lust for power—these were the true evils of war to Augustine. He maintained a just war was one that was reluctantly embarked upon, motivated instead by love and a desire to protect innocents.

Augustine's writings were one of several major religious sources used to create a coherent set of rules for the prosecution of a just war towards the end of the first millennium AD. Papal edicts in 989 and 1027 and the Second Lateran Council of 1139 helped to specify things like protected noncombatants and prohibited the use of certain weapons and actions, such as attacking a church. Catholic theologian St. Thomas Aquinas would later contribute important new ideas to the evolving theory. And today, religious thinkers continue to occupy a large space in the just war debate, even if they have gradually assumed a secondary role (Orend 2006, 9–27).

There is not necessarily an agreed upon set of *jus ad bellum* conditions for a conflict to be considered a just war. Still, some points in the various formulations overlap. For a war to be just, it must involve a *just cause* such as a direct response to aggression or the protection of human rights. It must be motivated by Augustine's *right intent*, meaning the war's aims should be in accord with the just cause and not be a product of vengeance or a desire to dominate. The war must also be *proportionate* to the cause; countries should not fight over small issues. It must be an instrument of a *legitimate authority* such as a state. The war must have a *reasonable prospect of success*. If a war is doomed to fail, it should not be entered into, since the suffering would lack purpose. And finally, a war must be an option of *last resort*. Peaceful alternatives should be sought first (see Johnson 1999, 27–38; Cook 2004, 27–32; Brown 2008, 46–47).

Bush's remarks demonstrated an awareness of these conditions. In a speech to the armed forces based near Dhahran, Saudi Arabia, Bush highlighted the just war aspects of the showdown (Bush 1990j). Bush focused on three different justifications for US intervention—standing up to aggression, ensuring the energy security of the United States, and protecting innocent life. This last point is an undeniably just cause for war. Bush made the case that Kuwaiti civilians were imperiled in the starkest of terms: "Number three, we're here because innocent lives are at stake. We've all heard of atrocities in Kuwait that would make the strongest among us weep. It turns your stomach when you listen to the tales of those that have escaped the brutality of Saddam, the invader. Mass hangings. Babies pulled from incubators and scattered like firewood across the floor. Kids shot for failing to display the photos of Saddam Hussein."

The president also argued that the United States was approaching war as a last resort, another of the criteria for a war to be considered just: "We have been patient. We've gone to the United Nations time and time again. I'm prepared to go another time. We still hope for a peaceful settlement, but the world is a dangerous place."

The third theme that can be located in Bush's remarks is the suggestion that the United States has the power of God behind it. Often, Bush would capitalize on days of prayers and holidays as a way to make this point.

On November 2, Bush issued a proclamation calling for a national day of prayer (Bush 1990h). Typically, such proclamations are routine. But this time, Bush focused his call for prayers entirely on events in the Gulf. In his message preceding the proclamation, Bush began by noting that "Throughout American history, the people of this Nation have depended on Almighty God for guidance and wisdom. Both Scripture and experience confirm that the Lord hears the prayers of those who place their trust in Him. Time and again, in peril and uncertainty, doubt and decision, we Americans have turned to God in prayer and, in so doing, found strength and direction."

The president then described the situation in the Middle East. Although he expressed gratitude for the bravery of the US forces, he nonetheless concluded that "military strength alone cannot save a nation or bring it prosperity and peace; as the Scripture speaks, 'Unless the Lord watches over the city, the watchman stays awake in vain.' With these grave concerns before us, we do well to recall as a Nation the power of faith and the efficacy of prayer."

With this realization in mind, Bush asked the country to "turn to Him, both as individuals and as a Nation," and to ask "the Lord to grant all leaders of nations involved in this crisis the wisdom and courage to work towards its just and speedy resolution." In the text of the proclamation, Bush urged the country to "give thanks to God for His mercy and goodness and humbly ask for His continued help and guidance in all our endeavors."

The proclamation is intriguing. No one thought war was imminent; recall that Bush had yet to even announce that he was doubling the number of troops in the Gulf. Still, Bush set aside a day for national prayer. In doing so, he made the point that America could not be successful in the Mideast without God's aid ("Unless the Lord watches over the city, the watchman stays awake in vain.")). Thankfully, though, Bush also implied that America need not worry about having his support because of the country's special relationship with God.

In a Thanksgiving trip, Bush also focused on the importance of God's support. Speaking to those aboard, the U.S.S. Nassau, the president said:

> I reminded some at an Army base a while ago that this reminds me a bit of a Thanksgiving that I spent 46 years ago on a carrier, U.S.S. San Jacinto CVL30, off the coast of the Philippines during World War II. I found then that the Lord does provide many blessings to men and women who face adversity in the name of a noble purpose. They are the blessings of faith and friendship, strength and determination, courage and camaraderie and dedication to duty. And I found that the Lord allows the human spirit the inner resolve to find optimism and hope amidst the most challenging and difficult times. He instills confidence when despair tries to defeat us and inspires teamwork when the individual feels overwhelmed . . .
>
> And so, I would like to close these remarks with a prayer.
>
> Lord, bless us and keep us. Show us your way, the way of liberty and love. Soften the hearts of those who would do us harm. Strengthen the hearts of those who protect and defend us. Sustain the hearts of those at home who pray for our safe return. We rely upon your guidance and trust in your judgment, for we are one nation under God. Amidst this threat of war, help us find the will to search for peace. As was said upon the Mount: "Blessed are the peacemakers, for they shall be called the children of God." Amen. (Bush 1990i)

In these remarks, Bush did more than merely request the help of God; akin to his earlier proclamation, Bush implied that the country already had him on their side. Bush explicitly claims that God provides "many blessings to men and women who face adversity in the name of a noble purpose." The context suggests that Bush is equating the noble purpose of WWII with the noble purpose that had brought the men on the ship to those far away waters.

Furthermore, Bush quotes from Christ's Sermon on the Mount, an influential sermon that Jesus addressed to his followers from the side of a mountain or hill in Galilee (see Matthew 5–7). The Sermon is seen as a summation of Jesus's most important teachings. It opens with the Beatitudes, a series of statements indicating categories of people who enjoy the blessing of God. The seventh Beatitude is the one Bush cited, "Blessed are the peacemakers, for they shall be called the children of God" (Matthew 5:9).

The way Bush uses Scripture in this speech leads to the conclusion that America is one of those blessed peacemakers. In the previous line, Bush asked God to help the country in its search for peace. Thus, the message of these passages is implicitly that America, a peacemaker, has God behind them.

Even though Bush had promised to do everything he could to avoid war, war did come. Baker's diplomacy had paid off in the form of UN Security Council Resolution 678, agreed to on November 29, which set a deadline of January 15, 1991 for Saddam's forces to vacate Kuwaiti territory. On January 9, Baker and his Iraqi counterpart, foreign minister Tariq Aziz, met in Geneva in a last ditch attempt to avert war. The meeting was a disaster, ending with Aziz proclaiming "We accept war." As the conflict began, Bush increasingly used all of his major religious arguments in conjunction with one another.

The United States began its air assault on January 16, 1991. It was the commencement of what would ultimately be six weeks of over 100,000 sorties preluding a general ground offensive. On the subsequent day, Bush appeared in public just one time, attending a religious service for government leaders at Memorial Chapel in Fort Myer, Virginia. Billy Graham spoke at the service.

"This was supposed to the Christian century. But it has been anything but the Christian century. Why can't we settle our problems in peace?" Graham asked. According to the preacher, the answer was because "there come times when we have to fight for peace." Graham spoke hopefully that out of the war "will come a new peace and, as has been stated by the president, a new world order" (Rosenfeld 1991). The service concluded with the singing of "Amazing Grace," after which Graham returned to the White House with the president for lunch. Graham had slept there the previous night. Graham's activities with Bush, occurring right as the war started, contributed to a religious aura surrounding the US mission.

In fact, Bush was about to attempt to enlist all of the nation's ministers in his campaign for public approval. With the air war already underway, it was essential that Bush maintain support during the long-run up to the US ground invasion. On January 28, for the fifth time, Bush addressed the annual convention of the nation's religious broadcasters (Bush 1991b). His speech received considerable media attention. Persuading these men and women, some of whom were skeptical about the necessity of war, could result in the president's message being carried by proxy to the broadcasters' thousands of listeners.

The majority of the address was a precise argument about how Operation Desert Storm, the code name for the military's offensive, met the criteria of a just war. First, though, Bush began with another recitation of the good versus evil duality at hand:

> The clergyman Richard Cecil once said, "There are two classes of the wise: the men who serve God because they have found Him, and the men who seek Him because they have not found Him yet." Abroad, as in America, our task is to serve and seek wisely through the policies we pursue.
>
> Nowhere is this more true than in the Persian Gulf where—despite protestations of Saddam Hussein—it is not Iraq against the United States, it's the regime of Saddam Hussein against the rest of the world. Saddam tried to cast this conflict as a religious war, but it has nothing to do with religion per se. It has, on the other hand, everything to do with what religion embodies: good versus evil, right versus wrong, human dignity and freedom versus tyranny and oppression. The war in the Gulf is not a Christian war, a Jewish war, or a Moslem war; it is a just war. And it is a war with which good will prevail.

Next, Bush discussed the origins of the principles of a just war, making reference to many of the intellectual luminaries discussed above such as Cicero, Augustine, and Aquinas. Then, Bush tested the conflict against several of the standards of a just war. "The first principle of a just war is that it support a just cause," Bush said. "Our cause could not be more noble. We seek Iraq's withdrawal from Kuwait—completely, immediately, and without condition; the restoration of Kuwait's legitimate government; and the security and stability of the Gulf. We will see that Kuwait once again is free, that the nightmare of Iraq's occupation has ended, and that naked aggression will not be rewarded. We seek nothing for ourselves."

Bush then turned to the criterion that "a just war must also be declared by legitimate authority" and noted that the coalition, composed of twenty-eight nations from six continents, was backed by twelve UN Security Council resolutions. He added that a "just war must be a last resort" and proved that this had been so by citing James Baker's extensive diplomatic efforts, "more than 200 meetings with foreign dignitaries; 10 diplomatic missions; 6 congressional appearances; over 103,000 miles traveled to talk with, among others, members of the United Nations, the Arab League, and the European Community." He also made reference to the *jus in bello* dictate that noncombatants be protected, pointing out that the United States would "make every effort possible to keep causalities to a minimum."

In closing, Bush once more articulated the notion that God was on America's team: "My fellow Americans, I firmly believe in my heart of hearts that times will soon be on the side of peace because the world is overwhelmingly on the side of God."

Admittedly, given that this speech was delivered to an audience of spiritual leaders, the high degree of religious rhetoric is unsurprising. Still, it has already been shown that Bush discussed the standoff in the context of just war principles on previous occasions in front of broader publics. It would not appear that that was a coincidence. This address provides proof that Bush was aware of these benchmarks and suggests that his earlier just war statements were not made haphazardly.

In fact, Bush would use just war rhetoric before the entire country the following evening in his State of the Union address (Bush 1991c). All three of Bush's major religious themes can be identified in this speech. Bush placed Iraq in a religious frame by the eighth paragraph:

> We in this Union enter the last decade of the 20th century thankful for our blessings, steadfast in our purpose, aware of our difficulties, and responsive to our duties at home and around the world. For two centuries, America has served the world as an inspiring example of freedom and democracy. For generations, America has led the struggle to preserve and extend the blessings of liberty. And today, in a rapidly changing world, American leadership is indispensable. Americans know that leadership brings burdens and sacrifices. But we also know why the hopes of humanity turn to us. We are Americans; we have a unique responsibility to do the hard work of freedom. And when we do, freedom works.
>
> The conviction and courage we see in the Persian Gulf today is simply the American character in action. The indomitable spirit that is contributing to this victory for world peace and justice is the same spirit that gives us the power and the potential to meet our toughest challenges at home. We are resolute and resourceful. If we can selflessly confront the evil for the sake of good in a land so far away, then surely we can make this land all that it should be.

First, Bush implies once more that God is on America's side. He says that it is up to America "to preserve and extend the blessings of liberty." This formulation is right out of Eisenhower's playbook. Bush calls liberty a "blessing," a literal gift from God. The inference is that by spreading liberty in Kuwait, America was helping to bring about God's plan for the world.

Second, Bush also makes use of another of the themes, the opposition of good and evil. The United States, Bush said, was "selflessly confronting the evil for the sake of good in a land so far away." A short while later, Bush would build on this dichotomy with the use of some well-timed light and dark imagery: "As Americans, we know that there are times when we must step forward and accept our responsibility to lead the world away from the dark chaos of dictators, toward the brighter promise of a better day." Hussein represents evil and "dark chaos," while America embodies good and the "brighter promise of a better day."

Third, the commander in chief used the just war theme in a passage toward the end of the speech.

> Each of us will measure within ourselves the value of this great struggle. Any cost in lives—any cost—is beyond our power to measure. But the cost of closing our eyes to aggression is beyond mankind's power to imagine. This we do know: Our cause is just; our cause is moral; our cause is right.
>
> Let future generations understand the burden and the blessings of freedom. Let them say we stood where duty required us to stand. Let them know that, together, we affirmed America and the world as a community of conscience.

Here, Bush defends the war on the just cause criteria: "Our cause is just; our cause is moral; our cause is right." Further, for a second time, he calls freedom a "blessing," one that "duty required" us to defend. As a smaller point, he also refers to the coalition as a "community of conscience," again alluding to the religious motivations behind the US offensive.

Bush had already declared one national day of prayer prior to the onset of hostilities. In February, he would declare another. Bush announced his intentions in his remarks at the national prayer breakfast on January 31 (Bush 1991d). Bush claimed on this occasion that America could not hope to be successful without God's assistance.

> You know, America is a nation founded under God. And from our very beginnings we have relied upon His strength and guidance in war and in peace. And this is something we must never forget . . . I have learned what I suppose every President has learned, and that is that one cannot be President of our country without faith in God

and without knowing with certainty that we are one nation under God . . . God is our rock and salvation, and we must trust Him and keep faith in Him.

And so, we ask His blessings upon us and upon every member not just of our Armed Forces but of our coalition armed forces, with respect for the religious diversity that is represented as these 28 countries stand up against aggression.

Today I'm asking and designating that Sunday, February 3rd, be a national day of prayer. And I encourage all people of faith to say a special prayer on that day—a prayer for peace, a prayer for the safety of our troops, a prayer for their families, a prayer for the innocents caught up in this war, and a prayer that God will continue to bless the United States of America.

The president publicized the event the following day in remarks he made to the community at Fort Stewart, Georgia (Bush 1991e). It is worth mentioning that, in his speech, Bush made reference to the good versus evil and just war rhetorical themes, too. At one point, Bush explained,

It began with Kuwait, but that wouldn't have been the end. What we've witnessed these last few weeks removed any last shred of doubt about the adversary that we face: the terror bombing, without military value—the terror bombing of innocent civilians with those Scud missiles; the brutal treatment—that brutal, inhumane treatment of our POW's; the endless appetite for evil that would lead a man to make war on the world's environment. All of us know what we're up against. All of you know why we're there.

We are there because we are Americans, part of something that's larger than ourselves. Our cause is right. Our cause is just. And because it is just, that world's cause will prevail.

The day of prayer was scheduled for February 3. Bush issued both a proclamation (Bush 1991f) and gave a national radio address (Bush 1991g) about the meaning of the day. What's remarkable about each is that Bush left the distinct impression that America already had found God's favor.

The proclamation began:

As one Nation under God, we Americans are deeply mindful of both our dependence on the Almighty and our obligations as a people He has richly blessed. From our very beginnings as a Nation, we have relied upon God's strength and guidance in war and peace. Entrusted

95

with the holy gift of freedom and allowed to prosper in its great light, we have a responsibility to serve as a beacon to the world—to use our strength and resources to help those suffering in the darkness of tyranny and repression.

Today the United States is engaged in a great struggle to uphold the principles of national sovereignty and international order and to defend the lives and liberty of innocent people. It is an armed struggle we made every possible effort to avoid through extraordinary diplomatic efforts to resolve the matter peacefully, yet—given no choice by a ruthless dictator who would wield political and economic hegemony over other nations through force and terror—it is a struggle we wage with conviction and resolve. Our cause is moral and just.

Bush claims that America has certain "obligations as a people He has richly blessed" and that "Entrusted with the holy gift of freedom . . . we have a responsibility to . . . use our strength and resources to help those suffering in the darkness of tyranny and repression." Like the State of the Union, the subtext is that America's mission in the Gulf is God's mission. At the same time, Bush yet again refers to the coalition's just cause ("Our cause is moral and just.").

The radio address opened along the same lines as the proclamation.

At this moment, America, the finest, most loving nation on Earth, is at war, at war against the oldest enemy of the human spirit: evil that threatens world peace.

At this moment, men and women of courage and endurance stand on the harsh desert and sail the seas of the Gulf. By their presence they're bearing witness to the fact that the triumph of the moral order is the vision that compels us. At this moment, those of us here at home are thinking of them and of the future of our world. I recall Abraham Lincoln and his anguish during the Civil War. He turned to prayer, saying: "I've been driven many times to my knees by the overwhelming conviction that I have nowhere else to go."

So many of us, compelled by a deep need for God's wisdom in all we do, turn to prayer. We pray for God's protection in all we undertake, for God's love to fill all hearts, and for God's peace to be the moral North Star that guides us. So, I have proclaimed Sunday, February 3rd, National Day of Prayer. In this moment of crisis, may Americans of every creed turn to our greatest power and unite together in prayer.

The good versus evil theme is present in the first line ("evil that threatens world peace"). But Bush is also claiming that America's actions in the Gulf are being driven by a "moral order," just like people usually take direction, he says, from God's "moral North Star." The motivations appear to be religious and Godly in each case.

On February 24, the coalition opened its ground attack. The outcome was never in doubt. Many of the enemy soldiers dropped their firearms and enthusiastically welcomed the advancing Americans, chanting "M-R-E," the US military slang for "Meals Ready to Eat." Others flashed victory signs in lieu of white flags. A cease fire was declared exactly 100 hours after the rout had begun.

Though, certainly, one combat loss is one too many, just 148 Americans died in action. That total was fewer than the number of Americans who were murdered in the United States during those same 100 hours (Greene 2000, 130). Desert Storm was a stunning military success, minting Gens. Norman Schwartzkopf and Colin Powell as national heroes overnight.

To review, beginning mid-fall, Bush mounted a vigorous religious rhetorical strategy as he worked to rally the country behind his war plans. Bush was responding to a serious deterioration in his position. Support for his leadership and his policy was on the decline, Congress was turning against him, and he was, all the while, in the process of escalating the conflict, making the backing of these actors more crucial than ever.

With his back to the wall, Bush reacted by declaring two national days of prayer. He shrewdly used Billy Graham to give the war a mantle of spiritual legitimacy. His rhetoric became marked by three consistent and easily identifiable religious themes: that the Gulf War was a conflict between good and evil; that the Gulf War was a just war; and that in the Gulf War America both needed and had God's support. What difference did all of this make?

As far as public opinion goes, a second look at Figure 3.1 would at first impress. In January, Bush's personal approval rating skyrocketed. The president hovered at over 80 percent approval for the second half of the month, and he maintained that lofty standing well into April. On February 28, he hit a high of 89 percent. Similarly, Figure 3.2 shows that, in the same time frame, Bush rose to a place where over 80 percent of the country approved of his handling of the Iraqi invasion.

This incredible upwelling of support cannot, however, in any way be attributed to the effect of Bush's religious rhetoric. Scholars of public opinion have long documented the existence of a "rally-round-the-flag effect." Broadly speaking, major foreign policy events trigger a short-term increase in presidential popularity as the country unites around its leader in a time of trial. This is especially so when it comes to war. Roosevelt was polling slightly above 50 percent until the country entered World War II; he soon found his numbers above 70 percent. Following the outbreak of the Korean War, Truman gained nine points. When the fighting in Vietnam escalated in 1966, Johnson received a boost of eight points. Even minor conflicts, like Reagan's quick invasion of Grenada, can benefit a president (Erikson and Tedin 2011, 120–21).

Therefore, Bush's remarkable New Year rise in the polls was merely a side effect of an understandable burst of patriotic pride that accompanied the country's first real military venture post-Vietnam. If we wish to evaluate the impact of Bush's rhetoric, it is wise to limit ourselves to examining opinion following his change in rhetoric (roughly beginning in November) but prior to the start of the fighting (and thus prior to the incidence of the rally-round-the-flag effect). And here, the record is less favorable for Bush.

Both Figures 3.1 and 3.2 show that the public was constant in terms of how they evaluated Bush's handling of the Iraq question. His switch to a religious rationale circa November 1990 did not appear to make a difference either way. In both graphs, the trend lines instead plateau for the remainder of the year. In this approximately three-month period, Bush's own approval rating, though it had its share of spikes, remained centered around 60 percent. If Bush's religious rhetoric had been influential, we'd expect to see positive trends on these graphs. The graphs instead show stability, providing evidence that Bush was unable to reacquire the higher level of support he enjoyed at the start of the crisis.

Bush did give one major speech where he framed the Gulf War in religious terms, his State of the Union address on January 29, 1991. Bush's approval rating before the address was measured at 74 percent on January 26. On January 30, his rating hit 82 percent. The eight-point increase would seem to indicate a statistically significant change.

However, there is an important qualification. Bush received the approval of 82 percent of respondents on January 19, and 83 percent of respondents on January 23. This makes us question whether the 74 percent mark he received on January 26 might not have been an aberration. Indeed, Bush would not poll that low again until May 2. The 82 percent support he received on January 30 was, therefore, in line with what Bush typically experienced during these early months of 1991.

As Table 3.1 clearly shows, the editorial reaction to Bush's religiously infused 1991 State of the Union address was shockingly out of step with the president's high approval ratings at the time. The average editorial was scored a solidly negative 2.10. Moreover, 67.5 percent of all pieces were negative in tone. This statistic is in striking contrast to the just 17.5 percent of op-eds that were supportive of Bush's Gulf War policies.

Table 3.1
Editorial coverage of Bush's 1991 State of the Union address

Date	Paper	Author	Title	Score
1/30/1991	*Chicago Tribune*	Staff Editorial	"To Defeat Saddam, Liberate Kuwait"	4
1/30/1991	*New York Times*	Leslie Gelb	"Gas, Germs and Nukes"	2
1/30/1991	*New York Times*	Tom Wicker	"The Key to Unity"	1
1/30/1991	*Washington Post*	Robert Hunter	"The Battle of Ideas"	1
1/30/1991	*Washington Post*	Robert Samuelson	"Don't Worry About the War's Cost"	5
1/31/1991	*Chicago Tribune*	Stephen Chapman	"The War and Its Critics"	1
1/31/1991	*Los Angeles Times*	Joshua Muravchik	"Striking a Balance With Evil"	5
1/31/1991	*Los Angeles Times*	John Mack and Jeffrey Rubin	"Is This Any Way to Wage Peace?"	1
1/31/1991	*New York Times*	Staff Editorial	"State of the War"	3
1/31/1991	*New York Times*	Anna Quindlen	"The Domestic Front"	1
1/31/1991	*New York Times*	William Safire	"Don't Throw Away Victory"	2

(continued on next page)

Table 3.1 (*continued*)

Date	Paper	Author	Title	Score
1/31/1991	*Washington Post*	Staff Editorial	"The Strength of Democracy"	1
1/31/1991	*Washington Post*	Richard Cohen	"Saddam Left Us No Choice"	5
1/31/1991	*Washington Post*	George Will	"Hard Work Avoided"	1
2/1/1991	*Chicago Tribune*	Mike Royko	"Clock is Running for America's Team"	1
2/1/1991	*Los Angeles Times*	Tim Rutten	"An Unhappy Era Comes to an End"	3
2/1/1991	*Los Angeles Times*	Staff Editorial	"Why U.S. Should Not Use Chemical Weapons"	3
2/1/1991	*New York Times*	A. Rosenthal	"Too Clever by Half"	1
2/1/1991	*New York Times*	Anthony Lewis	"The First Lesson"	2
2/1/1991	*Washington Post*	Stephen Rosenfeld	"Protest and the President"	4
2/2/1991	*New York Times*	Staff Editorial	"Why the Gulf War is Not Vietnam"	2
2/2/1991	*New York Times*	Tom Wicker	"An Opposition Leader?"	1
2/2/1991	*Washington Post*	A. Knighton Stanley and Andrea Young	"Race and War in the Persian Gulf"	1
2/2/1991	*Washington Post*	Eleanor Holmes Norton	"Race and War in the Persian Gulf"	1
2/2/1991	*Washington Post*	Constance Hilliard	"Race and War in the Persian Gulf"	5

(*continued on next page*)

Table 3.1 (*continued*)

Date	Paper	Author	Title	Score
2/3/1991	*Chicago Tribune*	Steve Daley	"Promise of a New World Order Doesn't Include the Old Problems at Home"	1
2/3/1991	*Los Angeles Times*	Martin Marty	"In a World of Shifting Rationales Can a War Be Just or Unjust?"	2
2/3/1991	*Los Angeles Times*	Staff Editorial	"Is Domestic Policy a Casualty of War?"	2
2/3/1991	*Los Angeles Times*	Judith Viorst	"A Prescription for Handling the War: Become an Activist"	1
2/3/1991	*Los Angeles Times*	Alexander Cockburn	"Bombs, the Moral Tools of the West"	1
2/3/1991	*New York Times*	Leslie Gelb	"The Next Surprise?"	3
2/3/1991	*Washington Post*	Robert Hunter	"Endgame: How the War Could Soon Be Over"	3
2/3/1991	*Washington Post*	Daniel Schorr	"Hypocrisy About Assassination"	1
2/3/1991	*Washington Post*	Colman McCarthy	"What the Children Understand"	1
2/3/1991	*Washington Post*	George Will	"Selective Morality"	1
2/4/1991	*Chicago Tribune*	Staff Editorial	"No Balance Sheet for War"	4

(*continued on next page*)

Table 3.1 (*continued*)

Date	Paper	Author	Title	Score
2/4/1991	*Los Angeles Times*	Jeffrey Garten	"Who's Sharing That Burden Now?"	3
2/4/1991	*New York Times*	Zbigniew Brzezinski	"Limited War, Maximum Advantage"	2
2/5/1991	*Los Angeles Times*	Tom Bethell	"Patriotism Doesn't Mean Mindlessness"	1
2/5/1991	*New York Times*	Victor Sidel and H. Jack Geiger	"Trip Wire of Armageddon"	1
Dates: **1/30 to 2/5**			**Average score**	**2.10**
			Positive articles	7 (17.5%)
			Negative articles	27 (67.5%)
			Mixed/neutral articles	6 (15.0%)

The president's critics shared a number of common concerns. One frequent complaint that echoed in many of these editorials was that Bush was pursuing a course of action that would inevitably lead to the use of chemical weapons, both by and against the United States (see Gelb 1991; Sidel and Geiger 1991).

A second group of critics fixated on what they saw as diplomatic bungling by the Bush Administration. Many felt that Bush and his State Department were not being candid about the country's objectives in Iraq. Rosenthal (1991), to cite an example, observed, "At a time when it is essential for the American public and the world to understand precisely what the U.S. is doing politically in the gulf and why, the word of the U.S. is becoming fuzzy, subject to different interpretations, and sometimes simply not believed" (see also Safire 1991).

A sizable collection of writers were also dismayed by the State of the Union's single-minded focus on the events happening in Iraq, which they felt came at the expense of other pressing domestic problems. Blasting the domestic parts of Bush's speech, Anna Quindlen (1991) argued that "If the President thinks only of war, the home front will have disintegrated, in some cases beyond repair" (see also Daley 1991).

Even reliable conservative George Will (1991a) was willing to castigate the Republican president on these grounds. Responding to Bush's claim that America was doing the "hard work of freedom" in Iraq, Will countered, "Providing such schools, sustaining such families and policing such streets—call that the hard work of freedom."

But, from the perspective of this study, the most interesting reaction to Bush's State of the Union address was the negative response writers had to its overt religious themes. Several commentators devoted column space solely for the purpose of attacking Bush's repeated religious justifications for the war. Mike Royko (1991), commenting on the "many Americans . . . convinced that God is always our side," wondered whether those same individuals "think he dozed off during the Vietnam War."

In a bitter piece, Colman McCarthy (1991) expanded on the same point. McCarthy claimed that Bush had been using Billy Graham as "the ultimate in evangelistic ground-and-air support" in order to "show that God is on our side." However, Graham and other "pious hawks," as McCarthy branded them, refused to admit their true purpose, which McCarthy claimed was "to fight for peace by saturation bombing, by slaughtering Iraqi civilians and further bankrupting our own economy while we do it."

In a more restrained critique, scholar Martin Marty (1991) considered Bush's just war claims in an essay printed in the *Los Angeles Times*. Marty believed that, through his rhetorical choices, "Bush took risks—and not only among the non-believing minority." "Many believers, even those who support Bush's course of action, are edgy about the sort of words he used," Marty wrote. Bush was ill-advised to claim that God was on America's side, even before an audience of religious leaders, because "As evangelists, they work on an opposite assumption: The world needs rescue and souls need saving precisely because the world is overwhelmingly *not* on the side of God." Indeed, Bush was not even correct to discuss the war in the terms of just war theory, Marty argued, because he was only doing so to "legitimize already-made choices," rather than to evaluate alternate courses of action.

George Will (1991b) chimed in on Bush's religious rhetoric, too. For Will, the issue was the application of Bush's principles. "The Bush administration's moralism has been in conspicuous abeyance regarding

China," Will observed. He continued, "When the Bush administration made defeating Saddam such a moral mission, critics worried that the rationale lacked a limiting principle: Would America become incontinently active in attempting to right all the world's wrongs? The administration's limp response to Gorbachev's intensified dictatorship suggests that the critics can relax." "The New World Order evidently rests on a moral principle with a single application," Will concluded.

In sum, Bush's religious rhetoric in his 1991 State of the Union address was unpersuasive so far as the media was concerned. Many writers simply looked past Bush's moralizing and harped on a series of pre-existing political shortcomings—Bush's evident lack of concern over possible chemical attacks, his lack of attention to domestic issues, and so on. Others reacted quite critically to Bush's religious language itself, disputing his categorizations of the Persian Gulf War as a just war being fought between the forces of good and evil.

In Congress, Bush's policy ultimately prevailed, but not absent heavy opposition. Bush decided to formally ask Congress for a vote authorizing the use of force against Iraq, pursuant to the demands of the earlier UN resolutions. This request went against the advice of many members of his cabinet, including Defense Secretary Dick Cheney, who worried that Congress might reject the measure. Bush did not think he needed such a resolution to act—indeed he was prepared to use force even were it to fail (Bush and Scowcroft 1998, 446). Still, Bush felt it important to have Congress on the record supporting the decision.

The resolutions, Solarz-Michel in the House and Dole-Warner in the Senate, were introduced on January 10, 1991. The debate was mostly civil despite having to be suspended several times on account of anti-war disruptions in the visitors' gallery. Still the president took a beating from the war's opponents.

"Just this morning I heard it said that there may be 'only' a few thousand American causalities. But for the families of those few thousand . . . the word will have no meaning," said Sen. George Mitchell (D-MN). "And the truly haunting question, which no one will ever be able to answer, will be: did they die unnecessarily? For if we go to war now, no one will ever know if sanctions would have worked if given a full and fair chance."

Sen. Barbara Boxer (D-CA) struck the same note, arguing that the country was "about to be sucked into a war in the area of the world known for violence, known for terrorism, known for blood baths, known for atrocities. We will never be the same again."

"There is still time to save the President from himself. And save thousands of American soldiers in the Persian Gulf from dying in the desert in a war whose cruelty will be exceeded only by the lack of any rational necessity for waging it," Sen. Ted Kennedy (D-MA) warned (445).

On January 12, both houses voted to support the resolution. Solarz-Michel passed 250-183, while Dole-Warner passed 52-47. These tight votes were a disappointment for Bush. Almost every member who the Administration felt was persuadable received multiple appeals. Bush desperately wanted a bipartisan, comfortable vote that would show "Saddam we were speaking as one voice" (Bush and Scowcroft 1998, 441). On these grounds, the president failed. The vote in the Senate was the closest in history for a declaration of war (Maynard 2008, 81).

The vote was also heavily partisan. In the House, 164 Republicans and 86 Democrats voted for the resolution. On the other side, 179 Democrats, 3 Republicans, and 1 independent voted against it. In the Senate, the majority was composed of forty-two Republicans and ten Democrats. Only two Republicans joined forty-five Democrats in the opposition. The picture that emerged was one of division. Given that the vote was entirely symbolic, even though Bush was on the winning side, we must see the resolution as a failure.

In the end, perhaps the biggest indictment of Bush's religious rhetoric was that it was not even successful in persuading those individuals most susceptible to this kind of rhetorical device. Several days before the onset of the air attack, the Society of Christian Ethics voted 97-20 that the use of force in the Gulf would not meet the criteria for a just war (*Washington Post* 1991). And major religious officials ranging from Pope John Paul II to George Weigel to the presiding bishop of the Episcopal Church, the Most Rev. Edmond L. Browning, remained steadfast in their opposition (Stepp 1991).

George W. Bush and the War on Terror

Bush's son's life changed course on the morning of July 28, 1986. The previous evening had featured a raucous, alcohol-fueled binge at the Broadmoor Hotel in Colorado Springs. When Bush attempted to go for his post-birthday run, he found himself unable to. Hungover and miserable, Bush vowed to never touch alcohol again. To his great credit, this was a vow he kept. Bush turned to God for help in abandoning liquor. Bush later admitted to a group of religious social workers, "I would not be president today if I hadn't stopped drinking 17 years ago. And I could only do that with the grace of God" (Smith 2006, 372).

Bush's acceptance of Christianity was a bit more gradual than this anecdote would lead one to assume (Smith 2006, 365–413; Aikman 2009). Meetings with Pentecostal evangelist Arthur Blessitt and Billy Graham also played a role. Regardless, Bush's change was lasting. Even in the midst of the multitude of crises he dealt with as a president, Bush made sure to find time for Bible study every day.

Bush understandably credits his faith with turning his life around. When asked during a December 1999 Republican primary debate who his favorite philosopher was, Bush famously answered Christ, "because he changed my heart." "When you turn your heart and your life over to Christ," Bush continued, "when you accept Christ as the Savior, it changes your life."

If Bush's life had changed course on July 28, 1986, Bush's presidency changed course on September 11, 2001. On that serene morning, nineteen men armed with little more than mace and box-cutters highjacked four airline flights. In the carnage that ensued, the terrorists destroyed both towers of the World Trade Center in New York, and did serious damage to the Pentagon in Washington. A fourth plane, United 93, crashed in a deserted field in Pennsylvania when the passengers heroically overwhelmed the terrorists in the cockpit. Around 3,000 people died on 9/11 in the worst attack ever on the United States.

Terrorism had not been high on the agenda for the new president. Neither Bush nor Democratic nominee Al Gore had discussed the issue much in the 2000 campaign. The issues the two debated were topics like health maintenance organizations and prescription drug coverage, school violence, and moral values. The Administration's first foreign policy discussions centered more on how to deal with Russia and China and missile defense, rather than what to do about religious fanatics thousands of miles away.

The attacks reordered Bush's priorities. Quickly, Bush declared that the country was at war with "terror." The country's goals in this new war were later formalized in National Security Presidential Decision 9, issued in October 2001. In this document, Bush set an ambitious standard for success: "the elimination of terrorism as a threat to our way of life." The war would start with al Qaeda, but that organization was only to be the first of many that would be targeted for eradication (Naftali 2010, 66).

The term "war on terror" is an amorphous one. Although thought to originate with Bush, it was Reagan who first began speaking of such a conflict. The precise objectives that the term encompasses are up for debate. Still, a broad definition of the War on Terror may nevertheless be possible. Most analysts would likely include the war in Afghanistan, the freezing of terrorist financial assets, the USA PATRIOT Act legislation, the creation of the Department of Homeland Security, and the war in Iraq as part of the collection of policies that Bush, at least, considered to comprise the War on Terror. These are the policies that I will pay the most attention to.

Many of the methods Bush adopted in the War on Terror were controversial (Anderson 2011). Bush spent much of his time in public defending the choices he had made. His speeches on terrorism typically featured a number of common points. He unfailingly would outline what some would label the "Bush doctrine," that being the idea that any state or regime that harbored terrorists should be considered as culpable as the terrorists themselves. Bush would frequently explain why he thought the terrorists hated America, how they resented the country's freedoms of speech, press, and religion. The president would tell audiences that their conceptions of America's security needed to evolve, that oceans no longer offered protection, and that America had to aggressively confront threats wherever they arose.

There also would be some bluster, like talk of a price to be paid, of individual terrorists who were "no longer a problem," or warnings of what happens to those who are guilty of "messing with" America. There would even be some strained attempts at humor. Bush's standard speech included a line that usually drew laughs where the president stated that the terrorists had miscalculated when they assumed that the United States was weak and materialistic. The terrorists must have, Bush would say, seen some "lousy movies." Or the terrorists wrongly believed that all the country would do is file a "couple of lawsuits" in retaliation.

Of course, religious language would be a prominent dimension of Bush's rhetoric on terrorism, too. The terrible events of September 11 without question qualify as a "crisis," which it is being argued seems to be a precondition for the appearance of religious rhetoric. In the introduction, the reader has already encountered a discussion of the first occasion on which Bush used coalitional religious rhetoric, his speech to the nation on September 20, 2001 (Bush 2001a).

In this address, Bush identified America's enemies and made clear his expectations for how the world should deal with them ("Every nation, in every region, now has a decision to make: Either you are with us, or you are with the terrorists"). But, as was said before, it was Bush's closing lines that were most remarkable. In these paragraphs, the president mixed overt invocations of God (i.e., "Freedom and fear, justice and cruelty have always been at war, and we know that God is not neutral between them") with a more subtly charged religious vocabulary (i.e., the use of words like "mission" and "patient justice").

From these beginnings, Bush's religious rhetoric would come to be defined by two basic trajectories. The first was that Bush consistently depicted the War on Terror as a massive ideological struggle between good and evil. Earlier in this chapter, I explained how good versus evil is one of the most recognized Biblical themes. Although this motif would be a constant in Bush's discourse, it would be most visible in the first year after 9/11.

The second religious theme marking Bush's rhetoric on terrorism would be the idea that America was fighting not just for its own safety, but for the preservation of freedom as well. Freedom, Bush always said, was God's "gift" to humanity. This religious theme would emerge as Bush moved to expand the War on Terror beyond Afghanistan in late 2002. Again, traces of this theme would remain visible in Bush's remarks until the last days of his Administration. I will consider each theme in turn.

Bush spoke of good and evil to a degree that is unprecedented among modern US presidents. The word evil or a word taking evil as its base (i.e., "evildoers") appears in 711 Bush public documents between 2001 and 2008. The events of 9/11 made some question America's place as a chosen nation. Bush moved to reassert this belief by focusing on the evil of America's enemies as contrasted with the own inherent goodness of the United States (Roof 2010).

In remarks he made to the Federal Bureau of Investigation (FBI) just two weeks after 9/11, Bush (2001b) expressed his understanding of the attacks: "I see things this way: The people who did this act on America and who may be planning further acts are evil people. They don't represent an ideology; they don't represent a legitimate political group of people. They're flat evil. That's all they can think about, is evil. And as a nation of good folks, we're going to hunt them down, and we're going to find them, and we will bring them to justice. Ours is a nation that does not seek revenge, but we do seek justice. And I don't care how long it takes to rout out terrorism, we're going to do it." The terrorists are "evil people" and "flat evil." The United States was a "nation of good folks." In the months immediately after the attacks, a similar version of these sentiments can be found in almost every single Bush transcript.

At times, Bush's fixation on good and evil could be overwhelming. For example, in an off the cuff speech he made to the State Department in late 2001, Bush (2001e) used the word "evil" or one of its variants nine separate times. Bush told the audience that the country intended to make it "clear to the evildoers that we reject you" that the upcoming fight would be "a war between good and evil," and he reminded them that "in order to overcome evil, the great goodness of America must come forth and shine forth." Bush would occasionally even call the military campaign a "war on evil" rather than his more common designation of a War on Terror (see, i.e., Bush 2001f).

Yet, Bush was careful to specify exactly *who* was evil. As it happens, Bush quite often defended Islam as a great and peaceful religion. The teachings of Islam, Bush once said, are the "exact opposite of the teachings of the Al Qaida organization, which is based upon evil and hate and destruction" (Bush 2001d). Instead, it was Osama bin Laden who was evil and not a true Muslim. When asked whether bin Laden was a religious or a political leader, Bush gave the following response:

> *Q.* Granted the extremism, do you—and I'd like to ask the imam the same question—do you consider bin Laden a religious leader or a political leader?
>
> *The President.* I consider bin Laden an evil man. And I don't think there's any religious justification for what he has in mind. Islam is a religion of love, not hate. This is a man who hates. This is a man who's declared war on innocent people. This is a man who doesn't mind destroying women and children. This is man who hates freedom. This is an evil man.
>
> *Q.* But does he have political goals?
>
> *The President.* He has got evil goals. And it's hard to think in conventional terms about a man so dominated by evil that he's willing to do what he thinks he's going to get away with. But he's not going to get away with it. (Bush 2001c)

No one could accuse Bush of failing to offer a moral vision. At the national prayer breakfast in 2002, Bush (2002b) explained how his own personal faith had led him to see the world in such absolutes: "At the same time, faith shows us the reality of good and the reality of evil. Some acts and choices in this world have eternal consequences. It is always and everywhere wrong to target and kill the innocent. It is always and everywhere wrong to be cruel and hateful, to enslave and oppress. It is always and everywhere right to be kind and just, to protect the lives of others, and to lay down your life for a friend."

Similarly, in a commencement address at West Point, Bush (2002g) noted that the United States had a long history of facing down evil in the world. The War on Terror was no different from the previous fight against communism. Bush believed that there were universal moral truths involved in each contest:

> Because the war on terror will require resolve and patience, it will also require firm moral purpose. In this way our struggle is similar to the cold war. Now, as then, our enemies are totalitarians, holding a creed of power with no place for human dignity. Now, as then, they seek to impose a joyless conformity, to control every life and all of life.
>
> America confronted imperial communism in many different ways, diplomatic, economic, and military. Yet, moral clarity was essential to our victory in the cold war. When leaders like John F. Kennedy and Ronald Reagan refused to gloss over the brutality of tyrants, they gave hope to prisoners and dissidents and exiles and rallied free nations to a great cause.
>
> Some worry that it is somehow undiplomatic or impolite to speak the language of right and wrong. I disagree. Different circumstances require different methods but not different moralities. Moral truth is the same in every culture, in every time, and in every place. Targeting innocent civilians for murder is always and everywhere wrong. Brutality against women is always and everywhere wrong. There can be no neutrality between justice and cruelty, between the innocent and the guilty. We are in a conflict between good and evil, and America will call evil by its name. By confronting evil and lawless regimes, we do not create a problem; we reveal a problem. And we will lead the world in opposing it.

At the same time, it was precisely because the United States stood for good against evil that the country could be confident of an eventual victory. Bush would often admit in his speeches that he saw a purpose behind history and that God was not, as Bush said in that September 20 address, neutral. Bush offered an example of this stream of thinking in his first address to the United Nations in November 2001 (Bush 2001g):

> But the outcome of this conflict is certain: There is a current in history, and it runs toward freedom. Our enemies resent it and dismiss it. But the dreams of mankind are defined by liberty: the natural right to create and build and worship and live in dignity. When men

and women are released from oppression and isolation, they find fulfillment and hope, and they leave poverty by the millions.

These aspirations are lifting up the peoples of Europe, Asia, Africa, and the Americas, and they can lift up all of the Islamic world.

We stand for the permanent hopes of humanity, and those hopes will not be denied. We're confident, too, that history has an author who fills time and eternity with His purpose. We know that evil is real, but good will prevail against it. This is the teaching of many faiths, and in that assurance we gain strength for a long journey.

One of the major criticisms leveled at Bush's response to 9/11 was the claim that the president did not call for enough sacrifice from the public. That he squandered a moment of unified purpose, asking no more than for people to continue to shop and take vacations. It is true that Bush called for people to spend money and go about their normal lives. But a close inspection of his good and evil rhetoric reveals that Bush also told ordinary citizens that one way in which they could aid the War on Terror was by doing good in their own communities.

Bush believed that out of the evil of the attacks, good might still come—a view he expressed to a meeting in Tennessee in the spring of 2002: "You know, I truly believe that out of this evil is going to come incredible good. I believe that by remaining strong in the face of terror, that we can lead the world to peace. I believe there's going to be some problems in the world that can be solved with American strength and American leadership and a coalition that refuses to bend when it comes to the defense of terror. And out of evil will come some incredible good in America, some incredible good" (Bush 2002e).

Bush offered concrete ideas about how an individual could help—by visiting an elderly neighbor, by mentoring a child, by feeding the hungry. All of this connected to Bush's overall view of the conflict. As Bush told the men and women stationed at an Air Force base in Alaska in early 2002, "As you probably figured out by now, I view this current conflict as either us versus them, and evil versus good. And there's no in-between. There's no hedging. And if you want to join the war against evil, do some good. If you want to be a part of our Nation's stand against those who murder innocent people for the sake of murder, for those who believe in tyranny, for those who hijack a noble religion—if you want to take a stand, love a neighbor like you'd like to be loved yourself" (Bush 2002c). Bush concluded most of his speeches in a similar fashion throughout his first several years in office (see, e.g., Bush 2002a, 2002d, 2002f).

The president did somewhat tone down the good and evil language in late 2002 as he increasingly turned to other themes. However, this bifurcated outlook on US foreign policy would re-emerge in full force in late 2005 and early 2006 as conditions began to unravel in Iraq. In a series of potent speeches, Bush made the case that it was precisely because the insurgents were so evil that it was necessary to finish the mission.

In Norfolk, Virginia, in October of 2005, for example, Bush (2005b) connected the insurgent leaders to the evil men of the past, observing "Some might be tempted to dismiss these goals as fanatical or extreme. They are fanatical and extreme, but they should not be dismissed. Our enemy is utterly committed. As Zawahiri (Zarqawi)* has vowed, 'We will either achieve victory over the human race, or we will pass to the eternal life.' And the civilized world knows very well that other fanatics in history, from Hitler to Stalin to Pol Pot, consumed whole nations in war and genocide before leaving the stage of history. Evil men, obsessed with ambition and unburdened by conscience, must be taken very seriously—and we must stop them before their crimes can multiply." At other points in his talk, Bush identified the insurgents as a version of "evil Islamic radicalism" and he described their goals as "evil but not insane" (for other examples, see Bush 2005c, 2005d).

Still, by late 2002, Bush had begun to prioritize in his rhetoric the preeminent importance of freedom. We can easily gather from Bush's speeches that the president sincerely believed that the expansion of human freedom was the best way to guarantee the long-term safety of America. He would remind his audiences that Europe had seen hundreds of years of war until the rapid spread of democracy across the continent in the latter half of the twentieth century. Or, he would point to Japan and explain how it was that the adoption of democratic institutions in that country had led to a long-term peaceful alliance with the United States, its former enemy. Bush believed that democracies did not go to war with each other, thereby subscribing to a theory that has been the subject of much empirical political science research (Ray 1998).

Freedom was especially important, Bush felt, in the Mideast. He often took his listeners inside the head of an Islamic radical and asked them how they would react if they had no opportunity, no rights, and no prospect of improving their circumstances. Sometimes, he could explain the rationale of a terrorist in the starkest of terms: "Our security depends on there to be an alternative to the ideology of hate. Because if there's resentment and hate, it's easier to recruit 19 kids to get on an airplane and kill 3,000 people" (Bush 2007).

Bush's views on freedom had a clear religious component to them. In a question and answer session in Manhattan, Kansas, in 2006, Bush succinctly presented his thoughts on this connection. He told the attendees that he believes that God created man to be free: "Part of my decision-making process is my firm belief in the natural rights of men and women, my belief that deep in everybody's soul is the desire to live free. I believe there's an Almighty, and I believe the Almighty's great gift to each man and woman in this world is the desire to be free. This isn't America's gift to the world; it is a universal gift to the world. And people want to be free. And if you believe that and if you believe freedom yields the peace, it's important for the United States of America, with friends, to lead the cause of liberty" (Bush 2006).

Hence, in addition to the practical reasons that exist for promoting freedom, Bush also claimed there was a spiritual rationale at work, as well. This merging of the practical and spiritual reasons for supporting political freedom was made plain in a much noted speech Bush made celebrating the twentieth anniversary of the National Endowment for Democracy when he observed, "Liberty is both the plan of heaven for humanity and the best hope for progress here on Earth" (Bush 2003h). The nation's and God's goals were aligned.

Although Bush would never publicly acknowledge it, the Bible is replete with stories of liberation, a good example being the travails of the Israelites in the Old Testament. The existence of this religious tradition made this rhetorical point culturally powerful (McAdams 2011, 195–230).

It would not be realistic to think that Bush pushed these claims simply because he believed them to be true, though. There is little evidence to suggest that Bush's God and freedom rhetoric was anything other than a strategic choice. Bush's presidency was one of the most carefully managed in modern history (Maltese 2009). Despite his outward disdain for polls, Bush relied heavily on surveys and focus groups, all the while cloaking these activities in secrecy. It is a little known fact that Bush increased the number of White House staff devoted to speech writing and spun off the Office of Media Affairs into its own separate department.

Bush's top speech writer, Michael Gerson, has admitted that the Administration gave ample consideration to the questions of when and how to use religion in the president's speeches. Gerson told a seminar of journalists in 2004 that Bush made so many religious references because these ideas were "our culture. They are literary allusions understood by millions of Americans" (Mattingly 2004).

More proof of the calculated nature of Bush's language is found in its timing. This theme only emerged as Bush began to campaign for military action in Iraq—a campaign that was itself an extremely well-coordinated media operation. Arguments for selling the war were developed as early as the summer of 2002. Bush's speech at West Point, a speech discussed above, was a field test of sorts. The only reason Bush did not begin his push until September was because, as White House Chief of Staff Andy Card candidly told *The New York Times*, "From a marketing point of view you don't introduce new products in August" (McClellan 2008, 119–47).

The first major example of Bush attempting to link the pursuit of freedom to God's intentions was his national address to the country from Ellis Island on the first anniversary of September 11 (Bush 2002h). Some of the president's religious rhetoric was communitarian. But the next day, Bush was scheduled to deliver an anticipated speech at the UN on Iraq. Bush left little doubt that his speech on the September 11 was the opening salvo when he said, "We are joined by a great coalition of nations to rid the world of terror. And we will not allow any terrorist or tyrant to threaten civilization with weapons of mass murder. Now and in the future, Americans will live as free people, not in fear and never at the mercy of any foreign plot or power."

In this address, Bush prefaced the religious rationale that would come to be a hallmark of his rhetoric about Iraq:

> Our deepest national conviction is that every life is precious, because every life is the gift of a Creator who intended us to live in liberty and equality. More than anything else, this separates us from the enemy we fight. We value every life. Our enemies value none, not even the innocent, not even their own. And we seek the freedom and opportunity that give meaning and value to life.
>
> There is a line in our time and in every time between those who believe that all men are created equal and those who believe that some men and women and children are expendable in the pursuit of power. There is a line in our time and in every time between the defenders of human liberty and those who seek to master the minds and souls of others. Our generation has now heard history's call, and we will answer it.

Bush was expanding the aims of the War on Terror by calling attention to the "line" between those who believe in "a Creator who intended us to live in liberty" and those who do not. In a way, this language is another iteration of the good versus evil contrast. However, Bush would not stop there, calling the defense of freedom the United States' "sacred promise." Bush announced that it was God who had assigned the country this task:

> We cannot know all that lies ahead. Yet, we do know that God has placed us together in this moment, to grieve together, to stand together, to serve each other and our country. And the duty we have been given, defending America and our freedom, is also a privilege we share. We're prepared for this journey, and our prayer tonight is that God will see us through and keep us worthy.

> Tomorrow is September the 12th. A milestone is passed, and a mission goes on. Be confident. Our country is strong, and our cause is even larger than our country. Ours is the cause of human dignity, freedom guided by conscience and guarded by peace. This ideal of America is the hope of all mankind. That hope drew millions to this harbor. That hope still lights our way. And the light shines in the darkness. And the darkness will not overcome it.

The reader should note the abundant smaller religious references present in these paragraphs, including the appeal to prayer, the location of the source of the cause as the guidance of conscience, and the light and dark imagery.

This speech was only the start of Bush's linkage between freedom, God and US policy toward Iraq. One only needs to examine a few of the many speeches Bush gave where he intertwined these three elements to get a sense of this aspect of his rhetorical strategy.

For instance, in Shreveport, Louisiana, in December 2002, Bush averred, "I believe that by doing what we need to do to secure the world from terrorist attack, to rid tyrants of weapons of mass destruction, to make sure that somebody like Saddam Hussein doesn't serve as a training base or a provider of weapons of mass destruction to terrorist networks—by doing our job, that the world will be more peaceful, by standing strong for what we believe, by remembering that freedom is not America's gift to the world, but God's gift to each and every human being, that we can achieve peace" (Bush 2002i).

In a slight contrast, in a speech in Grand Rapids, Michigan, in January, Bush chose to downplay the security rationale for invading

115

Iraq. Instead, such an action would be motivated by the country's most fundamental values, most significantly America's shared belief that freedom is mandated from above: "This great, powerful Nation is motivated not by power for power's sake but because of our values. If everybody matters, if every life counts, then we should hope everybody has the great God's gift of freedom. We go into Iraq to disarm the country. We will also go in to make sure that those who are hungry are fed, those who need health care will have health care, those youngsters who need education will get education. But most of all, we will uphold our values. And the biggest value we hold dear is the value of freedom. As I said last night, freedom and liberty, they are not America's gifts to the world. They are God's gift to humanity. We hold that thought dear to our hearts" (Bush 2003a, 2003d).

The values Bush identified were not just ascribed to Americans. Bush would from time to time attribute the same set of beliefs to the citizens of other democracies, too—one example being the impromptu remarks he made to the Australian people at the end of a press conference with their Prime Minister, John Howard, just before the onset of hostilities:

> I've thought long and hard about this issue. My job is to protect the American people from further harm. I believe that Saddam Hussein is a threat to the American people. I also know he's a threat to our friends and allies.
>
> The second thing—my message is, and I started speaking about this today, I also have got great compassion and concern for the Iraqi people. These are people who have been tortured and brutalized, people who have been raped because they may disagree with Saddam Hussein. He's a brutal dictator. In this country and in Australia, people believe that everybody has got worth, everybody counts, that everybody is equal in the eyes of the Almighty. So the issue is not only peace, the issue is freedom and liberty.
>
> I made it clear in my State of the Union—and the people of Australia must understand this—I don't believe liberty is America's gift to the world. I believe it is God's gift to humanity. (Bush 2003c)

The speeches excerpted above are just a sampling of the different ways in which Bush strove to link God's purposes with America's own interest in freedom (see also Bush 2003e, 2003f, 2003g). The truth is most readers will probably be familiar with this strain of religious rhetoric if for no other reason than Bush made freedom the focal point of his second inaugural address (Bush 2005a). It was, as could be expected, another extremely religious national address.[1] It was also quite possibly Bush's finest speech as president.

By the fifth paragraph, Bush had offered his thesis, saying, "We are led, by events and common sense, to one conclusion: The survival of liberty in our land increasingly depends on the success of liberty in other lands. The best hope for peace in our world is the expansion of freedom in all the world." Bush proceeded to note how the practical and spiritual rationales for freedom, arguments he had been making all along, had now merged so that "America's vital interests and our deepest beliefs are now one."

"From the day of our founding, we have proclaimed that every man and woman on this Earth has rights and dignity and matchless value, because they bear the image of the Maker of heaven and Earth," Bush went on. "Across the generations, we have proclaimed the imperative of self-government, because no one is fit to be a master and no one deserves to be a slave. Advancing these ideals is the mission that created our Nation. It is the honorable achievement of our fathers. Now, it is the urgent requirement of our Nation's security and the calling of our time."

Bush declared that America's "ideal of freedom" was a basic part of the country's spiritual tradition, a tradition "sustained in our national life by the truths of Sinai, the Sermon on the Mount, the words of the Koran, and the varied faiths of our people." Given this grounding, America's foreign policy, Bush maintained, served to "clarify the choice before every ruler and every nation, the moral choice between oppression, which is always wrong, and freedom, which is eternally right."

Additionally, Bush employed some carefully constructed light/dark imagery, a rhetorical tendency of the president that we have already encountered some evidence of. In this case, Bush explained how "And as hope kindles hope, millions more will find it. By our efforts, we have lit a fire as well, a fire in the minds of men. It warms those who feel its power. It burns those who fight its progress. And one day this untamed fire of freedom will reach the darkest corners of our world." It was America that represented the light, the fire, and the dictators of the world who represented those dark corners.

Similar to the good and evil theme, the fact that America was acting in pursuit of God's plans for the world once more led Bush to express optimism and assurance about the ultimate outcome of the struggle against terrorism.

> We go forward with complete confidence in the eventual triumph of freedom, not because history runs on the wheels of inevitability—it is human choices that move events; not because we consider ourselves a chosen nation—God moves and chooses as He wills. We have confidence because freedom is the permanent hope of mankind, the hunger in dark places, the longing of the soul. When our Founders declared a new order of the ages, when soldiers died in wave upon wave for a union based on liberty, when citizens marched in peaceful outrage under the banner "Freedom Now," they were acting on an ancient hope that is meant to be fulfilled. History has an ebb and flow of justice, but history also has a visible direction, set by liberty and the Author of Liberty.

Bush was often far more direct about the confidence that resulted from the knowledge that in promoting freedom America was doing God's work. Consider his speech to the national prayer breakfast in 2003 as a fitting example:

> We can be confident in America's cause in the world. Our Nation is dedicated to the equal and undeniable worth of every person. We don't own the ideals of freedom and human dignity, and sometimes we haven't always lived up to them. But we do stand for those ideals, and we will defend them.
>
> We believe, as Franklin Roosevelt said, that men and women born to freedom in the image of God will not forever suffer the oppressor's sword. We are confident that people in every part of the world wish for freedom, not tyranny, prefer peace to terror and violence. And our confidence will not be shaken.
>
> We can also be confident in the ways of providence, even when they are far from our understanding. Events aren't moved by blind change and chance. Behind all of life and all of history, there's a dedication and purpose, set by the hand of a just and faithful God. And that hope will never be shaken. (Bush 2003b)

Bush's rhetoric about Iraq was not limited to this one religious theme. Bush spoke just as often about the sixteen UN resolutions Saddam had defied, the threat that weapons of mass destruction posed, the ties between Saddam's regime and various terrorist organizations, and the need for the UN to be a meaningful actor. Still, religious rhetoric was a large part of the case Bush made for expanding the War on Terror into other states beyond Afghanistan.

I have documented that Bush's terrorism rhetoric featured two specific religious themes, a representation of the War on Terror as a struggle between good and evil, and an identification of the United States' practical interest in the expansion of freedom with God's own designs. Within each theme, multiple subsidiary religious elements have also been explored, such as the use of light/dark imagery and the expressions of confidence in the eventual outcome of the United States' efforts owing to their agreement with God's will. As I have repeatedly said, Bush continued to employ these two basic motifs until his last day in office.

In fact, Bush dedicated his farewell address to some final ruminations about these two topics (Bush 2009). Bush, for a last time, tried to connect freedom to God, remarking, "The battles waged by our troops are part of a broader struggle between two dramatically different systems. Under one, a small band of fanatics demands total obedience to an oppressive ideology, condemns women to subservience, and marks unbelievers for murder. The other system is based on the conviction that freedom is the universal gift of Almighty God, and that liberty and justice light the path to peace. This is the belief that gave birth to our Nation. And in the long run, advancing this belief is the only practical way to protect our citizens."

And, for one last time, Bush returned to his depiction of the War on Terror as an epic struggle between good and evil. "As we address these challenges and others we cannot foresee tonight, America must maintain our moral clarity. I've often spoken to you about good and evil, and this has made some uncomfortable," Bush admitted. "But good and evil are present in this world, and between the two there can be no compromise. Murdering the innocent to advance an ideology is wrong every time, everywhere. Freeing people from oppression and despair is eternally right. This Nation must continue to speak out for justice and truth. We must always be willing to act in their defense and to advance the cause of peace." Perhaps, no better evidence of Bush's commitment to message discipline can be found than his last address, seven long, hard years after the attacks of 9/11.

As the following pages will show, however, the import of Bush's religious language has been overstated, both by his political critics and by a few scholars (i.e., Domke 2004).

It is difficult to gauge the impact of Bush's rhetoric on his approval rating. His first major religious speech on September 20, 2001, cannot fairly be considered. Bush was the recipient of a massive rally-round-the-flag boost as his approval shot from 57 percent on August 16 to 90 percent on September 21. Obviously, that increase was due to the attacks and not Bush's rhetoric.

His other two major addresses, on the first anniversary and at his second inaugural, offer a mixed picture. Bush did witness an uptick in his approval marks after the former address. Bush went from 66 percent approval to 70 percent approval between September 5 and September 13, 2002. However, this increase is not enough to meet the 6 percent benchmark of statistical significance.

This benchmark was met for Bush's second inaugural. Bush's approval was clocked at 57 percent on February 2, 2005, whereas he registered only 51 percent approval in the last poll taken before the ceremony. Still, Bush's approval rating immediately fell back to 49 percent on February 7 and was then incredibly steady—51, 52, 52, and 52 percent—in the next four readings (Ragsdale 2009, 248–50). If Bush's second inaugural helped him, it did so only weakly.

More doubt about the impact of Bush's religious rhetoric can be found by means of an examination of issue specific opinion. Figures 3.3 and 3.4 track the opinion on questions related to the War on Terror. Each figure displays the same downward trend from 2003 onward.

In Figure 3.3, respondents were surveyed as to whether they approved or disapproved of Bush's "handling" of terrorism. At the start of the series, 71 percent of participants approved of Bush's performance. By the end of the series, that number had fallen almost twenty-five points. More Americans now disapproved of Bush's policies than supported them.

Figure 3.3
Gallup approval of Bush's handling of terrorism

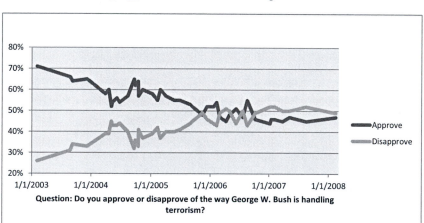

Figure 3.4
Pew center on decision to use force against Iraq

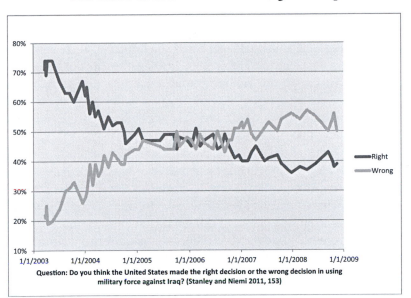

Question: Do you think the United States made the right decision or the wrong decision in using military force against Iraq? (Stanley and Niemi 2011, 153)

Indeed, healthy majorities questioned whether the war in Iraq was worthwhile, a fact made plain by Figure 3.4. In this graph, people were asked whether the United States made the "right decision or the wrong decision" in using military force in Iraq. At its peak, 74 percent of respondents felt that the right decision had been made. Yet by 2005 the pluralities had switched. By December 2007, just 36 percent of people felt the war in Iraq had been worth it, a precipitous fall of close to forty percentage points.

In reality, this selection of data underestimates Bush's loss of national support. In the run-up to the invasion of Iraq, roughly between September 2002 and March 2003, despite very concentrated religious rhetoric by Bush, opinion on a possible war did not budge. Indeed, a Pew poll found that, between mid-August and the end of October, support for military action *decreased* by nine points (Edwards 2007, 98–113).

Going forward, support for the war also atrophied more quickly than support for the Korean and Vietnam wars had. By August 2006, 55 percent of the country felt that the war had made America less safe from terrorism than it had been before, and 52 percent felt that it had distracted the United States from more pressing tasks in the fight against terror. When it comes to Iraq, it is George Edwards's judgment that "In essence, the president did not influence opinion at all" (111).

Bush's arguments did not change. What did change was the course of the War on Terror. The war in Afghanistan was initially seen as a stunning success. A multinational force encountered little resistance and suffered few casualties. Fewer than 4,000 American soldiers would see combat. Although the Taliban remained a nuisance in more than a few regions of the country, Afghanistan was, for a time, relatively peaceful and took some quick steps toward democracy, holding a constitutional convention as soon as 2002.

Then, the fighting in Iraq went equally smoothly at first, but complications developed shortly after the defeat of Hussein's armies. Poor planning by the Administration led to a confused start to the post-war occupation, where General Jay Garner was in short order replaced by diplomat Paul Bremer as head of the Coalition Provisional Authority. Following Bremer's ill-advised decision to disband the Iraqi military and Baathist political party, guerilla organizations sprouted for the purpose of launching attacks on US forces. Other militants flooded into the area for the opportunity to take shots at the American army. And the long-simmering conflict between the country's Sunni and Shia Muslims exploded into sectarian violence.

This proved to be a toxic brew for America's troops and prevented any drawdown in the country's forces. There were only 139 American fatalities during the invasion, but the country suffered the loss of over 800 soldiers in 2004, 2005, and 2006. The number of wounded annually averaged four to six times the number of deaths. Costs spiraled out of control. Prior to the war, Administration officials had testified that the war would cost less than $95 billion. In 2006, the cost had already reached four times that, surpassing the $400 billion mark. With signs of failure abounding, Bush doubled down and ordered an unpopular "surge" in troops in early 2007. Bush's decision was vindicated when the surge helped pacify the country. By 2008, American military causalities had returned to the levels not seen since the invasion (Schier 2009, 125–57).

The opinion in these graphs is, therefore, similar to how the public responded to Reagan's appeals for defense spending (see Chapter 2); citizens rationally evaluated both presidents' appeals in the context of their understanding of international affairs. For Bush, religious rhetoric could not overpower increasing casualties and political unrest in the Mideast after 2003.

The media coverage of Bush's religiously infused speeches mirrored the trend of public opinion; as conditions abroad worsened, Bush's speechifying was increasingly likely to be poorly received.

Bush's first major religious speech, his address to the nation on September 20, 2001, was for the most part highly praised. As Table 3.2 indicates, the op-ed pieces printed in response were, on average, positive, with a mean score of 3.37.

Table 3.2
Editorial coverage of Bush's national address on September 20, 2001

Date	Paper	Author	Title	Score
9/21/2001	*Chicago Tribune*	Staff Editorial	"A Call to Arms"	5
9/21/2001	*Los Angeles Times*	Staff Editorial	"Strong Words"	3
9/21/2001	*New York Times*	Staff Editorial	"Mr. Bush's Most Important Speech"	5
9/21/2001	*Washington Post*	Staff Editorial	"A Call to War"	4
9/21/2001	*Washington Post*	Jim Hoagland	"A Storm Out of the Gulf"	3
9/21/2001	*Washington Post*	David Broder	"Now Will We Pay Attention?"	2
9/21/2001	*Washington Post*	E. J. Dionne, Jr.	"No Time for Partisan Pleaders"	2
9/22/2001	*New York Times*	Anthony Lewis	"To Thine Own Self Be True"	3
9/22/2001	*New York Times*	Staff Editorial	"Calibrating the Use of Force"	4
9/22/2001	*Washington Post*	Staff Editorial	"The Money Trail"	3
9/22/2001	*Washington Post*	Richard Cohen	"Taking Command"	5
9/23/2001	*Chicago Tribune*	Staff Editorial	"Why Americans Go to War"	5
9/23/2001	*Chicago Tribune*	Clarence Page	"How to Catch an Elusive Terrorist"	2

(*continued on next page*)

Table 3.2 (*continued*)

Date	Paper	Author	Title	Score
9/23/2001	*Los Angeles Times*	John Balzar	"Sweet Land of Liberties"	4
9/23/2001	*Los Angeles Times*	Arthur Schlesinger	"Sand Trap"	2
9/23/2001	*Los Angeles Times*	Staff Editorial	"Follow the Money"	3
9/23/2001	*New York Times*	Maureen Dowd	"Autumn of Fears"	4
9/23/2001	*Washington Post*	Staff Editorial	"Rules of Engagement"	3
9/23/2001	*Washington Post*	Robert Kaplan	"U.S. Foreign Policy, Brought Back Home"	3
9/23/2001	*Washington Post*	Joel Achenbach	"No Preparation For Where We're Going"	4
9/23/2001	*Washington Post*	David Broder	"Echoes of Lincoln"	5
9/23/2001	*Washington Post*	Jim Hoagland	"Putting Doubts to Rest"	5
9/23/2001	*Washington Post*	George Will	"Battle Hymn"	3
9/24/2001	*Chicago Tribune*	Salim Muwakkil	"Military Might Not the Way to Win . . ."	1
9/24/2001	*New York Times*	Robert Wright	"America's Sovereignty in a New World"	1
9/24/2001	*New York Times*	Bob Herbert	"Leading America Beyond Fear"	5
9/24/2001	*Washington Post*	Otto Graf Lambsdorff	"We Are All Americans"	3
9/24/2001	*Washington Post*	Staff Editorial	"What to Fight For"	3
9/24/2001	*Washington Post*	Staff Editorial	"The Globalization of Justice"	3

(*continued on next page*)

Table 3.2 (*continued*)

Date	Paper	Author	Title	Score
9/24/2001	*Washington Post*	Fred Hiatt	"America's Attention-Deficit Disorder . . ."	3
9/25/2001	*Chicago Tribune*	Eric Zorn	"Peace Too Vital to be an Issue of Left or Right"	5
9/26/2001	*Chicago Tribune*	Kathleen Parker	"All is Fair in This War Except for Insensitivity"	5
9/26/2001	*Washington Post*	Staff Editorial	"Two Weeks Later"	3
9/26/2001	*Washington Post*	Michael Kelly	". . . Pacifist Claptrap"	5
9/27/2001	*Los Angeles Times*	James Pinkerton	"Nail Down Justice, But Don't Abandon . . ."	2
9/27/2001	*New York Times*	Staff Editorial	"Nation-Building in Afghanistan"	3
9/27/2001	*New York Times*	Jeff Madrick	"In Responding to Terrorism . . ."	1
9/27/2001	*Washington Post*	George Will	"Taking Down Enemy Territory"	3
Dates: **9/21 to 9/27**			**Average score**	**3.37**
			Positive articles	**15 (39.5%)**
			Negative articles	**8 (21.1%)**
			Mixed/neutral articles	**15 (39.5%)**

Even Bush's toughest opponents had hardly a negative word for the president. Bob Herbert (2001) remarked that Bush had "delivered a near-perfect speech," that he "got things exactly right," and that, all in all, it was a "splendid moment." Richard Cohen (2001) acknowledged that he thought Bush was unprepared until that Thursday night. Cohen wrote that Bush's "words were perfect, occasionally eloquent" and that he was "steadfast," "determined," and "the master of the moment."

The idea that the events of the past nine days had transformed Bush was a common one (i.e., Hoagland 2001).

In an unusual occurrence, no commentator took issue with Bush's religious tones, perhaps because this speech blended seamlessly with the communitarian rhetoric Bush had also been using at the time. One columnist, Kathleen Parker (2001), mocked those who expressed concern about Bush's references to God, his use of the word "crusade," and the naming of "Operation Infinite Justice." With disgust evident in her words, Parker wrote, "War demands much of a nation's citizenry, but only in America does war demand sensitivity training."

As a final note, it should be said that Bush remains in the background in a lot of these pieces. Many of the writers were trying to sort through how they felt about what had happened. Hence, a great many op-eds were structured around advice for the president, as opposed to positive or negative commentary on things he had done. Writers provided their perspective on everything from how the United States should counter the financial resources of the terrorists (*Washington Post* 2001) to what America's goals should be after they defeated the Taliban (Hiatt 2001). The overwhelming absence of Bush's actions in these editorials accounts for the unusually high percentage (39.5 percent) of neutral pieces.

For these reasons, the reaction to Bush's national address on the first anniversary of September 11 may be more revealing. Table 3.3 displays the results of these coding efforts. Editorial coverage of Bush's terrorism policies in the week after this address was surprisingly negative, given the context. The anniversary of 9/11 was a time of renewed national unity as well as a strong reminder of Bush's fine leadership in the days immediately after the attacks. But this appears to have mattered little; the average op-ed was scored a 2.62 and almost 54 percent of all pieces were negative in tone.

In a column appearing in the *Los Angeles Times*, James Pinkerton (2002) pointed out that Bush's "moral clarity" no longer "lined up" with the world's priorities. "The world has to some extent moved on," Pinkerton wrote, and the author worried that Bush was losing sight of the bigger picture. "In his speech at Ellis Island on Wednesday night," Pinkerton explained, "the president mentioned neither Bin Laden nor Al Qaeda. What was voiced instead were the unmistakable signs of 'mission creep'—toward war with Iraq, away from the consensus of Americans, even further away from international alliance."

Milton Viorst (2002), on the other hand, had a negative reaction to Bush's good and evil rhetoric. Viorst noted that there has always been

Table 3.3
Editorial coverage of Bush's address to the nation from Ellis Island, September 11, 2002

Date	Paper	Author	Title	Score
9/12/2002	*Los Angeles Times*	James Pinkerton	"We Cried and Remembered, Together"	2
9/12/2002	*New York Times*	Milton Viorst	"The Wisdom of Imagining the Worst-Case . . ."	1
9/12/2002	*Washington Post*	Mary McGrory	"Silence about Secrecy"	1
9/12/2002	*Washington Post*	Jim Hoagland	"Back and Forth with Bush"	4
9/12/2002	*Washington Post*	Michael Kelly	"In War, Limitations Have Their Place"	4
9/13/2002	*Chicago Tribune*	David Greising	"Bush's Bipolar Diplomatic Act May Backfire"	2
9/13/2002	*Chicago Tribune*	Staff Editorial	"Bush Challenges the U.N."	5
9/13/2002	*Los Angeles Times*	Wright and McManus	"Bush Veers From Unilateral Course . . ."	4
9/13/2002	*Los Angeles Times*	Staff Editorial	"No Case for Going in Alone"	3
9/13/2002	*New York Times*	Patrick Tyler	"A New Face in the Sights"	3
9/13/2002	*New York Times*	Staff Editorial	"The Iraq Test"	5
9/13/2002	*New York Times*	Madeleine Albright	"Where Iraq Fits in the War on Terror"	2
9/13/2002	*New York Times*	Nicholas Kristof	"The Guns of September"	1
9/13/2002	*Washington Post*	Staff Editorial	"Calling the U.N. Bluff"	3

(*continued on next page*)

Table 3.3 (*continued*)

Date	Paper	Author	Title	Score
9/13/2002	*Washington Post*	Robert Kagan	"Multilateralism, American Style"	2
9/13/2002	*Washington Post*	Charles Krauthammer	"Fictional Rift"	5
9/13/2002	*Washington Post*	E. J. Dionne, Jr.	"Getting Down to Coalition-Building"	1
9/14/2002	*New York Times*	Staff Editorial	"A Measured Pace on Iraq"	3
9/14/2002	*New York Times*	Frank Rich	"Never Forget What?"	1
9/14/2002	*Washington Post*	William Raspberry	"Bush's Worst-Case Scenario"	1
9/15/2002	*Chicago Tribune*	Wesley Clark	"USA-Iraq II: Necessity and Efficacy"	2
9/15/2002	*Los Angeles Times*	Robin Wright	"Dominoes on Iraq May Not Fall . . ."	1
9/15/2002	*Los Angeles Times*	William Arkin	"Why a War with Iraq Is Inevitable"	2
9/15/2002	*Los Angeles Times*	John Balzar	"Same Man, Same Ground"	1
9/15/2002	*New York Times*	Maureen Dowd	"W's Conflicts of Interest"	1
9/15/2002	*Washington Post*	James Baker	"The U.N. Route"	5
9/15/2002	*Washington Post*	Mary McGrory	"Time to Talk"	1
9/15/2002	*Washington Post*	George Will	"It's Not Too Late"	5
9/15/2002	*Washington Post*	Jim Hoagland	"Making the Case"	5
9/16/2002	*Chicago Tribune*	Dennis Byrne	"Why We Shouldn't Tiptoe Around Hussein"	5

(*continued on next page*)

Table 3.3 (*continued*)

Date	Paper	Author	Title	Score
9/16/2002	*Los Angeles Times*	Ronald Brownstein	"Bush May Have Won the Battle . . ."	2
9/16/2002	*New York Times*	William Safire	"Relying on Saddam"	3
9/16/2002	*Washington Post*	Sebastian Mallaby	"War, Then It Gets Hard"	1
9/17/2002	*Chicago Tribune*	Staff Editorial	"Bush's Prod to Multilateralism"	4
9/17/2002	*Washington Post*	Hank Perritt	"My Party Must Say No to War"	1
9/18/2002	*Chicago Tribune*	Clarence Page	"Haven't We Been Duped Once Before?"	3
9/18/2002	*New York Times*	Todd Purdum	"U.S. Hurries; World Waits"	2
9/18/2002	*New York Times*	Maureen Dowd	"Lemon Fizzes on the Banks of the Euphrates"	1
9/18/2002	*Washington Post*	Staff Editorial	"The Inspection Trap"	4
Dates: **9/12 to 9/18**			**Average score**	**2.62**
			Positive articles	**12 (30.8%)**
			Negative articles	**21 (53.8%)**
			Mixed/neutral articles	**6 (15.4%)**

evil in the world, but that does not mean the United States always has to do something about it. Viorst argued, "The cold war is a useful precedent. Saddam Hussein's power, and perhaps his evil too, pale next to that of Stalin. Yet even when we had clear military superiority we chose not to attack him."

Like most at the time, Viorst agreed with Bush that something needed to be done about Hussein. This was the consensus opinion of the four newspapers (i.e., see *New York Times* 2002). Rather, opposition at this point to Bush's Iraq policy centered on priorities. Why now? Why Iraq? Frank Rich (2002) concurred that Iraq was a "grave and gathering danger" but still asked "is it as grave a danger as the enemy that attacked America on 9/11 and those states that are its most integral collaborators?" In a point similar to the one Viorst offered, Rich continued "it's hard to find any doubter of the war who wants to appease Saddam or denies that he is an evil player. The question many critics are asking is why he has jumped to the head of the most-wanted list when the war on Al Qaeda remains unfinished and our resources are finite. "

These critics tried to find some explanation for why Bush was in such a hurry to go to war. E. J. Dionne (2002) speculated that electoral considerations were playing a role. Several other writers alluded to some psychological compulsion that may have been at work for Bush, an oedipal conflict of sorts with his father, the former president (Dowd 2002; McGrory 2002). Regardless of whether any of this commentary had merit or not, the important point is that Bush's religious rhetoric on September 11, 2002, did not guarantee positive editorial coverage of the War on Terror, despite the emotional circumstances of the week, and despite Bush's popularity at the time.

Bush's third and final major religious speech was his second inaugural. Again, the address seemed to come at an auspicious time for the president—the beginning of his second term, a fresh start for his Administration. However, the editorialists in all four papers were even more negative about the president's message than they were in the past. Table 3.4 reveals that 63 percent of the twenty-seven editorials published in the week after the ceremony were negative in tone and that the average score of any given article was 2.15, a mean that is low relative to the standards of other major presidential religious speeches.

We have seen in other speeches thus far that writers are quite often able to separate quality rhetoric, which they tend to like, from its attendant policy ideas, which they sometimes do not. That is exactly what happened in the case of Bush's second inaugural. Many commentators praised Bush's vocal expression of lofty ideals while criticizing his practice of those ideals.

E. J. Dionne (2005) was a critic of this address, too. Dionne wrote, "Every American will cheer the president's repeated references to the U.S. obligation to hold high the torch of freedom" and he granted that he "loved what the president said about our obligations to dissidents around the world." But, while appreciating Bush's language, Dionne nonetheless asked "whether the president has been candid about the

Table 3.4
Editorial coverage of Bush's second inaugural

Date	Paper	Author	Title	Score
1/21/2005	*Chicago Tribune*	Staff Editorial	"What Americans Believe"	4
1/21/2005	*Los Angeles Times*	Steve Lopez	"Mothers Mourn as the Elite Party On"	1
1/21/2005	*Los Angeles Times*	Staff Editorial	"No Country Left Behind"	1
1/21/2005	*New York Times*	Todd Purdum	"Focus on Ideals, Not the Details"	2
1/21/2005	*New York Times*	Staff Editorial	"The Inaugural Speech"	3
1/21/2005	*New York Times*	Bob Herbert	"Dancing the War Away"	1
1/21/2005	*New York Times*	William Safire	"Bush's 'Freedom Speech'"	5
1/21/2005	*Washington Post*	Staff Editorial	"The Rhetoric of Freedom"	2
1/21/2005	*Washington Post*	David Broder	"Big Goals, Unshakable Faith"	3
1/21/2005	*Washington Post*	E. J. Dionne, Jr.	"Visions in Need of a Little Realism"	2
1/22/2005	*New York Times*	Orlando Patterson	"The Speech Misheard Round the World"	1
1/22/2005	*New York Times*	David Brooks	"Ideals and Reality"	5
1/23/2005	*Chicago Tribune*	Charles Madigan	"Dancing in the Dark"	1
1/23/2005	*New York Times*	David Sanger	"A Speech About Nothing, Something, Everything"	2
1/23/2005	*New York Times*	Thomas Friedman	"Divided We Stand"	4
1/23/2005	*New York Times*	Maureen Dowd	"A Bunch of Krabby Patties"	1

(*continued on next page*)

Table 3.4 (*continued*)

Date	Paper	Author	Title	Score
1/23/2005	*Washington Post*	Jim Hoagland	"Leading vs. Managing"	3
1/23/2005	*Washington Post*	Courtland Milloy	"A Hunger for More than Rhetoric"	1
1/24/2005	*Los Angeles Times*	Ronald Brownstein	"For Democracy to Take Root, It Must Be the Work of Many Hands"	3
1/24/2005	*Washington Post*	Richard Haass	"Freedom Is Not a Doctrine"	1
1/25/2005	*Chicago Tribune*	Staff Editorial	"Promoting Democracy"	4
1/25/2005	*Los Angeles Times*	Robert Scheer	"1600 Pennsylvania Meets Madison Ave."	1
1/25/2005	*Washington Post*	E. J. Dionne, Jr.	". . . Oh, Never Mind"	1
1/25/2005	*Washington Post*	Richard Cohen	"Onward and Upward and . . ."	1
1/25/2005	*Washington Post*	Hanna Rosin	"Taking Liberty to Revise Famous Speeches"	1
1/26/2005	*Washington Post*	David Ignatius	"Reality Check for the Neo-Wilsonians"	3
1/27/2005	*Washington Post*	Art Buchwald	"On Second Thought"	1
Dates: 1/21 to 1/27			**Average score**	**2.15**
			Positive articles	**5 (18.5%)**
			Negative articles	**17 (63.0%)**
			Mixed/neutral articles	**5 (18.5%)**

costs of his all-embracing vision, about how to pay for it and raise the troops to fight for it." Dionne proceeded to fault Bush for the country's troubles in Iraq and for continuing to use 9/11 as justification for his "radical" decisions. "Stirring words, alas, cannot mask a flawed policy," Dionne concluded.

Similarly, the *Los Angeles Times* (2005) observed that "President Bush stood at the apogee of his life Thursday, and he rose to the occasion." The paper praised Bush for "eloquently weaving the big themes of his presidency and his life into a coherent philosophy and a bold vision of how he wants this country to spend the next four years." Yet they, too, worried about what these words might lead to: "It would be good if this country's foreign policy more closely tracked our professed ideals. It would be disastrous if self-righteous hubris led us into bloody and hopeless crusades, caused us to do terrible things that mock the values we are supposed to be fighting for, alienated us from an unappreciative world and possibly brought home more of the terrorism our neo-idealism is intended to suppress."

Other detractors chose to instead highlight the incongruence between Bush's grandiose address and the problems plaguing the country at the time. Steve Lopez (2005) contrasted the scene at the inaugural with the pain being suffered by two mothers who had lost their sons in Iraq. Charles Madigan (2005) drew attention to what individuals struggling to pay their healthcare bills or find work were doing on inauguration day. Courtland Milloy (2005) recounted a conversation he had recently had with some inner-city youth about the address. Milloy wrote that "Unlike Bush, those in my group want to see more of that (freedom) spread here at home before the United States goes off trying to change the rest of the world."

A final set of individuals questioned the sincerity of Bush's remarks. For instance, Robert Scheer (2005) argued that people who were worried about the policy implications of Bush's sweeping rhetoric were wasting their time. The inaugural, Scheer held, was little but a "political marketing device." "It takes a true demagogue to remorselessly cheapen the lovely word 'freedom' by deploying it 27 times in a 21-minute speech, while never admitting that its real-life creation is more complicated than cranking out a batch of Pepsi-Cola and selling it to the natives with a catchy 'Feeling Free!' jingle," Scheer wrote (see also Rosin 2005).

In sum, the editorial coverage of Bush's major usages of religious rhetoric on terror is marked by a clear downward trajectory, a fact visible simply in the change in the average score of the three addresses—from 3.37 to 2.62 to 2.15. Again, this pattern makes perfect sense given the increasing difficulties the country's military faced.

Where Bush had undeniable success in the War on Terror, however, was on the floor of Congress. Bush won legislative victories on basically every important issue.

In the weeks after the attacks, Congress passed the PATRIOT Act, a Bush priority, with almost no debate; the legislation was adopted by a 96-1 vote in the Senate. This act increased the government's domestic surveillance powers in a number of ways, one of the most notable being the National Security Letter (NSL) provisions that permitted the FBI to search telephone, email, and financial records of terrorist suspects without first obtaining a court order. Another provision allowed "sneak and peak searches," those searches where the subject is not immediately notified. The law also allowed the government to indefinitely detain any alien that the attorney general determined was a risk to launch a terrorist attack. Although the act became controversial and sparked a number of court challenges, Bush also persuaded Congress to reauthorize it in 2006.

Bush won the fight over the Department of Homeland Security. Congress was in favor of creating a new cabinet department for homeland security, but it was the president who was at first reluctant. Bush changed course in the summer of 2002 and proposed his own version of a Department of Homeland Security with one key difference from Congress' earlier proposals—Bush strove to keep the employees of the new agency out of the civil service. This aspect of the plan sparked a fierce debate with Senate Democrats and their union supporters. Still, Bush got what he wanted after the Democrats suffered losses in 2002 in races where the fate of Bush's plan had been made an issue.

In terms of Congressional involvement in the Iraq war, Bush easily carried the vote on a Congressional resolution authorizing the use of force against Iraq in October 2002 by margins of 77-23 in the Senate and 296-133 in the House.

A new House Democratic majority that took office following the 2006 midterms presented Bush with the stiffest challenge to his terror policies. The House Democrats made moves to potentially cut off funding for the war or, failing that, to at least include a timetable for withdrawal along with any additional authorizations. Yet, after a series of showdowns, including Bush's veto of spending bill with a deadline in May, Bush ultimately won funding for the surge, free of a withdrawal timetable, in December 2007.

It is more than fair to ask how much of Bush's legislative success was due to his rhetoric, though. Arguably, this success could have been anticipated regardless of what argument Bush chose to make for his terror policies. In domestic affairs, the president is often frustrated and forced to play a role subservient to Congress. It takes either great crises like the Depression or extraordinary Congressional majorities to get anything significant done. Even Franklin Roosevelt did not pass a significant piece of legislation after 1938.

In contrast, the president is much better positioned to dictate outcomes on foreign affairs. Both Congress and the public expect the president to lead in this arena and he has more formal powers at his disposal. On a major foreign policy issue where a president is serious and determined, the commander in chief is extremely unlikely to fail (Wildavsky 1966; see also Fleisher and Bond 1988; Edwards 1989; Canes-Wrone, Howell, and Lewis 2008).

If ever there were a good example of this phenomenon, it would be President Bush. Bush experienced some domestic successes, chiefly No Child Left Behind and his two tax cuts. But on many domestic issues, namely his highly publicized efforts at Social Security privatization and immigration reform, Bush was ignored by a recalcitrant Congress.

In contrast, the evidence is clear that he dominated policy in foreign affairs. This would be expected for any president who happened to be sitting in the Oval Office when the country was attacked, regardless of what rhetorical frames that man favored.

Conclusion

Like father, like son. Both Presidents George H. W. Bush and George W. Bush engaged in Middle Eastern wars. Both used religious rhetoric in support of their goals. Both failed to capture any benefit by doing so.

Born of crisis, with public support falling, Congressional opposition rising, and important military moves on the horizon, George H. W. Bush embraced a religious rhetorical strategy. This was atypical for a president who cared little for public relations and was kept at arm's length by many of the country's religious leaders.

Nevertheless, Bush consistently advanced three religious arguments about the Gulf War: that it was a conflict of good and evil, that it was just, and that God was on America's side. He called for two national days of prayer and shrewdly involved Billy Graham in his crusade.

All this appears inconsequential. Bush received no opinion benefits in the crucial November to January period that preceded his rally-round-the-flag boost, his religious rhetoric was rejected by the media, and his resolution in Congress was historically divisive.

It is hard to deny the powerful expressiveness of much of George W. Bush's religious rhetoric. It may well have proved soothing to the American public to hear a president talk so certainly of good and evil and of God and his plan for America. Many people were adrift after 9/11. They struggled to get a grasp on the dangerous new world they saw outside their windows. Bush's language probably helped some of us find our moorings. He promised there was order to a disordered world.

Yet, it is possible to admire George W. Bush's oratory and its potential civic value while questioning its political value. There is little evidence to suggest that Bush's religious rhetoric was any more useful to him than his father's was. Public opinion quickly and decisively turned against Bush's handling of the War on Terror. Far from the "echoing" press that some allege (Domke 2004; Gershkoff and Kushner 2005), the media also grew increasingly hostile toward the president. Finally, Bush did experience great success in Congress, but one would be hard-pressed to attribute that to language rather than the president's unique position in the American system as commander in chief.

Perhaps, the most persuasive point that casts doubt on the impact of Bush's religious rhetoric is this thought experiment. Imagine that Bush never once mentioned good and evil nor God. Would anything have been any different?

Another question is equally compelling. If religious rhetoric cannot help war-time presidents like both Bushes, when can it help *any* president?

Note

1. Interestingly, Bush's second inaugural was originally even more religious than it turned out to be. A quote from Leviticus was excised from the final draft (Safire 2005).

4

Protecting Our Blessings: Jimmy Carter and the Religious Rhetoric of Environmental Policy

For many, the story of creation is not only about Adam and Eve, it is also about nature. Numerous passages in the Bible praise the outcome of God's process (see, i.e., Genesis 1; Job 37–39; Psalm 104). These verses can lead to support for conservation. The thinking goes that, since the land, air, and water are all precious gifts from God, they must be protected.

In the second half of his term, President Jimmy Carter tried to play upon these feelings as he strove to build support for his energy and environment proposals. Carter would deliver jeremiads about consumerism, he would make repeated reference to the doctrine of stewardship, and he would attempt to co-opt the message of Pope John Paul II for his own benefit.

Carter's rhetorical strategy was well timed. American Protestantism became increasingly concerned with environmental protection between 1970 and 1990. Pioneers like Lutheran theologian Joseph Sittler and the National Council of Churches contributed to the spread of environmental concerns across religious communities. Even the conservative Southern Baptist Convention had taken a stand on the energy crisis by 1977 (Fowler 1995).

However, well-timed or not, this chapter will prove that Carter's rhetoric, most notably his famous "malaise" speech, failed to connect with the public, the media, or with Congress.

Jimmy Carter

Religion was a tricky issue for President Carter. Carter had to deal with what his chief political advisor Hamilton Jordan once memorably called the "weirdo factor" (Morris 1996, 5). Carter was a Southern Baptist, born again, and an evangelical. These were new things to the presidential politics of the 1970s.

Evangelical Protestantism had been a significant influence in American politics up until the 1920s, with evangelicals playing a key role in a number of important social movements like abolitionism. But the battle over evolution was a turning point. Many Christians passionately defended the Biblical account of creation found in Genesis. Further troubled by the social implications of Darwin's theories, the evangelical community reacted to the spread of these ideas by introducing anti-evolution bills in twenty different state legislatures in the 1920s.

However, events like the Scopes "monkey" trial, a sham proceeding intended to test the constitutionality of Tennessee's anti-evolution statute, led many religious Americans to rebel against the politicization of their faith. When combined with the failure of Prohibition, most decided they were better off sitting on the sidelines. In the middle of the century, evangelicals withdrew from politics in what historians have termed the "great reversal." They would only begin to remerge in the 1970s when certain local movements—a fight against textbooks in Kanawha County, West Virginia, a battle against a gay rights ordinance in Dade County, FL—had demonstrated their unrealized political potential (Wilcox and Larson 2006, 35–41; Wald and Calhoun-Brown 2011, 202–4).

Carter emerged in conjunction with the beginnings of this wider evangelical movement. Although he had publicly professed his faith by the age of eleven and had been ordained as a deacon in 1958, Carter had not been devout during his early life. Carter called his time in the Navy a "dormant phase" in his religious life (Carter 2002, 23). Partly, he had struggled to reconcile religious teachings with the technical training he had received as an engineer (Morris 2009, 324). But a third place finish in a 1966 Georgia gubernatorial primary would plunge Carter into a deep depression and prompt him to reassess his values.

Carter struggled to understand how God could let Lester Maddox, a segregationist best known for brandishing an ax handle in front of his restaurant, defeat him (Carter 2002, 202). Carter turned to his faith for solace but found little at first. He was particularly unsettled by a sermon he had heard that asked "If you were arrested for being a Christian, would there be enough evidence to convict you?" Carter's answer troubled him.

"Defending myself against the charge of being a Christian wouldn't be hard," Carter remembered. "I could imagine explaining with great conviction that, except during the Thanksgiving and Christmas seasons, I had rarely associated with the really poor citizens of our community ... As far as my church membership was concerned, there were obvious social and financial advantages . . . All in all, there was little evidence that I was anything other than a lukewarm follower of Christ" (208–9).

As a result of these revelations Carter was "born again." He took a new interest in the Bible, embarked on mission trips to Massachusetts and Pennsylvania, attended multiple religious conferences, and even organized the showing of a Billy Graham film in Americus, Georgia (Smith 2006, 294–95; Morris 2009, 325). Accounts indicate that Carter was personally involved in over fifty evangelical conversions (Holmes 2012, 153).

As a candidate, Carter had been reluctant to discuss his religious beliefs. That changed following an interview his sister gave to the *Washington Post* in March of 1976. Ruth Carter Stapleton was a curious figure. She ran an "inner healing" ministry that rather impractically tried to combine the insights of both psychology (based on her thirty hours of graduate study) and spirituality in attempt to heal an individual's emotional wounds.

In addition to discussing her own practice, Stapleton recounted to the *Post* in some detail the events of her brother's born-again experience (MacPherson 1976). Stapleton recalled walking through the woods with Carter after his defeat in 1966. Carter asked his sister what made her faith different from his own. Stapleton told the interviewer:

> I said, "Jimmy, through my hurt and pain I finally got so bad off I had to forget everything I was. What it amounts to in religious terms is total commitment. I belong to Jesus, everything I am." He said, "Ruth, that's what I want." So we went through everything he would be willing to give up. Money was no problem, nor friends, nor family. Then, I asked, "What about all political ambitions?" He said, "Ruth! You know I want to be governor. I would use it for the people!" I said, "No, Jimmy."
>
> But he really meant it and became connected with part-time religious work. So he went to Pennsylvania and New York ... Jimmy's a Baptist and to commit your life, Baptists think you have to go off and be a missionary somewhere.

The *Post* dispatched another reporter to confirm the story. Carter admitted that Ruth's account was "basically accurate." He proceeded to expand on Ruth's comments at a fundraiser later that evening. Carter spoke to his donors of a "deeply profound religious experience." He said, "I recognized for the first time that I lacked something very precious—a complete commitment to Christ, a presence of the Holy Spirit in my life in a more profound and personal way. And since then I've had an inner peace and inner conviction and assurance that transformed my life for the better" (Witcover 1976). In a subsequent speech, Ruth said that Jimmy had broken down and cried during his affirmation of faith (Carter 1984, 66).

Many Americans had little idea what any of this meant. As one network anchor felt compelled to say in a broadcast, "Incidentally, we've checked this out. Being 'born again' is not a bizarre experience of the voice of God from the mountaintop. It's a fairly common experience known to millions of Americans—especially if you're Baptist" (Balmer 2008, 80). The anchor was right, but Carter still had to be careful to manage the outside world's perceptions. Not only did he risk being seen as strange, his certain faith gave him an air of self-righteousness that his opponents often exploited at the first hint of hypocrisy (Hargrove 1988, 5).[1]

Sometimes, Carter fell short in pursuit of this goal. Perhaps, the most infamous example was his September 1976 interview with *Playboy* magazine. In trying to make the point that he did not believe himself "better" than anyone else because of his religiosity, Carter stumbled:

> I try not to commit a deliberate sin. I recognize that I'm going to do it anyhow, because I'm human and I'm tempted. And Christ set almost impossible standards for us. Christ said, "I tell you that anyone who looks on a woman with lust in his heart has already committed adultery."
>
> I've looked on a lot of women with lust. I've committed adultery in my heart many times. This is something that God recognizes that I will do—and I have done it—and God forgives me for it. But that doesn't mean that I condemn someone who not only looks on a woman with lust but who leaves his wife and shacks up with somebody out of wedlock.
>
> Christ says, Don't consider yourself better than someone else because one guy screws a whole bunch of women while the other guy is loyal to his wife. The guy who is loyal to his wife ought not to be condescending or proud because of the relative degrees of sinfulness. (Ribuffo 1989, 145–46)

Carter's comments upset everyone. The *Playboy* interview convinced many secular voters that Carter's faith was a legitimate concern. His comfortable lead over Ford disappeared in the aftermath of its publication. Yet, evangelicals were not pleased, either. As the Rev. Bailey Smith pointed out, "shacks up" and "screws" were not exactly "good Baptist" words (146).

So, more often than not, when it came to religion caution prevailed for Carter. According to Smith's (2006, 296) exhaustive research, Carter made fewer explicit references to the Bible or to his own faith than most other presidents, including Lincoln, Roosevelt, Eisenhower, and Reagan. He would regularly side-step opportunities to inject religion into the discussion of public policy issues. When a Polish journalist asked him in December 1977 how his evangelical principles helped him solve problems, he refused to give an example. When in March 1979 he was asked on what Scriptural basis he supported the Equal Rights Amendment (ERA), Carter responded that his position was in no way based on its wisdom (298). Carter continued to be visible in his religious practices—he taught Sunday school fourteen times as president—but there would be no repeat of his 1976 public self-examination (Bourne 1997, 377).

It was not just the "weirdo factor" that explained his reticence. One reason Carter avoiding talking about religion was because Baptists are some of the foremost defenders of the separation of church and state. Their commitment to this ideal is in many respects a product of the denomination's history. In colonial New England and Virginia, Baptists were disadvantaged in conflicts with the established churches. This experience made many early Baptists leading advocates for religious liberty (Brackney 2006, 39–42).

Carter's political record demonstrated his own commitment to this principle. As a state senator, Carter was practically alone in his opposition to a bill that stated all Georgians were free to worship God as they saw fit. Carter felt that the bill's presumption of God's existence violated the rights of atheists (Morris 2009, 325). As Governor of Georgia, Carter put an end to the religious services that had been held every morning in the state house. He also opposed the state's blue laws banning the sale of alcohol on Sundays (Glad 1980, 333).

As President, Carter declared his personal opposition to abortion, and did refuse to support the use of federal funds to pay for it, but he did not seek to overturn *Roe v Wade*. He consistently opposed school prayer and fought against tuition tax credits for parochial schools. He resisted regular meetings with religious groups and paid little attention to their concerns in order to avoid any appearance of favoritism (Smith 2006, 307–8). Additionally, he reneged on a promise to hire evangelicals for his White House staff. As a consequence of these decisions, Carter had strained relationships with most major religious leaders who would abandon him in droves in 1980 for the more responsive Ronald Reagan (Bourne 1997, 466–68).

Carter went as far as denying his role as a spiritual leader. At a February 18, 1978 town hall in Nashua, New Hampshire, a high school student named Bruce Prevost asked the president whether he would help America repent for the country's past immorality. Carter fumbled with his answer a bit, but he did demonstrate a precise understanding of the relationship between his faith and that of the country he led. Carter responded, "Well, my own religious faith is one that's much more personal . . . I don't consider myself to be the spiritual leader of this country. I'm the political leader. I have a right, I think, and a duty to be frank with the American people about my own belief. And I'm not a priest nor a bishop nor someone who, you know, fills a religious pulpit and is authorized nor asked to repent for the whole country" (Carter 1978b).

Carter's political complications with respect to religion and his reflexive commitment to the separation of church and state made him reluctant to embrace religious rhetoric. The energy crisis, a crisis that imperiled his presidency, would change his mind.

Carter was committed to resolving the country's energy problems. The price of foreign oil had doubled since the 1973 Yom Kippur War, from $6 to $12 a barrel, while the United States had come to depend on outside sources for around 50 percent of its supply (Kaufman 1993, 32). Fuel shortages ravaged the country during the winter of 1976 as schools and factories nationwide were shuttered owing to the inadequate availability of natural gas. Carter knew the solution rested in increasing the cost of energy so as to discourage waste, as well as in incentivizing the development of new sources. But these higher costs could not be so extreme as to invite a recession. Nor could the oil companies be seen as profiting from the American people's hardships.

Carter released his first energy plan in April of 1977. The main elements of the proposal were a variety of new taxes—on domestic oil production, on gas consumption over stated targets, on low fuel-efficiency cars and trucks, etc. Part of the tax revenue would be rebated to the public in the form of energy assistance for low-income citizens. The plan tilted more toward increasing conservation than it did toward encouraging production.

The legislation was enormously complicated. It consisted of 113 separate provisions, and had been drafted by Carter's energy advisor, James Schlesinger, in almost total secrecy. When printed the bill was five phonebooks thick (Morris 1996, 254). The Administration had to set up twenty-four separate legislative teams, each responsible for lobbying for a different aspect of the plan (Katz 1984, 100). The House and Senate were flummoxed by Carter's proposal and found themselves unable to resolve fundamental differences over the legislation in 1977, postponing action until the next session. A dispute over the question of natural gas deregulation continued to hold the program up throughout almost all of 1978.

After eighteen months, Carter's package did pass in October 1978. But the final law was hardly as the president had envisioned it. The bill now emphasized deregulation and tax credits, whereas Carter's initial proposal was centered on spurring conservation via taxation. Some of his taxes, such as the crude oil equalization tax and the standby gas tax, were abandoned entirely.

Perhaps then it is not a surprise that the legislation was unsuccessful in achieving its aims. The bill's flaws comprise some of the explanation, but the Iranian revolution was to blame as well. Domestic unrest brought Iran's oil production practically to a halt, severely impacting the world's supply. The United States imported only 5 percent of its oil from Iran so the seriousness of the situation was not immediately recognized (133). However, the Organization of the Petroleum Exporting Countries (OPEC) capitalized on the turmoil by raising the price of their oil by as much as 17 percent (Kaufman 1993, 136).

It is hard for someone who did not live through it to imagine, but by mid-May of 1979 motorists regularly waited an hour or more to reach the pumps. Some stations reported lines of up to a mile long. Many were forced to close on Sundays or to shorten their hours in order to conserve enough gas until their next delivery. The stations themselves were volatile locations, with fist fights and gun battles occasionally breaking out (Mattson 2009, 65).

It was in this context that President Carter unveiled what he termed "phase two" of his energy policy. Fifty percent of America's oil originated from domestic sources. But 70 percent of the oil from these reservoirs was subject to the Energy Policy and Conservation Act of 1975 (EPCA), which mandated price ceilings ranging from about \$5.50 to \$12.65 a barrel as compared to a world price of \$15.20 (Kaufman 1993, 137). Hence, a potentially easy solution to suppress consumption would be to remove the price controls and allow gas prices to rise naturally. This approach seemed a better option than the practical and political challenges inherent in rationing.

In an April 5, 1979 Oval Office address, Carter announced that he was phasing out all controls on oil by October 1981. Given that the oil companies stood to financially benefit from his decision, Carter also called for a windfall profits tax. The proceeds from the tax would be used to fund the development of alternative energy sources, to provide monetary assistance to families struggling with the price increases, and to build more fuel efficient mass transportation. The plan would have been a tough sell under any set of conditions, but it was especially so given the country's struggles with 14 percent annual inflation. The president's proposal promised that energy prices would rise even higher.

Carter's April 5 speech was the fourth major address he had given to the nation on energy (Carter 1977a, 1977b, 1977c, 1979a). It should not be shocking that the American public had begun to tune him out. About 80 million Americans had watched Carter's April 18, 1977 energy speech. His last address attracted an audience of only 30 million (Mattson 2009, 21).

Carter was in crisis. He had been fighting, mostly unsuccessfully, for energy reform for almost three years. He struggled to relate to Congress (Jones 1988). The nation was fed up. Their anger was visible every time a camera crew filmed a gas line. His audiences were shrinking, and his poll numbers were going down with them. That April marked the beginnings of a gradual strategic change in the president's approach toward selling his energy programs. It was a change that would culminate in Carter undertaking one of the most strenuous religious rhetorical campaigns in modern times.

On April 9, Carter's wunderkind pollster Pat Caddell came to the White House for a breakfast with the First Lady. Caddell briefed Rosalynn on his recent research, which showed an alarming increase in the number of what he called "long-term pessimists," those individuals who were losing faith in their country, their government, and themselves. Rosalynn was so moved by Caddell's presentation that she brought it up to her husband later that night. Carter was interested, and he requested that Caddell give him the information in a memo when he returned from his upcoming vacation (Mattson 2009, 23–25).

Caddell's final product was extraordinary. Weighing in at seventy-five pages, "Of Crisis and Opportunity" was mostly downbeat. Staffers joked that it really should have been named "Apocalypse Now" after the forthcoming film (46). As he tried to dissect the societal developments of the 1970s, Caddell warned Carter that a burgeoning "spiritual crisis" could lead "society to turn inward" (35). However, as the "opportunity" part of the title indicated, all was not lost. Caddell included a discussion of "covenant language" and quotes from the Rev. Jesse Jackson about "spiritual regeneration." He urged the president to deliver a jeremiad (46–47).

There should be little doubt that what Caddell was offering was political advice. Carter recalls, "His recent data had persuaded him that the American people had become completely inured to warnings about future energy shortages, convinced that both the government and the oil companies were either incompetent or dishonest—or both. In order for the people to support any energy proposals, the memorandum stated, their attention must somehow be focused on the facts, and the solutions must be cast in the form of a patriotic struggle to overcome a genuine threat to our country. Another recitation of my earlier themes would either put them to sleep or arouse in them a greater level of alienation and rejection" (Carter 1982, 114–15).

Carter did not take this advice at first. A fifth energy speech was planned for the evening of Thursday, July 5, 1979. On July 3, the president flew to Camp David and waited for a draft to arrive. The speech he received was so awful that Carter fell asleep reading it. The next morning, Carter phoned his staff in Washington, DC, and told them to cancel it. His aides were apoplectic. But when the president refused to change his mind, Carter's closest advisors grudgingly packed up and retreated to join him in Maryland. Before leaving, Carter's press secretary, Jody Powell, told reporters that the president was there "assessing major domestic policy issues" that "include but go beyond the question of energy." As Mattson (2009, 132) observes, "Not even Powell knew what that meant."

Over the next ten days, Carter remained secluded. The Administration had little communication with the press as different individuals came and went: labor leaders, college presidents, governors, businessmen, and ministers. Each gave the president their own opinion on what was wrong with America. Carter left Camp David by helicopter on two occasions in order to visit hardscrabble families in Pennsylvania and West Virginia so that he could get the perspective of the public first hand.

Over the course of that week and a half, Carter had been convinced that Caddell was right, that he *had* to deliver a jeremiad. Not all of his team agreed. Vice President Walter Mondale argued that to seem to blame the American people for the Administration's lack of a coherent energy policy was a recipe for disaster. Others wondered what in the world things like Carter's inability to find movies suitable for his daughter, or the contents of *People* magazine, had to do with energy. Both were brought up at Camp David, though.

Carter boarded a helicopter headed back toward the White House at 6 p.m. on Saturday, July 14. He had rescheduled his national address for 10 p.m. Sunday. The religious symbolism of Carter's time in the mountains was not lost on the media. In the Old Testament, Moses ascends Mt. Sinai to receive the Ten Commandments from God. Multiple outlets asked the president whether he saw himself playing a similar role (i.e., Broder 1979a; Smith 1979).[2]

Much of the key language in the address had been decided upon in a July 10 meeting with some of the nation's foremost religious leaders. All of the clerics counseled the president to face the problems of materialism and selfishness head on (Mattson 2009, 141–45).

Carter opened by telling the country that the question he was trying to answer was "Why have we not been able to get together as a nation to resolve our serious energy problem?" (Carter 1979b). The answer, the president suggested, was because "the true problems of our Nation are much deeper than gasoline lines or energy shortages, deeper even than inflation or recession."

Hands clasped before him, Carter proceeded to outline his own shortcomings, on the basis of what he heard while at Camp David. It was a confession of sins. He said he had been told he was not seen by the people enough, that he was managing instead of leading, that his cabinet was disloyal. But, as he said, "This kind of summarized a lot of other statements: 'Mr. President, we are confronted with a moral and a spiritual crisis.'"

This crisis had led to a "growing doubt about the meaning of our own lives." Now, Carter said:

> In a nation that was proud of hard work, strong families, close-knit communities, and our faith in God, too many of us now tend to worship self-indulgence and consumption. Human identity is no longer defined by what one does, but by what one owns. But we've discovered that owning things and consuming things does not satisfy our longing

for meaning. We've learned that piling up material goods cannot fill the emptiness of lives which have no confidence or purpose.

The causes of our dismay, according to the president, were the traumatic events of the past decade—the assassinations of the Kennedy brothers and Martin Luther King, Jr., Watergate, inflation, and Vietnam. The country had arrived at a fork in the road:

> There are two paths to choose. One is a path I've warned about tonight, the path that leads to fragmentation and self-interest. Down that road lies a mistaken idea of freedom, the right to grasp for ourselves some advantage over others. That path would be one of constant conflict between narrow interests ending in chaos and immobility. It is a certain route to failure.
>
> All the traditions of our past, all the lessons of our heritage, all the promises of our future point to another path, the path of common purpose and the restoration of American values. That path leads to true freedom for our Nation and ourselves. We can take the first steps down that path as we begin to solve our energy problem.
>
> Energy will be the immediate test of our ability to unite this Nation, and it can also be the standard around which we rally. On the battlefield of energy we can win for our Nation a new confidence, and we can seize control again of our common destiny.

After outlining his new policy initiatives, Carter summed up his overall message: "So, the solution of our energy crisis can also help us to conquer the crisis of the spirit in our country." In an overt Christian metaphor, in closing, the president asked that his country "commit ourselves together to a rebirth of the American spirit."

A jeremiad is what Caddell wanted and a jeremiad is what Carter delivered. Calling to mind the standard rhetorical structure of such an address (see Chapter 2), we find all the expected elements in the body of the text. Lamentations about decline abound in Carter's references to our loss of faith, to our materialism, and to the "emptiness of lives which have no confidence or purpose." The warnings of doom are present as well, both in the form of his frank talk about the consequences of energy dependence, as well in the discussion of the implications of taking that path of self-interest Carter spoke of in the passage excerpted above. At one point, Carter direly said "This is not a message of happiness or reassurance, but it is the truth and it is a warning." And, finally, he promises future glory if only we are willing to change.

147

By solving our energy crisis, we could solve our spiritual woes at the same time.

There is no other speech quite like this in the history of American politics. It is a speech where a president criticized his constituents for believing in "things" instead of God, for prioritizing themselves, instead of others. Moreover, this uncomfortable language was nevertheless still intended to draw support to Carter's revised energy plan, which now included three major elements.

The first was the windfall profits tax that the president had called for in April 1979. The second was an Energy Mobilization Board. The Board was a controversial idea. It was to have the authority to eliminate or modify the procedural restrictions that had slowed down the construction of nonnuclear energy facilities (Plotkin 1985). The irony of creating a government agency to cut through the red tape produced by other government agencies was apparently lost on Carter. The third major part of the plan was the creation of an Energy Security Corporation, which would coordinate the production of synfuels, alternatives to oil that are harvested from sources like coal, biomass, and shale. The Corporation would be independently managed by a seven-member board, and would be responsible for investing tens of billions of government funds outside of the normal appropriations process. The idea was inspired by the country's experience with synthetic rubber in World War II.

There can be little doubt that Carter made a strategic choice at this juncture. He deviated from the type of rhetoric he had become accustomed to using when speaking about energy for the previous two and a half years. He violated his earlier reluctance to make political use of his faith, a decision inconsistent with his Baptist philosophy and past political decisions. He risked raising anew the "weirdo factor." Above all, it was a decision made on the basis of polling data—data that claimed such an argument would be accepted. Yet Carter was in crisis, and that seems to be a precondition for the appearance of this style of rhetoric.

The "crisis of confidence" speech is better remembered by its derisive moniker, "malaise," a word not actually found in the text. What few know, however, is that Carter would continue to employ the same type of religious language as he advocated for his energy program throughout the remainder of 1979.

If anything, Carter's August 30, 1979 remarks at Emory University were even more spiritual than the crisis of confidence speech was (Carter 1979i). Once more, Carter highlighted the lack of meaning in an unchecked consumerism: "We can measure the grandeur of a person's house or the size of a bank account or the acreage of one's land, or how fast one's net worth increases each year. We tend to dwell too much on such things, for they tell us very little about the real meaning of life. For that, we must turn to things which cannot be seen or which cannot be measured, to things like honesty, integrity, the strength of conscience, the love of God, service to others, humility, wisdom."

In that jeremiad style, Carter also reminded his listeners that solving the energy crisis could bring greater, more intangible rewards:

> I pray that from our present material and spiritual crises, which are well recognized, that there may come a new sense of awakening and a new pursuit of more fulfilling ways to live and to work together as Americans.
>
> Let us confess our failures; let us marshal our inner resources and move on, upward. If we are guided by the best of our common mandates, renewal of American spirit will come.
>
> We in America will find a way to solve our material problems, and as we do, we can rejuvenate the spirit and the confidence of our country.

Despite his earlier protestations, Carter *had* become a spiritual leader, inviting his audience to "confess" and renew their spirit by overcoming America's energy challenges.

Well before his August speech at Emory, Carter had elected to follow up his July 15 address with a number of other speeches where he would express similar ideas and arguments. One such example was his July 19 appearance before the state presidents of the Future Farmers of America (Carter 1979c). Carter quickly picked up where he had left off just four days ago:

> A quality future of our lives is built on a strong today. We've got some weaknesses in our country that I tried to outline as best I could Sunday evening. Many things change rapidly in our world, and these changes upset people. New energy facts are hard to accept.
>
> For the first time, Americans have had to recognize the fact that there are limits, that we don't have the right anymore to squander the precious fuel reserves which our Nation possesses. We've got to husband those and to conserve those and to be good stewards over what we have been given. This is what comprises the proper attitude of an American citizen, to assess problems, to face them frankly, to let the truth be known, to search our own lives, our own hearts, our own influence, and say, "What can I do to make my life purer, better,

stronger, more admirable, and to let my life be felt meaningfully in the future of a nation which has been so good to me?"

The reference to stewardship is significant. This concept would be a common feature of much of Carter's energy rhetoric, and it is a concept with powerful Biblical referents. A steward is someone who looks over and cares for someone or something. In a parable that is also found in Luke (19:11–27), Matthew recalls the story of three servants who are entrusted with the wealth of their master while he is away. Two of the servants put the money to work and double its value; the other servant is afraid and buries his amount in the ground. For his poor management, this last servant is thrown out into the dark upon the master's return (Matthew 25:14–30). The parable's message is that being ready for Jesus's return requires taking proper care of what you have been given (see Keener 1999, 599–602).

The idea of stewardship has been traditionally connected with the environment (Fowler 1995, 76–90). Although the meaning of environmental stewardship is contested, its most straightforward interpretation is that God designated human beings as stewards over his creations. The most commonly cited Biblical passage in support of this view is Genesis 2:15: "The Lord God took the man and put him in the garden of Eden to till it and keep it."

Stewardship has been endorsed by churches ranging from the Assemblies of God to the Episcopal Church. The opinion that humans have to date been bad stewards is rarely challenged. As a consequence, talk of stewardship is often accompanied by intense feelings of guilt.

Carter uses all of these impulses to his advantage. His speech plays upon the feelings of guilt that accompany ideas of stewardship ("we don't have the right anymore to squander"). And the message is that the wonders of our environment are a gift from God (the implied source of "what we have been given"), so we are bound to look after them.

Carter's religious rhetoric accelerated the following month. In the middle of August, Carter announced that he would be taking a week-long trip down the Mississippi aboard the *Delta Queen*, a 285 foot, 188 passenger steamer (Broder 1979b). The trip was part vacation, part electioneering, but was sold to the public as, in Powell's words, "a campaign trip for the energy proposal" (*New York Times* 1979b). The president and his family personally paid the full $900 fare and joined the other passengers, all of whom had no idea when they booked their reservations that the leader of the free world would be accompanying them. The voyage, scheduled for August 17 through 24, would take the Carters from St. Paul to St. Louis, with stops in Wisconsin and Iowa in between. With a rumored primary challenge from Senator Ted Kennedy awaiting, the stop in Iowa was more than a coincidence.

The press critically referred to the trip as a "baby-kissing tour" (Coffey 1979). I would venture to suggest another description: Brother Jimmy's Traveling Salvation Show. For, at each stop, Carter made roughly the same speech with the same basic religious structure.

The first part involved reminding people how much God had blessed America. In Wabasha, Minnesota: "We are a nation which has indeed been blessed by God with blessings which exceed those of any other peoples on Earth. We're a nation of freedom. We're a nation of strength, of courage, of vitality. We're a nation which has always been able and eager to meet any challenge, no matter how difficult it might have been, to solve any problem, no matter how complex it might be, or to answer any question which confronts the people of the United States of America" (Carter 1979d).

In Prairie du Chien, Wisconsin: "God has blessed us above all other peoples with natural resources, not only a great river, one of the best avenues for traffic and also freight and also passengers in the whole world—one of the most enjoyable trips, I think, imaginable anywhere—but, of course, we've also been blessed with energy reserves. In our Nation we've got 25 percent of all the energy reserves in the whole world. All the OPEC nations in the Mideast put together only have 5 percent. So, God's blessed us with a strong nation and with a nation that has enough natural resources" (Carter 1979e).

In Muscatine, Iowa: "The last thing I want to say is don't ever forget, any of you, that we do live in a country where we've been blessed by God with almost every possible human need and every human advantage. We do have rich land. We do have freedom. We have a good free enterprise system. We've got a democracy" (Carter 1979f).

And at a town meeting in Burlington: "God's blessed us in many wonderful ways, with rich land, a democratic, free government, a pride in the individualism of each person, the right to be different, the right to speak our minds, the right to control our own Government, the right to unify ourselves in times of challenge . . ." (Carter 1979g).

The next step consisted of mildly criticizing America for taking God's beneficence for granted. In Wabasha: "and it's let us realize for the first time in our great country that we do have limits, and we cannot afford to waste any more, as we have wasted, what God gave us in the past"

151

(Carter 1979d). Or in St. Louis: "We've got so much to be thankful for. Sometimes we forget how much God has blessed us in the United States of America" (Carter 1979h).

On other occasions, Carter could be even more blunt. At a town meeting in Tampa a week after the conclusion of his trip, Carter said, "I think for us to recognize that we've got to save and not waste is really compatible with what the Bible teaches. God doesn't want us to waste what He gives. I think the fact that we have to now share with each other is a very good principle on which to base a family's style of living" (Carter 1979j).

The last step consisted of making the pitch for his program. Whether the real goal of the trip was to improve his positioning for November 1980 or not, Carter spoke extensively about energy and the environment at each stop.

Carter did not make much use of religious rhetoric that September. But he did re-introduce these themes in conjunction with a highly anticipated visit from Pope John Paul II in October. It was the charismatic new Pontiff's first visit to the United States. Carter was both impressed and moved by the outpouring of affection for the head of the Catholic Church, and he shrewdly chose to tie this reaction to the existence of the crisis he had alerted the country to in July. In Albuquerque on October 11, Carter reflected:

> I knew that they would have tens of thousands of people, maybe hundreds of thousands of people who would come out to meet him, but to see literally millions of people assembled on the streets of Chicago and Boston and Philadelphia and New York and even in the rural area of Iowa and, of course, in Washington, was a pleasant surprise and an exciting surprise for me.
>
> I think there's a hunger in our country for decency and commitment, for the binding of wounds, for unity, for mutual respect, for compassion, and for love; and this to me is heartening. And I think the reception that he got transcended any kind of minor religious differences we have, because we worship the same God. And this, I think, is a good solid base for Americans to meet any possible challenge to us. (Carter 1979k)

Having claimed that America's "hunger" for meaning and shared faith in "the same God" were "a good solid base" on which the country's problems might be solved, Carter transitioned into a discussion of the specific challenge of energy. He continued:

> We live in the greatest and the strongest nation on Earth. It's the strongest nation on Earth militarily. We need fear no one, and we will never be second to any other country in military strength. And, of course, we are the strongest nation on Earth economically, because God blessed us with such great natural resources. In the past, we've not always handled them carefully. We've not been constant good stewards of what we've inherited. But I really believe that the recent reminder that there is a limit to how much waste Americans can accept in our society is healthy for us.

Carter admitted that "it's not been possible for us in the past to marshal our great strength and to unify ourselves to meet a challenge that was not quite so easy to see—the threat to our security from the importation next year of $70 billion worth of foreign oil." But he did volunteer his hope that America was making progress. The reader should note the similarity between these remarks and those Carter made during his *Delta Queen* trip.

In remarks to an American Federation of Labor and Congress of Industrial Organizations (AFL-CIO) convention in San Diego, Carter spent about a fifth of his time discussing energy. Carter observed that the Pope's teachings illustrated how America's problems could only be solved if we abandoned our selfishness:

> The visit of Pope John Paul has given us a chance to reflect on our basic values and the challenges to them. We cannot permit this chance to slip away. Let's seize this opportunity and make the most of it.

> Perhaps the greatest gift the Pope gave us in his brief visit to our country was a chance to rethink what these four words mean, "One nation, under God." He lifted our eyes from petty concerns, sometimes selfish concerns, from the cynicism and the indifference that sometimes divides Americans one from another, to show us that we can unite for common purposes, as Americans, as children of God, or as citizens of a fragile world.

> Now let us rededicate ourselves to a simple truth that together we can shape a bright future . . . (Carter 1979l)

Carter continued to link John Paul II's message to his own energy goals before Catholic audiences (i.e., Carter 1979m). However, these were not the only occasions on which Carter explained before a religious gathering how energy related to faith. What is clear, though, is that Carter's January 10, 1980 remarks at a White House briefing held for religious leaders were nothing but a more direct statement of the same ideas he had been willingly discussing before the wider public for months.

> It might seem strange to some, not to you, that the conservation of oil has a religious connotation. But when God created the Earth and gave human beings dominion over it, it was with the understanding on the part of us, then and down through the generations, that we are indeed stewards under God's guidance, to protect not only those who are fortunate enough to grasp an advantage or a temporary material blessing or enjoyment but to husband those bases for enjoyment and for a quality of life for those less fortunate in our own generation and especially for those who will come after us.
>
> Our country is comprised of profligate wasters of the Earth's precious resources, not because of an innate selfishness, but because we've been overly endowed by God with those material blessings. We've seldom experienced limits on our lives because of a withholding of the production of food or fiber or building materials or energy itself. Access to warm oceans, wonderful climates, rich land—God has given us these things. But lately in the last few years, or particularly the last few months, we've begun to see that we not only have a responsibility to now and future Americans but also to those who live on Earth now and will live in the future. (Carter 1980a)

Carter's rhetoric on energy pivoted away from religion at the start of 1980. The main reason for this departure was that the international geopolitical climate had changed. Iranian radicals seized the US embassy in Tehran on November 4, 1979, taking sixty Americans hostage. Over Christmas, the Soviets invaded Afghanistan. The turmoil in the Mideast spread rapidly. In Saudi Arabia, religious fanatics took control of the Grand Mosque in Mecca, the holiest shrine of Islam. It took two weeks of fighting to evict the occupiers.

With so much of the oil producing world in chaos, it became easier to talk about energy in terms of national security as opposed to religious values. The change in emphasis was apparent in Carter's 1980 State of the Union address: "The crises in Iran and Afghanistan have dramatized a very important lesson: Our excessive dependence on foreign oil is a clear and present danger to our Nation's security. The need has never been more urgent. At long last, we must have a clear, comprehensive energy policy for the United States" (Carter 1980b).

Carter's energy campaign was a broad and diverse use of religious rhetoric. Carter made religious arguments over a period of six months. He delivered jeremiads. He openly discussed Biblical ideas

Figure 4.1
Carter 1979 public approval

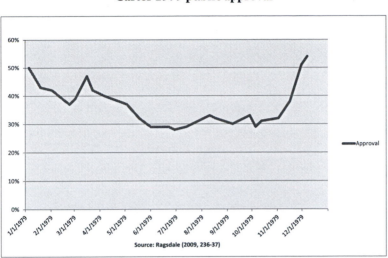

Source: Ragsdale (2009, 236-37)

like stewardship. He capitalized on Pope John Paul II's pilgrimage by linking the Pontiff's message on family and selflessness to his own policies. Yet, Carter's strategy did not produce the results he wanted.

For one, Carter's crisis of confidence speech fell flat with the public. On July 13, 1979, Carter received the support of 29 percent of Americans. On August 3, the first reading post-speech, he clocked in at 32 percent (Ragsdale 2009, 236). This change is less than the 6 percent that would lead us to be confident in its significance.

Plus, Carter's approval on August 3 was not unusual. As Figure 4.1 illustrates, Carter hovered in the range of 29 to 33 percent support for over five consecutive months. The event that finally changed the president's fortunes was the embassy seizure in Iran, which generated a strong rally-round-the-flag boost beginning in mid-November. So, in the longer term, it appears that Carter's religious rhetoric did little to dispel the negative vibes surrounding him at the time.

Even more troubling for Carter is the finding that his religious arguments, made repeatedly in the months after July 15, did not have any effect on the public's evaluation of his handling of the energy issue. Figure 4.2 tracks the ABC News/Harris polls on energy. The relatively flat lines indicate that over all of 1979 the public overwhelmingly disapproved of Carter's performance on energy. In every poll, between

Figure 4.2
ABC News/Harris on energy policy

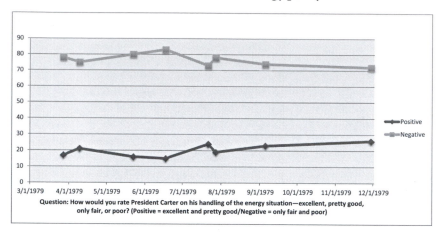

Question: How would you rate President Carter on his handling of the energy situation—excellent, pretty good, only fair, or poor? (Positive = excellent and pretty good/Negative = only fair and poor)

72 and 83 percent of respondents gave Carter a negative grade. His change in rhetoric did nothing to alter that pattern.

It should be said that Carter may have short-circuited any of the opinion benefits that he had been accruing following his July 15 address. A survey taken by Roger Seasonwein Associates, a New York based polling organization, reported that the number of respondents feeling that the president was doing a "good" job had risen from 21 percent on Saturday, July 14 to 30 percent on Monday, July 16 (*Washington Post* 1979). Likewise, the *New York Times*/CBS News Poll reported that Carter's approval had risen to 37 percent in the aftermath of the speech, as compared to a rating of 26 percent the week before (Clymer 1979).

The story is complicated by the turmoil within the White House later that week. One of the criticisms that Carter heard at Camp David was that he was being poorly served by members of his Administration. On July 17, the president requested that all members of his cabinet and senior staff submit their resignations. Carter said that he would then decide which ones to accept. He ultimately let five cabinet members go: Attorney General Griffin Bell, Secretary of the Treasury Michael Blumenthal, Secretary of Transportation Brock Adams, Energy Secretary James Schlesinger, and Health, Education, and Welfare Secretary Joseph Califano.

The changes were universally criticized. The departure of so many members at once made it seem as if the government was falling apart.

Carter made a bad situation worse by naming Hamilton Jordan chief of staff, another move widely seen as misguided. Jordan was disorganized, had little government experience, and was held in open contempt by some members of Congress, including Speaker Tip O'Neill. To the public, Jordan would mainly be known for allegations of unsavory personal behavior, including charges that he spat Amaretto and cream on a woman at a bar, that he made lewd comments about the cleavage of the wife of the Egyptian ambassador, and that he had used cocaine at New York's Studio 54.

It is reasonable to expect that these moves diminished the positive effects the malaise speech might have had on public opinion. Still, it should be said that not all of the polls supported the findings of the two positive surveys mentioned above. The NBC News/AP poll released on July 18, for instance, indicated that Carter's ratings had not moved at all (Clymer 1979). No matter what, if this increase in public support could not be sustained for more than a few days, it was not very meaningful.

An analysis of the editorial reaction to Carter's "Crisis of Confidence" speech also casts doubt on the persuasiveness of the president's religious rhetoric. As Table 4.1 shows, forty-nine editorials on energy appeared in the four newspapers in the week following the address. Fully 55 percent of these commentaries, twenty-seven articles in total, were negative toward Carter and received scores of 1 or 2. In contrast, just twelve articles (24.5 percent) were positive, receiving scores of 4 or 5. On average, any given article was scored a 2.35, indicating that Carter's editorial coverage was solidly negative.

Opinion writers seemed willing to praise Carter for his rhetoric, but they were consistently able to separate the merit of those arguments from the merit of the policies that Carter was arguing for. For instance, the *Chicago Tribune* (1979) wrote "It's hard to quarrel with his (Carter's) extended homily on our moral shortcomings; being reminded of our sins can have a therapeutic effect on the conscience . . ." But the *Tribune* then ripped Carter's policy prescriptions as "vague, trivial, of the 'appoint a commission' nature, or timed so as not to be painful until he was long out of office." The paper felt that parts of the plan were "utterly illogical" and "gimmicky," and it argued that the president had not asked enough from the country. In fact, they claimed "the greatest personal sacrifice demanded from Americans is the stretching of credulity and logic."

Nick Thimmesch (1979) was a second to voice approval of Carter's rhetoric while disapproving of his programs. For Thimmesch,

Table 4.1
Editorial coverage of Carter's "crisis of confidence" speech

Date	Paper	Author	Title	Score
7/16/1979	*New York Times*	Hedrick Smith	"Part Homily, Part Program"	3
7/16/1979	*Washington Post*	David Broder	"After 30 Months, Self-Criticism, Sense of Purpose"	4
7/16/1979	*Washington Post*	Meg Greenfield	"Report From Camp David"	2
7/16/1979	*Washington Post*	Rowland Evans and Robert Novak	"A National Revival"	1
7/17/1979	*Chicago Tribune*	Nicholas von Hoffman	"Economic Wickedness Unbearably Tempting"	3
7/17/1979	*Chicago Tribune*	Jack Mabley	"White House Fails to Set Good Example"	2
7/17/1979	*Chicago Tribune*	Staff Editorial	"Winning Neither Confidence . . . Nor More Oil"	1
7/17/1979	*Los Angeles Times*	Staff Editorial	"The Scramble Starts"	5
7/17/1979	*Los Angeles Times*	Mike Royko	"Why Hate the Arabs for Hustling a Buck?"	1
7/17/1979	*New York Times*	Steven Rattner	"For the Energy Plan, Uncertainties to Overcome"	1
7/17/1979	*New York Times*	Tom Wicker	"After the Thunder"	4
7/17/1979	*New York Times*	Staff Editorial	"Riding Casually to War"	1
7/17/1979	*Washington Post*	Joseph Kraft	"Carter: A Candidate Again"	1
7/17/1979	*Washington Post*	Martin Schram	"Carter: Back on the Track and Eager to Retake the Lead"	5

(*continued on next page*)

Table 4.1 (*continued*)

Date	Paper	Author	Title	Score
7/17/1979	*Washington Post*	Jim Hoagland	"Carter Plan Sketchy on Foreign Impact"	3
7/17/1979	*Washington Post*	Bill Gold	"The District Line"	3
7/17/1979	*Washington Post*	Staff Editorial	"The Right Commitment"	4
7/17/1979	*Washington Post*	Robert Samuelson	"Washington to Make Energy Moves"	3
7/18/1979	*Chicago Tribune*	Bob Wiedrich	"A President's Defeatist Message"	1
7/18/1979	*Los Angeles Times*	J. F. terHorst	"Camelot is Now Full of Weeds"	1
7/18/1979	*Los Angeles Times*	Staff Editorial	"Energy: The Chance to Conserve"	2
7/18/1979	*Washington Post*	Judy Mann	"No City Is an Island, Mister President"	1
7/18/1979	*Washington Post*	David Broder	"The Wife's Eye"	5
7/18/1979	*Washington Post*	Roger Ricklefs	"The Nation's 'Soul'"	1
7/18/1979	*Washington Post*	Rowland Evans and Robert Novak	"The Secretary's Stand"	1
7/19/1979	*Chicago Tribune*	Bob Wiedrich	"Great News—If Carter Meant It"	4
7/19/1979	*Washington Post*	Joseph Kraft	"A Genuine Outsider"	1
7/19/1979	*Washington Post*	George Will	"A Reluctant Broker"	1
7/19/1979	*Washington Post*	Hobart Rowen	"A Hollow Ring"	1
7/19/1979	*Washington Post*	Jack Anderson	"Fuel Plan Flies in the Face of History"	1

(*continued on next page*)

Table 4.1 (*continued*)

Date	Paper	Author	Title	Score
7/20/1979	*Chicago Tribune*	Jack Germond and Jules Witcover	"Can He Turn Back the Clock?"	3
7/20/1979	*Chicago Tribune*	Nick Thimmesch	"Mr. Carter on Energy: Sermon Better than the Program"	3
7/20/1979	*Los Angeles Times*	Staff Editorial	"It Gets Worse"	1
7/20/1979	*Washington Post*	Stephen Rosenfeld	"A Special Strain of Nationalism"	4
7/20/1979	*Washington Post*	Mary Russell	"On the Hill: One Step Forward for Carter—and One Back"	1
7/22/1979	*Chicago Tribune*	Aldo Beckman	"Carter Decides to Get Tough"	3
7/22/1979	*Chicago Tribune*	Bill Neikirk	"Moral Equivalent of Waffling"	1
7/22/1979	*Los Angeles Times*	Andrew Kopkind	"From the Left: Institutions Have Failed . . ."	1
7/22/1979	*Los Angeles Times*	Michael Novak	"From the Right: Statist Leaders Are the Problem"	1
7/22/1979	*Los Angeles Times*	Staff Editorial	"The Week That Was, Unfortunately"	1
7/22/1979	*New York Times*	Robert Howes	"Amid Our Crises, Church Silence"	5
7/22/1979	*New York Times*	Tom Wicker	"Carter's 'Different Road'"	5
7/22/1979	*New York Times*	Staff Editorial	"Running Against Himself"	2
7/22/1979	*New York Times*	Staff Editorial	". . . And His Energy Plan"	3

(*continued on next page*)

Table 4.1 (*continued*)

Date	Paper	Author	Title	Score
7/22/1979	*Washington Post*	Martin Schram	"A Stormy Week"	3
7/22/1979	*Washington Post*	Jack Anderson	"Working Things Out With Congress"	1
7/22/1979	*Washington Post*	David Broder	"Buying Time"	4
7/22/1979	*Washington Post*	George Will	"The Silverware Criterion"	1
7/22/1979	*Washington Post*	Bernard Nossiter	"The New Synfuel Offensive Can Win Carter's Energy War"	5
Dates: 7/16 to 7/22			**Average score**	**2.35**
			Positive articles	**12 (24.5%)**
			Negative articles	**27 (55.1%)**
			Mixed/neutral articles	**10 (20.4%)**

"President Carter really gave two speeches Sunday night. The first was a well-delivered sermon, one that could touch all but the most hedonistic or cynical American. The second offered a refurbished energy program, failed to resolve serious questions, and, in several ways, contradicted the first." Carter's moralizing, Thimmesch thought, "could move people to think about doing with less, to live more simply and more meaningfully, and to strengthen family and personal relationships." Yet, Thimmesch maintained that Carter's energy proposals failed to tackle the obstacles posed by environmental restrictions and the anti-nuclear lobby. This accusation of timidity was a common refrain for the president's critics (see Kraft 1979; Neikirk 1979; *New York Times* 1979a; Rowen 1979).

This is not to say that Carter's rhetoric was popular with everyone, though. Arguably, his words created as many enemies as they gained him friends. Rowland Evans and Robert Novak (1979) felt that Carter was following the path taken by Woodrow Wilson in blaming the country for his own personal failures. They accurately pointed out that, in the first two years of his presidency, Carter had said nothing about the impact of assassinations and Vietnam on the national psyche. It was "not until his own ratings tumbled," they wrote, "was there such intense concern with public morality."

Bob Wiedrich (1979) argued that the president's message was "defeatist." Wiedrich felt that Carter "should not have lectured the American people so severely about their materialistic instincts and other shortcomings. He should have looked instead to the failings of his own administration for the reasons behind the lack of confidence in government he so casually laid at all our doors." The president, Wiedrich said, is "supposed to be a leader, not a preacher."

Michael Novak (1979) went further. Playing off the Moses comparisons, Novak noted that "Moses did not go up on the mountain to consult a public relations delegation from the discontented and wandering people he was trying to lead." Novak felt that the president's performance was "disgusting" because "In the name of spiritual values, Carter tried to save himself." He had "shamefully" tried to use theology for "his own partisan purposes."

Beyond the pushback against the religiosity of the address, Carter was also hurt by the boomerang effect his cabinet dismissals created. The firings turned even initially supportive outlets against him. For instance, following the speech, the *Los Angeles Times* (1979a) printed one of the most supportive editorials that Carter would receive. However, the paper changed its tune following the shake-up. On July 20, the editorial board (1979b) wrote that the Administration's "theatrics" were "humiliating if not bizarre."

In sum, opinion writers were not favorable toward Carter in the week after the malaise speech. Those commentators who praised his rhetoric often criticized his policy prescriptions. Others attacked both. And the perception of Carter's energy program was altered for the worse after he decided to purge his administration.

Carter's religious strategy was most successful—though by no means entirely so—on the floor of Congress. In 1980, Congress took action on the major elements of Carter's second energy plan, the windfall profits tax, the Energy Mobilization Board (EMB), and the Energy Security Corporation (ESC). The legislature adopted the tax and the ESC but rejected the Board.

In the House, Carter resoundingly won the balloting on the windfall profits tax and the ESC by margins of 302-107 and 317-93. In the

Senate, the story is much the same. Carter won the windfall profits tax and ESC votes 66-31 and 78-12, respectively.

This is not to say everything was roses for Carter's energy plan in Congress. The EMB was put on the shelf on June 27, 1980, when the House voted to adopt an amendment by Rep. Samuel Devine that killed the House-Senate conference committee report. Carter lost this particular vote 232-131. This was one of Carter's worst showings that session.

It is important to mention one related vote. In early June, Congress overrode Carter's veto of a joint resolution that sought to bar the president from imposing a surcharge on imported oil. Carter included the charge as part of his March 14 anti-inflation program but it composed part of his energy policy as well. As it is, Congress was only given the authority to block the charge under the provisions of the recently passed windfall profits tax legislation. The House and Senate veto overrides were Carter's worst defeats of the year. He lost the votes with just ten Senators and merely thirty-four Representatives backing him.

Finally, Carter had to make some substantial concessions, too. In the final windfall profits bill, a variable rate replaced the flat rate Carter wanted, the revenues were marked for the general treasury fund rather than for specific energy purposes, and the tax was not made permanent but would instead expire no later than October 1993 (Carter 1982, 123).

Conclusion

Most historical accounts tend to treat the malaise speech as a one-time example of a devout president consciously examining the soul of his nation. This chapter has shown that that is an incomplete picture at best. In fact, the malaise speech was the starting point of a coherent and consistent religious rhetorical strategy that Carter used in trying to facilitate the adoption of his expensive energy/environment policies. The strategy was no more than partially successful.

Carter may have seen some immediate increase in his personal approval ratings but it was short-lived, doing nothing to arrest the long term cratering of his meager public support. His approval ratings for his handling of the energy issue never budged. Carter's editorial coverage in the week following the malaise speech was by and large critical. Even those who found themselves favorably disposed to his language attacked his policy ideas. Finally, Carter was well-supported on several key votes in the House and Senate—but then again he was less supported on others and he was served a crushing defeat when Congress failed to approve the EMB.

In some ways, the religious rhetoric that Carter used to sell his energy program was courageous. The president was right to point out the psychological problems that afflicted America after the traumas of the 1960s and the early 1970s. And the sacrifice Carter asked for seems to be needed even more today as the country continues to grapple with the same unresolved energy issues. Still, in other ways, Carter sounded ridiculous. It's hard not to agree with Roger Ricklefs (1979), who wrote at the time, "One person may spend the weekend in church while another spends it in a disco. It's hard to tell which contributes more to the energy crisis."

Notes

1. A reporter once asked Carter: "Do you have any doubts? About yourself? About God? About life?" Carter's answer: "I can't think of any" (see Katz 1984, 130).
2. For what it is worth, in a 1978 speech at a dinner in Atlanta, the president explicitly compared himself to Moses leading the Israelites in battle (Carter 1978a).

5

All God's Children: John Kennedy, Lyndon Johnson, and the Religious Rhetoric of Civil Rights

Civil rights are intended to prevent people from becoming victims of discrimination, whether at the hands of their fellow citizens or the state itself. This fact alone makes civil rights policy a likely fit for religious rhetoric, given that many religious precepts have the same underlying purpose. Love thy neighbor. Thou shall not bear false witness. Commandments like these are fundamentally about how people should treat one another.

In the following chapter, I will examine the religious rhetoric Presidents John Kennedy and Lyndon Johnson used as they tried to convince the country to support meaningful civil rights legislation. The two presidents made a wide array of religious claims. They would make pleas to morality, they would cite Scripture, they would invoke martyrs, they would warn of God's wrath, and they would call for days of prayer. Yet, in the end, I will argue that the Civil Rights Act of 1964 passed for reasons having little to do with religious rhetoric.

John Kennedy

John Kennedy was a reluctant advocate for civil rights. This was partly due to Kennedy's insular upbringing. Ben Bradlee, former editor of the *Washington Post*, was willing to bet that prior to his presidential campaign, "he (Kennedy) had never met a black person in his life." Bradlee continued, "I didn't—and I was on the WASP side of the same street—meet a black till I was sixteen. I think that Bobby (Kennedy)— St. Francis—felt that there was deep moral inequity, and I don't think that Jack felt that instinctively" (Strober and Strober 2003a, 287–88).

In addition to his privileged background, Kennedy had launched his political career in Massachusetts, a state that lacked a sizable African American population. And, further, his national aspirations had made him unduly sensitive to the Southern perspective. Kennedy would vote for the Southern jury trial amendment to the Civil Rights Act of 1957. He was also a vocal critic of Eisenhower's use of federal troops to integrate the Little Rock school system in 1957.

Upon becoming president, Kennedy continued to feel that taking a strong stand on civil rights had little to offer him politically. Kennedy had bested Nixon by just 118,574 votes. His margin of victory was the smallest since Grover Cleveland's 23,000 vote squeaker in 1884. When combined with accusations of voting fraud in Illinois and Texas, Kennedy was on shaky ground from day one. He had no mandate for action on any issue, let alone civil rights.

Kennedy was also confronted with a powerful conservative coalition that had the potential to frustrate a liberal agenda. After the 1960 election, the coalition included 285 of 437 House members and 59 of 100 Senators. Southern Democrats also headed twelve of twenty House committees and ten of sixteen Senate committees (Giglio 1991, 39). Given that, on any nondefense issue, Republican support could be expected to be minimal, Kennedy typically faced the challenge of persuading more than fifty conservative Southern Democrats in the House to vote for his bill, presuming he could even get it to the floor in the first place (O'Brien 2009, 133). The number problems were exacerbated by Kennedy's natural ineffectiveness when it came to dealing with Congress (Giglio 1991, 40–41). These dynamics created a strong incentive for Kennedy to avoid civil rights policies that could antagonize the Southern wing of his party.

Moreover, Kennedy was inclined to devote his time to foreign affairs as opposed to domestic ones regardless. As Kennedy once confided to Richard Nixon, "It really is true that foreign affairs is the only important issue for a president to handle, isn't it? I mean, who gives a shit if the minimum wage is $1.15 or $1.25 . . .?" (Isserman and Kazin 2004, 47).

One of Kennedy's common refrains was "Why fight if you are not sure to win?" (Reston 1966, 228). On civil rights, Kennedy seemed sure to lose, making him very unlikely to want to fight. His deputy attorney general Nicholas Katzenbach summed up Kennedy's initial position:

> There were times that civil rights issues preoccupied the president. The problems were hard to resolve and certainly occupied a great

deal of Bobby's time. Therefore the president spent more time on them, and they would talk a great deal about an issue that was on Bobby's mind. Yet I think other things were far more important. He was really interested in foreign policy and wanted to be involved in it. This caused problems with State; he wanted to be his own secretary of state.

He was always conscious of the closeness of the election, I always thought too conscious. He didn't feel he had a mandate, didn't feel he would succeed. In truth he didn't like working with Congress, even though he was a former senator and congressman. That's why he had Larry O'Brien, as opposed to LBJ, who reveled in working with Congress. Kennedy was inhibited about civil rights; he had all these demons going—the sit-ins, Meredith, Wallace. He wanted to get other things done. (Strober and Strober 2003a, 276–77)

As a consequence, Kennedy favored a strategy of executive action on civil rights. Over the first two and a quarter years of his administration, Kennedy's Justice Department would file forty-two lawsuits in support of Black voting rights (Dallek 2003, 591). He issued an order to create the President's Committee on Equal Employment Opportunity (PCEEO). Chaired by Vice President Johnson, the PCEEO had the power to conduct investigations and terminate government contracts if discrimination was found in its business partners. Kennedy also placed a high priority on appointing minorities to significant government positions. He appointed over forty African Americans to important posts and he nominated five Black federal judges, including Thurgood Marshall (Giglio 1991, 177).[1]

Yet, even in these smaller gestures, Kennedy was wary. During his presidential campaign, he had promised to end discrimination in federally financed public housing with the "stroke of the presidential pen." Once in office, though, Kennedy equivocated. The new president worried that such an order could weaken the chances that Congress would approve his proposed Department of Urban Affairs, an agency that he planned to appoint Robert Weaver to head as the first Black cabinet member. A limited order would not be announced until Thanksgiving of 1962. In the interim, the White House had been inundated with pens mailed by constituents angry that Kennedy had been reneging on his promise.

The history of Kennedy's administration is a timeline of tactics like the "Ink for Jack" drive. It is a timeline of increasing pressure on JFK—pressure that would force him to eventually take more assertive action. The Freedom Rides. The sit-ins. The riots over James Meredith's enrollment at Ole Miss in 1962. That kind of pressure would reach a critical mass in the spring of 1963. After events in Alabama, appointments and executive orders could no longer suffice.

At the beginning of 1963, Kennedy still believed that proposing a comprehensive civil rights program would be a mistake (O'Brien 2009, 158–59). The president held out hope that Congress might pass his tax, education, and healthcare bills, and he felt he needed to be on good terms with the Southern Democrats in order to do so.

In February, Kennedy called for action on civil rights in a message to Congress, but he failed to follow through with specific desegregation proposals. Kennedy also refused to back a movement to reform Rule XXII by reducing the threshold for ending a filibuster from two-thirds to three-fifths. This reform was viewed as instrumental to the cause of civil rights, an issue where filibusters were commonplace. In April, Kennedy took some additional heat for his rejection of a Civil Rights Commission recommendation that Mississippi's federal funding be cancelled until it complied with court orders mandating protection for Black citizens. But that same month, circumstances were about to change.

Martin Luther King Jr. and the Southern Christian Leadership Conference kicked off a campaign against segregation in Birmingham, Alabama, one of the most racist cities in the entire South. Birmingham had earned its reputation in large measure owing to the repressive police tactics of the city's commissioner, Eugene "Bull" Connor. Connor's forces were intertwined with the Klan and together they made life miserable for local minorities.

On the day after Connor lost the city's mayoral election, King began his protest, demanding an end to discrimination in hiring and the desegregation of public facilities. On Good Friday, King would be arrested for leading a march. It was while in solitary confinement that he wrote his famous "Letter from the Birmingham Jail," a potent disquisition on civil disobedience.

Tensions in Birmingham escalated following King's release. At the start of May, crowds of peaceful Black demonstrators, including children, were violently attacked by Connor's troopers. Connor used aggressive police dogs, nightsticks, and high-pressure fire hoses to scatter the marchers. These images, of dog bites and of people being knocked down by torrents of water, headlined news reports across the country. Upon seeing pictures of the chaos, Kennedy said they made him feel "sick" (Dallek 2003, 594).

In the near term, the administration was able to help negotiate a settlement to the standoff in Birmingham. The Southern Christian Leadership Conference won an agreement where a variety of facilities would be immediately desegregated, Blacks would be appointed to a number of white-collar jobs, and a committee would be established to deal with future racial problems. The ensuing calm would be short-lived, though; on May 11, bombs were set at the home of King's brother and at the hotel King stayed at while in town. The city's Black community responded with a four-hour riot.

Alabama's governor, George Wallace, was only making matters worse. Wallace, who had been elected on a pledge to defend segregation now and forever, was loudly opposing district court orders to desegregate the University of Alabama, the last segregated state university in the country. He planned to block the "school house" door himself if need be.

King's stated goal in Birmingham had been to "create a situation so crisis-packed that it will inevitably open the door to negotiation" (Giglio 1991, 191). The imbroglio with Wallace was merely the latest evidence that this scenario had come to fruition. In the ten weeks after the settlement, officials counted 758 racial demonstrations and 14,733 arrests in 186 cities (Branch 1988, 825). A survey by the attorney general had estimated that as many as thirty Southern cities were at risk of heavy violence over the course of the summer (Dallek 2003, 599).

Kennedy was acutely aware of the peril facing the country. He told one associate, "It's (unrest) going to be up North . . . This isn't any more just a Southern matter . . . It's Philadelphia and it's going to be Washington, DC, this summer, and we're trying to figure out what we can do to put this stuff in the courts and get it off the street because somebody's going to get killed" (Dallek 2003, 601). And so, on June 3, newspapers reported that Kennedy was prepared to ask Congress for a major civil rights law. Kennedy knew he was risking his presidency in the process. He told King in June, "We're in this up to the neck. The worst trouble of all would be to lose the fight in Congress . . . A good many programs I care about may go down the drain as a result of this—We may all go down the drain . . ." (Giglio 1991, 196).

Again, we see a president turning to religious rhetoric in crisis. This crisis, unfolding in riots and street violence, was more visible than most. However, for Kennedy the decision to embrace religious language was an intrinsically troublesome one because of his distinctive identity as a Catholic politician in 1960s America. It is ironic that Kennedy's faith would cause him so many difficulties, though, since as his wife Jackie once said, "I think it is unfair for Jack to be opposed because he is a Catholic. After all, he's such a poor Catholic" (Carty 2004, 4).

Kennedy's mother, Rose, had done her best to raise John within the Catholic tradition. Rose was a pious woman who attended mass daily and developed close relationships with figures within her church. She dragged her children to services every Sunday, demanded that they say grace before every meal, oversaw their nightly prayers, and reviewed their catechism lessons each week (Smith 2006, 260). Over the course of his adult life, John maintained his boyhood commitment to Catholic ritual, even to the point of fasting during Lent and attending confession.

But in a wider sense, Jackie was right about her husband's Catholic failings. Kennedy's faith was shallow. From a young age, Jack had sparred with his mother over her devotion to the church (Carty 2009, 285–86; Holmes 2012, 51). As his sister Eunice perceptively noted, "he was always a little less convinced about some (religious) things than the rest of us" (Smith 2006, 260).

Politically, Kennedy's relationship to Catholicism was equally complex. As an up and coming Representative from a heavily Catholic district in Massachusetts, Kennedy emerged as a vocal defender of Catholic interests. Jack fought for federally funded school busing and medical care, successfully so when he helped defeat two bills in 1950 that would have prevented aid from going to parochial schools.

Catholics were equally pleased by his votes on international affairs. Kennedy's foreign policy record was one of consistent support for Catholic countries fighting communist insurrections. He also defended Sen. Joe McCarthy's (R-WI) communist witch hunts. McCarthy enjoyed the strong backing of his co-religionists (Carty 2009, 288–89).

As Kennedy became a candidate for national office, however, he started to downplay his support for Catholic causes. He now stated his opposition to federal aid to parochial schools and he changed his stance on the question of whether the United States should appoint an ambassador to the Vatican, both reversals of his previous record (Smith 2006, 267).

Kennedy had good reason to tread lightly when it came to his religion. Despite the passage of thirty years since Al Smith's candidacy in 1928, many Protestants continued to be deeply suspicious of Catholic politicians. During Kennedy's run for the White House, pamphlets were distributed to voters filled with wild conspiracy theories about various Papal plots to overthrow the American government. Writers compared the act of voting for a Catholic to voting for a Nazi or a Fascist. In a moderated form, some of the same points would be made in bestselling books by author Paul Blanchard (Balmer 2008, 19–22).

Kennedy originally hoped that he had retired the religion issue with his decisive victory over challenger Hubert Humphrey in the West Virginia Democratic primary in May 1960; only 4 percent of West Virginians were Catholic. Still, religion continued to be an albatross around his neck. After a group of 150 Protestant ministers issued a public statement in early September questioning any Catholic's fitness for the presidency, Kennedy decided to forcefully respond. Before a somewhat hostile audience of the Greater Houston Ministerial Association on September 12, Kennedy gave a feisty speech on the subject of the separation of church and state (Kennedy 1960).

Kennedy argued that issues like Communism and poverty, not feelings about Roman Catholicism, should decide the election. But in a somewhat begrudging manner, he also acknowledged that he needed to explain what kind of role his faith would play in a potential Kennedy administration. The candidate said, "I believe in an America where the separation of church and state is absolute—where no Catholic prelate would tell the President, should he be Catholic, how to act, and no Protestant minister would tell his parishioners for whom to vote—where no church or church school is granted any public funds or political preference—and where no man is denied public office merely because his religion differs from the President who might appoint him or the people who might elect him." Kennedy pointedly reminded the ministers that when he and his late brother fought in World War II, "No one suggested then that we might have a 'divided loyalty,' that we did 'not believe in liberty' or that we belonged to a disloyal group that threatened the 'freedoms for which our forefathers died.'"

Ultimately, it is unclear whether Kennedy's campaign was helped or hurt by his religion. On the one hand, Kennedy only carried 34 percent of the White Protestant vote—the same amount that Adlai Stevenson had received in 1956 in an election in which he was trounced 57 to 42 percent by Eisenhower. On the other hand, Kennedy won 83 percent of the Catholic vote, whereas Stevenson won just 45 percent. Given that Protestants greatly outnumbered Catholics, these trends made for an exceptionally close popular vote, closer than it probably should have been. Nevertheless, Kennedy's Catholicism may have made the difference in states with sizable Catholic populations like New York, Pennsylvania, and Ohio (Casey 2009, 200–201).

Regardless, the legacy of the 1960 campaign is that Kennedy, much like Jimmy Carter, had to be cautious when it came to religion. Taking Kennedy's situation into account, it is logical that his standard rhetoric would not be marked much by religion. For sure, Kennedy would reference the Bible on occasion in his public remarks. Yet, these would be academic-style references. The Bible was a source of wisdom for the learned Kennedy, just like Shakespeare, ancient Chinese proverbs, Greek mythology, or philosophers like Francis Bacon (see Kennedy 1961a, 1961b, 1961c, 1963g). The Bible was not typically part of his larger rhetorical strategy. When Kennedy did cite it, his speechwriter Ted Sorenson says he did so only "as a matter of political convention" and "political necessity" (Holmes 2012, 70).

This is what makes the story of civil rights different. Every account acknowledges Kennedy's religious rhetoric in his televised speech on June 11, the day of the showdown at Alabama. Yet few consider what Kennedy said in the days surrounding his address.

On June 9, Kennedy spoke to the United States Conference of Mayors in Honolulu (Kennedy 1963b). Kennedy devoted his address to the "problem of race relations." At several points, JFK argued that the ultimate responsibility for better race relations rested with the mayors, and not the federal government. Indeed, Kennedy suggested several concrete steps that the civic leaders in attendance should take.

Yet, Kennedy also made a plea for his own forthcoming legislative proposals by spelling out a series of spiritual reasons why the mayors should support strong action on civil rights. For example, Kennedy approvingly quoted a Southern mayor who had attacked segregation as un-Christian. "Yesterday I read where Mayor David Schenck of Greensboro—and this is a story in the New York Times—appealed to all of the businessmen of the community in North Carolina and said, 'I say to you who own and operate places of public accommodation in the city, the hotels, motels and restaurants, that now is the time to throw aside the shackles of past customs. Selection of customers purely by race is outdated, morally unjust, and not in keeping with either democratic or Christian philosophy.' So spoke the Mayor of Greensboro, N.C. and I think it is good advice for all of us," said the president.

In closing, Kennedy also claimed that "Justice cannot wait for too many meetings" because "We face a moment of moral and constitutional crisis, and men of generosity and vision must make themselves heard in every section of this country." Clearly, Kennedy was already beginning to construct a moral and religious rationale for civil rights.

In fact, the next day, Kennedy would again use religious rhetoric to campaign for civil rights in a commencement address he delivered to the graduates of American University (Kennedy 1963c). This is a well-known address for other reasons. The subject of the speech was world peace. Kennedy made the case for improved Soviet-US relations and, in particular, for the adoption of a treaty banning nuclear testing. Kennedy had decided as early as May to use the American graduation ceremonies as his forum for presenting these ideas. The president wanted his olive branch to precede a Chinese-Soviet summit scheduled for July where China might be expected to pressure Khrushchev into rejecting any deals with Kennedy.

Kennedy knew that his softer tone would upset the hardliners in his administration so the text was mostly drafted in secrecy. Influential figures like Defense Secretary Robert McNamara and Secretary of State Dean Rusk did not even learn of it until June 8 when the president had already departed for his speaking tour. Today, nothing Kennedy said seems all that controversial. But, in 1963, praising the Soviets for their "many achievements—in science and space, in economic and industrial growth, in culture and in acts of courage" certainly was.

Historical commentary on this speech mostly overlooks the important comments Kennedy made about civil rights at American. The discussion of civil rights in a foreign policy address embodied Kennedy's constant concern about how racial violence in the United States could be exploited by Soviet propagandists (Dudziak 2000, 152–202). Kennedy told the graduates,

> Finally, my fellow Americans, let us examine our attitude toward peace and freedom here at home. The quality and spirit of our own society must justify and support our efforts abroad. We must show it in the dedication of our own lives—as many of you who are graduating today will have a unique opportunity to do, by serving without pay in the Peace Corps abroad or in the proposed National Service Corps here at home.
>
> But wherever we are, we must all, in our daily lives, live up to the age-old faith that peace and freedom walk together. In too many of our cities today, the peace is not secure because freedom is incomplete.
>
> It is the responsibility of the executive branch at all levels of government-local, State, and National—to provide and protect that freedom for all of our citizens by all means within their authority. It is the responsibility of the legislative branch at all levels, wherever that authority is not now adequate, to make it adequate. And it is the

responsibility of all citizens in all sections of this country to respect the rights of all others and to respect the law of the land.

All this is not unrelated to world peace. "When a man's ways please the Lord," the Scriptures tell us, "he maketh even his enemies to be at peace with him." And is not peace, in the last analysis, basically a matter of human rights—the right to live out our lives without fear of devastation—the right to breathe air as nature provided it—the right of future generations to a healthy existence?

While we proceed to safeguard our national interests, let us also safeguard human interests.

The audience was being cued to think of what had been happening in places like Birmingham when Kennedy said that in too many cities "peace is not secure because freedom is incomplete." Kennedy strongly claimed that the branches of government, and the people, had a responsibility to change this state of affairs. Kennedy then made a religious argument, based on Proverbs 16:7, that if each of these actors were to fight for equality, God might respond by removing the Soviet threat ("'When a man's ways please the Lord,' the Scriptures tell us, 'he maketh even his enemies to be at peace with him.'"). The inverse of Kennedy's point, of course, was that America's current treatment of its Black citizens was *displeasing* to the Lord, too.

Kennedy had resisted making a major address on civil rights for some time. In May, a reporter had asked him if he thought such an address might "serve a constructive purpose." Kennedy answered, "If I thought it would I would give one . . . But I made a speech the night of Mississippi—at Oxford—to the citizens of Mississippi and others. That did not seem to do much good . . ." (Kennedy 1963a).

Kennedy abruptly changed his mind about the matter. In the midst of the conflict with George Wallace on June 11, Kennedy received news of violent attacks on Black protestors in Danville, Virginia. Police brutality had hospitalized forty-eight of the sixty-five demonstrators. Martin Luther King telegrammed Kennedy about the incident, begging him to seek a "just and moral" solution to the crisis. "I ask you in the name of decency and Christian brotherhood to creatively grapple with Danville's and the nation's most grievous problem," King wrote.

Whether because of King's urging, or because of the Administration's success in forcing Wallace to capitulate, Kennedy suddenly decided to go on television that night to announce his civil rights legislation. Almost all of his advisors were against the idea; Ted Sorenson was given only two hours to write a draft. Kennedy would deliver a good part of his address off the top of his head—an astounding fact given the magnitude of the occasion (Branch 1988, 822–24; Dallek 2003, 603–4).

If the timing was not influenced by King, the religious message was (Kennedy 1963d). Kennedy informed the public that the standoff at the University of Alabama had been peacefully resolved, but, he said, "I hope that every American, regardless of where he lives, will stop and examine his conscience about this and other related incidents." Kennedy reminded his fellow Americans that they were committed to promoting the rights of oppressed peoples worldwide, so then "it ought to be possible" for students to attend college without the backing of the military, for consumers to have equal access to public accommodations, for voters to cast their ballot without interference.

Yet, Kennedy pointed out these things were not possible, and discrimination existed not just in the South, but "in every city, in every State of the Union." Civil rights were not a partisan or legal issue but, as Kennedy memorably claimed, "We are confronted primarily with a moral issue. It is as old as the scriptures and is as clear as the American Constitution. The heart of the question is whether all Americans are to be afforded equal rights and equal opportunities, whether we are going to treat our fellow Americans as we want to be treated. If an American, because his skin is dark, cannot eat lunch in a restaurant open to the public, if he cannot send his children to the best public school available, if he cannot vote for the public officials who represent him, if, in short, he cannot enjoy the full and free life which all of us want, then who among us would be content to have the color of his skin changed and stand in his place?" The reference to the issue being as "old as the scriptures" appears, based on context, to be a reference to the Golden Rule.

A little further into the address, Kennedy reiterated the moral dimension of the civil rights struggle: "We face, therefore, a moral crisis as a country and as a people. It cannot be met by repressive police action. It cannot be left to increased demonstrations in the streets. It cannot be quieted by token moves or talk. It is a time to act in the Congress, in your State and local legislative body and, above all, in all of our daily lives. It is not enough to pin the blame on others, to say this is a problem of one section of the country or another, or deplore the fact that we face. A great change is at hand, and our task, our obligation, is to make that revolution, that change, peaceful and constructive for all. Those who do nothing are inviting shame as well as violence. Those who act boldly are recognizing right as well as reality."

Kennedy's mentions of conscience, Scripture, and morality were moving. After watching the speech, King once more telegrammed Kennedy, this time to say, "I have just listened to your speech to the nation. It was one of the most eloquent, profound and unequivocal pleas for justice and the freedom of all men ever made by any president. You spoke passionately to the moral issues involved in the integration struggle" (Branch 1988, 824). Kennedy's proposal, outlined in his address, would ban discrimination in public accommodations like hotels, restaurants, and stores, and it would expand the powers of the Attorney General to enforce school desegregation orders. Tragically, Kennedy would not have much time left to fight for these policies. But in that short time, he would periodically restate these religious arguments.

In his special message to Congress on June 19, for example, Kennedy based much of his petition on religious themes (Kennedy 1963e). In the first line, Kennedy wrote "Last week I addressed to the American people an appeal to conscience—a request for their cooperation in meeting the growing moral crisis in American race relations." At another point, he termed racial discrimination "evil." At another, he observed that "religious leaders . . . recognize the conflict between racial bigotry and the Holy Word." And in closing, Kennedy asked for legislators to search within their "hearts" so that they might realize their responsibility to spread the "blessings of liberty," which was the only "right" thing to do: "I ask you to look into your hearts—not in search of charity, for the Negro neither wants nor needs condescension—but for the one plain, proud and priceless quality that unites us all as Americans: a sense of justice. In this year of the Emancipation Centennial, justice requires us to insure the blessings of liberty for all Americans and their posterity— not merely for reasons of economic efficiency, world diplomacy and domestic tranquility—but, above all, because it is right."

Another important example of religious rhetoric would be Kennedy's proclamation announcing a national day of prayer on October 8 (Kennedy 1963h). The day of prayer was tradition, authorized by Congress via a joint resolution in April 1952. However, Kennedy chose to direct the purpose of this year's day to supporting the civil rights struggle.

> On this day, let us acknowledge anew our reliance upon the divine Providence which guided our founding fathers. Let each of us, according to his own custom and his own faith, give thanks to his

Creator for the divine assistance which has nurtured the noble ideals in which this Nation was conceived. Most especially, let us humbly acknowledge that we have not yet succeeded in obtaining for all of our people the blessings of liberty to which all are entitled. On this day, in this year, as we concede these shortcomings, let each of us pray that through our failures we may derive the wisdom, the courage, and the strength to secure for every one of our citizens the full measure of dignity, freedom, and brotherhood for which all men are qualified by their common fatherhood under God.

The president's request was directly quoted in the Associated Press story on the proclamation, which also reported that he planned to attend services on the day of prayer as well (see, i.e., *New York Times* 1963e). Like George H. W. Bush, Kennedy had elected to turn a generic spiritual exercise into a vehicle that might advance his legislative agenda.

Over the course of the weeks lasting from June to October, Kennedy would occasionally use religious rhetoric in small doses, such as when he told a dinner hosted by the Italian president in July, "Of great importance today, we are trying to erase for all time the injustices and inequalities of race and color in order to assure all Americans a fair chance to fulfill their lives and their opportunity as Americans, and as equal children of God. I can neither conceal nor accept the discrimination now suffered by our Negro citizens in many parts of the country; and I am determined to obtain both public and private action to end it" (Kennedy 1963f).

More often, though, Kennedy was working behind the scenes, sometimes deputizing religious leaders to spread the gospel for him. On June 17, Kennedy met with around 250 religious leaders at the White House. Summing up his advice to them, Kennedy told the preachers, "I would hope each religious group would . . . underscore the moral position of racial equality" (O'Brien 2009, 162). Many of them would do this. Yet, after Kennedy's tragic assassination in November, it would be left to Lyndon Johnson to carry on the crusade for civil rights. And Johnson's religious rhetoric would make Kennedy's look timid by comparison.

Lyndon Johnson

When he was fifteen, Lyndon Johnson joined the Disciples of Christ church. Perhaps, his affection for a girl played a role in the decision, but Johnson had also been repelled by the harsh sermons of his mother's Baptist ministers, "real hell fire and damnation stuff," as he later described it. The gentler approach of the Disciples appealed to him (Woods 2006, 41).

Johnson would ultimately become a religious nomad. In the future, he would sometimes attend Episcopalian services with his wife, Lady Bird. As president, he became increasingly attracted to Roman Catholicism; Johnson's daughter, Luci, was a convert. During his final years in office, Johnson would from time to time visit the Catholic mission in Stonewall, TX or pray in the chapel at Saint Dominic's in Washington, DC, at the end of a trying day. In anguish over Vietnam, Johnson was known to attend as many as three different Sunday services (799). When asked by an aide why he could not just pick one sect and stick to it, Johnson gave an unconvincing response: "They all worship God, and just maybe by my attendance at different denominations, I will encourage others to attend the church of their choice" (Watson 2004, 132).

In an oral history interview with the staff of the Johnson Library, Billy Graham, a man who had ministered often to the president, paints a picture of a troubled follower (Transcript). "I think that he had a conflict within him about religion," Graham said. "He knew what it meant to be saved or lost, using our terminology, and he knew what it was to be born again. And yet he somehow felt that he had never quite had that experience. I think he tried to make up for it by having many of the outward forms of religion, in the sense of going to church almost fanatically, while he was president even."

On the one hand, Graham describes Johnson as a sincere Christian, a man who liked to have the Bible read to him, who would join Graham on his knees in prayer, and who loved to discuss the old sermons of his great grandfather. But on the other, Graham admits that part of Johnson's interest in religion was "political in this sense, I think he thought more about what the *Baptist Standard* said in Texas than the *Dallas Morning News*."

Johnson was not a saint. His personal behavior was frequently crude, he abused his aides, and he was a serial womanizer (Dallek 1998, 186–87, 408; Unger and Unger 1999, 371; Peters 2010, 138–39). But owing to his varied spiritual experiences, Johnson was at least consistently a saint in speech. The president carried lines from the Acts, Second Peter, and the Psalms around with him (Woods 2006, 685, 688). Those who followed Johnson closely knew that in public he commonly cited the words of Isaiah 1:18, "Come now, let us reason together" (see, e.g., Johnson 1964d, 1965a, 1967). Matthew 25 was another favorite passage (i.e., Johnson 1964m). Further, Johnson's speeches displayed an idiosyncratic fixation with prophets and prophesy; a simple search of the University of California, Santa Barbara public papers database returns ninety-two different speeches where the president used one or both of these words.

Indeed, at one time or another, it seems that Johnson used religious rhetoric in support of almost all of his policies. He defended his foreign aid packages by claiming that they were part of the country's "Christian duty" (Johnson 1964h). Medicare was framed as "the most noble of God's duties—the care of the sick and the helpless" (Johnson 1964o). The Highway Beautification Act of 1965 was praised because it would preserve "what God has gladly given" (Johnson 1965b). In one speech, Johnson would go as far as claiming that the impetus behind his entire Great Society agenda was a desire to translate Christian ethics into public policy (Johnson 1966).

But despite his obvious proclivity for religious language, Johnson would only turn to a religious rhetorical *strategy* one time—as a means for securing the passage of the Civil Rights Act of 1964. This was a continuation of the style of argument that Kennedy had earlier adopted. It was a choice Johnson made consciously. And it was at this time that Johnson was faced with a crisis of unmatched proportion. A president was dead. The country was a tinderbox. Johnson's own future was on the line. Religious rhetoric once more was a tool of the desperate.

President Kennedy was assassinated on November 22, 1963, while riding in a motorcade in downtown Dallas, Texas. Johnson had become president in the worst of circumstances. The country was shattered by Kennedy's death. Most major social and athletic events were immediately cancelled. Churches around the country held extra services that overflowed with mourners. Others remained glued to TV news broadcasts, weeping in private.

Johnson was not immune to these feelings himself. He told Doris Kearns (1976, 172) that he was concerned that the "enormity of the tragedy" could "overwhelm" him. He called himself a "man in trouble." On November 23, Johnson was so tormented that he insisted that Horace Busby, an old friend and current aide, spend the night in his bedroom. Busby sat watching the president try to sleep from an armchair. Twice during the night, he tried to slip away before Johnson called out for him to stay (Dallek 1998, 55).

Johnson's fears were more than just general anxieties about his new responsibilities; they also reflected specific political concerns. Johnson was stepping into a complex situation. The new president recognized that he had to act quickly on civil rights. Many saw the assassination as a consequence of the pernicious racial hate coursing through the country. Chief Justice Earl Warren added fuel to this fire when he issued a statement saying that Kennedy had died "as a result of the hatred and bitterness that has been injected into the life of our nation by bigots" (*Los Angeles Times* 1963a). Certain racist elements did little to dispel this impression by disgustingly cheering the news of Kennedy's death (Kotz 2005, 6–7). Action on civil rights was practically a matter of national security.

Civil rights were crucial to Johnson's own political future as well. Johnson's previous record on the issue was not flattering. He had been a consistent opponent of civil rights until 1957, at which point, he used his position as Senate majority leader to help guide through the underwhelming Civil Rights Acts of 1957 and 1960. Prior to then, Johnson had regularly bragged to constituents about his opposition to civil rights. In fact, Johnson's first speech on the floor as a Senator in March of 1949 was a denunciation of Harry Truman's civil rights proposals. Johnson had argued that they would "deprive one minority of its rights in order to extend rights to other minorities" (Stern 1991, 689).

By all accounts Johnson felt no personal animus toward African Americans, but was responding to the reality of being a Senator from racially segregated Texas. Johnson would explain to civil rights advocates that the only thing a supportive vote from him would accomplish was his defeat in the following election. Now, circumstances had changed. When one Senator asked Lady Bird to explain Johnson's unexpected turnabout she simply answered "The President has to take into consideration many things that a senator does not" (Bernstein 1996, 46).

Still, Johnson's background meant that he was naturally looked upon with skepticism from many quarters when he ascended to the top job. John Kenneth Galbraith warned the new president that "the whole liberal community" would be watching what he did on civil rights (Bornet 1983, 18–19). Shortly after Kennedy's death, a small but powerful group of liberal insiders began meeting privately to discuss whether it would be possible to deny Johnson the nomination in 1964. These individuals viewed Bobby Kennedy as JFK's rightful heir (Isserman and Kazin 2004, 107–8).

Johnson realized what these rumblings meant for civil rights: "I knew that if I didn't get out in front on this issue, they (the liberals) would get me. They'd throw up my background against me, they'd use it to prove that I was incapable of bringing unity to the land I loved so much . . . I couldn't let that happen. I had to produce a civil rights bill that was even stronger than the one they'd have gotten if Kennedy had lived. Without this, I'd be dead before I could even begin" (Kearns 1976, 191).

It is clear that Johnson was under a tremendous amount of pressure. The country was grieving a slain president, he was uncertain of his own ability to do the job, and civil rights loomed as a crucial problem for both the country and his own political future. And so in this uncertain time, Johnson turned to religious rhetoric as a means for selling the country on the need for legislation.

His rhetorical choice was eminently strategic. Johnson had already recommended the use of religious rhetoric to Kennedy. Johnson told Ted Sorenson in June of 1963 that the president should travel to a Southern city, look its residents "in the eye," and explain "the moral issue and the Christian issue" (Lawson 1981, 98).

Walt Rostow, a Kennedy security advisor, was aware of these conversations: "The point he (Johnson) was trying to make—and did drive home—was, if you want to carry the South on this thing and break the filibuster, there is only one appeal you can make: it is the right thing to do. You must appeal to morality, to their attachment to the Bible" (Strober and Strober 2003a, 288).

As usual, Johnson had his finger on the pulse of his constituents, "What Negroes are really seeking is moral force," the Vice President once said (Rorabaugh 2002, 116). Now, as president, Johnson had the opportunity to take his own advice. Johnson later remembered, "I knew that as President I couldn't make people want to integrate their schools or open their doors to blacks but I could make them feel guilty for not doing it and I believed it was my moral responsibility to do precisely that—to use the moral persuasion of my office to make people feel that segregation was a curse they'd carry with them to their graves" (Woods 2006, 475).

Johnson began his religious campaign for civil rights with his first national address, given to a joint session of Congress on the night of November 27, 1963 (Johnson 1963a). The setting of the speech was tinged with religious symbolism because it shared aspects in common with funeral ceremonies. Recall that this address was taking place just four days after the assassination. Still, this was also to be a policy address, a chance for Johnson to chart the course that he now intended to lead the nation on.

The new president emphasized that kind words for his predecessor would not be enough of a tribute. Civil rights legislation would be. "First, no memorial oration or eulogy could more eloquently honor

President Kennedy's memory than the earliest possible passage of the civil rights bill for which he fought so long," Johnson said.

In his inspiring conclusion, Johnson would closely link civil rights with religion via his rhetorical choices:

> We meet in grief, but let us also meet in renewed dedication and renewed vigor. Let us meet in action, in tolerance, and in mutual understanding. John Kennedy's death commands what his life conveyed—that America must move forward. The time has come for Americans of all races and creeds and political beliefs to understand and to respect one another. So let us put an end to the teaching and the preaching of hate and evil and violence. Let us turn away from the fanatics of the far left and the far right, from the apostles of bitterness and bigotry, from those defiant of law, and those who pour venom into our Nation's bloodstream.

> I profoundly hope that the tragedy and the torment of these terrible days will bind us together in new fellowship, making us one people in our hour of sorrow. So let us here highly resolve that John Fitzgerald Kennedy did not live—or die—in vain. And on this Thanksgiving eve, as we gather together to ask the Lord's blessing, and give Him our thanks, let us unite in those familiar and cherished words:

> America, America,
> God shed His grace on thee,
> And crown thy good
> With brotherhood
> From sea to shining sea.

A lot of interesting things are happening in these lines. To begin, Johnson makes a second call for progress on civil rights ("The time has come for Americans of all races and creeds and political beliefs to understand to respect one another") but, this time, he does so with the aid of a host of words with religious significance, words such as "preaching," "evil," "apostles," and "fellowship."

The sentence on fellowship merits additional comment. In the New Testament, fellowship is a description of the communal bond between Christians who have chosen to accept Christ as their savior (see 1 John 1:6–7). The existence of this fellowship indicates that believers share common experiences and a common hope for eternal life. In a way, fellowship is the Christian equivalent of the Jewish covenant that bound the Israelites together with each other and with God (Powell 2011, 285). Johnson's point is that to create such a fellowship requires action on civil rights.

From a broader perspective, Johnson was positioning Kennedy as a martyr for civil rights. The final paragraphs are about hatred and in them Johnson asks that the country resolve that Kennedy "did not live—or die—in vain." The suggestion—which, as I explained above, was already a powerful thought in the country—is that Kennedy's death was in some way connected to the battle over civil rights. Making Kennedy a martyr for the cause would be a potent image for Johnson to have at his disposal.

Martyrs have a long history in Christian tradition. By definition, a martyr is typically understood to be someone who died for their religious beliefs. Historically, Saints Paul, Peter, and many other influential early Christians died as victims of Roman persecution. Although the veneration of martyrs is something that mostly occurred in later years, the Bible does contain several examples of martyrs as well. Jesus would be the most notable example, but there are the cases of Stephen (Acts 22:20) and James (Acts 12:1–2), in addition to several other references to martyrdom found in the Book of Revelation.

Johnson would actively work to create the impression that Kennedy had been martyred for civil rights. As he once said, "Everything I had ever learned in the history books taught me that martyrs have to die for causes. John Kennedy had died. But his 'cause' was not really clear. That was my job. I had to take the dead man's program and turn it into a martyr's cause" (Dallek 2004, 148–49). In practice, this often meant paralleling Kennedy's death to Lincoln, a president who most certainly *did* die for the cause of racial justice.[2]

At a memorial service held for Kennedy at the Lincoln Memorial in Washington one month after his death (Johnson 1963e), Johnson opened his remarks by saying "Thirty days and a few hours ago, John Fitzgerald Kennedy, 35th President of the United States, died a martyr's death. The world will not forget what he did here. He will live on in our hearts, which will be his shrine. Throughout his life, he had malice toward none; he had charity for all. But a senseless act of mindless malice struck down this man of charity, and we shall never be the same."

The "malice toward none" and "charity for all" lines, not coincidentally, are adapted from Lincoln's second inaugural address, a speech that ruminated on the meaning of the Civil War and what would be needed if the combatants were to reconcile (see the introduction). The fact that the subject of Lincoln's speech was a racially motivated conflict is not insignificant. By following a reference to martyrdom with a reference to racial violence, Johnson implies that racial violence was the *cause* of Kennedy's martyrdom.

It is fitting, then, that Johnson concluded his remarks with a subdued plea for the civil rights package: "So let us here on this Christmas night determine that John Kennedy did not live or die in vain, that this Nation under God shall have a new birth of freedom, and that we may achieve in our time and for all time the ancient vision of peace on earth, good will toward all men." This is the same rhetorical structure as the address on November 22. Kennedy will have died in vain if we do not have "a new birth of freedom," a birth that could be accomplished by passing the civil rights law.

Similarly, in remarks to a cabinet meeting on May 28, 1964 (Johnson 1964p), one day before what would have been JFK's birthday, Johnson reminded his audience that "We would be untrue to the trust he (Kennedy) reposed in us, if we did not remain true to the tasks he relinquished when God summoned him." If it was not clear that Johnson had civil rights in mind, it would be soon. As the president continued: "John F. Kennedy called on many of the world's masters for his messages to us. But his favorite quotation was from a man who preceded him in martyrdom: Abraham Lincoln. 'I know there is a God and that He hates injustice. I see the storm coming, and I know His hand is in it. But if He has a place and a part for me, I believe that I am ready.'" Johnson did not have to mention the bill for his audience to know what he was talking about.

Johnson once more drew the linkage between Kennedy and Lincoln in a brief speech he delivered at an unveiling of a bust for Kennedy in November 1964 (Johnson 1964t). Johnson noted, "For all of us, the tragic anniversary of this weekend makes this a very sad and sober time. We can here reflect upon the irony that President Kennedy himself had placed in this room a bust of another martyred President, Abraham Lincoln. As was said of the Great Emancipator, we can say of our friend and our brother and our great leader: He belongs to the ages."

In sum, Johnson was unafraid to depict Kennedy as a martyr, a classification that has strong religious resonance (see also Johnson 1964q). In doing so, he would not hesitate to compare Kennedy to Lincoln, a president assassinated because of his efforts to advance the cause of racial justice. Both of these decisions helped to motivate the conclusion that Kennedy had been martyred for his support of civil rights. On each occasion, the audience was reminded that they must finish Kennedy's work.

Johnson gave another national address on November 28, the day after his appearance before Congress (Johnson 1963b). It was Thanksgiving Day. Some of the religious content of this speech was the standard communitarian style language we would expect to find. Yet, Johnson also made another eloquent statement about the need for racial progress. In the middle of the speech, Johnson remarked:

> In each administration the greatest burden that the President had to bear had been the burden of his own countrymen's unthinking and unreasoning hate and division.
>
> So, in these days, the fate of this office is the fate of us all. I would ask all Americans on this day of prayer and reverence to think on these things.
>
> Let all who speak and all who teach and all who preach and all who publish and all who broadcast and all who read or listen—let them reflect upon their responsibilities to bind our wounds, to heal our sores, to make our society well and whole for the tasks ahead of us.
>
> It is this work that I most want us to do: to banish rancor from our words and malice from our hearts; to close down the poison spring of hatred and intolerance and fanaticism; to perfect our unity north and south, east and west; to hasten the day when bias of race, religion, and region is no more; and to bring the day when our great energies and decencies and spirit will be free of the burdens that we have borne too long.

Toward the end of the speech, the president yet again re-emphasized the same point:

> On this Thanksgiving Day, as we gather in the warmth of our families, in the mutual love and respect which we have for one another, and as we bow our heads in submission to divine providence, let us also thank God for the years that He gave us inspiration through His servant, John F. Kennedy.
>
> Let us today renew our dedication to the ideals that are American. Let us pray for His divine wisdom in banishing from our land any injustice or intolerance or oppression to any of our fellow Americans whatever their opinion, whatever the color of their skins—for God made all of us, not some of us, in His image. All of us, not just some of us, are His children.

Johnson had thus made a strong religious argument about the need for equality ("God made all of us, not some of us, in His image"), and he had announced it as the "work that I most want us to do." He had done these things on a day, as he called it, "of prayer and reverence." He asked that the country "pray for His divine wisdom" about how best to eradicate prejudice. The last paragraph of this speech might as well have come from a minister.

When combined with his speech from a day earlier, Johnson's religious rhetorical campaign for civil rights was now well underway. In addition to the theme of martyrdom, Johnson's language would feature several other religious arguments for civil rights that bear individual discussions.

One such motif would be the importance of the Golden Rule: "In everything do to others as you would have them do to you; for this is the law and the prophets" (Matthew 7:12). Johnson would frequently call for civil rights by reference to this important dictate. He would tell his audience to place themselves in the shoes of a Black American and then consider how they would want to be treated. Johnson's speech to a group of Pittsburgh steelworkers in April 1964 serves as an example of this method of persuasion (Johnson 1964j).

Toward the latter half of his speech, Johnson transitioned from a discussion of economic policy and into a discussion of civil rights. Johnson forged ahead with a religious argument based on the Golden Rule:

> Just put yourself in the position of the man who gets up in the morning and walks the street all day looking for a job that can't be found, and he goes home and talks to his wife that night.
>
> You put yourself in that position and apply the Golden Rule and do unto others as you would have them do unto you and we will clear up a lot of these problems that are requiring a long debate in the Congress . . .
>
> There will be times when you will be frustrated and when you may even be irritated. But the best way in the world to get sobered up from that hangover is just put yourself in that other fellow's position and say, "How would I feel if I had been denied the job because of my religion or my race, or my color? How would I feel if I had been denied the right to buy a cup of coffee because of the color of my skin?" You ask yourself that question, and you will find the answer in your own heart.
>
> We are going to pass a civil rights bill if it takes us all summer long, and we are going to pass it with the votes of both parties. We don't want any Democratic labels on it. We want it to be an American bill, passed by Americans. We are going to keep this country at peace, if

God wills it, and we are doing our best. We are going to ask men of both parties to help us do that.

As the bill inched closer to passage, Johnson would not retreat from such phrasings. In fact, he would offer roughly the same rationale for civil rights at a fundraising dinner in Minneapolis that June (Johnson 1964r):

> Under the leadership of Hubert Humphrey and with an assist every now and then from some of the rest of us, we are about to pass the strongest and the best civil rights bill in this century. We are going on from this bill to give every American citizen, of every race and color, the equal rights which the Constitution demands and justice directs . . .

> And I would remind you good Americans tonight that there is a law more hallowed than the civil rights bill, more hallowed than even the Constitution of the United States. That law commands every man to respect the life and dignity of his neighbor; to treat others as he would be treated. That law asks not only obedience in our action, but it requires understanding in our heart. And may God grant us that understanding.

As it happens, Johnson often relied on the Golden Rule in remarks he made before business leaders. In so doing, the president was trying to persuade his audiences both to support his policies and to create additional opportunities for African Americans. One of the Johnson Administration civil rights initiatives was known as Plans for Progress. These were voluntary agreements large employers made whereby they promised to diversify their workforces. Johnson would make mention of the Golden Rule almost every time he spoke to one of these gatherings.

On December 12, 1963, for instance, Johnson said, "And I think, perhaps, the best way to quickly illustrate what is really in our hearts is to remind ourselves of the Golden Rule, 'Do unto others as you would have them do unto you.'" Johnson continued, "So when you're dealing with these people, in your company, or in your firm, or in your business, just remember they're some daughter's father, or some boy's mother, or someone's sister, or somebody's brother that you are dealing with. And except for the grace of God, it might be you—that they were dealing with you instead of you dealing with them" (Johnson 1963d).

On January 16, 1964, Johnson expressed similar feelings; only this time he did so more forcefully (Johnson 1964b). The president exhorted the businessmen in attendance to set an example that the rest of the country could follow: "If you men in this group can join the others that have already paved the way and cover six million employees and add to that total the group that you represent, we won't have to fight this battle in the streets. We will have fought it in our minds and we will have reached a logical and proper conclusion. And we will say that there is some truth in the statement that all men are created equal and there is some point in following the Golden Rule of doing unto others as you would have them do unto you."

From here, Johnson commented more broadly on the civil rights question beyond the immediate issue of the Plans for Progress program. Johnson went on, "So let's not rely upon our great economic power and the great wealth we possess to do justice. Let's do it ourselves, so when we go to bed we will have a clear conscience. And when we do that we will rightfully be entitled to lead the world. We'll lead them because of our moral standards and not because of our economic power." Emphatically, Johnson told the gathering, "it is up to you to pick up where Lincoln left off. It is up to you to achieve in the days ahead what we have been waiting for a hundred years."

Johnson's remarks to the Plans for Progress participants were equally broad on April 9 (Johnson 1964f). On this day, the president expressed optimism about the passage of his civil rights law, but he warned that "any law is insufficient unless it is supported . . . by the moral commitment of the people of the country." So, Johnson proceeded to urge the businessmen present to make that moral commitment themselves, in part by once more citing the Golden Rule: "Bear in mind that golden rule—'Do unto others as you would have them do unto you,' and examine your personnel department; examine your own conscience. See if you are doing unto others as you would have them do unto you. If you are, then we can say, 'Well done, thou faithful servant.' But until you can say that, until you can do that, until there is increased understanding, until there is a desire to put this bill into effect and make it work, we still have our job to do."

The second Biblical quote Johnson uses was another of his favorites. "Well done, thou faithful servant" is a line taken from Jesus's parable of the talents (Matthew 25:14–30), a passage I discussed last chapter. The parable's point is that believers are required to be true in performing the work they have been asked to do. Although the parable is a piece of New Testament wisdom, it includes the harsh consequences of failure found more commonly in the Old Testament; for his poor management, one servant is thrown out into the dark upon the master's return where "there will be weeping and gnashing of teeth" (Matthew 25:30). This is an overt symbol of damnation. And it is in this context that Johnson would typically use the quote as he warned people of what might happen were they *not* to support civil rights.

Indeed, warnings of eternal judgment were a third prominent aspect of LBJ's religious rhetoric on civil rights. A soft version of this kind of argument, one using that same line from the Gospels, can be found in Johnson's remarks at the twentieth conference of the Advertising Council in Washington on May 6, 1964 (Johnson 1964l). Johnson devoted almost half of his speech to civil rights. The objectives of the civil rights bill, Johnson said, were "moral objectives" and civil rights was a "moral problem." Johnson's appeal was entirely religious:

> Let us not wait for the day when the prophet will say that the harvest is past and the summer is ended, and we are not saved. Let us, instead, work together so that one day we may hear the benediction, "Well done, thou good and faithful servants."

> So I ask you this morning to resolve here, now, as individuals, not as a conference, to give us that help that is necessary, to passing this program that will give us a greater and a better society. Determine here that you will engrave your name on that honor roll of leaders of this Nation who in the 20th century sought to give finality to a proclamation that Lincoln issued a hundred years ago.

> It is true that a hundred years ago this year a great American President freed the slaves of their chains, but he did not free America of its bigotry, and he did not free us from the prejudice of color. Until education is blind to color, until employment is unaware of race, emancipation will be a proclamation but it will not be a fact.

> As the rest of the world looks upon this rich and strong Nation, let us not only pray and work for peace and good will toward all men, but let us determine that the sore spots here in our own social life can be wiped and washed away and we can set an example for the rest of the world.

The first line of this passage ("the harvest is past and the summer is ended, and we are not saved") is a Biblical quote found in the Book of Jeremiah (8:20). This section of Jeremiah, like the book itself, can confuse. The surrounding paragraphs are a long form poem that intersperses God's words with comments from both the people and the prophet himself. The main point of the poem, however, is the idea that the people have gone astray and as a result will be punished (Pixley 2004, 31–33).

The specific line Johnson chose to use is the lament of those facing God's wrath as a consequence of their actions. When combined with the reference to the parable of the talents, which, again, ends with a man consigned to torment for his failures, this part of Johnson's speech reads as a stark warning that God will be displeased with America should it fail to act on civil rights. It is not necessary to be aware of the context to grasp this message. Anyone can understand what Johnson is hinting at when he says "Let us not wait for the day when . . . we are not saved."

In fact, Johnson was even more direct with his Old Testament style admonitions in a speech he delivered to the members of the American Society of Newspaper Editors two weeks earlier (Johnson 1964g). Johnson reviewed his role in the American political system at considerable length. He spoke of the awesome responsibility a president has to lead the people not just for today but in preparation for the future. Civil rights was the first policy Johnson mentioned when he said they were a "moral, national commitment." Johnson continued to speak about other issues like the War on Poverty, Medicare, and a government pay bill. But then, Johnson had some strong religious words for his listeners in closing:

> And from our science and our technology, from our compassion and from our tolerance, from our unity and from our heritage, we stand uniquely on the threshold of a high adventure of leadership by example and by precept. "Not by might, nor by power, but by my spirit, saith the Lord." From our Jewish and Christian heritage, we draw the image of the God of all mankind, who will judge his children not by their prayers and by their pretensions, but by their mercy to the poor and their understanding of the weak.

> We cannot cancel that strain and then claim to speak as a Christian society. To visit the widow and the fatherless in their affliction is still pure religion and undefiled. I tremble for this Nation. I tremble for our people if at the time of our greatest prosperity we turn our back on the moral obligations of our deepest faith. If the face we turn to this aspiring, laboring world is a face of indifference and contempt, it will rightly rise up and strike us down.

> Believe me, God is not mocked. We reap as we sow. Our God is still a jealous God, jealous of his righteousness, jealous of his mercy, jealous for the last of the little ones who went unfed while the rich sat down to eat and rose up to play. And unless my administration profits the present and provides the foundation for a better life for all humanity, not just now but for generations to come, I shall have failed.

> If there is judgment in history, it rests on us, according to our generosity or our disdain. These are the stakes, to make a world in which all of God's children can live or to go into the dark. For today as we meet here in this beautiful rose garden under the shadows of atomic power it is not rhetoric but it is truth to say that we must either love each other or we must die.

It is difficult to be sure what specific policies Johnson had in mind in these paragraphs. On the one hand, he was certainly referencing his foreign aid goals. In the paragraph preceding the excerpt, Johnson highlighted the plight of the "Two-thirds of the teeming masses of humanity" who were struggling "fitfully to assert its own initiative." In the excerpt, as well, Johnson mentions the "aspiring, laboring world."

However, the remarks read broader than that single objective alone. Indeed, Johnson returns in this section to the basic theme of his speech, the need to set the stage for the future of the country. Civil rights had already been positioned as a key part of that project. Others interpreted this speech as such. Hedrick Smith (1964) of the *New York Times* made the plea for civil rights the focus of his entire piece on the address.

Regardless, such a lengthy thought places a religious frame around all of the content in the speech, whether intentionally or not. Again, what is important to note is that Johnson was issuing a warning. He depicts a God who will judge America. "God is not mocked." "We reap as we sow." Johnson "trembles" for the nation. The implication is that the passage of the civil rights bill was crucial if the country hoped to avoid a terrible fate.

Johnson's speech was addressed to a secular audience of newspaper editors, some of whom had to be surprised at the extent of the religious rhetoric they encountered. This is in contrast to Johnson's talks with religious leaders, where spiritual rhetoric on civil rights was to be expected. On this point, Johnson did not disappoint. In his remarks to members of the Southern Baptist Christian Leadership Seminar on March 25, 1964, Johnson demonstrated his ability to put the cause of civil rights in terms the faithful were familiar with (Johnson 1964e):

> The most critical challenge that we face today is the struggle to free men, free them from the bondage of discrimination and prejudice. This administration is doing everything it possibly can do to win that struggle . . .

> In the long struggle for religious liberty, Baptists have been prophets. Your forebears have suffered as few others have suffered, and their

suffering was not in vain. This cause, too, this cause of human dignity, this cause of human rights demands prophets in our time, men of compassion and truth, unafraid of the consequences of fulfilling their faith. There are preachers and there are teachers of injustice and dissension and distrust at work in America this very hour. They are attempting to thwart the realization of our highest ideals. There are those who seek to turn back the rising tide of human hope by sowing half-truths and untruths wherever they find root. There are voices crying peace, peace, peace, when there is no peace.

Help us to answer them with truth and with action. Help us to pass this civil rights bill and establish a foundation upon which we can build a house of freedom where all men can dwell. Help us, when this bill has been passed, to lead all of our people in this great land into a new fellowship.

Let the acts of everyone, in Government and out, let all that we do proclaim that righteousness does exalt the Nation.

Very clearly, Johnson is claiming that the religious beliefs of Baptists should compel them to support civil rights. At the same time, Johnson supplements this call for action with numerous religious references to concepts like "prophets" and another reference to "fellowship." Finally, the last line ("Let the acts of everyone . . . proclaim that righteousness does exalt the Nation") is drawn from Proverbs 14:34.

Johnson voiced similar feelings to a group of civil rights leaders that April (Johnson 1964k):

All that this bill will do is to see to it that service and employment will not be refused to individuals because of their race or their religion or where their ancestors were born. This bill is going to pass if it takes us all summer, and this bill is going to be signed and enacted into law because justice and morality demand it . . .

It is your job as prophets in our time to direct the immense power of religion in shaping the conduct and the thoughts of men toward their brothers in a manner consistent with compassion and love. So help us in this hour. Help us to see and do what must be done. Inspire us with renewed faith. Stir our consciences. Strengthen our will. Inspire and challenge us to put our principles into action.

For the future of our faith is at stake, and the future of this Nation is at stake.

As the Old Testament pleads, "Let there be no strife, I pray, between you and me, and between my herdmen and your herdmen, because we are brothers." So do we plead today.

> Yes, we are all brothers, and brothers together must build this great
> Nation into a great family, so that a hundred years from now in this
> house every man and woman present today will have their name
> pointed to with pride because in the hour of our greatest trial, we
> were willing to answer the roll and to stand up and be counted for
> morality and right.

Notably, Johnson uses a Biblical quote from Genesis 13:8 ("Let there be no strife . . . because we are brothers"). The quote points to the importance of brotherhood, another religious concept with great significance (see Chapter 2).

A final theme that marked Johnson's religious discourse on civil rights was his varied use of universal moral statements. This was a habit of the president, which we have already encountered much evidence of. Johnson would offer these moral claims whether the audience was religious, as in the last two speeches above, or not. In some places, these statements would have explicit connections to religion, and in others, they would be more general articulations of standards of right and wrong.

At a meeting of the AFL-CIO: "Before the Congress also is a civil rights bill that is denied a hearing in the Rules Committee. The endless abrasions of delay, neglect, and indifference *have rubbed raw the national conscience.* We have talked too long. We have done too little. And all of it has come too late. You must help me make civil rights in America a reality" (Johnson 1963c).

In his 1964 State of the Union address: "Let me make one principle of this administration abundantly clear: All of these increased opportunities—in employment, in education, in housing, and in every field—must be open to Americans of every color. As far as the writ of Federal law will run, we must abolish not some, but all racial discrimination. For this is not merely an economic issue, or a social, political, or international issue. *It is a moral issue,* and it must be met by the passage this session of the bill now pending in the House" (Johnson 1964a).

As he was interviewed on TV and radio by the major broadcasters: "I think great progress has been made under the leadership of President Kennedy and the Attorney General and others in the last year is getting all the people of the Nation to accept their *moral responsibility* and take some leadership in this field where there has been so much discrimination. And I know of nothing more important for this Congress to do than to pass the Civil Rights Act as the House passed it" (Johnson 1964c).

At a press conference in April 1964 in response to a question on civil rights demonstrations: "I think the most important thing we can do to ease this situation is to act with promptness and dispatch on the very good civil rights bill that is now pending in the Senate . . . I have a deep faith that *whatever may have been our sins of the past*, we are going to try to do our best in our lifetime, and we are making progress" (Johnson 1964i).

And, finally, in a powerful address to legislature of Georgia: "My ancestors felt free to ask their fellow Georgians for the help of their neighbors when they needed it. In the same way, I come here this morning at the invitation of your Governor to pay tribute and honor to your great legislature, and I come also to ask for your help and to *ask for your prayers* in a task that is shared by the people, sustained by the labor, and strengthened by the freedom of all the people of these United States. *In God's praise and under God's guidance*, let all of us resolve this morning to help heal the last fading scars of old battles. Let us match united wills to boundless means, so that many years from now men will say it was at that time, in that place of free men, that the possibilities of our past turned to the grandeur of our future" (Johnson 1964n).

In terms of sheer quantity of religious rhetoric, Johnson's campaign for civil rights legislation is almost unmatched. From the time he took office in November 1963 until when he signed the Civil Rights Act on July 2, 1964, LBJ hammered home a religious rationale for civil rights. He did so by making Kennedy a martyr, by citing the Golden Rule, by warning of Old Testament style judgment, and by virtue of generalized moral claims. All of these themes were the product of a conscious choice Johnson had made to, as he put it, make people "feel guilty." And, like every case in this book, Johnson made the decision to turn to religious rhetoric in a time of crisis.

As we have seen, both Kennedy and Johnson made strong religious arguments for the bill over the course of the time period between June 1963 and July 1964. As such, it makes sense to treat the efforts of each Administration as one continuous campaign. The question that we now turn to is how much did these rhetorical constructions matter? The answer is less than some might think.

The opinion data that is available does not suggest that religious rhetoric was of much use to either man. Both Kennedy and Johnson delivered major addresses on civil rights, Kennedy on June 11, 1963, and Johnson on November 27 and 28, 1963. It is impossible to estimate what impact Johnson's addresses may have had on his approval; Gallup's first poll was not taken until December 5. But for Kennedy his June 11 address probably hurt him. Kennedy's approval rating before the address, measured on May 23, was 64 percent. In the first poll taken after the address, Kennedy clocked in at 61 percent on June 21 (Ragsdale 2009, 230). This margin of decline is not enough to be statistically significant. However, there is additional evidence that taking a strong position on civil rights worked to Kennedy's detriment.

For instance, Kennedy's own data showed an immediate decline in his standing following his address. Although no one has ever located the specific source, Kennedy told civil rights leaders gathered at the White House on June 22 that he had just been given a new poll that showed approval of his administration had fallen from 60 to 47 percent (Dallek 2003, 642).

Further, as Figure 5.1 illustrates, beginning in late May, Kennedy's approval gradually fell about ten points by September. Civil rights had a lot to do with this change. An October *Newsweek* poll estimated that about 4.5 million White voters had abandoned Kennedy as a consequence of civil rights, leading the researchers to report that the issue might cost him re-election (O'Brien 2009, 164–65). Obviously, most of these defectors were from the South; Kennedy's approval in these states had dropped from 60 percent in March to 44 percent in September (Giglio 1991, 202). So, overall, Kennedy's religious arguments for civil rights do not appear to have protected him from the political fallout from his proposals.

Figure 5.1
Kennedy 1963 public approval

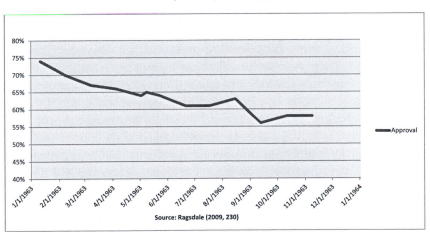

Source: Ragsdale (2009, 230)

Issue-specific data is even harder to come by. Few identical questions on civil rights were asked and no question was asked with a frequency that would allow us to gain meaningful traction on the change in opinion over this roughly one-year period. It must be said that there is some hint that Kennedy and Johnson's religious rhetoric may have benefited their cause. On three occasions, in June 1963, August 1963, and January 1964, Gallup asked the following: "How would you feel about a law which would give all persons—Negro as well as white—the right to be served in public places such as hotels, restaurants, theaters, and similar establishments—would you like to see Congress pass such a law, or not?" Over the course of those three readings, those responding "yes" increased from 49 to 54 to 61 percent (Gallup Organization 1963a, 1963b, 1964). How much we can take from this finding is debatable, though, as more comprehensive analysis on civil rights opinion must make us question the influence of any president's rhetoric.

Borrowing from Victor Hugo, Republican Senate leader Everett Dirksen (R-IL) said in 1964: "Stronger than all the armies is an idea whose time has come." The story of civil rights opinion is one of a consistent and gradual movement toward increasing tolerance. Support for school integration, for example, was 31 percent in 1942, 50 percent in 1956, 66 percent in 1963, 71 percent in 1965, 76 percent in 1970, 88 percent in 1980, and 93 percent in 1985. Questions on related issues like public accommodations, employment, and housing segregation reveal similar trends. Unlike some other issues like foreign policy, when it comes to civil rights there is scant evidence of dramatic changes in opinion that can be associated with specific events. The trend toward integration is visible even well before the landmark *Brown v Board of Education* school desegregation ruling in 1954 (Page and Shapiro 1992, 69).

What seems most likely is that Kennedy and Johnson's moralizing did not convince people that the "time had come" for civil rights; rather, people were in the process of finally realizing that truth for themselves. Indeed, the causal relationship between Kennedy's rhetoric and civil rights opinion is likely the inverse. Kennedy's words did not cause opinion to change; opinion caused his words to change. Kennedy's public statements contained few references to civil rights prior to 1963. It was only when public opinion began to indicate that civil rights had become an issue of national, instead of regional, importance did Kennedy's rhetoric become more supportive of the cause (Stevens 2002).

As far as the media goes, the editorial reaction that greeted Kennedy's June civil rights address was rather muted. Over the course of the

Table 5.1
Editorial coverage of Kennedy's June 11, 1963 civil rights speech

Date	Paper	Author	Title	Score
6/12/63	*New York Times*	James Reston	"Kennedy and King Canute of Alabama"	4
6/12/63	*New York Times*	Staff Editorial	"Troops at Tuscaloosa"	5
6/12/63	*Washington Post*	Roscoe Drummond	"Will the Bill Pass?"	3
6/13/63	*New York Times*	Staff Editorial	"Racial Assassination"	5
6/14/63	*New York Times*	James Reston	"A Time for Reflection and Vigilant Calm"	3
6/14/63	*New York Times*	Cabell Phillips	"New Rights Legislation"	3
6/14/63	*Washington Post*	Chalmers Roberts	"Today's Race Issue Moves Senate . . ."	3
6/16/63	*New York Times*	Staff Editorial	"Civil Rights: 'The Fiery Trial'"	5
6/16/63	*New York Times*	James Reston	"No Longer a 'Problem' but a Revolution"	2
6/16/63	*Los Angeles Times*	Sen. Barry Goldwater	"Kennedy Should Settle the Race Issue . . ."	1
6/17/63	*Washington Post*	Joseph Alsop	"Politics and the Race Crisis"	3
6/18/63	*New York Times*	Staff Editorial	"Equal Rights, Not Politics"	5
6/18/63	*Los Angeles Times*	Roscoe Drummond	"Hope of Avoiding Race Violence Rises . . ."	5
Dates: 6/12 to 6/18			**Average score**	**3.62**
			Positive articles	**6 (46.2%)**
			Negative articles	**2 (15.4%)**
			Mixed/neutral articles	**5 (38.5%)**

subsequent week, just thirteen editorials appeared in the four major papers under study (Table 5.1). Kennedy's civil rights proposals were somewhat overshadowed by other important events that were taking place at the same time. Some writers chose to focus their columns on Kennedy's foreign policy address at American University. Others stuck to discussing George Wallace's antics without mentioning Kennedy's legislative response. Others preferred to ride their normal horses; on June 12 the fiscally conservative *Chicago Tribune* (1963) printed a staff editorial on tax policy, not on civil rights.

What little commentary appeared was slightly positive; the average score of these articles was 3.62. But, this score also indicates that the enthusiasm was tempered. For sure, different outlets heaped praise on Kennedy's rhetoric. The *New York Times* (1963a) wrote that Kennedy "spoke both to and for the American conscience in his moving address." By making his moral commitment clear, the paper claimed, it would become less likely that "there will be . . . battles in the street to establish the rights that are an American's by birth."

In a follow-up editorial, the *Times* argued that Kennedy's speech "matched his magnificent Inaugural Address in idealism and fervor" and applauded the "luminousness of his challenge to the white conscience" (*New York Times* 1963b). The *Times* board printed two additional editorials that week supporting Kennedy (*New York Times* 1963c, 1963d).

In truth, not a single author came out in express opposition to Kennedy's call for new civil rights laws. What held the praise back was only a sober estimation of the challenges facing Kennedy's program. For example, Joseph Alsop (1963) worried that the end result of the racial crisis would be a marked increase in the strength of the conservative coalition, to the detriment of many of Kennedy's goals. James Reston (1963), on the other hand, thought that continued demonstrations might fracture the emerging consensus for civil rights.

There is even less to say about the media reaction to Johnson's speeches on civil rights following Kennedy's death. Only nine editorials made reference to the new president's remarks (Table 5.2). The editorial silence is easily explained; Kennedy had barely been laid to rest at the time. Indeed, some of the commentary that did appear seemed ready to write off the remainder of the year altogether. As the *Los Angeles Times* (1963b) wrote, "Most major legislation is dead for this session, as the President knows. While he forcefully appealed for passage of Mr. Kennedy's top requests, Mr. Johnson set no timetable. In this he was being only realistic" (see also Donovan 1963). Whatever little commentary there was slanted in favor of the president; Johnson averaged a 4.11 score—though, again, that number is based on just nine articles.

Table 5.2
Editorial coverage of Johnson's first Congressional address and his Thanksgiving speech

Date	Paper	Author	Title	Score
11/28/63	*New York Times*	Staff Editorial	"A Time for Action"	3
11/28/63	*New York Times*	James Reston	"The Office and the Man"	5
11/29/63	*New York Times*	Staff Editorial	"A Strong Start"	5
11/29/63	*Los Angeles Times*	Staff Editorial	"The President and the Congress"	3
11/30/63	*Chicago Tribune*	Walter Trohan	"Pause for Mourning, Then Politics Goes On"	2
12/1/63	*New York Times*	Staff Editorial	"Look Now to the Future"	4
12/1/63	*Washington Post*	Robert Estabrook	"Civil Rights Aid View of Johnson"	5
12/1/63	*Los Angeles Times*	Robert Donovan	"Formidable Candidate Shaping Up"	5
12/3/63	*New York Times*	Staff Editorial	"Too Much Delay on Civil Rights"	5
Dates: 11/28 to 12/4			**Average score**	**4.11**
			Positive articles	**6 (66.7%)**
			Negative articles	**1 (11.1%)**
			Mixed/neutral articles	**2 (22.2%)**

Still, the positive reaction to Johnson's civil rights speeches was to be expected and likely had little to do with anything that he said. Johnson, as a new president taking office under tragic circumstances, was the beneficiary of a pronounced honeymoon period. His first approval rating was 78 percent (Ragsdale 2009, 230). This is natural. Every new president begins with a period free of the criticism of the media, other politicians and the public (Erikson and Tedin 2011, 119–20).

The country is remarkably fair about giving its new leaders a chance. Therefore, Johnson's positive media coverage had little to do with the religious rhetoric he used in support of civil rights and much more to do with the timing of his speeches.

Finally, we can hazard some guesses about the extent of the impact of JFK's and LBJ's religious rhetoric on Congress. On November 20, the Judiciary Committee in the House approved Kennedy's bill by a 20-14 vote, a significant early victory. Would Kennedy ultimately have gotten the law—or at least something resembling it—through Congress had he lived? It is difficult to say, but there is ample reason to doubt it.

For one, Kennedy's advocacy for civil rights poisoned his relations with Congress. Shortly after Kennedy's June address, Carl Albert (D-OK) told him that the White House had lost an important vote on a public works bill in retaliation and that civil rights was threatening to overwhelm other bills on mass transit and agriculture as well. In 1963, Congress passed 27 percent of Kennedy's proposals, one of the lowest percentages in modern times (Rorabaugh 2002, 116).

Two, after leaving the Judiciary Committee, the bill was then referred to the Rules Committee, chaired by Howard Smith (D-VA), an arch segregationist. In 1957, with civil rights legislation pending before his committee, Smith had simply disappeared, ostensibly returning to his farm to examine fire damage to one of his barns. A Republican on the committee wryly noted, "I knew the Judge (Smith) was opposed to the civil rights bill. But I didn't think he would commit arson to beat it" (Bernstein 1996, 48).

Needless to say, Smith vowed never to let Kennedy's civil rights package reach the House floor. But if Smith succeeded only in stalling its passage, that might have been enough. The upcoming elections in 1964 would have likely changed the political calculations for many members, reducing their willingness to cast a risky vote. And, even if the bill had made it through the House, the more formidable prospect of defeating a Senate filibuster still loomed.

Three, owing to the above realities, Kennedy immediately began preparing himself and others to accept a watered down law. Senate Democratic leader Mike Mansfield (D-MT) had advised the president to abandon the public accommodations section of the bill in order to speed adoption of the rest of it. "The assumption is that it is better to secure passage of as much of the Administration's legislative proposals on civil rights as is possible rather than to run the very real risk of losing all in an effort to obtain all," Mansfield told Kennedy (Dallek 2003, 641).

Fear of making such a bargain more difficult led Kennedy to initially oppose the great March on Washington in August. He reluctantly collaborated once he accepted its inevitability. At a meeting with civil rights leaders subsequent to the day's activities, however, Kennedy deliberately scaled back expectations. He presented those in attendance with his staff's projected vote count. The picture was not pretty, especially in the upper chamber. By October, Kennedy was so depressed over this lack of progress that he privately confessed he "felt like packing his bags and leaving" (648).

Of course, Johnson faced the same obstacles. Yet, he had better success overcoming them. The legislative process for the Civil Rights Act was tortuous, marked by a blizzard of arcane legislative maneuvers. But the short history of the Civil Rights Act is that it was a smashing victory for the new president. The bill passed 290 to 130 in the House in February, and 73 to 27 in the Senate in June after months of filibustering. Both tallies featured bipartisan support. Johnson was intimately involved in the process of assembling these majorities.

But as far as the impact of religious rhetoric goes, it is crucial to keep one fact in mind. Both Kennedy and Johnson offered similar, and similarly religious, rationales for the bill. Kennedy struggled mightily in Congress. He was pessimistic about his chances at the time of his death and the forecast for the bill looked bleak. Johnson, in contrast, steamrolled his opposition. Basic social science tells us a constant (the same style of religious rhetoric) cannot explain a variable (the different outcomes in Congress). If each president used the same argument, the argument cannot explain why one had more success in Congress than the other. Other factors, like Johnson's superior bargaining skills and Kennedy's death, loom as far more important to the bill's final triumph than the religious arguments that were made for it.

The truth is the legislative history of civil rights parallels the evolution of public opinion. Scholars have tended to treat the years between the two "reconstructions," generally speaking the 1880s to 1950s, as a time when civil rights disappeared from the public agenda. However, from 1900 until 1940 Congress debated well over a hundred bills that would have protected Blacks from lynching and other forms of mob violence. In three cases, a bill passed the House only to fail in the Senate owing to Southern obstructionism. The legislative progress toward the Civil Rights Act was much more gradual than one might think (Jenkins, Peck, and Weaver 2010). The time had come for civil rights in Congress, just like it had come for them in the public.

Conclusion

The Civil Rights Act was signed in a jubilant ceremony on July 2, 1964. Johnson gave a television address to mark the occasion (Johnson 1964s). In his speech, the president told the country that the significance of the law was that "those who are equal before God shall now also be equal in the polling booths, in the classrooms, in the factories, and in hotels, restaurants, movie theaters, and other places that provide service to the public." Knowing that passing the law did not mean the nation's work was complete, Johnson asked, "Let us close the springs of racial poison. Let us pray for wise and understanding hearts. Let us lay aside irrelevant differences and make our Nation whole. Let us hasten that day when our unmeasured strength and our unbounded spirit will be free to do the great works ordained for this Nation by the just and wise God who is the Father of us all."

The sentiments Johnson offered on this occasion were entirely in keeping with what he, and President Kennedy, had been saying about civil rights for the past year. The two presidents had campaigned for civil rights by referencing morality and conscience, by citing Scripture, by creating martyrs, by warning of heavenly judgment, and by calling for days of prayer. Few policies were ever couched in stronger religious terms.

This is one case where it is tempting to ascribe an important role to religious rhetoric. However, a closer examination must lead us to question whether these types of claims had any sort of discernable impact. In terms of approval, although Johnson's speeches cannot fairly be analyzed, Kennedy's religious rhetoric on June 11 did not provide any boost and, indeed, may actually have caused a deterioration in his support instead. When it comes to opinion on the issue, the greater likelihood is not that religious rhetoric was persuasive, but that American attitudes were in the midst of a long term, gradual movement toward greater acceptance.

In terms of the media, none of the major speeches attracted much attention. Johnson's coverage may have been positive, but this was expected given the typical media response to a president in a honeymoon period.

Finally, in Congress, each president made the same kind of religious arguments, which makes it very doubtful that this language was important to the outcome. Johnson was much more successful than Kennedy, even though they embraced the same religious themes. Other factors are, therefore, needed to explain the difference.

In the end, the passage of the Civil Rights Act of 1964 was a tremendous achievement for both men and one that they each deserve some amount of credit for. But this chapter concludes there is little reason to suspect that in another universe, where religious arguments were not made, the result would have been any different.

Notes

1. Even so, the impact of these appointments was somewhat nullified by the many segregationists Kennedy also appointed to the bench in the South (Dallek 2003, 493–94, 590–91).

2. Interestingly, Johnson also appeared to view himself as somewhat of a martyr. In his interviews with Doris Kearns, Johnson frequently lamented the fact that he had to sacrifice his presidency for Vietnam—and that he received no credit for doing so. "I knew from the start that I was bound to be crucified either way I moved. If I left the woman I really loved—the Great Society—in order to get involved with that bitch of a war on the other side of the world, then I would lose everything at home. All my programs. All my hopes to feed the hungry and shelter the homeless. All my dreams to provide education and medical care to the browns and the Blacks and the lame and the poor. But if I left that war and let the Communists take over South Vietnam, then I would be seen as a coward and my nation would be seen as an appeaser and we would find it impossible to accomplish anything for anybody anywhere on the entire globe" (Kearns 1976, 251–52). Genuinely believing these things, Johnson confessed in the dark days of the war, "It's hard to sleep these days. I'm beginning to feel like a martyr; misunderstood, misjudged by friends at home and abroad" (Dallek 1998, 259).

6

I Have Sinned: Gerald Ford, Bill Clinton, and the Religious Rhetoric of Scandal

The fundamental goal of the Christian faith is to be saved from one's sins. And while Muslims and Jews may not share the same goal of salvation, they do share with Christians some concern about sin (Prothero 2010). As a result, the day-to-day practices of many religions have been structured around how to deal with this problem. For example, as far back as the sixth century, Irish monks wrote handbooks for the Catholic faithful to use as reference materials so that they could identify all the different ways in which they had sinned, and then know the appropriate ways to atone for them (Weaver 2003).

Of course, presidents sin, too. Any timeline of presidential history is a timeline of inevitable presidential scandal. The Petticoat Affair. Credit Mobilier. Teapot Dome. Sherman Adams. Bert Lance. Iran-Contra. Valerie Plame. These events can be thought of as the sins of presidents and their associates. Thus, it makes sense that presidents would draw on religious language as they attempt to make things right with the American people.

This chapter will consider two such rhetorical strategies. The first part of the chapter will identify and analyze the religious rhetoric Gerald Ford used as justification for his explosive decision to pardon the former president, Richard Nixon, for all Watergate-related criminal activity. Ford would discuss the importance of being merciful, a concept with great religious power, and would frame the pardon as a matter between him and God.

The second part of the chapter will highlight the religious rhetoric Bill Clinton used after earlier attempts to dismiss his affair with Monica Lewinsky had failed. Clinton would talk about forgiveness, playing upon the Lord's Prayer as he did so. He would explain that his errors could be a blessing for the country. He would prefer religious words like "atone" and "repentance" over secular alternatives.

However, the conclusion of this chapter will be the same as that of the previous four: Ford and Clinton's religiosity would all be for naught. In fact, there is strong reason to believe their choice of words actually made matters worse for each man.

Gerald Ford and the Nixon Pardon

Gerald Ford died on December 26, 2006. Ford's passing was accompanied by glowing appraisals of his time in office, all of which highlighted the bold foresight Ford had displayed when he pardoned President Richard Nixon in September 1974. Praise for the pardon was freely offered by leading political figures ranging from Republican Bob Dole (2006) to liberal Justice John Paul Stevens (Stout and Zeleny 2006).

In truth, the perception of the pardon had begun to change well before Ford's death. The best evidence of this change was that in 2001 Ford received the John F. Kennedy Profile in Courage award for his decision. Senator Ted Kennedy made the presentation. Kennedy had been a fierce critic of the pardon at the time. Now, with the benefit of hindsight, Kennedy had a different view: "President Ford recognized that the nation had to get on with its business and could not, if there was a continuing effort to prosecute the former president Nixon. So he made a tough decision and pardoned Richard Nixon. I was one of those who spoke out against his action. But time has a way of clarifying things, and now we see he was right" (Feldman 2002).

It is instructive to compare the acclaim surrounding the pardon in 2006 with the reaction that it originally provoked in 1974 (Berthelsen 1974). The *New York Times* (1974a) argued that Ford had "failed in his duty to the Republic, made a mockery of the claim of equal justice before the law, promoted renewed historical discord, made possible the clouding of the historical record, and undermined the humane values he sought to invoke." When the president appeared in Pittsburgh the day after, an angry crowd greeted him with chants of "Jail Ford, Jail Ford, Jail Ford!" Ford's press secretary, Jerald terHorst, a friend of the president's for over a quarter of a century and his very first appointment, self-servingly resigned in protest. And so it went.

Ford chose a religious rhetorical strategy to persuade the country that the time had come to let go of Watergate. These anecdotes provide only the briefest glimpse at just how spectacularly this strategy failed.

Ford may not have been the most inspiring orator among the postwar presidents, but he was one of the most consistently religious. A devout Episcopalian, Ford was comfortable speaking the language of faith. He often demonstrated his aptitude for communitarian language when speaking about the nation's Bicentennial. In his speech in Philadelphia on July 4, 1976, Ford at some length explained the meaning of the little known Biblical verse found on the Liberty Bell (Ford 1976d). Ford located the Bicentennial in the Christian and Jewish calendars in the opening to his 1976 State of the Union address (Ford 1976a). He also made the event the dominant theme of his remarks to that year's national prayer breakfast (Ford 1976b) and religious broadcasters' convention (Ford 1976c).

Ford's religious rhetoric on Watergate, on the other hand, was quintessentially political. The word "Watergate" has morphed into a catchall term representing a variety of Nixon Administration misdeeds, including the illegal wiretapping of news reporters, the political abuse of the Internal Revenue Service, the creation of a White House "enemies list," and the raiding of the office of Daniel Ellsberg's psychiatrist. It was Ellsberg who had leaked the damaging Pentagon Papers, a document that exposed Vietnam War deceptions, to the press.

The break-in itself occurred in the early morning of Saturday, June 17, 1972. Acting on a night watchman's tip, Washington, DC police apprehended five men inside the Democratic National Committee (DNC) headquarters in the Watergate complex. The men were wearing surgical gloves and were attempting to install or modify electronic surveillance equipment inside the offices. Two other men were located across the street running logistics at the Howard Johnson Hotel.

Four of the men arrested in the DNC offices were past Cuban employees of the Central Intelligence Agency. The fifth, James McCord, was a former agent who was also the chief of security for the president's re-election organization, the Committee to Re-elect the President, later known by the unfortunate acronym CREEP. Howard Hunt and G. Gordon Liddy were the men across the street. Both had worked for the White House, and Liddy had been counsel to CREEP's finance committee. These lines running from the break-in back to the Administration were publicly revealed by Bob Woodward and Carl Bernstein in a *Washington Post* story two days later.

No one seemed to care at first. Nixon's contemptuous press secretary Ron Ziegler labeled the crime a "third-rate burglary attempt"—and this characterization seemed more apt to the public than George McGovern's claim that the Nixon White House was "the most corrupt

Administration in our national history." Despite the indictment of all seven of the perpetrators on September 15, Nixon cruised toward re-election. He would destroy McGovern 61 to 38 percent, losing only Massachusetts and the District of Columbia.

The good times would be short-lived. In February 1973, the Senate voted to establish the Select Committee on Presidential Campaign Activities, led by Democratic Senator Sam Ervin. Soon after, McCord wrote a letter to the judge presiding over his case, John Sirica, claiming that political pressure had been applied to coerce him and his fellow defendants into remaining silent. He alleged that others who had been involved had not been identified.

To some observers this was the turning point in the scandal. After Sirica's tough-love sentences were handed down on the Watergate defendants, Nixon's aides scrambled to negotiate deals with prosecutors. With pressure mounting, at the end of April, Nixon was forced to accept the resignations of H. R. Haldeman, his chief of staff; John Ehrlichman, his top domestic advisor; and Richard Kleindienst, his attorney general. By May, the Ervin committee had opened its hearings with damaging testimony from McCord and others. And in June, White House counsel John Dean testified that there had been a massive cover-up of the break-in, and Nixon himself had been at the center of it.

After the existence of a secret White House taping system was revealed in July, the scandal transitioned into a protracted fight for the tapes. Those tapes would prove who was telling the truth, Nixon or Dean. After negotiations over the tapes fell apart in October, Robert Bork, the No. 3 employee in the Justice Department, fired special prosecutor Archibald Cox on Nixon's orders after Attorney General Eliot Richardson and his subordinate William Ruckelshaus both had resigned rather than doing so. The resignations and the firing became known as the "Saturday Night Massacre." Impeachment at this point was close to inevitable.

The fight over which tapes would be provided and whether transcripts would be considered sufficient, however, continued well into the summer of 1974. But then on July 24, in a unanimous decision, the Supreme Court ruled in *United States of America v. Richard M. Nixon, President* that executive privilege cannot supersede the demands of due process and a fair administration of criminal justice. Nixon had to turn over the tapes.

On August 5, the White House released transcripts of the June 23, 1972 meetings between Nixon and Haldeman, the "smoking gun" tapes, which provided incontrovertible evidence that the two had conspired to block the probe of the Federal Bureau of Investigation into Watergate. Whatever support remained for Nixon was gone. The president announced his resignation at 9 p.m. on August 8. A little after noon the next day, Nixon flashed his famous "V" for victory signal and hopped in a helicopter, flying off into exile (Ambrose 1991).

Ford did not enter this story until the fall of 1973. At that time, Vice President Spiro Agnew was under investigation for crimes unrelated to Watergate. Prior to joining Nixon's team, Agnew had accepted more than $100,000 in kickbacks for public works contracts awarded while he was a Baltimore County executive and Governor of Maryland. Facing forty indictable charges, Agnew cut a deal and resigned on October 10. Nixon nominated Ford as his replacement three days later.

Ford was mostly kept in the dark about the happenings within the Nixon White House. His main role was to travel the country and make speeches proclaiming Nixon's innocence. Unfortunately for Ford, Watergate ultimately became his mess. It was up to him to move the country forward after over two years of scandal. This was arguably his most essential task as the new president.

Ford later remembered spending "about 25 percent of my time listening to lawyers argue what I should do with Mr. Nixon's papers, his tapes, et cetera. At the very same time, our country was faced with serious economic problems, inflation, higher interest rates, unemployment going up. And we had allies that were uncertain as to what would happen. And the Soviet Union—we never knew what they might do in this change of presidency" (Mieczkowski 2005, 30). Ford could not deal with any of these questions with the ghost of Watergate hovering over him.

Ford was stepping into a difficult situation in other ways as well (Werth 2006). His vice-presidency was unelected. Ford was confronted with the urgent task of building up the support he would need to govern and be re-elected in just two short years. "I have no solid coalition of support outside of southwestern Michigan and no working relationships outside of the House," Ford candidly acknowledged (Smith and Smith 1994b, 122). This was a reality that had to change if his presidency was to be successful.

So, again, the crisis condition is met. Ford was inheriting a country in turmoil owing to an unprecedented presidential scandal, pressing problems could not be addressed so long as that scandal lingered, and he had a meager political base from which to operate from. The stage was set for the appearance of religious rhetoric.

Ford began his campaign to move the country past Watergate with his first speech as president (Ford 1974a). Shortly after Nixon had departed, a select group gathered in the East Room of the White House to witness Ford's swearing in by Chief Justice Warren Burger. The speech is mainly remembered for Ford's classic line, "My fellow Americans, our long national nightmare is over." But it was also an address packed with powerful religious references.

Ford began by noting the unusual circumstances. Reflecting on the fact that he had not been elected, Ford beseeched the country for its spiritual support instead: "I am acutely aware that you have not elected me as your President by your ballots, and so I ask you to confirm me as your President with your prayers. And I hope that such prayers will also be the first of many."

After some brief comments on the type of relationships he wished to construct with Congress and the world, Ford made a sincere plea for mercy on the behalf of Nixon:

> Our Constitution works; our great Republic is a government of laws and not of men. Here the people rule. But there is a higher Power, by whatever name we honor Him, who ordains not only righteousness but love, not only justice but mercy.[1]

> As we bind up the internal wounds of Watergate, more painful and more poisonous than those of foreign wars, let us restore the golden rule to our political process, and let brotherly love purge our hearts of suspicion and of hate.

> In the beginning, I asked you to pray for me. Before closing, I ask again your prayers, for Richard Nixon and for his family. May our former President, who brought peace to millions, find it for himself. May God bless and comfort his wonderful wife and daughters, whose love and loyalty will forever be a shining legacy to all who bear the lonely burdens of the White House.

This section of the address was a brave choice. By speaking openly about his former boss, Ford was reminding the country that he, too, had been a member of the fallen Administration. Nevertheless, Ford calls for the country to be merciful toward Nixon, reminding the public that "a higher Power" demands this of them.

Mercy is an unmistakable religious theme (Metzger and Coogan 1993, 512–13). Often, in the Bible, mercy is depicted as an attribute of God, who will be merciful toward his flock and forgive their sins (Exodus 34:6–7; Psalm 86:15). For humans, mercy means taking compassion on the downtrodden, particularly when their suffering is undeserved. In many instances, Jesus acts in a merciful way himself. A woman whose daughter is tormented by a demon requested Christ's mercy and, after her persistence, he healed the child (Matthew 15:21–28). A father asked Christ to have mercy on his epileptic son and Jesus cured him, too (Matthew 17:14–20). Jesus also cleansed ten lepers (Luke 17:11–19) and restored sight to a blind man (Luke 18:35–43), simply because they had faith and called for his mercy.

The link between the two Biblical themes—God's mercy and Christ's acts of mercy—is that Jesus was teaching his followers that if they want mercy from God, they need to grant it first. In the parable of the unforgiving servant (Matthew 18:23–35), Jesus tells the story of a king settling accounts with his slaves. One man owed him a great sum that he could not pay, so the king ordered that the man, his wife, his children, and all his possessions be sold. The man begged for patience, and the king relented, forgiving the debt. However, that same slave later encountered a fellow servant owing him money, but he refused the other man's pleas for leniency. When the king found out, he grew angry and had the slave tortured. The message of the parable lies in the question the king asked, "Should you not have had mercy on your fellow slave, as I had mercy on you?" (see also James 2:13; Matthew 5:7).

By speaking forcefully about the need for mercy, Ford's rhetoric transfused with religious precepts that a majority of Americans would be familiar with. Lord have mercy. Christ have mercy. One can hear these sayings in churches across the country every single Sunday. As we shall soon see, Ford would return to this specific argument on several later occasions when speaking about his ultimate move to pardon Nixon.

In the section excerpted above, Ford also invokes the Biblical terminology of the golden rule when he asks for an infusion of "brotherly love" into the country's politics. In a sense, these words stand as a denunciation of Nixon and his dirty tricks. It would be hard to say that Nixon treated others as he wished to be treated himself. "Suspicion" and "hate" came to define Nixon's political career.

Ford was making this point, though, in a forward-looking manner. Ford was not fixated on the lessons of the past; rather, he was highlighting what the country could do in the future "As we bind up the internal wounds of Watergate." This, of course, was Ford's intent.

Therefore, these phrases have another purpose; a call for *everyone* to let bygones be bygones, to, again, show compassion for Nixon and in doing so to "purge our hearts of . . . hate" that we felt for *him*. Hence, the usage of the concepts of brotherly love and the golden rule has two effects; it reminded the audience that Nixon failed to do these things while asking that they not repeat the former president's mistakes themselves.

At his first press conference on August 28, Ford (1974c) revealed that he was open to a pardon: "I am not ruling it out. It is an option and a proper option for any President." He refused to commit to issuing one, saying only that he would consider the matter later. However, Ford had apparently already concluded that a pardon was his only road out of the Watergate morass. Ford's thinking on the matter had evolved since he unequivocally stated his opposition to a pardon at his confirmation hearings in 1973.

Before ascending to the office, Ford had met with Alexander Haig, Haldeman's replacement as chief of staff, on August 1, 1974. Haig laid out a number of possible scenarios for the upcoming weeks, the final one being that Nixon would agree to leave office in return for a promise of a pardon. Ford did not immediately reject the idea, but he did call Haig the following day, with witnesses present, to emphasize that there would be no deal.

The situation was no less complicated a month later. Ford knew that a preemptive pardon, made before Nixon had been put to trial, would hint that a bargain had been made. Ford felt he had to take this risk anyways. He later remarked, "I felt I had come to the conclusion that I had an obligation—which was my own decision—to spend 100 percent of my time on the problems of 230 million people, rather than 25% of my time on the problems of one man" (Brinkley 2007, 73).

The only issue unresolved was how to present his decision. Early on the morning of Sunday, September 8, the White House informed the press to expect a major announcement from the president. Ford proceeded to take Communion during services at St. John's Episcopal Church in Washington. "I wanted to go to church and pray for guidance and understanding before making the announcement," Ford said (Cannon 1994, 382). He specifically chose to speak on Sunday, it was later revealed, to symbolically represent that the pardon was an act of mercy (Herbers 1974). As Ford left the church, a reporter asked him what was up. Ford cryptically answered, "You will find out soon enough" (Greene 1995, 52). At 11:00 a.m., the president appeared on national television in a prerecorded broadcast (Ford 1974d).

Two things immediately jump out about this speech. The first is how consistently Ford framed his decision to pardon Nixon as a matter between him and his God. In fact, Ford's opening line was, "I have come to a decision which I felt I should tell you and all of my fellow American citizens, as soon as I was certain in my own mind and in my own conscience that it is the right thing to do." Later, in a key section, Ford continued along this line of reasoning:

> I have asked your help and your prayers, not only when I became President but many times since. The Constitution is the supreme law of our land and it governs our actions as citizens. Only the laws of God, which govern our consciences, are superior to it.
>
> As we are a nation under God, so I am sworn to uphold our laws with the help of God. And I have sought such guidance and searched my own conscience with special diligence to determine the right thing for me to do with respect to my predecessor in this place, Richard Nixon, and his loyal wife and family.
>
> Theirs is an American tragedy in which we all have played a part. It could go on and on and on, or someone must write the end to it. I have concluded that only I can do that, and if I can, I must.

Further into the speech, Ford would again emphasize how much of a role his conscience played in leading him to this decision.

> As President, my primary concern must always be the greatest good of all the people of the United States whose servant I am. As a man, my first consideration is to be true to my own convictions and my own conscience.
>
> My conscience tells me clearly and certainly that I cannot prolong the bad dreams that continue to reopen a chapter that is closed. My conscience tells me that only I, as President, have the constitutional power to firmly shut and seal this book. My conscience tells me it is my duty, not merely to proclaim domestic tranquility but to use every means that I have to insure it.
>
> I do believe that the buck stops here, that I cannot rely upon public opinion polls to tell me what is right.
>
> I do believe that right makes might and that if I am wrong, 10 angels swearing I was right would make no difference.

The word "conscience" appears in the body of the speech seven times. "God" is used five times. Ford presented the pardon as a decision made on the basis of prayer, not on political or judicial considerations.

Ford was claiming that his relationship with God more or less made the decision for him. His conscience could allow nothing else. It was a provocative argument to make. Every American would have an opinion on what should happen to Nixon now that he had abdicated his office. But Ford was almost saying that only his own sense of morality counted.

The second significant aspect of this speech is that Ford reiterated the pleas for mercy that he had first made on August 9. At various times throughout the address, Ford spoke of a number of hardships that continued prosecution would impose on the former president. Ford pointed out, "it is common knowledge that serious allegations and accusations hang like a sword over our former President's head, threatening his health as he tries to reshape his life, a great part of which was spent in the service of this country and by the mandate of its people." He argued that in a public trial, "instead of enjoying equal treatment with any other citizen accused of violating the law, (Nixon) would be cruelly and excessively penalized either in preserving the presumption of his innocence or in obtaining a speedy determination of his guilt in order to repay a legal debt to society." Ford also expressed his opinion "that Richard Nixon and his loved ones have suffered enough and will continue to suffer, no matter what I do, no matter what we, as a great and good nation, can do together to make his goal of peace come true."

Having built up sympathy for Nixon with these references to the ex-president's health, to a trial being a cruel and excessive penalty, and to his suffering, Ford finally made the point that if we want mercy from God ourselves, we must be prepared to give it first. "I do believe, with all my heart and mind and spirit, that I, not as President but as a humble servant of God, will receive justice without mercy if I fail to show mercy," Ford said. Listeners at home were once more led to make the connection that not only Ford, but they, too, had to be merciful toward Nixon.

One hint that this was a strategic argument lies in what Ford did *not* say. Ford's real reasons for issuing the pardon had little to do with the dictates of his own conscience and everything to do with the burden Nixon's unresolved status was placing on his administration. Ford's own words serve as testament to that fact. But Ford did not talk about the 25 percent of his time that he was spending on the problems of one man. He talked about religion instead, presumably because he felt the American people would be more receptive to such thinking.

The pardon speech is one of the most religious speeches in all of American presidential history; from its setting, on a Sunday morning right after the president had gone to worship, to its abundant references to God, conscience, and mercy. As the later opinion and media analyses will show, the speech should be considered a public relations disaster. It must be acknowledged, though, that this is likely at least partly owing to the surprise nature of the announcement.

White House staffers unanimously agreed that the suddenness of the pardon undercut Ford's credibility with the press and the public (Rozell 1993, 465–76). Ford was thought to be an open politician and the pardon had been a closed process. As a Ford aide, John Hushen, admitted, "we delivered it to the country like Pearl Harbor" (467). It was this kind of lack of acuity with the press that allowed Ford, an all-American lineman at Michigan and the most athletic man ever to sit in the Oval Office, to become caricaturized as a stumbling klutz.

Regardless, the pardon had made a bad situation worse and Ford spun into damage control. Ford held his second press conference on September 16 (Ford 1974e). The conference was nationally televised. As Ford remembers, he was "hoping to explain the pardon rationale more clearly" (Ford 1979, 180). The pardon dominated the questioning; seventeen of the twenty-two questions had at least something to do with Nixon. Before any of those questions could be posed, however, Ford opened the conference with an unusual statement:

> Ladies and gentlemen, this press conference is being held at a time when many Americans are observing the Jewish religious New Year. It begins a period of self-examination and reconciliation. In opening this press conference, I am mindful that the spirit of this holy day has a meaning for all Americans.
>
> In examining one's deeds of the last year and in assuming responsibility for past actions and personal decisions, one can reach a point of growth and change. The purpose of looking back is to go forward with a new and enlightened dedication to our highest values.
>
> The record of the past year does not have to be endlessly relived, but can be transformed by commitment to new insights and new actions in the year to come.
>
> Ladies and gentlemen, I am ready for your questions.

Ford, like Clinton after him (see later in this chapter), had branched into religious rhetoric outside the bounds of Christianity. The president's mention of the Jewish New Year was a reference to start of the High Holy Days that began with Rosh Hashanah, an observance falling on the same day as the press conference. As Ford correctly said, for

Jewish Americans, the following ten days would be ten days of prayer, repentance, and self-examination. This is not necessarily a joyous time for Jews, but a serious one, a time in which they think deeply about their relationship with God and consider ways that they can better themselves in the year to come. The Rosh Hashanah service itself is marked by the sounding of a shofar, an ancient wind instrument made from the horn of a ram. This call symbolizes worshippers being reawakened to their moral responsibilities.

By making a rhetorical connection between the pardon and these religious rituals, Ford was re-emphasizing his message that it was time to move beyond Watergate, time to, metaphorically speaking, begin a "new year." All of his comments in this opening statement were forward-looking. For instance, "The purpose of looking back is to go forward with a new and enlightened dedication to our highest values." Or, "The record of the past year does not have to be endlessly relived, but can be transformed by commitment to new insights and new actions in the year to come."

During the conference, Ford did stress the fact that the distractions a trial would pose were the primary reason he granted Nixon a pardon. However, he also continued to prioritize the role his own conscience played in the decision-making process. In response to one query, Ford defended himself by claiming "Every action I have taken . . . is predicated on my conscience without any concern or consideration as to favor as far as I am concerned." Toward the end of the availability, Ford emphasized, "And since I was the only one who could make that decision, I thought I had to search my own soul after consulting with a limited number of people."

Nevertheless, Ford was unsuccessful in his efforts to quiet the unrest his actions had caused. In mid-September, Congresswoman Bella Abzug (D-NY) led a group of representatives who submitted a House resolution calling for more information on the pardon. John Conyers (D-MI) followed suit with a similar resolution of his own. William Hungate (D-MO), chair of the Judiciary Committee's Subcommittee on Criminal Justice, responded to these resolutions with a written request to the president, asking that he answer a number of specific questions. Ignoring the advice of almost all of his staff, Ford agreed to respond to the questions in person before the Committee. This was a move almost without historical precedent; no president had testified in person before Congress in the post-Civil War era (Greene 1995, 57).

The two-hour hearing was held on October 17 and was broadcast live nationally (Ford 1974f). Ford opened the hearing with a lengthy statement. He had made a strong religious argument by the sixth paragraph:

> We would needlessly be diverted from meeting those challenges if we as a people were to remain sharply divided over whether to indict, bring to trial, and punish a former President, who already is condemned to suffer long and deeply in the shame and disgrace brought upon the office he held. Surely, we are not a revengeful people. We have often demonstrated a readiness to feel compassion and to act out of mercy. As a people, we have a long record of forgiving even those who have been our country's most destructive foes.
>
> Yet, to forgive is not to forget the lessons of evil in whatever ways evil has operated against us. And certainly the pardon granted the former President will not cause us to forget the evils of Watergate-type offenses or to forget the lessons we have learned that a government which deceives its supporters and treats its opponents as enemies must never, never be tolerated.

On yet another high-profile occasion, Ford had emphasized the importance of being merciful. Mainly, though, the questioning and Ford's comments focused on precise issues of information, dates, etc. Mostly, the appearance was cordial, with the exception of freshman Representative Elizabeth Holtzman (D-NY) who berated the president with a series of long-winded, accusatory "questions." In a climactic moment, Ford interrupted the Congresswoman's tirade with visible anger, pounding the table as he exclaimed, "there was no deal, period, under no circumstances."

After his testimony, Ford did not exert much more effort in defense of the pardon. Ford had certainly used a religious rhetorical strategy up until then. His public statements on Nixon repeatedly diverged from his actual rationale for pardoning the ex-president, highlighting religious ideals like mercy and conscience over the argument that the prospect of a trial was occupying too much of his and the country's important time. But, as I've alluded to throughout this section, neither the public, nor the press, nor Congress was buying it.

Most damaging to Ford in the long term was the impact that the pardon had on his public approval. As the trend lines in Figure 6.1 show, the pardon triggered a steep decline in Ford's support that he never recovered from. In Gallup's first poll, Americans approved of Ford's performance after one week in office by a margin of 71 to 3 percent. By September 27, Ford was down to 50 percent. He had fallen twenty-one

Figure 6.1
Ford August 1974–March 1975 approval

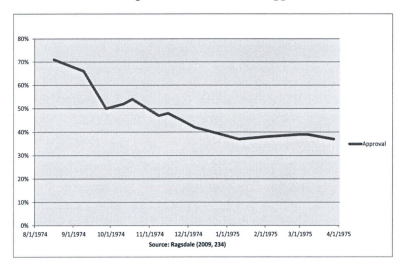

Source: Ragsdale (2009, 234)

points. Ford's religious rhetoric announcing the pardon on September 8 was met with a swift decline in his approval. Despite Ford's articulation of religious arguments on national television on a number of occasions—the press conference on September 16, his Congressional testimony on October 17—the tide did not change.

Issue-specific data are limited in this case. Yet, what is available is revealing. In a survey taken the week of September 6, two days before the pardon would be issued, Louis Harris and Associates (1974a) asked the public, "Do you think President Ford should pardon former President Nixon on the grounds he has suffered enough, or do you think such a pardon would be wrong?" Respondents opposed a pardon made for this reason by a margin of 57 to 35 percent.

After the pardon was granted, Harris and Associates (1974b) asked whether survey participants felt that Ford's actions were "right or wrong?" Sixty percent of respondents said the pardon was "wrong," while only 33 percent of people said it was "right." These numbers are similar to the data collected right before the pardon, indicating that Ford's religious justifications had failed to change many minds.

Other outlets reported similar findings. Roper Organization (1974) found that 54 percent of people disapproved of the pardon at the end of September versus the 30 percent who approved of it. The results continued to be stable throughout the coming months. Over the first week of November, Harris and Associates (1974c) again asked the interviewees how they felt about the pardon. Sixty-one percent gave Ford negative marks for it; thirty-three percent gave the president positive marks for it.

What emerges then is a picture of a public that opposed a pardon by a margin of about 60 to 35 percent over the duration of Ford's religious rhetorical strategy. His pleas to be merciful seem to have been ignored. Worst of all for Ford is that opinion on his overall objective, ending Watergate, went against him as well. In that same final survey, Harris also asked whether participants agreed or disagreed with the following statement: "Now that Nixon has been pardoned, the country can rightfully close the book on the Watergate case." The respondents overwhelmingly disagreed by a margin of 66 to 27 percent.

Before moving on, it is worth looking at two other representations of public opinion for some further insight. The results of subsequent elections can stand as an imperfect indicator of the impact of the pardon on public opinion. In the 1974 midterms, with the pardon not even two months in the past, the Democrats picked up forty-three seats in the House, three in the Senate, and four more governorships. This tidal wave left the Democrats with a Senate majority of 23 and a House majority of 147. More striking is that Ford most certainly lost the 1976 election as a result of his decision. Ford lost the popular vote to Jimmy Carter by just 2 percent. In exit polls, 7 percent of respondents said they voted against Ford because of the pardon (Small 1999, 301).

As a last piece of opinion information, mail and call counts are a questionable statistic, but they may contribute to the overall picture nonetheless. For what it is worth, the White House received 4,000 letters the week after the announcement. Less than 700 complimented the president's decision (Ford 1979, 180). Out of 30,000 messages in total, six of every seven would take a stand against Ford (Mieczkowski 2005, 30). Calls were even worse; the switchboard ran eight to one against the pardon (Brinkley 2007, 68). Letters sent to the *Los Angeles Times* (1974b) followed the same basic pattern. On September 14, the paper reported having received 1,186 letters criticizing the pardon. In contrast, the paper received just fifty-eight letters supporting it.

In sum, Ford's own approval rating tanked, the public consistently opposed the pardon, his party took a shellacking in the upcoming election, and calls and mail flooded the White House and major papers expressing their opposition. It would be hard to find religious rhetoric that was more unsuccessful with the public than this.

Although Ford addressed Watergate with religious language in three nationally televised events, it only makes sense to analyze the media coverage that pertains to his pardon announcement speech. Ford's August 9 speech was his first as president and the coverage was logically dominated by information about Nixon, not Ford. And Ford's remarks to open the Congressional hearing on October 17 were qualitatively different than a typical major speech. Therefore, I have coded only the articles surrounding Ford's speech on September 8.

In short, the editorial reaction to Ford's pardon announcement was as bad as could be imagined. Table 6.1 summarizes the carnage. The average score of the editorials printed in the four papers was 1.73,

Table 6.1
Editorial coverage of Ford's pardon announcement on
September 8, 1974

Date	Paper	Author	Title	Score
9/9/1974	*Los Angeles Times*	John Lawrence	"Ford and Nixon Both Could Be Scarred by Controversial Move"	2
9/9/1974	*Los Angeles Times*	Staff Editorial	"The Pardoning of Nixon"	1
9/9/1974	*New York Times*	Staff Editorial	"The Failure of Mr. Ford"	1
9/9/1974	*New York Times*	Anthony Lewis	"The System Scorned"	1
9/10/1974	*Chicago Tribune*	Staff Editorial	"A Pardon Mishandled"	1
9/10/1974	*Chicago Tribune*	Bob Wiedrich	"Pardon Too Early to Meet Approval"	1
9/10/1974	*Los Angeles Times*	Robert Donovan	"Overnight, Widespread Doubts About Mr. Ford"	2
9/10/1974	*New York Times*	Tom Wicker	"A New Kind of Cover-Up"	1
9/10/1974	*New York Times*	Fred Hechinger	"Nixon's 'Mistakes'"	1
9/10/1974	*New York Times*	Staff Editorial	"Pardon for What?"	1

(*continued on next page*)

Table 6.1 (*continued*)

Date	Paper	Author	Title	Score
9/10/1974	*Washington Post*	Marquis Childs	"... And Reopened the Watergate Scandals"	1
9/10/1974	*Washington Post*	Joseph Kraft	"Gerald Ford: 'An Ordinary Pol' ..."	2
9/10/1974	*Washington Post*	Staff Editorial	"The Presidential Pardon"	1
9/10/1974	*Washington Post*	George Will	"... Who Has Eroded Respect for Law ..."	1
9/11/1974	*Chicago Tribune*	Staff Editorial	"The High Cost of Miscalculation"	1
9/11/1974	*Los Angeles Times*	Staff Editorial	"An Affront, a Mockery"	1
9/11/1974	*Los Angeles Times*	Joseph Alsop	"The Pardon: No Spur-of-the-Moment Decision"	5
9/11/1974	*New York Times*	Staff Editorial	"Growing Dossier"	1
9/11/1974	*New York Times*	Staff Editorial	"Nightmare Compounded"	1
9/11/1974	*New York Times*	William Shannon	"The End or Foreword?"	1
9/11/1974	*Washington Post*	William Raspberry	"Mr. Ford's No-Return Decision"	1
9/11/1974	*Washington Post*	Rowland Evans and Robert Novak	"'Somebody Got to President Ford'"	1
9/12/1974	*Chicago Tribune*	Bob Wiedrich	"Did Ford Foresee the Pardon Furor?"	1
9/12/1974	*Chicago Tribune*	Staff Editorial	"Putting Pardons in Perspective"	4
9/12/1974	*Los Angeles Times*	Paul Halpern	"What the Pardon Tells Us About Mr. Ford"	3
9/12/1974	*New York Times*	Staff Editorial	"Back to Politics"	1
9/12/1974	*New York Times*	Anthony Lewis	"Out of the Wreckage"	2

(*continued on next page*)

Table 6.1 (*continued*)

Date	Paper	Author	Title	Score
9/12/1974	*Washington Post*	Joseph Kraft	"Prolonging the National Nightmare . . ."	2
9/12/1974	*Washington Post*	Rowland Evans and Robert Novak	". . . With an 'Expected' Pardon"	3
9/13/1974	*Chicago Tribune*	Clarence Petersen	"Begging Your Pardon, Sir"	1
9/13/1974	*New York Times*	William Shannon	"Flying Into the Storm"	3
9/13/1974	*New York Times*	Arthur Liman and Steven Rosenfeld	"Rockefeller, Attica and Pardons"	1
9/13/1974	*Washington Post*	Joseph Alsop	"Behind the Nixon Pardon"	5
9/13/1974	*Washington Post*	William Greider	"Presidential Words and Deeds"	1
9/13/1974	*Washington Post*	Staff Editorial	"The Unfinished Business"	2
9/14/1974	*Washington Post*	Clayton Fritchey	"Ford: Maintaining His Record"	1
9/15/1974	*Chicago Tribune*	Nick Thimmesch	"Nixon Pardon is Best for America"	5
9/15/1974	*Chicago Tribune*	Jack Mabley	"Too Many Using God's Name Lightly"	1
9/15/1974	*Los Angeles Times*	Charles Wiggins	"A Good President Must Act Decisively"	5
9/15/1974	*Los Angeles Times*	Martin Marty	"Ford's Talk of God: Do Religion and Politics Mix?"	2
9/15/1974	*Los Angeles Times*	Staff Editorial	"The President and His Problems"	2
9/15/1974	*New York Times*	David Rosenbaum	". . . And What Everyone Else May Now Never Find Out"	1

(*continued on next page*)

Table 6.1 (*continued*)

Date	Paper	Author	Title	Score
9/15/1974	*New York Times*	Anthony Lewis	"Mercy Was Satisfied, But the Constitution Requires Justice"	1
9/15/1974	*New York Times*	Staff Editorial	"Mr. Ford's Folly"	1
9/15/1974	*Washington Post*	George Reedy	"The Politics of Secrecy and Surprise"	1
Dates: 9/9 to 9/15			Average score	1.73
			Positive articles	5 (11.1%)
			Negative articles	37 (82.2%)
			Mixed/neutral articles	3 (6.7%)

the lowest mean to be found in any of this book's case studies. Fully thirty-seven of forty-five editorials (82.2 percent) were negative in tone. What is worse, twenty-nine of these pieces were scored a "1," indicating that they were entirely hostile toward the president.

This subtotal includes the immediate reactions published by the editorial boards of all four papers. The *New York Times* (1974a) has already been quoted earlier. The *Los Angeles Times* (1974a) called the pardon "a serious mistake" and wrote that "this ending goes against the principle of equal application of the law." The first two lines of the *Chicago Tribune*'s (1974) staff editorial were: "Dismay and regret. These are the two words that best describe our reaction to the manner and timing of President Ford's announcement of a full pardon for Richard Nixon." Finally, the *Washington Post* (1974) commented that "But for those of us who believe that the consequences of Watergate were public consequences having to do with an office and a system of government which were not Mr. Nixon's personal property, then this newest use of the powers of the presidency to curtail inquiry and to relieve Mr. Nixon of responsibility for this action will strike you as nothing less than a continuation of a cover-up."

One only needs to scan the titles in the table to get a sense of how poisonous the atmosphere was for Ford in the days afterward: "The Failure of Mr. Ford," "The System Scorned," "A New Kind of Cover-Up," "An Affront, a Mockery," "Nightmare Compounded," "Mr. Ford's Folly," etc.

Many criticized the pardon on the grounds that it undermined the principle of equality before the law. These individuals worried about the message the pardon would send. They believed that message would be that there is one set of laws for the rich and powerful, and one for everyone else, including those co-conspirators in the Watergate mess who Ford had not pardoned. Some took this concern to its logical extreme by speculating about the consequences this signal could have for the judicial system at large (i.e., Wiedrich 1974). Clarence Petersen (1974) facetiously suggested "Let our new President temper justice with mercy for all and pardon everyone! Our burglars, stickup men, tax cheaters, embezzlers, rapists, and murderers—all of them hounded into jail by hostile policemen and prosecutors—have suffered enough."

A second criticism of the pardon highlighted the circumstances under which it had been issued. Many felt that Ford had acted too soon and that the process had been too secretive. A lot of these writers expressed openness to a pardon had it occurred later on down the road, but they rejected such a move as premature at this stage. Some also faulted Ford for not obtaining a statement where Nixon admitted guilt in return for his immunity from future prosecution. As the *New York Times* (1974b) lamented, "Now, by President Ford's ill-considered action, the nation is in danger of losing even that note of clarity in a morass which has confused and divided a frustrated populace for two long years. Without the firm seal of a conclusive judgment by constitutional institutions, the way will be open wide for a subsequent demagogic rewriting of history that could poison the political atmosphere for generations to come."

A third criticism maintained that the pardon was counterproductive. Ford wanted to put Watergate in the past by pardoning Nixon. Instead, these men and women objected, all he was doing was reopening old wounds (i.e., Childs 1974).

It must also be said that quite a few editorialists found Ford's religious justifications for the pardon to be deeply offensive. Jack Mabley (1974) noted that the pardon speech "was virtually a religious production, with frequent references to 'a humble servant of God' and a decision reached 'with the help of God.'" "Well, it was a lousy decision and I don't think God had much to do with it," Mabley added. Summing his feelings up, Mabley observed, "Religious faith is a very precious thing, and it is cheapened and endangered by this casual tossing around of God's name . . ."

Likewise, Martin Marty (1974) wrote in the *Tribune* that "whenever people invoke the gods for their political causes, all the stakes on both sides are raised and the danger of incivility increases." He cited the Crusades and religious warfare in India and Israel as support for this contention. Though praising Ford for the sincerity of his beliefs, Marty warned, "Americans will be better off if the religious community not only rejoices in its leaders' faith but also joins all the biblical prophets in being instinctively suspicious of the pious claims of the powerful."

Last, the pardon was not greeted by any better of a reception in Congress. Congress could not overturn the decision, but they expressed their displeasure in a variety of other ways. There was some vocal discussion about resuming the impeachment proceedings against Nixon, which had been halted following his resignation, though Representative Peter Rodino, Jr. (D-NJ), chairman of the House Judiciary Committee, indicated he had little interest in doing so. Nevertheless, Senator Walter Mondale (D-MN) declared his intention to propose a constitutional amendment permitting Congress to overturn any future pardon by a two-thirds vote (Rich and Russell 1974). And ultimately, the Senate, by a vote of fifty-five to twenty-four, did pass a resolution calling for Ford to refrain from pardoning any other Watergate defendants before those individuals had been tried.

The resolutions in the House that led to Ford's appearance have been covered earlier. Congress' response was so toxic that when congressional liaison William Timmons sent Haig a sampling of statements that Senators had made on the pardon, Haig asked that Ford not be allowed to see the document (Greene 1995, 55).

Remember that Ford's objective in pardoning Nixon was to move past Watergate. What this flurry of activity proves is that he actually renewed Congressional interest in re-fighting these past battles.

Bill Clinton and Impeachment

Twenty-one-year-old White House intern Monica S. Lewinsky arrived in Washington in the summer of 1995. Lewinsky had obtained a position in chief of staff Leon Panetta's office with the assistance of Walter Kaye, a millionaire insurance executive, a friend of Lewinsky's mother, and a major Democratic contributor. The intern and the president interacted several times that summer and fall, though never substantially.

In November 1995, a conflict between Clinton and the House Republicans over the budget forced a government shutdown. Lewinsky, by now a paid staffer in the Office of Legislative Affairs, was part of a skeletal crew of employees that came in to answer the phones and help out during the closure. On November 15, the second day of the impasse, Clinton and Lewinsky flirted from a distance over the course of the work day. Early that evening, Lewinsky walked by the door to the inner office of the West Wing and saw Clinton standing alone. She quickly lifted the jacket of her pantsuit to reveal her thong underwear. As John Harris (2005, 223) amusingly puts it, "Somehow he interpreted this delicate signal as an invitation."

Around 8 p.m., long after most of the other volunteers had called it a day, Clinton saw Lewinsky in the hallway and invited her into George Stephanopoulos's office. The office was connected via a back door to a hallway leading to Clinton's study. There, the president asked the intern if he could kiss her. She said yes.

This was the start of a sixteen-month affair, one finally ending in May 1997. The couple exchanged gifts and notes. They had furtive weekend liaisons, including one on Easter Sunday. They shared graphic telephone conversations. All in all, in the words of Clinton aide Rahm Emanuel, it was "less than sex but more than kissy-face" (Wilentz 2008, 382). Still, the transgressions would almost be enough to end Clinton's presidency.

Clinton's indiscretions were incomprehensible in many ways, not the least of which was that they occurred at the same time that he was fighting a sexual harassment suit that had been filed against him by Paula Jones in May 1994. Jones, a former Arkansas state employee, alleged that as Governor Clinton had unwelcomely propositioned her in a hotel room in Little Rock in 1991. Clinton's lawyers argued that, as a civil matter, the resolution of the suit should have been postponed until after the completion of his time in office. However, in *Clinton v. Jones*, the Supreme Court unanimously held that the suit should be allowed to proceed.

Jones's lawyers began to dig into Clinton's past to see whether they could unearth any other similar accusations. As Gil Davis, one of Jones's counsels explained, "Showing a pattern or habit of sexual advances to women, particularly in private circumstances of some related nature, would be a method of showing that this was a characteristic of the president. So, yes, we were announcing that. Made no bones about it" (Gormley 2010, 241).

The Jones camp had the details about Clinton's affair fall unexpectedly into their laps. After being transferred to the Pentagon, Lewinsky had befriended an older woman, Linda Tripp, with whom she shared details of her relationship with the president. Tripp was a Republican partisan who harbored a strong personal dislike of the Clintons. On the advice of Lucianne Goldberg, herself a former White House secretary and Nixon ally, Tripp began to secretly record her conversations with Lewinsky. Goldberg later shared those tapes with Jones's attorneys, and helped funnel the information to the staff of independent prosecutor Kenneth Starr.

Starr's investigation into the Whitewater real estate development had hit a wall. But on the basis of what he learned, Starr realized that he had solid grounds for charging Clinton with suborning perjury and obstruction of justice. He soon received formal permission from Attorney General Janet Reno to expand his investigation to include charges related to the *Jones v. Clinton* case. Clinton's two long-running nuisances, the Paula Jones suit and Whitewater, had merged into one spectacular problem.

The president was deposed in the Jones case on Saturday, January 17, 1998, in his attorney's offices, only two blocks from the White House. Clinton knew that the deposition had not gone well. The specific nature of the questions—about gifts, about Lewinsky's job search—revealed that some in the outside world knew what he had been doing behind closed doors. On top of that, the president also recognized that his answers, though possibly not perjury by the technical definition, were not entirely truthful, either.

On that same Saturday, after much internal debate, *Newsweek* decided not to publish a story on the affair by reporter Michael Isikoff. But the Drudge Report, at that time an obscure gossip chasing website, did it for them in a post that identified Lewinsky by name. On Tuesday evening, the *Washington Post* and ABC News simultaneously became the first mainstream outlets to cover the story. George Stephanopoulos, in his new role as an ABC News commentator, was one of the first to publicly discuss the possibility of impeachment. His coworker Sam Donaldson predicted a resignation, perhaps by the end of the week.

Clinton wavered on how he should respond. He turned to his former political guru Dick Morris, architect of Clinton's strategy of "triangulation," for advice. Morris himself was no stranger to sex scandals; he had been forced out of the White House after stories emerged prior to the 1996 election linking him to a prostitute.

Morris surreptitiously took a small poll. His results revealed that, whereas people might forgive Clinton for his adultery, they would not be so forgiving when it came to perjury. Thirty-five percent of respondents felt the president should go to jail if he lied. Morris summed up his findings: "They're just too shocked by this. It's just too new, it's just too raw. They're just not ready for it." Clinton blusteringly replied, "Well, we just have to win then" (Harris 2005, 308).

On January 26, at an appearance in the Roosevelt Room for his child care policy, Clinton issued his infamous, finger wagging denial: "But I want to say one thing to the American people. I want you to listen to me. I'm going to say this again. I did not have sexual relations with that woman, Miss Lewinsky. I never told anybody to lie, not a single time—never. These allegations are false. And I need to go back to work for the American people" (Clinton 1998a).

Clinton's combative posture worked to temporarily quiet the storm. He further helped his case by delivering a well-received State of the Union address shortly thereafter. Starr's investigation continued, but over the next several months, Clinton was mostly able to focus on the work of his Administration unimpeded.

That was no longer possible as the summer came to an end. Lewinsky negotiated an immunity deal with Starr's office at the end of July, in the process turning over the evidence she had in her possession, including the rumored blue dress. Clinton had his blood drawn for DNA testing and agreed to a deposition with Starr's team in the White House on August 17. With physical evidence in Starr's possession, the stonewalling could not continue unless Clinton was determined to commit perjury.

In his deposition, Clinton read a prepared statement where he finally confessed to an inappropriate physical relationship with Lewinsky, though he defended his answers at the prior Jones deposition as accurate under the agreed to definition of sexual relations. That night, at 10 p.m. in the Map Room of the White House, Clinton addressed the nation (Clinton 1998b).

For a master politician with such finely tuned political antennae as Clinton, this speech was a shocking misstep. He was angry and defiant. In a very short statement (the total address was only ten paragraphs long), Clinton chose to lash out at his opponents rather than apologizing to the country.

As he tried to explain why he had misled people about his relationship with Lewinsky, Clinton noted "The fact that these questions were being asked in a politically inspired lawsuit which has since been dismissed was a consideration, too." He went on to rip into Starr's office, adding "I had real and serious concerns about an Independent Counsel investigation that began with private business dealings 20 years ago—dealings, I might add, about which an independent Federal agency found no evidence of any wrongdoing by me or my wife over two years ago. The Independent Counsel investigation moved on to my staff and friends, then into my private life. And now the investigation itself is under investigation. This has gone on too long, cost too much, and hurt too many innocent people."

Furthermore, Clinton said that the affair was irrelevant, anyways. "It's nobody's business but ours," Clinton argued, "Even Presidents have private lives. It is time to stop the pursuit of personal destruction and the prying into private lives and get on with our national life. Our country has been distracted by this matter for too long." Never once did Clinton say sorry.

The problem was that Clinton could not bring himself to say what he did not feel. Clinton admitted to his intimates that he did not regret having lied. It was Clinton's view that the lie saved his presidency. By giving people time to process the allegations, most had come to accept that something untoward had happened between Clinton and Lewinsky. And Clinton, like his wife, really did believe that a coterie of enemies lurked just outside the White House, plotting his downfall.

Hence, after his testimony with Starr, Clinton was "in a shaking rage" (Harris 2005, 342). In her memoirs, Hillary described him as "deeply angry" after the questioning (Clinton 2003, 467). Clinton gathered his advisors in the White House solarium to work on his speech, but the scene was pure chaos. As one witness put it, "this was like halftime at an NFL game" (Gormley 2010, 552). Some Clintonites urged the president to be repentant; others played into Clinton's feelings of persecution and argued that he should go on the attack. In the end, Clinton looked to the First Lady. Hillary coldly replied, "It's your speech, Bill. Say whatever you want" (Harris 2005, 344). Regrettably for Clinton, he did just that.

The first family departed for their summer vacation in Martha's Vineyard the next morning. The scene was a painful one as Chelsea Clinton walked between her parents on the trek across the White House lawn, taking each of their hands. Clinton would spend most of his vacation alone in the guest room, working the phone, trying to assess the damage. There the magnitude of his troubles sunk in.

Clinton's standing with his own party was shaky at best, to say nothing of his problems with the Republicans. Neither of the Democratic congressional leaders—in the Senate, Tom Daschle, and in the House, Dick Gephardt—would accept Clinton's phone calls (Gormley 2010, 556). Gephardt would raise the possibility of impeachment in a speech on August 25 (Gillon 2008, 236). Dianne Feinstein (D-CA), one of Clinton's strongest supporters, was another Democrat furious about his August 17 speech. "I was present in the Roosevelt Room in January when the President categorically denied any sexual involvement with Monica Lewinsky. I believed him. His remarks last evening leave me with a deep sense of sadness in that my trust in his credibility has been badly shattered," Feinstein fumed (Berke 1998a).

With a midterm election upcoming, many of the rank and file felt that Clinton's adultery had jeopardized not just his, but their own careers as well. And many were emboldened to further distance themselves from the president following a speech Senator Joe Lieberman (D-CT) delivered on the Senate floor on September 3. Reading calmly from his prepared text, Lieberman criticized Clinton for behavior that was "not just inappropriate," Lieberman said, but "immoral." The Senator worried that Clinton's actions were harmful because they send "a message of what is acceptable behavior to the larger American family—particularly our children—which is as influential as the negative messages communicated by the entertainment culture." Lieberman's willingness to break ranks inspired others, such as Daniel Patrick Moynihan of New York and Bob Kerrey of Nebraska, to break their own silences and follow Lieberman with their own denunciations from the chamber floor (Berke 1998b).

For Clinton's staff, this dissension among Democrats was alarming. One aide remembered, "The lesson from Watergate was—it wasn't when the Democrats wanted Nixon to leave; it's when [the Senate Republicans] told him 'it's time.' So we always saw the Democrats as our biggest vulnerability" (Gormley 2010, 556). Drawing on these parallels, some compared Lieberman's remarks to those delivered by James Buckley, a New York Senator who was the first conservative Republican to demand Nixon's resignation. In early September, it appeared as if this doomsday scenario might be once more close to fruition. Senator Kent Conrad (D-ND) at one point told the Clinton legal team, "You are about three days from having the senior Democrats come down and ask for the president's resignation" (Harris 2005, 347).

A similar reaction was playing out at the same time within the White House itself. Clinton faced the possibility of an all-out staff revolt. White House aides Doug Sosnick and John Podesta had found that the women working within the Administration had grown increasingly upset about the president's conduct while he was away at the Vineyard. There was a real chance that a high-profile feminist such as Health and Human Services Secretary Donna Shalala or Secretary of State Madeleine Albright might quit in protest.

Clinton's standing with the media was no better than his standing with his party or his staff. Soon after he admitted his relationship with Lewinsky, over 140 newspapers called for his resignation (Johnson 2001, 378). The media demanded to know why Clinton was not being more contrite about his failures.

At a press conference with Russian President Boris Yeltsin on September 2, a reporter asked Clinton, "You know, there have been some who have expressed disappointment that you didn't offer a formal apology the other night when you spoke to the American people. Are you—do you feel you need to offer an apology? And in retrospect now, with some distance, do you have any feeling that perhaps the tone of your speech was something that didn't quite convey the feelings that you had, particularly your comments in regard to Mr. Starr?" Clinton refused to back down, answering, "I think the question of the tone of the speech and people's reaction to it is really a function of—I can't comment on that. I read it the other day again, and I thought it was clear . . . And I was commenting that it seemed to be something that most reasonable people would think had consumed a disproportionate amount of America's time, money, and resources and attention . . ." (Clinton 1998d).

This was not going to be good enough for a rabid press. The consensus was voiced by the *New York Times* (1998a) in its staff editorial on September 9. The paper wrote, "Mr. Clinton faces a rapid erosion of support that imperils his Presidency. As an astute politician and adroit card player, Mr. Clinton must by now realize that his incomplete explanations about Ms. Lewinsky are a losing hand. If Mr. Clinton wants to regain some control over his political situation, he must change course decisively and quickly. The country demands a serious Presidential discussion about the Lewinsky case . . ."

Clinton did ultimately come to agree with this editorialist. His friends and allies did not have any qualms telling him these difficult truths (see McAuliffe 2007, 163). In his memoirs, Clinton (2004, 803) owns up to his poor performance: "I believed every word I said, but my anger hadn't worn off enough for me to be as contrite as I should have been."

Most of the presidents in these pages faced policy crises. Their own jobs were not at stake. In that sense, Clinton was the most desperate of all. His job *was* at stake, and he responded by turning to religious rhetoric as a means for both saving his soul and his presidency.

Speaking the language of religion came easily to Clinton for he had sought comfort in his faith from a young age. Clinton's biological father had died in a car accident three months before Bill was born in 1946.

Clinton's mother, Virginia Kelley, had remarried a divorcee named Roger Clinton in 1950 and moved her family with him to Hot Springs, Arkansas. Bill, originally given the last name Blythe, would adopt his stepfather's name. Yet, Clinton's relationship with Roger was far from smooth. Roger Clinton was a drinker and abusive. Once, Roger assaulted Virginia at a community dance. On another occasion, in the midst of a fight about visiting a sick relative, he fired a gun in her direction.

One can imagine how church could be Clinton's means of escape from this turmoil. Every Sunday he would walk to the local Baptist church by himself, as neither his stepfather nor his mother were regular worshippers. Clinton was actively involved in the church's community. It was no surprise when he was asked to be the prayer leader of his high school's graduation ceremony. Clinton was especially influenced by the sermons of Billy Graham, and he secretly mailed a part of his allowance to the preacher as a donation.

Clinton combined his Southern Baptist traditions with the experiences he had with other Christian faiths throughout his life. He spent several years of elementary school being taught by the nuns at St. John's Catholic School. Financial pressures forced the family to place him back in the public school system, but the time spent at St. John's left its mark on Clinton.

Later, Clinton attended Georgetown University, a school run by the Catholic Jesuit order. In addition to the religious instruction he received from his classes, Clinton was known to attend Mass with his fellow Catholic students (Hamilton 2003, 132). During college, he also would frequently accompany his friend, Kit Ashby, to First Presbyterian Church (Espinosa 2009, 439).

Clinton began to draw on all this religious experience at the end of August, beginning with a speech he gave on August 28 in Oak Bluffs, Massachusetts (Clinton 1998c). The president was in town visiting a simple, one-room, wooden chapel for the purpose of commemorating the thirty-fifth anniversary of the civil rights March on Washington. The original draft of Clinton's speech dealt solely with the issue of civil rights but the president sensed an opportunity to broaden its scope. Clinton drafted his remarks on the fly, writing them in part on his ride to the church and even while sitting backstage prior to ceremonies (Seelye 1998).

Clinton began by sharing his own memories of the speech. Where things got interesting, though, is when Clinton began to discuss what he had learned about forgiveness from Dr. King and the marchers:

All of you know, I'm having to become quite an expert in this business of asking for forgiveness. It gets a little easier the more you do it. And if you have a family, an administration, a Congress, and a whole country to ask, you're going to get a lot of practice.

But I have to tell you that, in these last days, it has come home to me, again, something I first learned as President, but it wasn't burned in my bones, and that is that in order to get it, you have to be willing to give it.

And all of us—the anger, the resentment, the bitterness, the desire for recrimination against people you believe have wronged you, they harden the heart and deaden the spirit and lead to self-inflicted wounds. And so it is important that we are able to forgive those we believe have wronged us, even as we ask for forgiveness from people we have wronged. And I heard that first—first—in the civil rights movement: "Love thy neighbor as thyself."

Obvious religious references abound in this passage. For one, Clinton speaks of the importance of forgiveness. This is one of the most commonly broached subjects in the Bible (Metzger and Coogan 1993, 232); there are approximately 125 direct references to forgiveness in its pages (Ryken, Wilhoit, and Longman III 1998, 302). Even those wholly unfamiliar with religion could be expected to have some awareness of the image of a forgiving God.

In a more specific way, Clinton talks about forgiveness in the context of the Lord's Prayer, playing upon it when he says, "As so it is important we are able to forgive those we believe have wronged us, even as we ask for forgiveness from people we have wronged." The Lord's Prayer, also called the Our Father or the Paternoster, is the central prayer of the Christian faith (Stevenson 2004). Though its text has varied across time and place, the prayer has a scriptural basis, found in two different New Testament accounts of Jesus' teachings (Luke 11:2–4; Matthew 6:9–13). Clinton's words sound similar to lines of the prayer as it appears in each gospel. In Matthew, "And forgive us our debts, as we also have forgiven our debtors" (6:12). And in Luke, "And forgive us our sins, for we ourselves forgive everyone indebted to us" (11:4).

What Jesus is saying in these gospels is easy to grasp; it is that forgiveness of our own sins depends on our willingness to forgive the sins of others. He is quoted making this point explicit following the prayer's appearance in Matthew: "For if you forgive others their trespasses, your heavenly Father will also forgive you; but if you do not forgive others, neither will your Father forgive your trespasses" (Matthew 6:14–15).

Hence, the subtext of Clinton's phrasing is that he now realizes that if he wants to be forgiven for his affair, he must first be willing to forgive Starr for his excesses. There was precious little of that in his speech on August 17.

Further, Clinton uses the phrase "harden the heart." Many who would read these lines in their morning papers would recognize the words. In addition to being the basis for many popular church hymnals, the admonition to *not* harden one's heart is found in several places in the Bible. For instance, in Hebrews 3:15, the Holy Spirit is quoted as warning, "Today, if you hear his voice, do not harden your hearts. . ." The phrase is repeated at other places throughout Hebrews (i.e., 3:7–8; 4:7) and is found in Psalm 95 (7–8) as well.

Finally, Clinton concludes with yet another Biblical quotation, "Love thy neighbor as thyself." This commandment can be found in the Old Testament (Leviticus 19:18) as well as in the New. According to Christ, it is the second most important requirement of faith, trailing only loving God with all that you have (see Mark 12:28–34).

Given the context of the quote—it appears in a section where Clinton is discussing his "desire for recrimination against people you believe have wronged you"—Clinton is again intimating that he must be kinder to his political opponents, including Starr. In a meaningful way, Clinton used these religious references to renounce his earlier comments as a betrayal of his beliefs.

Clinton continued his steps toward penance in a private meeting with his cabinet at the White House on September 10. Clinton told his secretaries that he realized that he had cheated on his wife out of anger. His anger at his political opponents had made him emotionally vulnerable and susceptible to self-destructive behavior. Clinton apologized to his Administration and explained, with tears in his eyes, how he had now turned to Scripture for strength in overcoming this ordeal.

Some were sympathetic to what he was saying. Transportation Secretary Rodney Slater and Labor Secretary Alexis Herman spoke up afterward in Clinton's defense, themselves pointing to the Bible's message of forgiveness and redemption. Bruce Babbit, Secretary of the Interior and a practicing Catholic, spoke to Clinton about the therapeutic effects of confession. Others, however, were less convinced. Shalala and Albright loudly expressed their disappointment and anger.

According to Clinton, it was at this cabinet meeting that the gravity of the scandal dawned on him. He remembers, "Listening to my cabinet, I really understood for the first time the extent to which the exposure of my misconduct and my dishonesty about it had opened a Pandora's box of emotions in the American people" (Clinton 2004, 809). That night, Clinton did not sleep. He spent the late evening and early morning hours scribbling on a legal pad what he would say in an appearance the next morning at the annual White House prayer breakfast.

The prayer breakfast speech meets our criteria for being considered a major address since it was carried live by the networks. Clinton announced early in his remarks that this speech would be his confession, saying "I agree with those who have said that in my first statement after I testified, I was not contrite enough. I don't think there is a fancy way to say that I have sinned. It is important to me that everybody who has been hurt know that the sorrow I feel is genuine: first and most important, my family; also my friends, my staff, my Cabinet, Monica Lewinsky and her family, and the American people. I have asked all for their forgiveness" (Clinton 1998e).

Clinton moved on to explain the changes he was prepared to make: "But I believe that to be forgiven, more than sorrow is required—at least two more things: first, genuine repentance, a determination to change and to repair breaches of my own making—I have repented; second, what my Bible calls a 'broken spirit,' an understanding that I must have God's help to be the person that I want to be, a willingness to give the very forgiveness I seek, a renunciation of the pride and the anger which cloud judgment, lead people to excuse and compare and to blame and complain." There are several notable religious aspects to this paragraph.

The phrase "broken spirit" appears to be a quotation taken from Psalm 51:17, which reads "The sacrifice acceptable to God is a broken spirit; a broken and contrite heart, O God, you will not despise." If so, it was a thoughtful choice. Psalm 51 is a prayer for cleansing and pardon (Terrien 2003, 400–410). The Psalm likely was composed sometime in the sixth century BC and is meant to recall when David, the first king of Israel, had an affair with Bathsheba, the wife of Uriah (see 2 Samuel 11–12). David had spotted Bathsheba bathing from his roof. Struck by her beauty, he sent a messenger to procure the woman for him. But Bathsheba became pregnant and David had to have her husband killed in order to take her as his own wife. David's actions upset God, who afflicted the child with a terrible sickness as punishment. David wept, prayed, and fasted for a week, but still the child died. In the Psalm, the singer is begging for forgiveness for these sins, which are admitted to be attacks against God himself.

The particular words "broken spirit" are meant to capture the idea that the singer is abandoning his ego and ambition and thereby giving himself up entirely to God. Clinton, by choosing this to cite these lines, is at once expressing his remorse for his David-like adultery, while announcing his commitment to changing his ways.

Additionally, "repair breaches" is a phrasing that would certainly register with the ministers in attendance, if not as much with the outside world, perhaps. The label "repairer of the breach" is a well-known term found in Isaiah 58. Isaiah 58 is about the difference between false and true worship (Hanson 1995, 204–7). It is a polemic directed against a group that is pious and meticulous in religious practices, but hypocritical in their actions. They fast and bow their heads, but they still oppress their workers, act selfishly, quarrel, and fight. If, however, the people abandon their selfishness, if they aid their fellow neighbors in need, the Lord will guide and protect them. Only then, they "shall be called repairer of the breach, restorer of streets to live in." Many Christian groups and schools have been so inspired by this message that they have included it as part of their nomenclature.

By using the phrase "repair breaches," Clinton could have been signaling that he knew that up until this point he, too, was pursuing his own interest at the expense of God's. The president may have gone to church, he may have talked publicly about the importance of family values, but these things did not square with his private behavior. However, this phrasing was also a curious choice since, as many critics would point out, this whole speech—on TV, in front of a sympathetic audience, from a president who only adopted a confessional tone once his Administration seemed at a point of maximum peril—could be accused of being an example of exactly the kind of false religion Isaiah decries.

A final important facet of this part of the address was that Clinton again picks up on the theology of the Lord's Prayer, pointing once more to the importance of giving "the very forgiveness I seek."

After thanking people for their support, and asking for their prayers, Clinton speculated whether or not this entire sordid episode might in the end have a silver lining:

> Nevertheless, in this case, it may be a blessing, because I still sinned. And if my repentance is genuine and sustained, and if I can maintain both a broken spirit and a strong heart, then good can come of this for our country as well as for me and my family.

> The children of this country can learn in a profound way that integrity is important and selfishness is wrong, but God can change us and make us strong at the broken places. I want to embody those lessons for the children of this country, for that little boy in Florida who came up to me and said that he wanted to grow up and be President and to be just like me. I want the parents of all the children in America to be able to say that to their children.

Needless to say, it is quite debatable whether the president cheating on his wife was a "blessing" and "good" for the children of the country. That being said, this was not the only occasion on which Clinton voiced these sentiments. At a press conference with Andres Pastrana of Colombia on October 28, Clinton spoke of how children might learn from him that if they make mistakes, they should be humble, trust in God, and he will help them grow stronger as a result (Clinton 1998i). Clinton told the reporters,

> I was talking about—on the first question you asked, I think what people ought to say to their children is that when someone makes a mistake, they should admit it and try to rectify it and that this is an illustration of the fact that those rules should apply to everyone, but that when people do that, if they do it properly, they can be stronger in their personal lives and their family lives and in their work lives.

> And many of us in life can cite examples where if we went through a period of assessing, that we grew stronger from it, and we actually did better. With a humble spirit, with the grace of God, and with a lot of determination, I think that happens. And I think in that sense, the lesson is a good one, that it should apply to everyone, from the President on down.

A final unique aspect of Clinton's speech on September 11 was that the president's rhetoric went beyond the typical Christian-centrism of most presidents. In the last section of the speech, Clinton recited an extensive passage from the Yom Kippur liturgy in a Jewish prayer book called "Gates of Repentance." The theme of the liturgy was about the time for "turning." Turning for leaves, birds, and animals, the prayer reads, comes instinctively. But the prayer makes note of the special difficulties humans face as they try to break old habits, admit wrong, and start all over again.

In concluding, Clinton ended his speech with a sentimental prayer of his own:

I ask you to share my prayer that God will search me and know my heart, try me and know my anxious thoughts, see if there is any hurtfulness in me, and lead me toward the life everlasting. I ask that God give me a clean heart, let me walk by faith and not sight.

I ask once again to be able to love my neighbor—all my neighbors—as myself; to be an instrument of God's peace; to let the words of my mouth and the meditations of my heart and, in the end, the work of my hands, be pleasing. This is what I wanted to say to you today.

Thank you. God bless you.

The ritual of confession is most commonly associated with Roman Catholicism. The Fourth Lateran Council, convened by Pope Innocent III in 1215, marked a change in practice as the Church began for the first time to emphasize the verbal act of confession rather than public penance. In Canon 21, annual confession in private to a parish priest was made an obligation on all the community. It stands today as one of the seven sacraments of the Catholic Church. Typically termed penance or reconciliation, confession joins baptism, confirmation, receiving the Eucharist, anointing of the sick, holy orders, and matrimony as one of the most important activities a Catholic is called to participate in.

Although not as formalized as the Catholic practice, confession still has an important role in the Protestant traditions as well. Part of the rationale for the Protestant Reformation was outage over confessional abuses. Priests were in the practice of selling indulgences in return for the forgiveness of sins. These payments were bribes or blackmail, depending on how one looked at them. As a consequence, many Protestant churches have a history of skepticism when it comes to individual confession, instead preferring that all attendees perform a general confession during services. Similarly, in Judaism, the community as a whole confesses their sins, much of it in plural language, on Yom Kippur, the Day of Atonement (see Hymer 1995).

The point is that a great majority of Americans had some experience with what Clinton was doing on the 11th. They could relate in a personal way to this political performance.

A few days later, a press conference that Clinton held with President Vaclav Havel of the Czech Republic was hijacked with questions about Lewinsky (Clinton 1998f). Clinton mostly tried to stick to the foreign policy issues he had intended to discuss. Still, a few of his answers are significant for the reason that they provide strong evidence of his change in tone since August 17. His responses were remorseful and gave the impression of someone who was seeking the country's forgiveness.

Twice, Clinton lamented the "pain" he had caused and noted the "work" he was doing to heal it. Clinton also used a word with strong religious connotations when, at another point, he spoke of his intent to "atone" for his behavior: "On last Friday at the prayer breakfast, I laid out as carefully and as brutally honestly as I could what I believe the essential truth to be. I also said then, and I will say again, that I think that the right thing for our country and the right thing for all people concerned is not to get mired in all the details here but to focus—for me to focus on what I did, to acknowledge it, to atone for it; and then to work on my family, where I still have a lot of work to do, difficult work; and to lead this country . . ."

The choice of words like "atone" is key because, like the use of the term "sin" before, these words carry more weight than other, less religious synonyms such as "apologize" and the like. In fact, Clinton repeatedly opted for these religious words over other available alternatives throughout the impeachment process.

For example, in his remarks to the Congressional Black Caucus Foundation on September 19, Clinton began by saying to his supporters, "I have a speech I want to give, but first I'd like to say something from the heart. I want to thank you for standing up for America with me. I want to thank you for standing up for me and understanding the true meaning of repentance and atonement" (Clinton 1998g).

Similarly, Clinton would make a statement much like the one above at the press conference with Andres Pastrana at the end of October: "I hope the American people have seen in me over these last few weeks a real commitment to doing what I told them I would do from the beginning, to try to atone to them for what happened and to try to redouble my efforts to be a good President" (Clinton 1998i).

The final element of Clinton's religious rhetorical strategy was the expression of some rather fatalistic impulses. One of the ways Clinton justified ignoring the ongoing controversy in favor of other presidential business was that the whole matter was up to God to decide. This line of argument was forcefully advanced in his brief remarks to reporters following the vote on impeachment on October 8 (Clinton 1998h). Clinton told the press, "First of all, I hope that we can now move forward with this process in a way that is fair, that is constitutional, and that is timely. The American people have been through a lot on this, and I think that everyone deserves that. Beyond that, I have nothing to say.

It is not in my hands; it is in the hands of Congress and the people of this country, ultimately in the hands of God. There is nothing I can do." Clinton returned to this theme at the end of the availability, answering a follow-up question by claiming, "Personally, I am fine. I have surrendered this. This is beyond my control. I have to work on what I can do."

Overall, Clinton mostly avoided discussing the prospect of impeachment. Between his August 17, 1998 speech and February 19, 1999, a week after his acquittal by the Senate, Clinton mentioned impeachment on only twenty-eight occasions. Moreover, fourteen of the twenty-eight were brief statements where Clinton addressed the issue by saying he would not be addressing the issue (Hart and Sawyer 2003, 198). Thus, the rhetoric that has been analyzed above represents a healthy percentage of all President Clinton was ever to say about Monica Lewinsky.

It appears safe to claim that Clinton's religious rhetoric was a strategic choice made at a crucial point in his presidency. Clinton turned to religion only after his previous attempts at short-circuiting the controversy had failed, alienating the media, his fellow Democrats and even his own staff in the process. Quite simply, he was responding to demands for contrition by being more contrite. Clinton confessed his "sin" before a group of ministers, he directly quoted religious texts from multiple faiths on several occasions, and he regularly elected to use meaningful religious words like "atone" and "repentance" instead of other secular alternatives.

It would seem that Clinton's religious pivot was successful. After all, he did manage to avoid being removed from office. However, a closer look at the evidence reveals a more complicated picture.

Public opinion must be a major part of any discussion of Clinton's impeachment. Clinton's high marks were one of the main reasons the Republicans were not able to attract the votes needed to remove him from office. Figure 6.2 shows the extraordinary stability of Clinton's approval ratings.

On January 28, 1998, two days after Clinton's first public denial, the president received the support of 67 percent of Americans in the Gallup Poll. By February 19, 1999, one week after his acquittal, Clinton was still clocking in at 66 percent. Never at any point between these dates did the president fall below 60 percent. Never at any point did he rise above 73 percent. Ironically, Clinton's high was reached on the very day, December 19, that the House voted for two articles of impeachment.

What these findings mean is that Clinton's religious rhetoric did not have much, if any, impact on his standing. He was in good standing

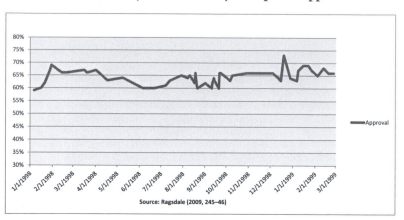

Figure 6.2
Clinton January 1998–February 1999 public approval

Source: Ragsdale (2009, 245–46)

to begin with and his shift to religious language in late August did not change this, one way or the other. A variable (his type of rhetorical defense) cannot explain a constant (his high ratings).

Also, Clinton received only a 3 percent bump from his major speech to the prayer breakfast on September 11, 1998. His approval was 60 percent on September 10 and improved to 63 percent by September 12. This increase is too small to be sure that the movement was statistically significant and his ratings for that week did not move any further upward; his approval was measured at 64 percent on September 13 and 63 percent on September 14 (Ragsdale 2009, 246).

A glance at the more specific polling displayed in Figure 6.3 muddles, but does not change, this first impression.

ABC News tracked whether Americans felt Clinton should remain in office or resign owing to his personal misconduct. His support was high on this issue, as well. At no point did a majority of Americans favor his resignation. However, there is a clear trend visible in this graph. The gap between those who wanted Clinton to continue as president and those who preferred that he step aside visibly narrowed in the middle of September. The explanation for this development is probably the fallout from the gratuitous Starr report, a document that boldly detailed the president's sexual dalliances. The Starr report was released to the public on the afternoon of September 11.

There are two ways one could interpret this data with respect to the effects of Clinton's religious rhetoric. On the one hand, one could

Figure 6.3
ABC News polling on Lewinsky scandal

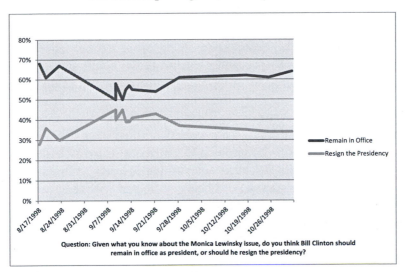

Question: Given what you know about the Monica Lewinsky issue, do you think Bill Clinton should remain in office as president, or should he resign the presidency?

argue that his religious rhetoric helped him climb back to his original position. By the end of the time series, there is again a difference of around 30 percent in the percentages of those saying they wished him to remain in office versus those saying they wanted him to resign. On the other hand, however, one could argue that his religious rhetoric did little to arrest the damaging consequences of the Starr report's release. A poll taken on the afternoon of September 11, after Clinton's speech to the ministers, was the closest in the set; fifty percent of respondents supported him, and 45 percent of respondents wanted his resignation.

In truth, the opinion data are even more confounding when one considers that the public was at the same time convinced of Clinton's guilt. In a December 1998 poll, for example, 80 percent of Americans answered yes to the question, "Just your best guess—do you think Clinton did or did not lie under oath about having an affair with Lewinsky?" (ABC News/Washington Post 1998). Clinton was seen as a man of integrity by fewer people than Richard Nixon was just two weeks before Nixon resigned (Renshon 2002b, 422).

A variety of explanations have been offered to account for these massive contradictions. One thought is that the public, having earlier been exposed to Gennifer Flowers and the history of Clinton's draft-era evasions, had already come to terms with Clinton's lapses in morality. Another possibility is that Americans are traditionally ambivalent when it comes to the private lives of their politicians (Renshon 2002a, 2002b). This may be even more relevant given that Clinton was so much more skilled and likable than all the other major players in the scandal (Sonner and Wilcox 1999). Certainly, the fact that the country was prosperous and at peace stood in Clinton's favor, too (Zaller 1998).

It is also possible that the public did not care about the scandal because they were not even paying attention to it. Americans ranked the story as less important than other concurrent events like Columbine and the death of John F. Kennedy Jr. Only one-third of individuals reported following the Lewinsky scandal very closely (Bennett 2002).

So, perhaps, Clinton's religious rhetoric helped with the public. But a more likely conclusion is that none of this—whether Clinton's arguments or the scandal itself—left much of an impression on the country. In the end, we can be sure that larger forces were at work beyond the persuasive power of religion.

In contrast to the apparent stability of public opinion during the scandal, Clinton's religious rhetoric on impeachment produced a solidly negative response from the editorialists of the four papers. Table 6.2 displays the results. Of the fifty-five editorials published in the week after Clinton's prayer breakfast speech, thirty-two were negative in tone (58.2 percent). Moreover, the average score was 2.22, a mark falling well into negative territory.

Clinton's religiosity at the breakfast led to an avalanche of scorn. Many writers were skeptical, if not outright offended, by Clinton's rhetorical strategy. For the *New York Times* (1998b), the most important characteristic of Clinton's speech was not the words he chose but its poor timing: "He (Clinton) attempted to repair the damage yesterday at the White House prayer breakfast with his most aggressive speech of contrition. With its unmitigated confession, its declaration of repentance, its forthright apology to Ms. Lewinsky, this was a striking speech. But its most striking feature was its lateness. The same words delivered in January, when he lied, or on Aug. 17, when he equivocated and hurled blame, might have lifted Mr. Clinton on to a road of guaranteed survival. He has no such guarantee today."

Fred Hiatt (1998), in turn, took issue with one specific point of Clinton's—the president's claim that his affair might wind up being a blessing for the country. Hiatt ripped Clinton for "the brazenness with which he invites us all to join in his healing" and he asked the president

Table 6.2
Editorial coverage of Clinton's national prayer breakfast speech on
September 11, 1998

Date	Paper	Author	Title	Score
9/12/1998	*Los Angeles Times*	Staff Editorial	"A Jury of Millions"	1
9/12/1998	*New York Times*	Michiko Kakutani	"An American Drama Replete With Ironies"	2
9/12/1998	*New York Times*	Staff Editorial	"Shame at the White House"	1
9/12/1998	*Washington Post*	Colbert King	"Dreams Destroyed"	1
9/13/1998	*Chicago Tribune*	James Coates	"It's Lurid, But Important—And Available to All"	3
9/13/1998	*Chicago Tribune*	Mary Schmich	"Starr Report Goes Against Alien Ideals"	5
9/13/1998	*Chicago Tribune*	Charles Madigan	"About 30% of American Voters . . ."	4
9/13/1998	*Chicago Tribune*	Michael Tackett	"Sex, Power—The Volatile Mix"	3
9/13/1998	*Los Angeles Times*	William Schneider	" It's Politics, Stupid"	2
9/13/1998	*Los Angeles Times*	Bruce Schulman	"Clinton's Reaganite Legacy"	2
9/13/1998	*Los Angeles Times*	Mike Downey	"How Long Will His Friends Stand By Their Man?"	2
9/13/1998	*New York Times*	Maureen Dowd	"Pulp Nonfiction"	2
9/13/1998	*Washington Post*	E. J. Dionne, Jr.	"Democrats' Dilemma: Step in It, or Throw It?"	3
9/13/1998	*Washington Post*	Staff Editorial	"Low Crimes and Misdemeanors"	2
9/13/1998	*Washington Post*	Richard Cohen	"Starr's Fault"	2

(*continued on next page*)

Table 6.2 (*continued*)

Date	Paper	Author	Title	Score
9/13/1998	*Washington Post*	Jim Hoagland	"A Couch for the President"	3
9/13/1998	*Washington Post*	Fred Hiatt	"The Contrition Campaign"	1
9/13/1998	*Washington Post*	Liza Mundy	"Chelsea's World"	3
9/14/1998	*Chicago Tribune*	John Kass	"Time for Clinton to Look for Work . . ."	1
9/14/1998	*Chicago Tribune*	Eric Zorn	"In the Book of Love . . ."	3
9/14/1998	*Los Angeles Times*	Shawn Hubler	"Explaining to the Children"	3
9/14/1998	*Los Angeles Times*	Staff Editorial	"A Defense Without Sense"	1
9/14/1998	*Los Angeles Times*	Gerald Uelmen	"Why Struggle to Defend So Lame a Duck?"	1
9/14/1998	*New York Times*	Staff Editorial	"Justice or Mercy for Bill Clinton?"	1
9/14/1998	*New York Times*	William Safire	"Starr's Unfinished Business"	2
9/14/1998	*New York Times*	Josef Joffe	"Where Europe Draws the Line"	1
9/14/1998	*Washington Post*	Meg Greenfield	"No Harmless Dirty Joke"	2
9/14/1998	*Washington Post*	William Raspberry	"In the Beginning, Monica Was 5"	3
9/15/1998	*Chicago Tribune*	Staff Editorial	"The President's Last Chance at Honor"	1
9/15/1998	*Chicago Tribune*	John Kass	"Sure Clinton's Tryst is a Private Matter . . ."	1
9/15/1998	*New York Times*	Anthony Lewis	"Muddying the Waters"	5
9/15/1998	*New York Times*	Katie Roiphe	"Monica Lewinsky, Career Woman"	4

(*continued on next page*)

Table 6.2 (*continued*)

Date	Paper	Author	Title	Score
9/15/1998	*New York Times*	Orlando Patterson	"What is Freedom Without Privacy?"	5
9/15/1998	*New York Times*	Clyde Haberman	"Contrition Doesn't Right All Wrongs"	1
9/15/1998	*Washington Post*	Staff Editorial	". . . And the Ability to Govern"	1
9/15/1998	*Washington Post*	Staff Editorial	"The Fast Track . . ."	3
9/15/1998	*Washington Post*	E. J. Dionne, Jr.	"Censure-Plus"	3
9/15/1998	*Washington Post*	David Broder	"With 28 Months to Go"	1
9/15/1998	*Washington Post*	Donna Britt	"An Affair Too Common to Forget"	2
9/16/1998	*Los Angeles Times*	Jim Mann	"Scandal Sidetracks Another Nation"	2
9/16/1998	*Los Angeles Times*	Thomas Baker	"There's No Basis for Censure"	3
9/16/1998	*New York Times*	Maureen Dowd	"The Wizard of Is"	1
9/16/1998	*Washington Post*	Michael Kelly	"Hairsplitting . . ."	1
9/17/1998	*Chicago Tribune*	Staff Editorial	"The Republican Imperative"	4
9/17/1998	*Los Angeles Times*	Staff Editorial	"A Test of Fairness"	3
9/17/1998	*Los Angeles Times*	Robert Reich	"Clinton's Challenge: Restore Trust"	1
9/17/1998	*Washington Post*	Richard Cohen	"Gatekeepers No More"	3
9/17/1998	*Washington Post*	Gene Weingarten	"The Unexpurgated Clinton"	1
9/18/1998	*Chicago Tribune*	R. Dold	"A Behind-the-Scenes Look at Democracy"	3

(*continued on next page*)

Table 6.2 (*continued*)

Date	Paper	Author	Title	Score
9/18/1998	*Chicago Tribune*	Mary Schmich	"Mired in Scandal . . ."	3
9/18/1998	*New York Times*	Staff Editorial	"Rancorous Diversions in Congress"	3
9/18/1998	*New York Times*	Elliot Richardson	"Sometimes, Evidence of Guilt Isn't Everything"	4
9/18/1998	*New York Times*	James Wilson	"Clinton, Nixon and What It Means to Obstruct"	1
9/18/1998	*New York Times*	A. Rosenthal	"The Three Questions"	1
9/18/1998	*Washington Post*	Charles Krauthammer	"Resignation, Then Pardon"	1
Dates: 9/12 to 9/18			**Average score**	**2.22**
			Positive articles	7 (12.7%)
			Negative articles	32 (58.2%)
			Mixed/neutral articles	16 (29.1%)

to have the "decency" to not make the country "endure further lectures on how it had all been to the good—our good." Hiatt was skeptical of most of Clinton's speech, admitting that, to him, how the ministers in attendance "could be so certain of the president's sincerity was hard to fathom."

Indeed, the sincerity of Clinton's religious appeals was a point of objection raised by many writers. William Safire (1998) wrote that "the central fact making a mockery of his misty-eyed 'repentance' is this: He refuses to admit, even now, that he and Monica Lewinsky had a sexual relationship." Clyde Haberman (1998) sounded a similar note. Derisively calling Clinton "The First Supplicant," Haberman argued that Clinton had not done enough to atone for his conduct. He observed, "the President would have been well warned that here, as elsewhere, contrition has its limits. Apologies do not absolve all sins, even when they are offered right away and with apparent feeling, not on the installment plan that Mr. Clinton has preferred."

John Kass (1998) was incensed by the legal defense that was also embedded in Clinton's speech. For this author, such statements served to undermine the rest of the message. Kass argued, "While making public contrition, he ordered his lawyers and mouthpieces to attack and confuse and spin. The idea is to shape public opinion. These aren't the actions of a contrite sinner seeking redemption. They are the tactics of a desperate man who would damage his nation to win a political fight." Kass concluded his column with four words of advice for Clinton: "Spare us. Get out."

Even the reliable liberal Maureen Dowd (1998) was not buying Clinton's confession. Dowd mocked Clinton's penchant for treating language as subjective, for disputing what words such as "is" and "alone" really mean. Quoting George Orwell, Dowd wrote that "the great enemy of clear language is insincerity." Along those lines, she could not believe what Clinton had said at the prayer breakfast: "Mr. Clinton's supporters are upset that he did not give his groveling prayer breakfast speech 25 days earlier, on the night he made his defiant television address. But the petulant and angry TV address was the authentic Clinton moment. The repentant and lip-biting prayer breakfast speech was the contrived Clinton moment. We no longer expect this President to be sincere. We just expect him to fake better, fake sooner."

There were precious few commentators rushing to Clinton's defense. Only seven positive editorials were printed in the week following Clinton's apology. Those pieces that received positive scores did not praise Clinton—not a single piece even hazarded to compliment his prayer breakfast speech—but they chose to strike at other targets like Clinton's political opponents (Madigan 1998), the Americans who voted for Clinton (Hubler 1998), Lewinsky (Roiphe 1998), or Kenneth Starr (Lewis 1998; Patterson 1998; Schmich 1998).

Finally, Clinton appears to have had mixed success persuading Congress that the punishment for his affair was a matter between him and God instead of between him and the government. After the Republicans surprisingly lost seats in the midterm elections, they nonetheless decided to continue to pursue impeachment. Party leaders decided that they were too far in at this point to back down. As Representative Henry Hyde, chairman of the House Judiciary Committee, told his fellow committee members, "What can we do? Can we sweep it under the rug?" (Wilentz 2008, 397). Still, as fall turned to winter, there was little question that the votes for removing Clinton were not there.

On Saturday, December 19, the House voted on four articles of impeachment. The outcome was not positive for Clinton. He lost two of the four impeachment votes, on Article I (grand jury perjury) and Article III (obstruction of justice), meaning he would go to trial in the Senate. These were embarrassing defeats. The votes for all four articles were exceptionally close: 228-206, 205-229, 221-212, and 148-285, in order.

At the same time, another key vote was the House's vote to release the Starr report to the public. Clinton was livid about this particular vote and he rants against the injustice of it in his memoirs (see Clinton 2004, 809). Clinton lost this vote by a huge margin, 363-63.

Following the House's actions, the Senate trial of President Clinton formally opened on January 7, 1999. After several weeks of testimony, the Senate began deliberating behind closed doors on February 9. On February 12, the Senate acquitted the president on both articles of impeachment, coming up well short of the two-thirds majority needed for conviction. The perjury charge was rejected 45-55, the obstruction charge 50-50.

We should also take note of one other specific vote. On January 27, Robert Byrd (D-WV), made a motion to dismiss the impeachment proceedings altogether. The motion was rejected, 44-56. It was a vote that could have saved Clinton much greater humiliation.

Most importantly, Clinton's religious rhetoric did not spare him the indignity of a Senate trial. And other votes that could have greatly improved his situation, the vote against the release of the Starr report and for the Byrd dismissal motion, went decisively against him.

Conclusion

Neither Ford nor Clinton's religious rhetoric helped them accomplish their goals. Ford turned to religious rhetoric as a way to temper the country's obsession with Watergate. The pardon decision was a means to this end. But Ford wound up having the exact opposite effect of what he had intended. His public support was shattered, surveys showed that the country consistently opposed his handling of the issue, the media excoriated his performance, and Congress ultimately spent even *more* time on Watergate. His religious rhetoric was an unmitigated failure.

As far as Clinton goes, it is impossible to know whether what some called his "contrition campaign" was a sincere attempt at atonement or not. What Clinton truly felt is somewhat immaterial, though. We do know that Clinton only turned to religious rhetoric as a strategic maneuver after his earlier comments on the affair, namely his speech on

August 17, had fallen flat. And we do know that this religious rhetoric did not improve his chances of survival.

Public opinion was stable, whether Clinton was defiant or penitent. Clinton's ratings showed no change after he embraced religious rhetoric, he received a statistically insignificant boost from his major address on September 11, and more people wanted him to resign *right after* that speech than at any other time. The media was hostile, choosing to hammer away at Clinton's confessional language at the prayer breakfast on September 11. Last, in Congress, Clinton could not avoid a series of disappointing and embarrassing defeats on several impeachment votes, including votes on related issues like the release of the Starr report in the House and the motion to dismiss the proceedings in the Senate. Despite the obvious unpopularity of the impeachment proceedings, Clinton's religious rhetoric did nothing to stop them. So, sincere or not, as a strategic choice, Clinton's use of religious rhetoric was a dubious choice at best.

The significance of the failure of Ford and Clinton's rhetorical pleas should not be discounted. To the end, Ford felt that his inability to convince the country that the pardon was the right call was one of his biggest shortcomings as president. "I thought people would consider his (Nixon's) resignation from the Presidency as sufficient punishment and shame. I thought there would be greater forgiveness. It was one of the greatest disappointments of my Presidency that everyone focused on the individual instead of on the problems the nation faced" (Ford 1979, 178–79).

Similarly, Clinton did not have a single major domestic accomplishment in the two years following his trial. Clinton's vice president, Al Gore, actively tried to distance himself from his predecessor during the 2000 campaign—and for good reason. Election night exit polls showed that most voters approved of Clinton's job performance but held negative feelings about him as a person. As a result, Gore captured only 63 percent of the votes from those individuals who were happy with the job Clinton had done—a much smaller number than one would normally expect (Norpoth 2001, 48).

So, in the end, no amount of religious speechifying could undo the damage of Watergate and Monica.

Note

1. As an aside, Ford would reuse these exact lines a little over a week later when he announced his clemency program for those who had avoided the draft (Ford 1974b).

7

An Experimental Evaluation of Religious Rhetoric

The previous case study chapters have all contributed the same basic insight: religious rhetoric is of limited value for a president who is trying to achieve his goals. Time and time again, we have seen such language be rejected by public opinion, be eviscerated by critics in the media, and be ignored by members of the US Congress.

Why have these appeals failed? Is it because this kind of speech is not persuasive? Or does it have something to do with the context in which such rhetoric has appeared? In each case study, a president only embraced religious arguments when in crisis. Bill Clinton is staring down impeachment, so he says he has sinned. Jimmy Carter's popularity craters, so he begins to discuss the meaning of life. George H. W. Bush sees support for his Gulf policy disintegrate at a key strategic moment, so he starts to frame the conflict as test of good and evil. It is possible that, if only a president were to use religious rhetoric in more favorable circumstances, then perhaps he would witness a more favorable outcome. The experiment that follows is designed to adjudicate between these two explanations. The evidence suggests it is more likely that the former is correct than it is the latter.

Indeed, the experimental results will offer the following conclusions. First, exposure to a religious policy argument has no effect on an individual's opinion. Second, exposure to secular rhetoric is slightly more impactful than exposure to religious rhetoric. Secular rhetoric is further shown to be considered as a stronger type of argument. Finally, third, ideology and partisan affiliation are more important than exposure to either type of rhetoric when it comes to explaining policy opinions, as one might reasonably expect to begin with.

Experimental Design

Two hundred and fifty-three individuals participated in this experiment over the course of the fall of 2011. The study's population was composed of Columbia University and Barnard College undergraduates. The research design was approved by the institutional review board of Columbia University (protocol IRB-AAAI5503). Students were invited to participate in the study during a regularly scheduled meeting of one of three political science lecture classes: an introductory course in American politics, an introductory course in comparative politics, and an upper level course on the role of labor in American politics. Despite the setting, participation was optional. No compensation or extra credit was offered in exchange.

Those students who did choose to participate received one of three versions of a questionnaire that was distributed throughout each class at random. Those receiving questionnaires marked #1 read a series of consecutive policy speeches that included examples of strong religious rhetoric. Participants were only told that they were about to read a "selection of 5 speeches made by past U.S. presidents, some Republicans and some Democrats." Crucially, these sample speeches were designed to mimic the way coalitional religious rhetoric has been used by American presidents. The topics of the speeches are the same issues where presidents have historically made religious arguments. The corresponding themes of the speeches are the same themes that presidents have actually employed.

The first speech made the case for the importance of fully funding America's foreign aid programs. The religious rhetoric in this treatment was an amalgam of points made at different times by a number of different presidents. The major source of this material, however, was Dwight Eisenhower. The speech principally highlights the importance of brotherhood, which in Chapter 2 was shown to be a key Eisenhower motif. The speech also references the Sermon on the Mount, a passage of Scripture that several presidents, namely Gerald Ford and George H. W. Bush, have drawn from in support of their policies.

The second speech was an argument about the need for additional civil rights legislation. This speech was constructed to reflect the type of religious arguments both John Kennedy and Lyndon Johnson had chosen to utilize. For example, the treatment references the Golden Rule and the possibility of an unfavorable eternal judgment if the country fails to live up to its obligations. Johnson repeatedly expressed these ideas. I do use a broader definition of civil rights in the speech, one that includes gender, sexual orientation, and national origin, to reflect the fact that the meaning of the term has become more encompassing over time.

The third religious speech contained an argument for stronger environmental standards. This speech was wholly based on Carter's rhetoric. The first paragraph includes arguments about steward-ship and protecting what God has given to America. The second paragraph is meant to capture the jeremiad style of Carter's malaise speech.

The fourth speech consists of a president defending himself after having admitted to an extramarital affair. This rhetorical treatment echoed Clinton's religious rhetoric, in particular his comments from August 28, 1998, and his major speech at the national prayer breakfast on September 11, 1998.

Finally, the fifth and final speech was a religion-based argument for government provision of healthcare. This issue has not been one on which presidents have used religious rhetoric, but it easily could have been given the high priority many faiths place on taking care of the sick. It would be interesting to know if Harry Truman, Bill Clinton, or Barack Obama would have had more success had they offered a strong religious rationale for their healthcare programs. This last speech is meant to explore this hypothetical. I crafted the religious argument in these paragraphs by means of my own reading of documents produced during the recent healthcare debates by various religious organizations like Faith for Health.

Hence, as one easily can see, these speeches are not just religious arguments that presidents *might* use, they are the religious arguments that presidents have *already* used.

After reading a speech, a participant would be presented with a set of three questions. First, they would be asked about their opinion on the policy content of the speech they had just read. For instance, after reading a religious argument by an adulterous president begging for forgiveness, participants were asked whether any president who admits to an affair should resign from office. Next, participants were asked the following: "On a scale of 1 to 5, with 1 being very weak and 5 being very strong, how strong an argument do you feel the president is making?" Finally, participants were asked: "Do you think this president was a Republican or a Democrat?"

The second section of the questionnaire consisted of a series of demographic queries. Students were surveyed on their sex, their race, whether they grew up in the South, their ideology, their partisanship, and their political interest and knowledge. Participants were also asked a set of questions about their religious beliefs and practices, including what denomination they identify with, how often they go to church, and whether they believe in God and the Bible or not. The wording of almost all of these questions, including the policy questions that follow the speeches, was taken verbatim from questions previously asked by either the General Social Survey or the National Election Studies. The political knowledge questions were chosen on the basis of the five-point scale recommended by Michael Delli Carpini and Scott Keeter (1993, 1996).

A second group of students received questionnaire 2. The structure of questionnaire 2 was almost identical to that of questionnaire 1—a series of five speeches on foreign aid, civil rights, the environment, an affair, and healthcare, each followed by the same three questions, and then a final section of the same demographic and religious measures. The major difference between the two versions is that, in questionnaire 2, the speeches offered secular, rather than religious, arguments. The secular arguments were constructed on the basis of research into the kinds of claims different individuals and organizations supporting such policies most commonly make. For example, the civil rights secular speech is drawn in large part from a review of the American Civil Liberties Union's platform. The secular speech for foreign aid is in large part drawn from an analysis of different articles in magazines like *Foreign Affairs*.

Thus, each religious speech in questionnaire 1 has a matching secular speech in questionnaire 2. The pairs are more or less identical in terms of word count and each pair contains the same number of lines of text, thereby controlling for any potential length effects. All of the ten speeches range from 240 to 280 words, a length meant to approximate a "whistle stop" type of address. Both the religious and the secular speech on an issue use the same introduction and the same conclusion. It is only the argument in the body of the text that provides the variation. Table 7.1 provides an illustration of the interrelationship between the two questionnaires, as well as examples of the religious and secular treatments.

A final group received questionnaire 3. These students were not exposed to any speeches. Instead, this group was only asked the policy,

Table 7.1
Sample speech treatment and question

Common Introduction

I'd like to quickly talk to you today about the energy bill that's currently being debated in Congress. You may have heard about it. It will require some sacrifice, whether in the form of slightly increased prices or the reductions in consumption each of us will have to make. But there's a lot of misconceptions out there which I'd like to clear up. The simple truth is that we have to do a better job conserving and protecting our environment.

Religious Argument

Sometimes I worry that we lose track of how many blessings have been bestowed upon this country. God has given us an abundant and fertile land, plentiful natural resources, great rivers, clean air. These are all gifts from God. Where would we be without them? I simply believe that it is incompatible with what the Bible teaches to waste what He has given to us. The time has come for us to recognize that there are limits and that we don't have the right to squander our natural resources. We have to be good stewards of the environment.

Too often, though, I feel people are selfish and short-sighted. Too many of us now worship materialism and consumption and self-indulgence. We need to solve this energy problem together. Let's search our own lives and hearts and ask what we can do to make them better, purer and more meaningful.

OR Secular Argument

We have to sacrifice because the planet is warming and if we don't rein in our energy usage the consequences will be catastrophic. If current trends continue, increases in ozone will exacerbate breathing problems, causing additional serious respiratory illnesses and hospitalizations. As ice sheets melt, rising oceans will flood coastal areas around the globe. We have all unfortunately seen the devastating impact severe weather can have on our communities. But if we fail to act, in the future our coasts will be more frequently threatened by storms and hurricanes that are likely to become stronger.

Additionally, as all this happens, a number of species will be dislocated and some, such as polar bears, may be threatened with eventual extinction if ice continues to disappear. That is a tragic loss we could never replace.

Common Conclusion

We must adopt a new, comprehensive energy policy. We owe it to our children. Please call your Representatives and your Senators and ask them to support the energy bill.

Thanks, and have a great afternoon.

Matching Opinion Question

Some people think that current regulations to protect the environment are already too much of a burden on business. Suppose these people are at one end of the scale, at point 1. Others think we need much tougher government regulations on business in order to protect the environment. Suppose these people are at the other end of the scale, at point 5. And, of course, some other people have opinions somewhere in between.

Where would you place yourself on this scale?

demographic, and religious background questions. Questionnaire 3 is a control group that will allow me to estimate what the impact of reading a speech is on an individual's opinion.

If religious rhetoric is meaningful, the expectation would be that those exposed to a religious speech will report higher support for that policy than those who did not read a speech. By including tests of secular rhetoric, we will also be able to determine whether there is anything distinctive about religious language relative to other types of

Table 7.2
Selected summary statistics on three questionnaires

Variable	Questionnaire 1 Religious Speeches ($N = 81$)	Questionnaire 2 Secular Speeches ($N = 85$)	Questionnaire 3 Control ($N = 87$)
Female (%)	51.85	56.47	59.77
Southern (%)	17.28	23.53	11.49
Caucasian (%)	58.44	56.47	52.33
Average ideology	3.18	2.84	2.82
Average partisanship	3.07	2.76	2.81
Political knowledge	4.16	4.22	4.20
Average church attend	3.85	4.04	3.78
Average belief in God	3.82	3.42	3.80

argumentation. If religious rhetoric is meaningful, it should produce a greater increase in opinion than secular rhetoric.

Eighty-one students completed questionnaire 1, eighty-five students completed questionnaire 2, and eighty-seven students completed questionnaire 3. Table 7.2 displays the summary statistics for each group.

Results

The first step in the analysis involved a series of difference of means tests, the results of which are reported in Tables 7.3–7.5.

Table 7.3 compares the mean issue opinion between those students who were not exposed to a speech, and the group that had read the religious speeches. Values on all five questions range from 1 to 5, where higher scores indicate greater support for the speaker's position.

For example, the environmental speech included in questionnaire 1 made a religious argument about the need for muscular environmental protections. A response of 5 on the environmental question that followed signified strong support for such regulations and reflected agreement with the speech's message. If religious rhetoric has an effect, the means in the religious treatment group should be significantly higher than the means in the control group.

That turns out not to the case. In fact, there is no significant difference between the two groups on any of the five issues. On healthcare, the two means are practically identical, both being rounded off to 3.82.

Table 7.3
Difference of means—control group versus religious treatment

Issue	Control (N = 87)	Religious Treatment (N = 81)
Foreign aid	4.00 (0.11)	3.80 (0.11)
Civil rights	4.24 (0.10)	4.19 (0.13)
Environment	4.01 (0.10)	3.93 (0.11)
Affair	3.86 (0.13)	4.00 (0.12)
Healthcare	3.82 (0.11)	3.82 (0.14)

Note: Standard errors in parentheses. Values represent the score on the matching five-point issue opinion question; higher scores indicate greater support for the president's position.
**$p < 0.01$; *$p < 0.05$; two-tailed test.

Table 7.4
Difference of means—control group versus secular treatment

Issue	Control (N = 87)	Secular Treatment (N = 85)
Foreign aid	4.00 (0.11)	4.05 (0.11)
Civil rights	4.24 (0.10)	4.33 (0.12)
Environment	4.01 (0.10)	4.11 (0.09)
Affair	3.86* (0.13)	4.19* (0.11)
Healthcare	3.82 (0.11)	4.01 (0.12)

Note: Standard errors in parentheses. Values represent the score on the matching five-point issue opinion question; higher scores indicate greater support for the president's position.
**p < 0.01; *p < 0.05; two-tailed test.

Table 7.5
Difference of means—strength of argument

Issue	Religious Argument Strength (N = 81)	Secular Argument Strength (N = 84)
Foreign aid	2.22** (0.10)	3.00** (0.11)
Civil rights	3.40 (0.11)	3.57 (0.12)
Environment	2.72** (0.11)	3.65** (0.10)
Affair	3.06 (0.12)	3.31 (0.13)
Healthcare	3.25* (0.12)	3.64* (0.11)

Note: Standard errors in parentheses. Values represent the score on the matching five-point strength of argument question; higher scores indicate that a respondent found the argument more persuasive.
**p < 0.01; *p < 0.05; two-tailed test.

Table 7.4 repeats the same analysis, but this time, the means of the control group and those of the group that read the secular speeches are compared. What this table reveals is that secular rhetoric appears to be slightly more powerful than religious rhetoric.

On one of the five issues, we do find a significant difference in opinion. If a participant was exposed to a speech that argued that a presidential affair was a private matter between a president and his wife, and further that by focusing on such matters the nation was distracting itself from more pressing problems, then an individual was significantly more likely to disagree with the statement that any president who admits to an affair should resign from office.

More evidence suggesting that secular rhetoric is more powerful than religious rhetoric can be found in Table 7.5.

Table 7.5 presents the results for a difference of means test on the prompt that asked participants to evaluate "how strong an argument" they felt the president was making. Responses ran from 1 to 5 with 1 being "very weak" and 5 being "very strong." As the table shows, the secular arguments were uniformly seen as the stronger of the two. On three of five issues—foreign aid, environmental protection, and government support for healthcare—the differences between the two groups were statistically significant.

Overall, these tables imply that religious rhetoric is inconsequential and that it pales in comparison to the potential force of secular rhetoric. However, more in-depth analysis still needs to be conducted. These three tables do not address the possibility that religious rhetoric may only appeal to certain types of individuals. In theory, the effect of exposure to religious rhetoric may be limited to religious people, those who are most familiar with the language and most likely to take it seriously.

It should be acknowledged that, if true, this effect would still not be a strong endorsement for coalitional religious rhetoric. The types of policy changes presidents have sought via religious rhetoric, things like landmark civil rights laws and support for wars, were, by definition, major initiatives. The success of these campaigns demanded the support of all Americans, and not just that of the faithful. Still, it is a question worth asking.

The best method to address this issue is by means of regression models using interaction terms. Akin to how a cup of coffee only becomes sweeter if you add sugar *and* stir—either one of these actions by itself fails to change the flavor of the coffee—it may be that a speaker needs to be exposed to a religious speech *and* have a high degree of confidence in the Bible or the like. The use of interaction terms, which is common to experimental methodology, can help us to identify such effects if they exist (Gelman and Hill 2007, 167–98).

Tables 7.6–7.10 estimate five sets of regression models that take the five policy opinion questions that were answered by all participants as their dependent variables. Two dummy variables were created to indicate whether a participant was exposed to a religious speech or a secular speech. For each, a value of 1 indicates that the participant read

Table 7.6
Predictors for opinion on US engagement with the world

Independent Variable	Model 1	Model 2	Model 3
Religious speech	−0.07 (0.16)	0.01 (0.16)	0.87 (1.19)
Secular speech	0.05 (0.15)	0.14 (0.15)	0.13 (0.15)
Female	0.29* (0.13)	0.23 (0.13)	0.20 (0.13)
South	−0.01 (0.17)	0.07 (0.17)	0.11 (0.17)
Minority	−0.07 (0.13)	−0.13 (0.14)	−0.14 (0.14)
Ideology	−0.04 (0.07)	−0.08 (0.07)	−0.08 (0.08)
Party	−0.09 (0.06)	−0.12* (0.06)	−0.13* (0.06)
Political interest	0.17 (0.09)	0.16 (0.09)	0.14 (0.10)
Political information	0.02 (0.06)	0.05 (0.06)	0.06 (0.06)
Protestant	−	0.23 (0.21)	0.45 (0.26)
Catholic	−	0.12 (0.19)	0.21 (0.24)
Jewish	−	0.05 (0.24)	0.22 (0.29)
Church attendance	−	−0.15* (0.07)	−0.10 (0.09)
Belief in the Bible	−	−0.19 (0.11)	−0.19 (0.14)
Belief in God	−	−0.12 (0.06)	−0.14* (0.07)
Religious speech × Protestant	−	−	−0.67 (0.45)
Religious speech × Catholic	−	−	−0.38 (0.41)
Religious speech × Jewish	−	−	−0.55 (0.50)
Religious Speech × church attendance	−	−	−0.21 (0.15)
Religious speech × belief in the Bible	−	−	−0.01 (0.25)
Religious speech × belief in God	−	−	0.07 (0.13)
Constant	3.56** (0.41)	5.07** (0.68)	4.99** (0.75)
R^2	0.08	0.14	0.16
N	245	235	235

Note: Entries are unstandardized ordinary least squares regression coefficients. Standard errors are in parentheses.
**$p < 0.01$; *$p < 0.05$.

Table 7.7
Predictors for opinion on civil rights

Independent Variable	Model 1	Model 2	Model 3
Religious speech	0.17 (0.15)	0.12 (0.16)	0.92 (1.19)
Secular speech	0.12 (0.15)	0.09 (0.15)	0.10 (0.15)
Female	0.52** (0.13)	0.50** (0.13)	0.50** (0.13)
South	0.04 (0.16)	0.01 (0.17)	−0.00 (0.17)
Minority	0.15 (0.13)	0.14 (0.14)	0.13 (0.14)
Ideology	−0.26** (0.07)	−0.24** (0.08)	−0.24** (0.08)
Party	−0.06 (0.06)	−0.08 (0.06)	−0.09 (0.06)
Political interest	−0.05 (0.09)	−0.10 (0.09)	−0.10 (0.10)
Political information	0.09 (0.06)	0.06 (0.06)	0.06 (0.06)
Protestant	–	0.16 (0.21)	0.13 (0.26)
Catholic	–	−0.09 (0.20)	0.08 (0.24)
Jewish	–	0.05 (0.24)	0.04 (0.29)
Church attendance	–	−0.10 (0.07)	−0.17 (0.09)
Belief in the Bible	–	−0.04 (0.12)	0.11 (0.14)
Belief in God	–	−0.14* (0.06)	−0.12 (0.07)
Religious speech × Protestant	–	–	0.19 (0.45)
Religious speech × Catholic	–	–	−0.30 (0.41)
Religious speech × Jewish	–	–	0.06 (0.50)
Religious speech × church attendance	–	–	0.18 (0.15)
Religious speech × belief in the Bible	–	–	−0.46 (0.25)
Religious speech × belief in God	–	–	−0.09 (0.14)
Constant	4.57** (0.40)	5.89** (0.68)	5.65** (0.75)
R^2	0.26	0.27	0.29
N	245	235	235

Note: Entries are unstandardized ordinary least squares regression coefficients. Standard errors are in parentheses.
**$p < 0.01$; *$p < 0.05$.

Table 7.8
Predictors for opinion on environmental regulation

Independent Variable	Model 1	Model 2	Model 3
Religious speech	0.02 (0.13)	−0.00 (0.13)	1.84 (0.95)
Secular speech	0.11 (0.12)	0.06 (0.13)	0.09 (0.12)
Female	0.11 (0.11)	0.16 (0.11)	0.16 (0.11)
South	−0.13 (0.14)	−0.15 (0.14)	−0.12 (0.13)
Minority	0.10 (0.11)	0.09 (0.11)	0.04 (0.11)
Ideology	−0.23** (0.06)	−0.22** (0.06)	−0.24** (0.06)
Party	−0.10 (0.05)	−0.08 (0.05)	−0.07 (0.05)
Political interest	−0.07 (0.07)	−0.13 (0.08)	−0.13 (0.08)
Political information	0.05 (0.05)	0.07 (0.05)	0.07 (0.05)
Protestant	–	−0.17 (0.17)	0.08 (0.21)
Catholic	–	−0.12 (0.16)	0.35 (0.19)
Jewish	–	−0.21 (0.20)	−0.14 (0.23)
Church attendance	–	−0.03 (0.06)	0.00 (0.07)
Belief in the Bible	–	−0.01 (0.10)	0.06 (0.11)
Belief in God	–	−0.08 (0.05)	−0.06 (0.06)
Religious speech × Protestant	–	–	−0.89* (0.36)
Religious speech × Catholic	–	–	−1.40** (0.33)
Religious speech × Jewish	–	–	−0.50 (0.40)
Religious speech × church attendance	–	–	−0.21 (0.12)
Religious speech × belief in the Bible	–	–	−0.13 (0.20)
Religious speech × belief in God	–	–	−0.04 (0.11)
Constant	4.88** (0.34)	5.43** (0.57)	4.95** (0.60)
R^2	0.25	0.31	0.37
N	245	235	235

Note: Entries are unstandardized ordinary least squares regression coefficients. Standard errors are in parentheses.
**$p < 0.01$; *$p < 0.05$.

Table 7.9
Predictors for opinion on if a president should resign due to an affair

Independent Variable	Model 1	Model 2	Model 3
Religious speech	0.17 (0.15)	0.14 (0.16)	0.11 (1.19)
Secular speech	0.24 (0.15)	0.19 (0.15)	0.19 (0.15)
Female	0.12 (0.13)	0.13 (0.13)	0.16 (0.13)
South	0.36* (0.16)	0.37* (0.17)	0.35* (0.17)
Minority	0.07 (0.13)	0.15 (0.14)	0.16 (0.14)
Ideology	−0.24** (0.07)	−0.18* (0.07)	−0.18* (0.08)
Party	−0.05 (0.06)	−0.05 (0.06)	−0.05 (0.06)
Political interest	0.10 (0.09)	0.09 (0.09)	0.10 (0.10)
Political information	0.23** (0.06)	0.24** (0.06)	0.25** (0.06)
Protestant	–	−0.14 (0.21)	−0.16 (0.26)
Catholic	–	−0.09 (0.19)	0.09 (0.24)
Jewish	–	0.09 (0.24)	−0.13 (0.29)
Church attendance	–	0.03 (0.07)	0.04 (0.09)
Belief in the Bible	–	−0.03 (0.11)	−0.03 (0.14)
Belief in God	–	−0.08 (0.06)	−0.08 (0.07)
Religious speech × Protestant	–	–	0.03 (0.45)
Religious speech × Catholic	–	–	0.03 (0.41)
Religious speech × Jewish	–	–	0.67 (0.50)
Religious speech × church attendance	–	–	−0.01 (0.15)
Religious speech × belief in the Bible	–	–	−0.01 (0.25)
Religious speech × belief in God	–	–	0.00 (0.14)
Constant	3.24** (0.40)	3.33** (0.68)	3.21** (0.75)
R^2	0.25	0.29	0.30
N	245	235	235

Note: Entries are unstandardized ordinary least squares regression coefficients. Standard errors are in parentheses.
**$p < 0.01$; *$p < 0.05$.

Table 7.10
Predictors for opinion on government provision of healthcare

Independent Variable	Model 1	Model 2	Model 3
Religious speech	0.18 (0.14)	0.20 (0.14)	0.04 (1.07)
Secular speech	0.18 (0.14)	0.23 (0.14)	0.22 (0.14)
Female	0.16 (0.12)	0.15 (0.12)	0.09 (0.12)
South	−0.00 (0.15)	0.02 (0.15)	0.07 (0.15)
Minority	0.23* (0.11)	0.20 (0.13)	0.18 (0.13)
Ideology	−0.34** (0.06)	−0.37** (0.07)	−0.38** (0.07)
Party	−0.20** (0.05)	−0.19** (0.06)	−0.20** (0.06)
Political interest	0.07 (0.08)	0.06 (0.09)	0.02 (0.09)
Political information	0.01 (0.05)	0.01 (0.06)	0.03 (0.06)
Protestant	–	−0.21 (0.19)	0.08 (0.23)
Catholic	–	−0.15 (0.18)	0.03 (0.22)
Jewish	–	−0.23 (0.22)	0.07 (0.26)
Church attendance	–	−0.11 (0.07)	−0.17* (0.08)
Belief in the Bible	–	0.09 (0.11)	0.19 (0.12)
Belief in God	–	0.02 (0.06)	−0.05 (0.06)
Religious speech × Protestant	–	–	−0.68 (0.41)
Religious speech × Catholic	–	–	−0.45 (0.37)
Religious speech × Jewish	–	–	−0.77 (0.45)
Religious speech × church attendance	–	–	0.10 (0.14)
Religious speech × belief in the Bible	–	–	−0.26 (0.23)
Religious speech × belief in God	–	–	0.19 (0.12)
Constant	4.92** (0.37)	5.18** (0.62)	5.45** (0.67)
R^2	0.44	0.47	0.50
N	244	234	234

Note: Entries are unstandardized ordinary least squares regression coefficients. Standard errors are in parentheses.
**$p < 0.01$; *$p < 0.05$.

the speech, a value of 0 indicates that they did not. Additional dummy variables were created to capture whether a respondent was female (1 = yes, 0 = no), whether a respondent has lived in the US South for five or more years (1 = yes, 0 = no) and whether a respondent self-identified as a racial or ethnic minority (1 = yes, 0 = no).

Other variables measured a participant's ideology and partisan affiliation. These two measures were the standard seven-point, self-placement scales used throughout much of the political science literature. Higher values indicate that a student was more conservative or more Republican. Two variables also represent a participant's political interest and political information. The political interest variable is a scale from 1 to 4, where higher values indicate greater interest in government affairs. The political knowledge variable is the Delli Carpini and Keeter (1993, 1996) five-question scale. A score of 5 on this variable would indicate that a respondent provided correct answers to all five knowledge questions.

Last, the models include six different variables meant to capture a participant's religious affiliation, religious behavior, and religious beliefs. Dummy variables were generated to indicate if a participant self-identified as Protestant, Catholic, or Jewish (for all, 1 = yes, 0 = no). A variable was also created to measure church attendance. This variable runs from 1 to 5 where lower scores indicate that a respondent reported attending services more often. A variable was created to measure a participant's belief in the Bible. Four statements were offered and participants were asked to select the one that was closest to their own view. Values run from 1 to 4, and lower values suggest an individual places more weight on the contents of the Bible. Finally, a similar variable was constructed to measure an individual's beliefs about God. This variable ranges from 1 to 6, where higher values signify greater faith in God.

In this sequence of tables, the key models are the fully specified ones found in the third column. In each, the dummy variable for a religious speech is interacted with the six other religious variables, i.e., religious speech × church attendance.

An examination of the results from these regressions yields some important observations. As expected given the results from the difference of means tests, in not a single one of the fifteen different models are any of the speech dummy coefficients significant. Exposure to a speech of either type does not predict an individual's opinion on any of these five issues.

Importantly, the interaction terms fare no better. In four of the five models, all six of the interaction terms are insignificant. The only exception is found in the model predicting opinion on environmental regulation. Here, the interactions between exposure to a religious speech and both the Catholicism and Protestantism dummies are significant. Indeed, the coefficient for religious speech × Catholic is substantively large and significant at the 0.01 level.

However, the negative signs of both terms are in the wrong direction. If a participant self-identified as a member of either faith and received a religious speech they were actually *less* likely to agree with the speaker's policy position. This result, therefore, undermines the premise that religious individuals might respond more positively to religious arguments. What instead could be happening is that, perhaps, these individuals were reacting negatively to what they viewed as a crass manipulation of their faith. In the end, these models suggest that religious rhetoric may possibly alienate religious individuals.

It is valuable to consider what variables *do* predict opinion on these issues. What emerges from these models is a sense of the pre-eminent importance of ideology and partisanship. The coefficient for ideology is significant in all of the models, mostly at the 0.01 level, with the exception of the three models that estimate opinion on United States' engagement with the world. Intuitively, though, this result seems to make sense. It is hard to detect an ideological direction to opinion on foreign aid. Conservatives, for example, are thought to be split between isolationists and a more robust, internationally oriented neoconservative wing (Kagan 2006).

In all of the other models, the signs of the different ideology coefficients are in the right direction. These values show that, as an individual becomes more conservative, he or she becomes more likely to think the country has gone too far in pushing civil rights, that environmental regulations are too much of a restriction on business, that a president who admits to an affair should resign his office, and that healthcare should not be a government responsibility. These are logical findings.

Partisanship proves to be almost equally important in explaining issue opinion. An individual's self-identification with either party is key to understanding his or her opinion on isolationism and healthcare. The coefficients show that as an individual becomes more Republican, he or she becomes less supportive of a vibrant international role for America and less supportive of government provision of healthcare. These findings, too, are logical.

Thus, rhetoric does not appear to matter, but ideology and partisanship do. Putting aside the similar findings of the case studies, we should not be surprised by these results. The credibility of the source of a communication can impact whether a person will be receptive to it or not (Druckman 2001). More to the point, if there is an ideological or partisan mismatch between the source of a communication and its recipient—say a conservative Republican voter hears a speech by a liberal Democratic president—persuasive effects are unlikely to be found (Zaller 1992, 45; Hartman and Weber 2009).

Along those lines, Table 7.11 suggests important insights that may account for why these rhetorical appeals were apparently ignored.

Table 7.11 reports the suspected partisan affiliation of the speaker for all five issues in both the religious and secular speech groups. It is clear that the respondents tended to weakly associate religious language with Republican presidents. When given a secular speech on civil rights, just 5.88 percent of participants thought the president was a Republican. When given a religious speech, however, 24.69 percent of the sample thought the president was a Republican, an increase of almost 19 percent. On environmental protection, when given a secular speech, just 10.59 percent of students thought the president was a Republican. When given a religious speech, however, that same figure soars to 36.71 percent, an increase of over 26 percent. This finding is interesting because the actual presidents the frames were based on were Democrats in three of the five cases.

At the same time, for four of these issues, individuals nonetheless detected a clear partisan direction to the policies. The civil rights,

Table 7.11
Suspected partisan affiliation of president by treatment

Issue	Religious Treatment Republican (%) / Democrat (%)	Secular Treatment Republican (%) / Democrat (%)
Foreign aid	70.00 / 30.00	34.94 / 65.06
Civil rights	24.69 / 75.31	5.88 / 94.12
Environment	36.71 / 63.29	10.59 / 89.41
Affair	25.00 / 75.00	11.90 / 88.10
Healthcare	8.75 / 91.25	2.38 / 97.62

environment, affair, and healthcare policies were all thought to be Democratic initiatives, and by wide margins. On healthcare, for example, 97.62 percent of those receiving a secular speech and 91.25 percent of those receiving a religious speech associated the arguments with the Democrats. Likewise, on civil rights, 94.12 percent of those receiving a secular speech and 75.31 percent of those receiving a religious speech associated the arguments with the Democrats.

What this means is that participants were able to detect partisan and ideological cues in the speeches, despite not being told who the president was or what party he belonged to. These data help us to understand why ideology and partisanship were so important in explaining the results. When over 90 percent of subjects associate an issue with the Democrats, it makes sense that opinions toward that party and its ideas would guide an individuals' response. It is no secret that partisanship is one of the single most important factors determining political behavior (Green, Palmquist, and Schickler 2002).

Notably, the one issue where these cues did not seem to be available was foreign aid. Here, by a strong margin, those receiving the secular speech thought the speaker was a Democrat (65.06 to 34.94 percent). In contrast, those who received the religious speech thought the speaker was a Republican by an equally large margin (70.00 to 30.00 percent). Thus, it is not surprising that it was only in the regression models for foreign aid that the coefficients for ideology and partisanship failed to reach statistical significance.

When an individual listens to a president speak, they know who he is, what he stands for, and what he is trying to accomplish. And when individuals can evaluate the credibility and partisan and ideological disposition of a source, they are more than capable of resisting attempts at persuasion. Such has been the case here. Respondents, despite not being told, had strong presumptions of the identity of the presidential speakers. These feelings then guided their opinions on the policy issues. The findings of this experiment are thus in tune with the idea that the acceptance of political communications is a deliberative, contingent process (i.e., Nelson and Oxley 1999; Brewer 2001; Druckman 2001).

Conclusion

This chapter has presented a possible causal explanation for the repeated failures of religious rhetoric that are documented in the case studies: religious rhetoric is inherently unpersuasive. Difference of means tests have shown that exposure to a religious speech did not lead to a significant change in opinion on any of the five issues that were being tested. Secular rhetoric was slightly more promising. Exposure to a secular speech caused a significant opinion change on a presidential affair and the secular arguments were judged by respondents to be significantly stronger than their religious counterparts.

Still, regression analysis showed that issue opinion was mainly driven by ideology and partisanship. Although religious rhetoric was slightly more likely to be seen as a Republican tactic, participants recognized strong source cues from the speech that led them to see all but one of the issues as a Democratic policy. With this information at hand, respondents were well positioned to screen the speeches' messages.

Admittedly, some will want to dismiss these results because the subject population was made up of college students, and, moreover, students at secular and liberal Columbia University. If a person wishes to dismiss research for the sole reason that it is based on student subjects, they will have to cast a very wide net. From 1990 through 2006, one quarter of all experimental articles published in top-tier political science journals used student subjects (Kam, Wilking, and Zechmeister 2007). It is not enough, however, to point to the commonality of student subjects as a defense. This skepticism is not justified for several more important reasons.

The rationale for being skeptical of student subject research is sensible enough. College students are characterized by their questionable sense of self and their strong need for peer approval. Their political and social attitudes are known to be less stable than those of older adults. When combined with the unique features of a laboratory setting, a number of biases may be introduced. For instance, a core finding of psychology is that individuals are easily influenced. But maybe, this finding is only a product of the database from which it was discovered—students who are known to have weakly formed attitudes to begin with (Sears 1986).

In an unusual twist, though, this reasoning adds to the assurance one can have about the results reported from this experiment. If college students are so easily influenced, this study should have been biased toward identifying a number of effects from political speech. The opposite occurred. Religious rhetoric was not important in explaining opinions, even among the most religious individuals. Thus, the use of student subjects should actually make one more confident about the validity of the findings.

A second defense for the use of student subjects is that the differences between students and the general population have been overblown. In most cases, college students and the general population are indistinguishable when it comes to important political characteristics like partisanship, belief in limited government, views on homosexuality, social trust, and political interest (Druckman and Kam 2011). Students also tend to process information in the same ways that older adults do, too (Kuhberger 1998).

A last criticism of the experimental design may highlight the use of not just student subjects, but Columbia student subjects. The claim could be made that Columbia is a setting biased against religious rhetoric. True, Columbia in some ways is not representative. The entire sample of 253 students had an average ideology score of 2.94, which is just to the left of "slightly liberal." When this question is asked by the American National Election Studies (ANES), typically the national mean comes out to somewhere between 4, that is "moderate," and 5, that is "slightly conservative." And in the experiment sample, the mean of the church attendance variable was 3.89, which translates to most students reporting that they attend religious services only "a few times a year."

However, recall that the inclusion of interaction terms in the regression models was meant to explore the possibility that religious rhetoric was more appealing to the churched. This did not turn out to be the case. And, if Columbia does not look exactly like America now, America is likely to look ever more like Columbia in the future owing to the growing secularization of younger Americans. Any president's rhetoric will increasingly be aimed at a secular audience. I'll discuss the implications of this development further in the conclusion.

Conclusion

This book began by arguing that presidents can choose to use either of two distinct types of religious rhetoric.

One form represents religion's potential to bring a community together, something scholars of religion like Durkheim have long been aware of. By using bland, nondescript religious phrases, presidents build on their natural role in defining who counts as an American. I labeled such language communitarian religious rhetoric.

Although aware of this style of expression, I was far more concerned with a different style of religious rhetoric—coalitional religious rhetoric. This term is meant to capture the strategic use of religious arguments for political goals and objectives, like passing a bill or ending a scandal. This kind of religious rhetoric is very unlike communitarian religious rhetoric. It can upset people, it can offend people, and, owing to its attachment to political motivations, it most certainly will divide people. However, in choosing to embrace such language, presidents are making a calculated gamble that these words will ultimately attract more than they alienate, and thus allow a president to assemble the winning coalition that he needs to prevail.

Every president except Harry Truman and Richard Nixon has used this latter style of language, but only in certain areas. Coalitional religious rhetoric has clustered on four issues where religion is easily applicable: foreign policy, environmental policy, civil rights, and presidential scandals. Each of the case study chapters explored one of these areas.

Table 8.1 provides a summary of the major religious themes that were highlighted in these chapters. Be aware that this list is a simplified one. A number of smaller features of the religious rhetoric of different presidents are not included, such as George H. W. Bush's calls for days of prayer or Gerald Ford's discussion of the import of Rosh Hashanah. This table is meant to only capture the most prominent themes marking each president's religious discourse.

Table 8.1
Summary of major religious themes

Policy Type	President	Objective	Major Religious Themes
Foreign policy	Dwight Eisenhower	Mutual security funding	• Cold war as a battle between atheism and religion • Christian brotherhood • Jeremiads on selfishness
Foreign policy	Ronald Reagan	Defense spending	• Cold war as a battle between atheism and religion • Biblical support found in the Psalms, Luke • General spiritual descriptions of purposes of defense spending
Foreign policy	George H. W. Bush	Persian Gulf War	• Conflict as an example of good versus evil • War meets criteria of just war theory • God supports the US mission
Foreign policy	George W. Bush	War on Terror	• Conflict as an example of good versus evil • United States is fighting for freedom/God's purpose
Environment	Jimmy Carter	Energy reform	• Jeremiads on materialism/consumerism • Stewardship/environment is a blessing from God • Co-opting of message of John Paul II
Civil rights	John Kennedy	Civil rights	• Segregation is immoral and conflicts with scripture
Civil rights	Lyndon Johnson	Civil rights	• Kennedy as a martyr figure • Relevance of the golden rule • Warnings of eternal judgment • General moral statements about civil rights
Scandal	Gerald Ford	Nixon pardon	• Importance of being merciful • The pardon as a matter of God and conscience

(continued on next page)

Table 8.1 (*continued*)

Policy Type	President	Objective	Major Religious Themes
Scandal	Bill Clinton	Lewinsky scandal	• Personal forgiveness depending on his willingness to forgive others • Scandal as a blessing for the country • Preference for religious words like "sin," "atone," and "repent" over secular alternatives

What is interesting is how little overlap there is between the cases. Some themes did recur in the rhetoric of multiple presidents. For instance, both Dwight Eisenhower and Ronald Reagan depicted the Cold War as a battle against atheism. Both George H. W. Bush and his son spoke of good and evil. But mostly presidents constructed religious rationales that were specific to their goals. Ford talked of the importance of being merciful because it made sense to do so in the context of the pardon. Mercy would not be appropriate to a discussion of defense spending or the War on Terror.

This observation underscores the fundamental perspective of this study—that being that religious rhetoric has often been a strategic tool for the president. The case studies contain ample evidence that each president chose his religious rhetoric carefully.

In Chapter 3, we saw how George H. W. Bush built an extensive communications operation that was designed to build grassroots support for his Gulf War policy. When Bush's pollster told the president that the administration's rhetoric was too unfocused, Bush responded by playing up the more clear-cut religious argument for action.

We learned in Chapter 4 that Jimmy Carter's jeremiads on energy were a direct byproduct of a polling report produced by one his top advisors.

In Chapter 5, I discussed how Johnson came to use religious rhetoric on civil rights because he felt that a Christian, moral appeal was the only one Southerners would respond to. We also learned how Johnson consciously built Kennedy up into a martyr so as to associate his predecessor's death with his own causes.

In other chapters, I have surveyed how presidents could, in general, be extraordinarily shrewd when it came to religion. For example, Reagan would speak to anti-abortion protesters every year on the anniversary of *Roe v. Wade*, but only by telephone so as to ensure that he would not be seen at the rally when it was covered on the evening news.

In an age of speechwriters, press secretaries, and focus groups, it is taken for granted that presidents choose their words carefully. Nevertheless, when this evidence is combined with the impression one gains from Table 8.1, one realizes that presidents do not use coalitional religious rhetoric simply because they are comfortable speaking in these terms; they use coalitional religious rhetoric because they think they can benefit by calling to mind the American people's most sacred beliefs. Each president narrowly interpreted traditional religious doctrine for their own strategic purposes.

In fact, this book has shown that many presidents are actually *not* comfortable talking about religion. Consider John Kennedy as a fitting illustration. As a young Representative from a heavily Catholic district in Massachusetts, Kennedy was initially a prominent defender of Catholic interests. Yet, as he emerged as a candidate for national office, Kennedy started to downplay his support for Catholic causes, changing his stance on issues such as aid to parochial schools. Kennedy later faced a great deal of bigotry during his run for the White House in 1960, forcing him to proclaim his belief in an inviolate separation of church and state before the Greater Houston Ministerial Association. JFK wanted to distract people from his religion, not draw attention to it by peppering his public remarks with spiritual content.

Carter, on the other hand, did not exactly hide his Christian faith. He continued to teach Sunday school as president. But he, too, tried to walk a tightrope on religion. Carter's evangelical beliefs were unfamiliar to many Americans. Moreover, as a Baptist, Carter also was committed to a strict separation of church and state. So as president, he promised to uphold *Roe v. Wade*, he consistently opposed school prayer, and he fought against tuition tax credits for parochial schools. He resisted regular meetings with religious groups and paid little attention to their concerns. Therefore, it is little surprise that Carter made fewer explicit references to the Bible or to his own faith than most other presidents (Smith 2006, 296).

Along these lines, it has been proved that a crisis was a necessary, if not a sufficient, condition for the appearance of religious rhetoric. In each case, a president faced a visible deterioration in his political circumstances before beginning to voice religious arguments for his policy. Reagan was buffeted by recession, deficits, and plunging approval ratings. Kennedy confronted protestors in the streets, police brutality, and a country coming apart at the seams. Ford had the albatross of Nixon's unresolved situation hanging around his neck, swallowing up all his time. Bill Clinton was days away from the Congressional Democrats asking for his resignation.

The most significant finding of this book, however, is that religious rhetoric does not work. The case studies evaluated the effect of religious rhetoric on three different actors—the public, the media, and Congress. The results all tend in the same direction.

Opinion, most commonly, was nonresponsive. Most speeches did not impact a president's approval ratings. On average, a major religious speech led to less than a 1 percent increase. Issue specific opinion was even more obstinate.

The media consistently criticized both the presidents' ideas and the religious content of their appeals. The mean editorial score for all coded speeches was a negative 2.63. On average, 51.1 percent of all commentaries on a speech were negative in tone, meaning they were scored a 1 or a 2 on the five-point scale.

Similarly, Congress was unlikely to embrace the president's proposals. Money was cut, proposals were rejected, and investigations continued. Overall, the case studies range from outright failures (Eisenhower, Kennedy, Ford, Carter, Reagan) to those where no reasonable argument can be made that religious rhetoric had a positive effect on a president's fate (Johnson, Clinton).

The experimental chapter was needed to determine why religious rhetoric typically fails. Potentially, the answer could lie in the context in which such language has appeared. In each case study, a president used religious arguments when in crisis. It, therefore, was an open question whether a president would witness a more favorable outcome if he were to use religious rhetoric in more favorable circumstances. The experiment, mimicking the actual religious arguments presidents have historically used, resolved this puzzle.

Difference of means tests revealed that exposure to a religious speech did not lead to a significant change in opinion on any of the issues that were tested. In contrast, exposure to a secular speech caused a significant change on the presidential affair issue, while the secular arguments were also judged by respondents to be significantly stronger than the religious ones.

Nonetheless, regression analysis showed that issue opinion was instead driven by ideology and partisanship. Although religious rhetoric was slightly more likely to be seen as a Republican tactic, participants picked up on strong source cues in each speech that led them to see all but one of the issues as Democratic policies. With this information at hand, respondents were well-positioned to screen the messages contained in each speech.

To sum up: Presidents can use either communitarian or coalitional religious rhetoric. Mainly for personal reasons, most presidents have hesitated to use religious rhetoric to further their goals. A crisis has been needed to help them overcome their reluctance but they have only overcome it slightly. They have restricted their use of religious rhetoric to those issues were religion is most closely identified. In the end, it does not much matter. Religious rhetoric typically does not persuade the public, the media, or the Congress to support the president. Likely, the reason this is so is that religious language is inherently unpersuasive.

These findings have serious implications for anyone who seeks to understand presidential power or the role of religion in American politics.

I began this study open to the possibility that religious rhetoric was different. It turns out that religious rhetoric is much the same. I join the growing chorus of voices who question the effectiveness of any kind of presidential oratory (i.e., Jacobs and Shapiro 2000; Edwards 2003; Wood 2009).

God Wills It is an important contribution to this discussion because it explores a type of rhetoric that has been mostly overlooked to date, despite its prominence in presidential leadership. And, further, previous research argues that religious rhetoric can be powerful, given certain conditions (Shogan 2006). The analysis in this book should replace this view.

It bears repeating that, even though we expect a president to lead, the formal powers of the office guarantee nothing more than clerkship. A successful president must use his status and authority to persuade and bargain (Neustadt 1960). Unfortunately, it does not seem that religious rhetoric will help these leaders as they do so. Presidents are constrained, hamstrung, and limited. They frequently find it difficult to act. Strategically using religious speech cannot change the fundamentals of the office.

The Language of Our Past

This has been a study of the role of religious rhetoric in modern presidential leadership. So, one question this book cannot fairly answer is whether or not religious rhetoric has always been so ineffectual.

That said, the religious rhetoric of the pre-modern presidents likely was more meaningful. Benjamin Harrison, a remarkably active speaker for his time, seems to have been able to use religious rhetoric as part of a nuanced appeal for the Republican economic program (Calhoun 1993). Andrew Jackson is another who appears to have successfully used religious rhetoric (Langston 1993). So, when Abraham Lincoln used religious rhetoric in those miserable final days of the Civil War, his words probably did resonate more with his listeners than those same words would resonate with an audience today.

There is ample reason to suspect that the force of religious rhetoric has become weaker over time as the religious foundations of American society have begun to crumble. The end of 1950s marked the beginning of a long decline in American religion (Putnam and Campbell 2010). A variety of factors had contributed to a renewed interest in spirituality in the immediate postwar years. The unsettling memories of combat had reawakened many soldiers' spiritual convictions. When those soldiers later got back to the states, they settled down and had children—two activities strongly associated with church attendance. The consequences of these experiences would be dramatic. Among those under thirty years of age, weekly church attendance soared from 31 percent in 1950, all the way to 51 percent in 1957 (84).

The heightened religiosity of the 1950s would not last, though. The dawning of the 1960s brought with them changing sexual mores, recreational drugs, and a willingness to question all authority, including religious ones. By 1966, *Time* magazine was famously asking, "Is God dead?" The number of Americans who said that religion was "very important" to them had fallen from 75 percent in 1952, down to 52 percent by 1978 (98).

It is no secret that recent decades have continued to present enormous difficulties for America's major religious institutions. Just between 1990 and 2000 alone, the Presbyterian USA denomination lost 11.6 percent of its total membership. The United Church of Christ fared even worse, losing 14.8 percent of its membership (Fowler et al. 2010, 39).

Indeed, today, 20 percent of the US public declines to identify with any religious denomination. The rise of these "nones" is most pronounced among the young. Currently, 32 percent of adults under thirty years of age have no affiliation (Pew Forum on Religion and Public Life 2012b).

Unsurprisingly, these changes have influenced the basic contours of religious belief in American society. In the 1960s, around 65 percent of people believed the Bible was the literal word of God. Now, just 30 percent of people think that way (Putnam and Campbell 2010, 112). America has changed from a society where it was impossible to question God or the Bible, to one where believing in them is just one option among many. As a result, the challenges of sustaining one's faith have become exponentially greater (Taylor 2007).

The truth is that these trends have hurt all religious organizations that have relaxed their expectations in order to accommodate modern society. Growth has only been seen in smaller, demanding sects like Mormonism and Pentecostalism. In these faiths, the rewards of participation, things like community and spiritual direction, are still high enough to make the costs of religious life worthwhile (Finke and Stark 2005). They are the exceptions to the rule.

I am not trying to make the case that America is heading the way of Western Europe, or at least not yet. Even most of the "nones" continue to believe in God and describe themselves as religious or spiritual people (Pew Forum on Religion and Public Life 2012b). But what is happening is that religion is being transformed into something less formal, and more personal. Recent generations have been generations of "seekers." Their spiritual life has been less tied to institutions. The content of their beliefs has become more fluid as more individuals are open to experimenting with alternatives like astrology or the occult (Roof 1993).

What these changes mean for politicians who would use religious rhetoric is unclear. But the work of Robert Bellah et al. (1996) suggests an answer. In their influential book *Habits of the Heart*, this diverse collection of scholars warn of the dangers of modern individualism. Individualism values independence, self-reliance, and self-expression. It is embodied in the US tradition of expecting children to leave home once they reach a certain age, a practice not shared with many other peoples in the world. In its softer form, individualism is embodied in our culture's preference for therapy, for focusing on "finding oneself."

Religious practice and belief have not been spared from the influence of individualism. In one of their most famous anecdotes, Bellah et al. recount an interview they conducted with Sheila Larson, a young woman they not so subtly identify as a long-time therapy patient. Larson takes self-centrism to its logical extreme by naming her religious faith after herself: "I believe in God. I'm not a religious fanatic. I can't remember the last time I went to church. My faith has carried me a long way. It's Sheilaism. Just my own little voice" (221).

Because, like Larson, each individual is trying to construct their own meaning to the world, the authors argue that Americans have lost their ability to contextualize their lives in terms of Biblical tradition. When asked big questions about life, the authors' interview subjects can do little more than fall back on weak abstractions.

Habits of the Heart opens with the tale of Wayne Bauer, a social justice activist in California (17–20). Wayne is outraged that landlords in Santa Monica repeatedly bully their immigrant tenants with threats of deportation. He wants to empower the poorer citizens in his community. Yet, when asked to what end, he stammers. He says he wants to make the world "better," but when questioned what he means by that, he replies, "I'm probably not the best person to ask."

The authors' point is that Wayne cannot explain a concept like social justice because he no longer has access to the religious cultural resources that would allow him to do so. It stands to reason that when average citizens, even churchgoing ones like Wayne Bauer, cannot explain themselves using religious language, then they will struggle mightily to connect to a politician who uses religious language to explain their own.

But the limitations of religious rhetoric in modern society go even further than this. Just consider the types of words we might instead identify as most powerful in contemporary American life. "Progress." "Fact." "Science." These are kinds of words that now carry the highest blessing. These are the kind of words that now can compel people to accept great sacrifices in pursuit of the ideals they are associated with (Weaver 1953, 211–32).

So, we explain societal developments as the workings of "progress." In the past, we might have attributed such things to "Providence" instead. We accept arguments based on the "facts," and no longer on religious truth. And even if a politician wishes to contest climate change or evolution, they will do so by pointing to contrasting studies or gaps in the fossil record. They still make their argument based on what "science" does or does not say.

However resilient religious belief appears to be in American culture, the language of religion is slipping from our grasp. Religious rhetoric is the political language of our past, not our future. Goal-oriented presidents would do well to keep that in mind.

The Value of Religious Rhetoric to the Modern President

I have said repeatedly that I think the governing view is that presidents can manipulate the public by means of religious rhetoric. For example, in a piece appearing in *Presidential Studies Quarterly*, Douglas Kellner (2007) assigns almost superhuman power to George W. Bush's religious rhetoric. Focusing on Bush's good versus evil discourse, Kellner argues that Bush, working with the media, "created tremendous fear in the population, which made the public look anxiously to the government for protection, rendering the population malleable to manipulation" (627). Interchangeably, Kellner describes Bush's rhetoric as "Orwellian," "fascist," and an example of the "the Goebbels-Hitler strategy." This book should cause the reader to dismiss these kinds of critiques as exaggerations.

That does not mean that there is no reason to be concerned about presidential religious rhetoric, though. If presidents cannot manipulate the public—which, assuredly, they cannot—there might still be other consequences to worry about. Religion often hardens political divisions. It can be difficult to find common ground on social issues like abortion and homosexuality once religious values have been introduced into the discussion. Worse, sometimes religious values can lead to violence. Over the course of American history, fanatics have often selectively found justification for their extremism in religious texts (Marty and Moore 2000).

A related issue is that those outside the Abrahamic tradition are increasingly prone to feeling excluded by presidential displays of religiosity. It has been noted that President Bush systematically overlooked Hindus, one of the fastest growing religious communities in America, in his post-9/11 religious statements. This neglect may have contributed to a burgeoning Hindu nationalism that publicly attacked Islam in an attempt to differentiate the two religions (Kurien 2006).

Still, I would hazard to counter that presidents should continue to freely discuss religious beliefs in public, whether it is useful for their agenda or not.

For one, at least communitarian religious rhetoric has undeniable social value. Communitarian rhetoric often will accompany moments of national trial and religion can help people endure those challenging times. Greater religiousness is associated with the onset of fewer symptoms of depression (Smith, McCullough, and Poll 2003), lower levels of suicidal behavior (Gearing and Lizardi 2009), and positive posttraumatic growth (Shaw, Joseph, and Linley 2005). Hence, by referencing religious values during moments of despair, a president could conceivably make a meaningful difference in the lives of some Americans who might be struggling to cope with depression and anxiety.

In a more abstract sense, though, I think we should be cautious when it comes to any attempt to separate religious values from public life. Richard John Neuhaus (1984) has written intelligently of the "naked public square"—"naked" because it has been stripped of all references to religion. Yet, law by its very nature distinguishes right from wrong. Even if legislators deny it, by acting, they are making moral judgments. So, if law is to be seen as legitimate, it must be backed by morality.

This truism has been recognized since de Tocqueville (1990, 307), who wrote, "Despotism may govern without faith, but liberty cannot. Religion is much more necessary in the republic which they set forth in glowing colors than in the monarchy which they attack; it is more needed in democratic republics than in any others. How is it possible that society should escape destruction if the moral tie is not strengthened in proportion as the political tie is relaxed?"

Even more insidious, however, is that Neuhaus points out how the public square cannot remain naked for long. Something inevitably must take religion's place. Throughout history, Neuhaus argues, "something" has been the state. The Soviet Union, Hitler's Germany, Mao's China—these were all naked public squares. But they were also places of diminished rights and individual liberties. Far better for presidents and other political leaders to continue to engage with religious beliefs and values. Pluralism of ideas and faiths is one of the biggest reasons why the American democratic experiment has been so successful, and will continue to be so in the future.

The Last Word

It is rare for a work of political science to cite the Bible as much as I have. So being, it is only fitting to conclude with one last verse of Scripture, this one from Proverbs 14:23, "In all toil there is profit, but mere talk leads only to poverty." Words only get you so far, both in life and in politics.

It may be nice to think that a president could step up to the microphone, turn on the TV cameras, and deliver an eloquent sermon that would cause Americans everywhere to shout Hallejuahs to the heavens. That is how the presidency works in the movies, after all. But, as we all know, movies represent presidential fantasy. When presidents make a religious appeal for a political goal, they are far more likely to find political damnation, rather than political salvation.

The title of the book is meant to call to mind Pope Urban II, who launched the First Crusade at the Council of Claremont in 1095 with the rousing call of "Deus vult!"—"God wills it!" But instead of *God Wills It*, I might have been better served had I titled this book *God Doesn't Will It*. That, at least, would have been a fitting description of the role that presidential religious rhetoric plays in American politics.

References

ABC News/Washington Post. 1998. Survey Conducted December 12–December 13. Retrieved from the iPOLL Databank, Roper Center for Public Opinion Research, University of Connecticut.

Achtemeier, Paul J., ed. 1996. *The HarperCollins Bible Dictionary*. San Francisco, CA: HarperSanFrancisco.

Aikman, David. 2009. "Religion and the Presidency of George W. Bush." In *Religion and the American Presidency*, ed. Gaston Espinosa. New York: Columbia University Press.

Albertson, Bethany. 2006. *Dog-Whistle Politics, Coded Communication and Religious Appeals*. American Political Science Association and International Society of Political Psychology. Princeton, NJ: Princeton University.

Alsop, Joseph. 1963. "Politics and the Race Crisis." *Washington Post*, June 17, A15.

Alsop, Stewart. 1957. "Ike Fights Back and Moves Ahead." *Washington Post*, May 26, E5.

Altschuler, Glenn C. 2003. "Apathy, Apocalypse and the American Jeremiad." *American Literary History* 15 (Spring): 162–71.

Ambrose, Stephen E. 1984. *Eisenhower: The President*. New York: Simon and Schuster.

———. 1991. *Nixon: Ruin and Recovery, 1973–1990*. New York: Simon and Schuster.

Anderson, Terry H. 2011. *Bush's Wars*. New York: Oxford University Press.

Apple, R. W., Jr. 1990. "Bush Sure-Footed on Trail of Money." *New York Times*, September 29, 8.

———. 2001. "A Clear Message: 'I Will Not Relent.'" *New York Times*, September 21, A1.

Arnal, William E., and Russell T. McCutcheon. 2013. *The Sacred Is the Profane: The Political Nature of "Religion."* New York: Oxford University Press.

Aune, James Arnt, and Enrique D. Rigsby, eds. 2005. *Civil Rights Rhetoric and the American Presidency*. College Station, TX: Texas A&M University Press.

Balmer, Randall. 2008. *God in the White House: A History; How Faith Shaped the Presidency from John F. Kennedy to George W. Bush*. New York: HarperOne.

Barilleaux, Ryan J., and Mark J. Rozell. 2004. *Power and Prudence: The Presidency of George H. W. Bush*. College Station, TX: Texas A&M University Press.

Bartels, Larry M. 1994. "The American Public's Defense Spending Preferences in the Post-Cold War Era." *The Public Opinion Quarterly* 58 (Winter): 479–508.

Bell, Lauren Cohen, Joan L. Conners, and Theodore F. Sheckels. 2008. *Perspectives on Political Communication*. Boston, MA: Pearson.

Bellah, Robert N. 1967. "Civil Religion in America." *Daedalus* 96 (Winter): 1–21.

———. 1992. *The Broken Covenant: American Civil Religion in Time of Trial.* 2nd ed. Chicago, IL: University of Chicago Press.

Bellah, Robert N., and Phillip E. Hammond. 1980. *Varieties of Civil Religion.* San Francisco, CA: Harper & Row.

Bellah, Robert N., Richard Madsen, William M. Sullivan, Ann Swidler, and Steven M. Tipton. 1996. *Habits of the Heart: Individualism and Commitment in American Life.* Updated Ed. Berkeley, CA: University of California Press.

Bennett, Stephen Earl. 2002. "Another Lesson about Public Opinion During the Clinton-Lewinsky Scandal." *Presidential Studies Quarterly* 32 (June): 276–92.

Benze, James G., Jr. 2005. *Nancy Reagan: On the White House Stage.* Lawrence, KN: University Press of Kansas.

Beres, Louis Rene. 1982. "Reagan Calls It MX: Actually, It's M-Hex." *New York Times*, November 26, A27.

Bergman, Jerry. 2009. "Religion and the Presidency of Dwight D. Eisenhower." In *Religion and the American Presidency*, ed. Gaston Espinosa. New York: Columbia University Press.

Berke, Richard L. 1998a. "Scathing and Sad, Democrats React to Clinton Speech." *New York Times*, August 19, A1.

———. 1998b. "Senate Democrat Rebukes Clinton." *New York Times*, September 4, A1.

Bernstein, Irving. 1996. *Guns or Butter: The Presidency of Lyndon Johnson.* New York: Oxford University Press.

Berthelsen, John. 1974. "Group Assails Ford on Pardon." *Washington Post*, September 10, A1.

Bornet, Vaughn Davis. 1983. *The Presidency of Lyndon B. Johnson.* Lawrence, KN: University Press of Kansas.

Bortolini, Matteo. 2012. "The Trap of Intellectual Success: Robert N. Bellah, the American Civil Religion Debate, and the Sociology of Knowledge." *Theory and Society* 41 (March): 187–210.

Bourne, Peter G. 1997. *Jimmy Carter: A Comprehensive Biography from Plains to Postpresidency.* New York: Lisa Drew/Scribner.

Boyle, Peter G. 2005. *Eisenhower.* Harlow, UK: Pearson Longman.

Brackney, William H. 2006. *Baptists in North America: An Historical Perspective.* Malden, MA: Blackwell Publishing.

Branch, Taylor. 1988. *Parting the Waters: American in the King Years, 1954–1963.* New York: Simon and Schuster.

Brewer, Paul R. 2001. "Value Words and Lizard Brains: Do Citizens Deliberate about Appeals to Their Core Values?" *Political Psychology* 22 (March): 45–64.

Briggs, Kenneth A. 1985. "Theologians Fault Reagan on Bible Arms Lesson." *New York Times*, February 6, D14.

Brinkley, Douglas. 2007. *Gerald R. Ford.* New York: Times Books.

Broder, David S. 1979a. "Carter Seeking Oratory to Move an Entire Nation." *Washington Post*, July 14, A1.

———. 1979b. "President, Rosalynn and Amy Planning a Trip on the Riverboat Delta Queen." *Washington Post*, August 10, A2.

Brown, Davis. 2008. *The Sword, the Cross, and the Eagle: The American Christian Just War Tradition.* Lanham, MD: Rowman and Littlefield Publishers, Inc.

Burke, Kenneth. 1989. *On Symbols and Society.* Chicago, IL: University of Chicago Press.

Busch, Andrew E. 1997. "Ronald Reagan and the Defeat of the Soviet Empire." *Presidential Studies Quarterly* 27 (Summer): 451–66.

Bush, George H. W. 1990a. "Remarks and a Question-and-Answer Session with the Magazine Publishers of America." July 17. http://www.presidency.ucsb.edu/ws/index.php?pid=18685&st=&st1=#axzz1PGLxGEyI (accessed June 14, 2011).

———. 1990b. "Remarks and an Exchange with Reporters on the Iraqi Invasion of Kuwait." August 2. http://www.presidency.ucsb.edu/ws/index.php?pid=18726&st=&st1=#axzz1M3I3UgOo (accessed May 11, 2011).

———. 1990c. "Remarks and an Exchange with Reporters on the Iraqi Invasion of Kuwait." August 3. http://www.presidency.ucsb.edu/ws/index.php?pid=18738&st=&st1=#axzz1M3I3UgOo (accessed May 11, 2011).

———. 1990d. "Address to the Nation Announcing the Deployment of United States Armed Forces to Saudi Arabia." August 8. http://www.presidency.ucsb.edu/ws/index.php?pid=18750&st=&st1=#axzz1Lb52i79K (accessed May 6, 2011).

———. 1990e. "Remarks at the Annual Conference of the Veterans of Foreign Wars in Baltimore, Maryland." August 20. http://www.presidency.ucsb.edu/ws/index.php?pid=18774&st=evil&st1=#axzz1LszydTpI (accessed May 9, 2011).

———. 1990f. "Address Before a Joint Session of the Congress on the Persian Gulf Crisis and the Federal Budget Deficit." September 11. http://www.presidency.ucsb.edu/ws/index.php?pid=18820&st=&st1=#axzz1Lb52i79K (accessed May 6, 2011).

———. 1990g. "Remarks to Officers and Troops at Hickam Air Force Base in Pearl Harbor, Hawaii." October 28. http://www.presidency.ucsb.edu/ws/index.php?pid=18972&st=&st1=#axzz1Lg1H9lhj (accessed May 7, 2011).

———. 1990h. "Proclamation 6221 – For a National Day of Prayer, November 2, 1990." November 2. http://www.presidency.ucsb.edu/ws/index.php?pid=1926&st=&st1=#axzz1LszydTpI (accessed May 9, 2011).

———. 1990i. "Remarks During a Thanksgiving Day Service on Board the U.S.S. Nassau in the Persian Gulf." November 22. http://www.presidency.ucsb.edu/ws/index.php?pid=19087&st=&st1=#axzz1M3I3UgOo (accessed May 11, 2011).

———. 1990j. "Remarks to Allied Armed Forces Near Dhahran, Saudi Arabia." November 22. http://www.presidency.ucsb.edu/ws/index.php?pid=19088&st=&st1=#axzz1M3I3UgOo (accessed May 11, 2011).

———. 1991a. "Open Letter to College Students on the Persian Gulf Crisis." January 9. http://www.presidency.ucsb.edu/ws/index.php?pid=19205&st=&st1=#axzz1M3I3UgOo (accessed May 11, 2011).

———. 1991b. "Remarks at the Annual Convention of the National Religious Broadcasters." January 28. http://www.presidency.ucsb.edu/ws/index.php?pid=19250&st=&st1=#axzz1M3I3UgOo (accessed May 12, 2011).

———. 1991c. "Address Before a Joint Session of the Congress on the State of the Union." January 29. http://www.presidency.ucsb.edu/ws/index.php?pid=19253&st=&st1=#axzz1M3I3UgOo (accessed May 12, 2011).

———. 1991d. "Remarks at the National Prayer Breakfast." January 31. http://www.presidency.ucsb.edu/ws/index.php?pid=19261&st=&st1=#axzz1M3I3UgOo (accessed May 12, 2011).

———. 1991e. "Remarks to Community Members at Fort Stewart, Georgia." February 1. http://www.presidency.ucsb.edu/ws/index.php?pid=19269&st=&st1=#axzz1M3I3UgOo (accessed May 12, 2011).

———. 1991f. "Proclamation 6243—For a National Day of Prayer, February 3, 1991." February 1. http://www.presidency.ucsb.edu/ws/index.php?pid=47257&st=&st1=#axzz1M3I3UgOo (accessed May 12, 2011).

———. 1991g. "Radio Address to the Nation on the National Day of Prayer." February 2. http://www.presidency.ucsb.edu/ws/index.php?pid=19270&st=&st1=#axzz1M3I3UgOo (accessed May 12, 2011).

Bush, George W. 2001a. "Address Before a Joint Session of the Congress on the United States Response to the Terrorist Attacks of September 11." September 20. http://www.presidency.ucsb.edu/ws/index.php?pid=64731&st=&st1=#axzz-1j5E3L3kL (accessed January 10, 2012).

———. 2001b. "Remarks to Federal Bureau of Investigation Employees." September 25. http://www.presidency.ucsb.edu/ws/index.php?pid=65083&st=&st1=#axzz1i2eh9yi6 (accessed December 31, 2011).

———. 2001c. "Remarks Prior to Discussions with Muslim Community Leaders and an Exchange with Reporters." September 26. http://www.presidency.ucsb.edu/ws/index.php?pid=64877&st=&st1=#axzz1i2eh9yi6 (accessed December 31, 2011).

———. 2001d. "Remarks Prior to Discussions with King Abdullah II of Jordan and an Exchange with Reporters." September 28. http://www.presidency.ucsb.edu/ws/index.php?pid=64217&st=&st1=#axzz1i2eh9yi6 (accessed December 31, 2011).

———. 2001e. "Remarks to Department of State Employees." October 4. http://www.presidency.ucsb.edu/ws/index.php?pid=65086&st=&st1=#axzz1i2eh9yi6 (accessed December 31, 2011).

———. 2001f. "Remarks to the Community at Travis Air Force Base, California." October 17. http://www.presidency.ucsb.edu/ws/index.php?pid=64258&st=&st1=#axzz1i2eh9yi6 (accessed December 31, 2011).

———. 2001g. "Remarks to the United Nations General Assembly in New York City." November 10. http://www.presidency.ucsb.edu/ws/index.php?pid=58802&st=&st1=#axzz1i2eh9yi6 (accessed December 31, 2011).

———. 2002a. "Remarks on Arrival in Charleston, West Virginia." January 22. http://www.presidency.ucsb.edu/ws/index.php?pid=63417&st=&st1=#axzz1i2eh9yi6 (accessed January 1, 2012).

———. 2002b. "Remarks at the National Prayer Breakfast." February 7. http://www.presidency.ucsb.edu/ws/index.php?pid=58750&st=&st1=#axzz1i2eh9yi6 (accessed December 31, 2011).

———. 2002c. "Remarks to the Troops at Elmendorf Air Force Base in Anchorage, Alaska." February 16. http://www.presidency.ucsb.edu/ws/index.php?pid=73257&st=&st1=#axzz1i2eh9yi6 (accessed January 1, 2012).

———. 2002d. "Remarks to Employees of the Printer, Inc., in Des Moines." March 1. http://www.presidency.ucsb.edu/ws/index.php?pid=72979&st=&st1=#axzz1i2eh9yi6 (accessed January 1, 2012).

———. 2002e. "Remarks on the Citizens Corp in Knoxville." April 8. http://www.presidency.ucsb.edu/ws/index.php?pid=62742&st=&st1=#axzz1i2eh9yi6 (accessed January 1, 2012).

———. 2002f. "Remarks at Logan High School in La Crosse, Wisconsin." May 8. http://www.presidency.ucsb.edu/ws/index.php?pid=73292&st=&st1=#axzz1i2eh9yi6 (accessed January 1, 2012).

———. 2002g. "Commencement Address at the United States Military Academy in West Point, New York." June 1. http://www.presidency.ucsb.edu/ws/index.php?pid=62730&st=&st1=#axzz1i2eh9yi6 (accessed December 31, 2011).

———. 2002h. "Address to the Nation from Ellis Island, New York, on the Anniversary of the Terrorist Attacks of September 11. September 11. http://www.presidency.ucsb.edu/ws/index.php?pid=62948&st=&st1=#axzz1ibG1JRr9 (accessed January 5, 2012).

———. 2002i. "Remarks in Shreveport, Louisiana." December 3. http://www.presidency.ucsb.edu/ws/index.php?pid=73189&st=&st1=#axzz1ibG1JRr9 (accessed January 5, 2012).

———. 2003a. "Remarks in Grand Rapids, Michigan." January 29. http://www.presidency.ucsb.edu/ws/index.php?pid=64591&st=&st1=#axzz1ibG1JRr9 (accessed January 5, 2012).

———. 2003b. "Remarks at the National Prayer Breakfast." February 6. http://www.presidency.ucsb.edu/ws/index.php?pid=58749&st=&st1=#axzz1ibG1JRr9 (accessed January 6, 2012).

———. 2003c. "Remarks Following Discussions with Prime Minister John Howard of Australia and an Exchange with Reporters." February 10. http://www.presidency.ucsb.edu/ws/index.php?pid=172&st=&st1=#axzz1ibG1JRr9 (accessed January 5, 2012).

———. 2003d. "Remarks in Kennesaw, Georgia." February 20. http://www.presidency.ucsb.edu/ws/index.php?pid=147&st=&st1=#axzz1ibG1JRr9 (accessed January 5, 2012).

———. 2003e. "The President's News Conference." March 6. http://www.presidency.ucsb.edu/ws/index.php?pid=119&st=&st1=#axzz1ibG1JRr9 (accessed January 6, 2012).

———. 2003f. "Remarks Following a Visit with Troops Wounded in Operation Iraqi Freedom and an Exchange with Reporters in Bethesda, Maryland." April 11. http://www.presidency.ucsb.edu/ws/index.php?pid=62956&st=&st1=#axzz1ibG1JRr9 (accessed January 6, 2012).

———. 2003g. "Remarks to Employees at the Army Tank Plant in Lima, Ohio." April 24. http://www.presidency.ucsb.edu/ws/index.php?pid=64005&st=&st1=#axzz1ibG1JRr9 (accessed January 6, 2012).

———. 2003h. "Remarks on the 20th Anniversary of the National Endowment for Democracy." November 6. http://www.presidency.ucsb.edu/ws/index.php?pid=844&st=&st1=#axzz1ibG1JRr9 (accessed January 5, 2012).

———. 2005a. "Inaugural Address." January 20. http://www.presidency.ucsb.edu/ws/index.php?pid=58745&st=&st1=#axzz1ibG1JRr9 (accessed January 6, 2012).

———. 2005b. "Remarks on the War on Terror in Norfolk, Virginia." October 28. http://www.presidency.ucsb.edu/ws/index.php?pid=73776&st=&st1=#axzz1i2eh9yi6 (accessed January 1, 2012).

———. 2005c. "Remarks on the War on Terror in Tobyhanna, Pennsylvania." November 11. http://www.presidency.ucsb.edu/ws/index.php?pid=64753&st=&st1=#axzz1i2eh9yi6 (accessed January 1, 2012).

———. 2005d. "Remarks on the War on Terror in Anchorage, Alaska." November 14. http://www.presidency.ucsb.edu/ws/index.php?pid=65071&st=&st1=#axzz1i2eh9yi6 (accessed January 1, 2012).

———. 2006. "Remarks on the War on Terror and a Question-and-Answer Session in Manhattan, Kansas." January 23. http://www.presidency.ucsb.edu/ws/index.php?pid=65144&st=&st1=#axzz1iVGEO2EK (accessed January 4, 2012).

———. 2007. "Remarks to Military Personnel and Their Families at Fort Benning, Georgia." January 11. http://www.presidency.ucsb.edu/ws/index.php?pid=24435&st=&st1=#axzz1i2eh9yi6 (accessed January 1, 2012).

———. 2009. "Farewell Address to the Nation." January 15. http://www.presidency.ucsb.edu/ws/index.php?pid=85423&st=&st1=#axzz1jBkqalA2 (accessed January 11, 2012).

Bush, George, and Brent Scowcroft. 1998. *A World Transformed.* New York: Alfred A. Knopf.

Calfano, Brian Robert, and Paul A. Djupe. 2009. "God Talk: Religious Cues and Electoral Support." *Political Research Quarterly* 62 (June): 329–39.

Calhoun, Charles W. 1993. "Civil Religion and the Gilded Age Presidency: The Case of Benjamin Harrison." *Presidential Studies Quarterly* 23 (Fall): 651–67.

Campbell, Angus, Philip Converse, Warren Miller, and Donald Stokes. 1960. *The American Voter.* New York: John Wiley and Sons, Inc.

Campbell, Karlyn Kohrs, and Kathleen Hall Jamieson. 2008. *Presidents Creating the Presidency: Deeds Done in Words.* Chicago, IL: University of Chicago Press.

Canes-Wrone, Brandice. 2006. *Who Leads Whom? Presidents, Policy, and the Public.* Chicago, IL: The University of Chicago Press.

Canes-Wrone, Brandice, William G. Howell, and David E. Lewis. 2008. "Toward a Broader Understanding of Presidential Power: A Reevaluation of the Two Presidencies Thesis." *Journal of Politics* 70 (January): 1–16.

Cannon, James. 1994. *Time and Chance: Gerald Ford's Appointment with History.* New York: HarperCollins.

Cannon, Lou. 1991. *President Reagan: The Role of a Lifetime.* New York: Simon and Schuster.

Carter, Jimmy. 1977a. "Report to the American People—Remarks from the White House Library." February 2. http://www.presidency.ucsb.edu/ws/index.php?pid=7455&st=&st1= (accessed February 22, 2011).

———. 1977b. "The Energy Problem: Address to the Nation." April 18. http://www.presidency.ucsb.edu/ws/index.php?pid=7369&st=&st1= (accessed February 22, 2011).

———. 1977c. "National Energy Plan: Address to the Nation." November 8. http://www.presidency.ucsb.edu/ws/index.php?pid=6904&st=&st1= (accessed February 22, 2011).

———. 1978a. "Atlanta, Georgia Remarks at the Southern Salute to the President Dinner." January 20. http://www.presidency.ucsb.edu/ws/index.php?pid=31044&st=&st1= (accessed February 23, 2011).

———. 1978b. "Nashua, New Hampshire Remarks and a Question-and-Answer Session at a Town Meeting with New Hampshire High School Students." February 18. http://www.presidency.ucsb.edu/ws/index.php?pid=30389&st=&st1= (accessed February 23, 2011).

———. 1979a. "Energy Address to the Nation." April 5. http://www.presidency.ucsb.edu/ws/index.php?pid=32159&st=&st1= (accessed February 22, 2011).

———. 1979b. "Address to the Nation on Energy and National Goals: 'The Malaise Speech.'" July 15. http://www.presidency.ucsb.edu/ws/index.php?pid=32596&st=&st1= (accessed February 23, 2011).

———. 1979c. "Future Farmers of America Remarks to the Organization's State Presidents." July 19. http://www.presidency.ucsb.edu/ws/index.php?pid=32610&st=&st1= (accessed February 24, 2011).

———. 1979d. "Wabasha, Minnesota Remarks on Arrival at the City." August 18. http://www.presidency.ucsb.edu/ws/index.php?pid=32770&st=&st1= (accessed February 24, 2011).

———. 1979e. "Prairie du Chien, Wisconsin Remarks at a Picnic Sponsored by the Minnesota Mining and Manufacturing Company." August 19. http://www.presidency.ucsb.edu/ws/index.php?pid=32773&st=&st1= (accessed February 24, 2011).

———. 1979f. "Muscatine, Iowa Remarks on Arrival at the City." August 21. http://www.presidency.ucsb.edu/ws/index.php?pid=32781&st=&st1= (accessed February 24, 2011).

———. 1979g. "Burlington, Iowa Remarks and a Question-and-Answer Session at a Town Meeting." August 22. http://www.presidency.ucsb.edu/ws/index.php?pid=32783&st=&st1= (accessed February 24, 2011).

———. 1979h. "St. Louis, Missouri Remarks on Arrival at the City." August 24. http://www.presidency.ucsb.edu/ws/index.php?pid=32786&st=&st1= (accessed February 24, 2011).

———. 1979i. "Atlanta, Georgia Remarks at Emory University." August 30. http://www.presidency.ucsb.edu/ws/index.php?pid=32818&st=&st1= (accessed February 23, 2011).

———. 1979j. "Tampa, Florida Remarks and a Question-and-Answer Session at a Town Meeting." August 30. http://www.presidency.ucsb.edu/ws/index.php?pid=32819&st=&st1= (accessed February 24, 2011).

———. 1979k. "Albuquerque, New Mexico Remarks at a Meeting with Civic and Community Leaders." October 11. http://www.presidency.ucsb.edu/ws/index.php?pid=31509&st=&st1= (accessed February 24, 2011).

———. 1979l. "San Diego, California Remarks at the Annual Convention of the Building and Construction Trades Department, AFL-CIO." October 11. http://www.presidency.ucsb.edu/ws/index.php?pid=31510&st=&st1= (accessed February 24, 2011).

———. 1979m. "Kansas City, Missouri Remarks at the Annual Convention of the National Conference of Catholic Charities." October 15. http://www.presidency.ucsb.edu/ws/index.php?pid=31532&st=&st1= (accessed February 24, 2011).

———. 1980a. "Energy Conservation Remarks at a White House Briefing for Religious Leaders." January 10. http://www.presidency.ucsb.edu/ws/index.php?pid=33011&st=&st1= (accessed February 24, 2011).

———. 1980b. "The State of the Union Address Delivered Before a Joint Session of the Congress." January 23. http://www.presidency.ucsb.edu/ws/index.php?pid=33079&st=&st1= (accessed February 24, 2011).

———. 1982. *Keeping Faith: Memoirs of a President*. New York: Bantam Books.

———. 2002. *The Personal Beliefs of Jimmy Carter*. New York: Three Rivers Press.

Carter, Rosalynn. 1984. *First Lady from Plains*. Boston, MA: Houghton Mifflin.

Carter, Stephen L. 1993. *The Culture of Disbelief: How American Law and Politics Trivialize Religious Devotion*. New York: Anchor Books.

Carty, Thomas J. 2004. *A Catholic in the White House? Religion, Politics, and John F. Kennedy's Presidential Campaign*. New York: Palgrave Macmillan.

————. 2009. "Religion and the Presidency of John F. Kennedy." In *Religion and the American Presidency*, ed. Gaston Espinosa. New York: Columbia University Press.

Casey, Shaun A. 2009. *The Making of a Catholic President: Kennedy vs. Nixon 1960*. New York: Oxford University Press.

Chapman, Stephen. 1982. "How to Cut the Defense Budget." *Chicago Tribune*, November 25, 22.

Chapp, Christopher B. 2012. *Religious Rhetoric and American Politics: The Endurance of Civil Religion in Electoral Campaigns*. Ithaca, NY: Cornell University Press.

Chappell, David L. 2004. *A Stone of Hope: Prophetic Religion and the Death of Jim Crow*. Chapel Hill, NC: University of North Carolina Press.

Chernus, Ira. 2008. *Apocalypse Management: Eisenhower and the Discourse of National Insecurity*. Stanford, CA: Stanford University Press.

Chicago Tribune. 1957a. "Inaugural Message." January 22, 18.

————. 1957b. "For Whom the Bell Tolls." January 24, 10.

————. 1957c. "Lobbyist in the White House." May 23, 12.

————. 1957d. "Mr. Eisenhower's Friend Tito." May 26, 24.

————. 1957e. "The 80 Year Old 'Emergency.'" May 26, 24.

————. 1959. "Santa's Competitor." December 9, 14.

————. 1960. "Moral Imperatives." January 10, 20.

————. 1963. "Out of Chaos, Some Sense." June 12, 16.

————. 1974. "A Pardon Mishandled." September 10, 8.

————. 1979. "Winning Neither Confidence . . . Nor More Oil." July 17, B2.

————. 1983. "Panic vs. Prudent Defense." March 15, 18.

Childs, Marquis. 1974. ". . . And Re-opened the Watergate Scandals." *Washington Post*, September 10, A21.

Clinton, Bill. 1998a. "Remarks on the After-School Child Care Initiative." January 26. http://www.presidency.ucsb.edu/ws/index.php?pid=56257&st=&st1=#axzz1Gghf9J2V (accessed March 15, 2011).

————. 1998b. "Address to the Nation on Testimony Before the Independent Counsel's Grand Jury." August 17. http://www.presidency.ucsb.edu/ws/index.php?pid=54794&st=&st1=#axzz1HKqCFE91 (accessed March 22, 2011).

————. 1998c. "Remarks on the 35th Anniversary of the March on Washington in Oak Bluffs, Massachusetts." August 28. http://www.presidency.ucsb.edu/ws/index.php?pid=54823&st=&st1=#axzz1HQvWktrP (accessed March 24, 2011).

————. 1998d. "The President's News Conference with President Boris Yeltsin of Russia in Moscow." September 2. http://www.presidency.ucsb.edu/ws/index.php?pid=54841&st=&st1=#axzz1HQvWktrP (accessed March 23, 2011).

————. 1998e. "Remarks at a Breakfast with Religious Leaders." September 11. http://www.presidency.ucsb.edu/ws/index.php?pid=54886&st=&st1=#axzz1HjRiXcrj (accessed March 26, 2011).

————. 1998f. "The President's News Conference with President Vaclav Havel of the Czech Republic." September 16. http://www.presidency.ucsb.edu/ws/index.php?pid=54916&st=&st1=#axzz1HjRiXcrj (accessed March 26, 2011).

————. 1998g. "Remarks to the Congressional Black Caucus Foundation." September 19. http://www.presidency.ucsb.edu/ws/index.php?pid=54941&st=&st1=#axzz1HjRiXcrj (accessed March 26, 2011).

———. 1998h. "Remarks on the Impeachment Inquiry Vote and an Exchange with Reporters." October 8. http://www.presidency.ucsb.edu/ws/index.php?pid= 55050&st=&st1=#axzz1HjRiXcrj (accessed March 26, 2011).

———. 1998i. "The President's News Conference with President Andres Pastrana of Colombia." October 28. http://www.presidency.ucsb.edu/ws/index.php?pid= 55165&st=&st1=#axzz1HjRiXcrj (accessed March 27, 2011).

———. 2004. *My Life*. New York: Alfred A. Knopf.

Clinton, Hillary Rodham. 2003. *Living History*. New York: Simon & Schuster.

Clymer, Adam. 1979. "Speech Lifts Carter Rating to 37%; Public Agrees on Confidence Crisis." *New York Times*, July 18, A1.

Coffey, Raymond. 1979. "Carters' Boat Trip Baby-Kissing Tour." *Chicago Tribune*, August 20, 5.

Cohen, Jeffrey E. 1995. "Presidential Rhetoric and the Public Agenda." *American Journal of Political Science* 39 (February): 87–107.

———. 2010. *Going Local: Presidential Leadership in the Post-Broadcast Age*. New York: Cambridge University Press.

Cohen, Richard. 2001. "Taking Command." *Washington Post*, September 22, A29.

Coleman, John A. 1970. "Civil Religion." *Sociological Analysis* 31 (Summer): 67–77.

Congressional Quarterly. 1958a. "Mutual Security Act Sets Up Loan Fund." In *CQ Almanac 1957*, 13th ed. Washington, DC: Congressional Quarterly.

———. 1958b. "Mutual Security Funds." In *CQ Almanac 1957*, 13th ed. Washington, DC: Congressional Quarterly.

———. 1960. "Congress Authorizes $3,556,200,000 for Mutual Security." In *CQ Almanac 1959*, 15th ed. Washington, DC: Congressional Quarterly.

———. 1982. "Defense 1981: Overview." In *CQ Almanac 1981*, 37th ed. Washington, DC: Congressional Quarterly.

———. 1983. "Defense 1982: Overview." In *CQ Almanac 1982*, 38th ed. Washington, DC: Congressional Quarterly.

———. 1984. "Defense 1983 Overview." In *CQ Almanac 1983*, 39th ed. Washington, DC: Congressional Quarterly.

———. 1985. "Defense 1984: Overview." In *CQ Almanac 1984*, 40th ed. Washington, DC: Congressional Quarterly.

———. 1986. "Defense 1985: Overview." In *CQ Almanac 1985*, 41st ed. Washington, DC: Congressional Quarterly.

———. 1987. "Defense 1986: Overview." In *CQ Almanac 1986*, 42nd ed. Washington, DC: Congressional Quarterly.

———. 1988. "Defense 1987: Overview." In *CQ Almanac 1987*, 43rd ed. Washington, DC: Congressional Quarterly.

———. 1989. "Defense 1988: Overview." In *CQ Almanac 1988*, 44th ed. Washington, DC: Congressional Quarterly.

Conine, Ernest. 1983. "Reagan's Good-vs.-Evil Blunder." *Los Angeles Times*, March 14, C5.

Cook, Martin L. 2004. *The Moral Warrior: Ethics and Service in the U.S. Military*. Albany, NY: State University of New York Press.

Daley, Steve. 1991. "Promise of a New World Order Doesn't Include the Old Problems at Home." *Chicago Tribune*, February 3, 4.

Dallek, Robert. 1998. *Flawed Giant: Lyndon Johnson and His Times*. New York: Oxford University Press.

———. 2003. *An Unfinished Life: John F. Kennedy, 1917–1963.* Boston, MA: Little, Brown and Company.

———. 2004. *Lyndon B. Johnson: Portrait of a President.* New York: Oxford University Press.

Dalton, Russell J., Paul A. Beck, and Robert Huckfeldt. 1998. "Partisan Cues and the Media: Information Flows in the 1992 Presidential Election." *The American Political Science Review* 92 (March): 111–26.

Deaver, Michael K. 2001. *A Different Drummer: My Thirty Years with Ronald Reagan.* New York: Harper Collins.

Delli Carpini, Michael X., and Scott Keeter. 1993. "Measuring Political Knowledge: Putting First Things First." *American Journal of Political Science* 37 (November): 1179–206.

———. 1996. *What Americans Know about Politics and Why It Matters.* New Haven, CT: Yale University Press.

Diamos, Jason. 2001. "Rangers Game Halted for President's Speech." *New York Times,* September 21, D1.

Dionne, E. J., Jr. 2002. "Getting Down to Coalition-Building." *Washington Post,* September 13, A39.

———. 2005. "Visions in Need of a Little Realism." *Washington Post,* January 21, A17.

Dole, Bob. 2006. "Profile in Decency." *Washington Post,* December 28, A27.

Domke, David. 2004. *God Willing? Political Fundamentalism in the White House, the "War on Terror," and the Echoing Press.* London: Pluto Press.

Domke, David, and Kevin Coe. 2008. *The God Strategy: How Religion Became a Political Weapon in America.* New York, NY: Oxford University Press.

Donovan, Robert J. 1963. "Formidable Candidate Shaping Up." *Los Angeles Times,* December 1, M1.

Dowd, Maureen. 1998. "The Wizard of Is." *New York Times,* September 16, 29.

———. 2002. "W's Conflicts of Interest." *New York Times,* September 15, A15.

Druckman, James N. 2001. "On the Limits of Framing Effects: Who Can Frame?" *Journal of Politics* 63 (November): 1041–66.

Druckman, James N., and Cindy D. Kam. 2011. "Students as Experimental Participants: A Defense of the 'Narrow Data Base.'" In *Cambridge Handbook of Experimental Political Science,* ed. James N. Druckman, Donald P. Green, James H. Kuklinski, and Arthur Lupia. New York: Cambridge University Press.

Druckman, James N., and Michael Parkin. 2005. "The Impact of Media Bias: How Editorial Slant Affects Voters." *The Journal of Politics* 67 (November): 1030–49.

Dudziak, Mary L. 2000. *Cold War Civil Rights: Race and the Image of American Democracy.* Princeton, NJ: Princeton University Press.

Durkheim, Emile. 1971. *The Elementary Forms of the Religious Life.* London: George Allen & Unwin Ltd.

Edelman, Murray. 1964. *The Symbolic Uses of Politics.* Urbana, IL: University of Illinois Press.

———. 1977. *Political Language: Words That Succeed and Policies That Fail.* New York: Academic Press.

Edwards III, George C. 1989. *At the Margins: Presidential Leadership of Congress.* New Haven, CT: Yale University Press.

———. 2003. *On Deaf Ears: The Limits of the Bully Pulpit.* New Haven, CT: Yale University Press.

———. 2007. *Governing by Campaigning: The Politics of the Bush Presidency*. New York: Pearson Longman.

Edwards III, George C., Andrew Barrett, and Jeffrey Peake. 1997. " The Legislative Impact of Divided Government." *American Journal of Political Science* 41 (April): 545–63.

Ehrman, John. 2005. *The Eighties: America in the Age of Reagan*. New Haven, CT: Yale University Press.

Eisenhower, Dwight D. 1953a. "Address 'The Chance for Peace' Delivered Before the American Society of Newspaper Editors." April 16. http://www.presidency. ucsb.edu/ws/index.php?pid=9819&st=&st1= (accessed February 3, 2011).

———. 1953b. "The President's News Conference." June 17. http://www.presidency.ucsb.edu/ws/index.php?pid=9611&st=&st1= (accessed January 25, 2011).

———. 1954. "Radio and Television Address to the American People on the State of the Nation." April 5. http://www.presidency.ucsb.edu/ws/index.php?pid=10201&st=&st1= (accessed February 2, 2011).

———. 1955. "Annual Message to Congress on the State of the Union." January 6. http://www.presidency.ucsb.edu/ws/index.php?pid=10416&st=&st1= (accessed February 2, 2011).

———. 1956a. "The President's News Conference." March 21. http://www.presidency.ucsb.edu/ws/index.php?pid=10759&st=&st1= (accessed February 2, 2011).

———. 1956b. "Address and Remarks at the Baylor University Commencement Ceremonies, Waco, Texas." May 25. http://www.presidency.ucsb.edu/ws/index.php?pid=10499&st=&st1= (accessed February 2, 2011).

———. 1957a. "Special Message to Congress on the Situation in the Middle East." January 5. http://www.presidency.ucsb.edu/ws/index.php?pid=11007&st=&st1= (accessed February 2, 2011).

———. 1957b. "Second Inaugural Address." January 21. http://www.presidency. ucsb.edu/ws/index.php?pid=10856&st=&st1= (accessed January 25, 2011).

———. 1957c. "Radio and Television Address to the American People on the Need for Mutual Security in Waging the Peace." May 21. http://www.presidency.ucsb. edu/ws/index.php?pid=11042&st=&st1= (accessed January 26, 2011).

———. 1958. "Remarks and Address at Dinner of the National Conference on the Foreign Aspects of National Security." February 25. http://www.presidency.ucsb.edu/ws/index.php?pid=11308&st=&st1= (accessed January 26, 2011).

———. 1959a. "Radio and Television Address to the American People Before Leaving on Good Will Trip to Europe, Asia, and Africa." December 3. http://www.presidency.ucsb.edu/ws/index.php?pid=11590&st=&st1= (accessed January 26, 2011).

———. 1959b. "Radio and Television Remarks on the Good Will Tour Delivered at the Pageant of Peace Ceremonies." December 23. http://www.presidency. ucsb.edu/ws/index.php?pid=11653&st=&st1= (accessed January 26, 2011).

———. 1960a. "Annual Message to the Congress on the State of the Union." January 7. http://www.presidency.ucsb.edu/ws/index.php?pid=12061&st=&st1= (accessed January 26, 2011).

———. 1960b. "Address at a Dinner Sponsored by the Committee for International Economic Growth and the Committee to Strengthen the Frontiers of Freedom." May 2. http://www.presidency.ucsb.edu/ws/index.php?pid=11766&st=&st1= (accessed January 26, 2011).

Erickson, Paul D. 1985. *Reagan Speaks: The Making of An American Myth*. New York: New York University Press.

Erikson, Robert S., and Kent L. Tedin. 2011. *American Public Opinion*. 8th ed. Boston, MA: Longman.

Espinosa, Gaston. 2009. "Religion and the Presidency of William Jefferson Clinton." In *Religion and the American Presidency*, ed. Gaston Espinosa. New York: Columbia University Press.

Evans, Rowland, and Robert Novak. 1979. "A National Revival." *Washington Post*, July 16, A19.

Fairbanks, James David. 1981. "The Priestly Function of the Presidency: A Discussion of the Literature on Civil Religion and Its Implications for the Study of Presidential Leadership." *Presidential Studies Quarterly* 11 (Spring): 214–32.

Feldman, Trude B. 2002. "Ford Says Pardon of Nixon Now Feels 'Even More Right.'" *Washington Times*, July 16, A2.

Finke, Roger, and Rodney Stark. 2005. *The Churching of America, 1776–2005*. New Brunswick, NJ: Rutgers University Press.

Finkel, Steven. 1993. "Reexamining the 'Minimal Effects' Model in Recent Presidential Campaigns." *The Journal of Politics* 55 (February): 1–21.

Fiorina, Morris. 1981. *Retrospective Voting in American National Elections*. New Haven, CT: Yale University Press.

Fleisher, Richard, and Jon Bond. 1988. "Are There Two Presidencies? Yes, But Only for Republicans." *Journal of Politics* 50 (August): 747–67.

Ford, Gerald. 1974a. "Remarks on Taking the Oath of Office." August 9. http://www.presidency.ucsb.edu/ws/index.php?pid=4409&st=&st1=#axzz1JVX39sQC (accessed April 14, 2011).

———. 1974b. "Remarks to the Veterans of Foreign Wars Annual Convention, Chicago, Illinois." August 19. http://www.presidency.ucsb.edu/ws/index.php?pid=4476&st=&st1=#axzz1K4nAm4et (accessed April 20, 2011).

———. 1974c. "The President's News Conference." August 28. http://www.presidency.ucsb.edu/ws/index.php?pid=4671&st=&st1=#axzz1JVX39sQC (accessed April 14, 2011).

———. 1974d. "Remarks on Signing a Proclamation Granting Pardon to Richard Nixon." September 8. http://www.presidency.ucsb.edu/ws/index.php?pid=4695&st=&st1=#axzz1JVX39sQC (accessed April 14, 2011).

———. 1974e. "The President's News Conference." September 16. http://www.presidency.ucsb.edu/ws/index.php?pid=4717&st=&st1=#axzz1JVX39sQC (accessed April 14, 2011).

———. 1974f. "Statement and Responses to Questions from Members of the House Judiciary Committee Concerning the Pardon of Richard Nixon." October 17. http://www.presidency.ucsb.edu/ws/index.php?pid=4471&st=&st1=#axzz1Jy-h59vKH (accessed April 19, 2011).

———. 1976a. "Address Before a Joint Session of the Congress Reporting on the State of the Union." January 19. http://www.presidency.ucsb.edu/ws/index.php?pid=5677&st=&st1=#axzz1KXiC5vM3 (accessed April 25, 2011).

———. 1976b. "Remarks at the National Prayer Breakfast." January 29. http://www.presidency.ucsb.edu/ws/index.php?pid=5877&st=&st1=#axzz1KXiC5vM3 (accessed April 25, 2011).

———. 1976c. "Remarks at the Combined Convention of the National Religious Broadcasters and the National Association of Evangelicals." February 22.

http://www.presidency.ucsb.edu/ws/index.php?pid=5606&st=&st1=#axzz-1KXiC5vM3 (accessed April 25, 2011).

———. 1976d. "Remarks in Philadelphia, Pennsylvania." July 4. http://www.presidency.ucsb.edu/ws/index.php?pid=6183&st=&st1=#axzz1KXiC5vM3 (accessed April 25, 2011).

———. 1979. *A Time to Heal: The Autobiography of Gerald R. Ford.* New York: Harper & Row, Publishers.

Fowler, Robert Booth. 1995. *The Greening of Protestant Thought.* Chapel Hill, NC: University of North Carolina Press.

Fowler, Robert Booth, Allen D. Hertzke, Laura R. Olson, and Kevin R. Den Dulk. 2010. *Religion and Politics in America: Faith, Culture, and Strategic Choices.* Boulder, CO: Westview Press.

Friedland, Michael B. 1998. *Lift Up Your Voice Like a Trumpet: White Clergy and the Civil Rights and Antiwar Movements, 1954–1973.* Chapel Hill, NC: University of North Carolina Press.

Gallup, George. 1957. "Eisenhower 'Loses' Aid Plea." *Washington Post,* May 26, K10.

Gallup Organization. 1958. Survey Conducted March 6–March 11. Retrieved from the iPOLL Databank, Roper Center for Public Opinion Research, University of Connecticut.

———. 1959. Survey Conducted throughout August. Retrieved from the iPOLL Databank, Roper Center for Public Opinion Research, University of Connecticut.

———. 1963a. Survey Conducted June 21–June 26. Retrieved from the iPOLL Databank, Roper Center for Public Opinion Research, University of Connecticut.

———. 1963b. Survey Conducted August 15–August 20. Retrieved from the iPOLL Databank, Roper Center for Public Opinion Research, University of Connecticut.

———. 1964. Survey Conducted January 2–January 7. Retrieved from the iPOLL Databank, Roper Center for Public Opinion Research, University of Connecticut.

Gearing, Robin E., and Dana Lizardi. 2009. "Religion and Suicide." *Journal of Religion and Health* 48 (September): 332–41.

Gelb, Leslie. 1991. "Gas, Germs and Nukes." *New York Times,* January 30, A23.

Gellner, David N. 1999. "Anthropological Approaches." In *Approaches to the Study of Religion,* ed. Peter Connolly. London: Cassell.

Gelman, Andrew, and Jennifer Hill. 2007. *Data Analysis Using Regression and Multilevel/Hierarchical Models.* New York: Cambridge University Press.

Germond, Jack, and Jules Witcover. 1982. "Reagan Meets Political Reality." *Chicago Tribune,* November 23, 17.

Gershkoff, Amy, and Shana Kushner. 2005. "Shaping Public Opinion: The 9/11-Iraq Connection in the Bush Administration's Rhetoric." *Perspectives on Politics* 3 (September): 525–37.

Gerstle, Gary. 2001. *American Crucible: Race and Nation in the Twentieth Century.* Princeton, NJ: Princeton University Press.

Giglio, James N. 1991. *The Presidency of John F. Kennedy.* Lawrence, KN: University Press of Kansas.

Gillon, Steven M. 2008. *The Pact: Bill Clinton, Newt Gingrich and the Rivalry That Defined a Generation.* New York: Oxford University Press, Inc.

Glad, Betty. 1980. *Jimmy Carter: In Search of the Great White House*. New York: W. W. Norton & Company.

Gonzalez, Justo L. 2010. *Luke*. Louisville, KY: Westminster John Knox Press.

Goodman, Ellen. 1982. "The Words Race." *Washington Post*, November 27, A15.

Gormley, Ken. 2010. *The Death of American Virtue: Clinton vs. Starr*. New York: Crown Publishers.

Green, Donald, Bradley Palmquist, and Eric Schickler. 2002. *Partisan Hearts and Minds: Political Parties and the Social Identities of Voters*. New Haven, CT: Yale University Press.

Greene, John Robert. 2000. *The Presidency of George Bush*. Lawrence, KN: University Press of Kansas.

Greenstein, Fred I. 1982. *The Hidden-Hand Presidency: Eisenhower as Leader*. New York: BasicBooks.

Haberman, Clyde. 1998. "Contrition Doesn't Right All Wrongs." *New York Times*, September 15.

Hamilton, Nigel. 2003. *Bill Clinton: An American Journey; Great Expectations*. New York: Random House.

Hanson, Paul D. 1995. *Isaiah 40–66*. Louisville, KY: John Knox Press.

Hargrove, Edwin C. 1988. *Jimmy Carter as President: Leadership and the Politics of the Public Good*. Baton Rouge, LA: Louisiana State University Press.

Harlow, Rachel Martin. 2006. "Agency and Agent in George Bush's Gulf War Rhetoric." In *The Rhetorical Presidency of George H. W. Bush*, ed. Martin J. Medhurst. College Station, TX: Texas A&M University Press.

Harris, John F. 2005. *The Survivor: Bill Clinton in the White House*. New York: Random House.

Hart, Roderick P. 2002. "Why Do They Talk That Way? A Research Agenda for the Presidency." *Presidential Studies Quarterly* 32 (December): 693–709.

Hart, Roderick P., and J. Kanan Sawyer. 2003. "Resurrecting the Clinton Presidency: A Linguistic Profile." In *Images, Scandal, and Communication Strategies of the Clinton Presidency*, ed. Robert E. Denton Jr. and Rachel L. Holloway. Westport, CT: Praeger Publishers.

Hartman, Todd K., and Christopher R. Weber. 2009. "Who Said What? The Effects of Source Cues in Issue Frames." *Political Behavior* 31 (March): 537–58.

Heclo, Hugh. 2003. "Ronald Reagan and the American Public Philosophy." In *The Reagan Presidency: Pragmatic Conservatism and Its Legacies*, ed. W. Elliot Brownlee and Hugh Davis Graham. Lawrence, KN: University Press of Kansas.

Herbers, John. 1974. "No Conditions Set." *New York Times*, September 9, 73.

Herbert, Bob. 2001. "Leading America Beyond Fear." *New York Times*, September 24, A31.

Hiatt, Fred. 1998. "The Contrition Campaign." *Washington Post*, September 13, C7.

———. 2001. "America's Attention-Deficit Disorder . . ." *Washington Post*, September 24, A21.

Hill, Kim Quaile. 1998. "The Policy Agendas of the President and the Mass Public: A Research Validation and Extension." *American Journal of Political Science* 42 (October): 1328–34.

Hoagland, Jim. 2001. "Putting Doubts to Rest." *Washington Post*, September 23, B7.

Holmes, David L. 2012. *Faiths of the Postwar Presidents: From Truman to Obama*. Athens, GA: University of Georgia Press.

Howell, William G. 2003. *Power without Persuasion: The Politics of Direct Presidential Action.* Princeton, NJ: Princeton University Press.

Hubler, Shawn. 1998. "Explaining to the Children." *Los Angeles Times,* September 14, 1.

Hulsether, Mark D. 2005. "Like a Sermon: Popular Religion in Madonna Videos." In *Religion and Popular Culture in America,* ed. Bruce David Forbes and Jeffery H. Mahan. Berkeley, CA: University of California Press.

Hurst, Steven. 2004. "The Rhetorical Strategy of George H. W. Bush During the Persian Gulf Crisis 1990–91: How to Help Lose a War You Won." *Political Studies* 52 (June): 376–92.

Hymer, Sharon. 1995. "Therapeutic and Redemptive Aspects of Religious Confession." *Journal of Religion and Health* 34 (Spring): 41–54.

Isserman, Maurice, and Michael Kazin. 2004. *America Divided: The Civil War of the 1960s.* 2nd ed. New York: Oxford University Press.

Jacobs, Lawrence R., and Robert Y. Shapiro. 2000. *Politicians Don't Pander: Political Manipulation and the Loss of Democratic Responsiveness.* Chicago, IL: University of Chicago Press.

Jenkins, Jeffery A., Justin Peck, and Vesla M. Weaver. 2010. "Between Reconstructions: Congressional Action on Civil Rights, 1891–1940." *Studies in American Political Development* 24 (April): 57–89.

Johnson, Haynes. 2001. *The Best of Times: America in the Clinton Years.* New York: James H. Silberman.

Johnson, James Turner. 1999. *Morality and Contemporary Warfare.* New Haven, CT: Yale University Press.

Johnson, Lyndon B. 1963a. "Address Before a Joint Session of the Congress." November 27. http://www.presidency.ucsb.edu/ws/index.php?pid=25988&st=&st1=#axzz1QftZt1Rz (accessed June 29, 2011).

———. 1963b. "The President's Thanksgiving Day Address to the Nation." November 28. http://www.presidency.ucsb.edu/ws/index.php?pid=25999&st=&st1=#axzz1QftZt1Rz (accessed June 29, 2011).

———. 1963c. "Remarks at a Meeting with the AFL-CIO Executive Council." December 4. http://www.presidency.ucsb.edu/ws/index.php?pid=26110&st=&st1=#axzz1RElDmiff (accessed July 6, 2011).

———. 1963d. "Remarks to New Participants in 'Plans for Progress' Equal Opportunity Agreements." December 12. http://www.presidency.ucsb.edu/ws/index.php?pid=26310&st=&st1=#axzz1RElDmiff (accessed July 5, 2011).

———. 1963e. "Remarks at a Candlelight Memorial Service for President Kennedy." December 22. http://www.presidency.ucsb.edu/ws/index.php?pid=26576&st=martyr&st1=#axzz1QftZt1Rz (accessed June 29, 2011).

———. 1964a. "Annual Message to the Congress on the State of the Union." January 8. http://www.presidency.ucsb.edu/ws/index.php?pid=26787&st=&st1=#axzz-1RElDmiff (accessed July 6, 2011).

———. 1964b. "Remarks to New Participants in 'Plans for Progress' Equal Opportunity Agreements." January 16. http://www.presidency.ucsb.edu/ws/index.php?pid=25990&st=&st1=#axzz1RElDmiff (accessed July 5, 2011).

———. 1964c. "Transcript of Television and Radio Interview Conducted by Representatives of Major Broadcast Services." March 15. http://www.presidency.ucsb.edu/ws/index.php?pid=26108&st=&st1=#axzz1RElDmiff (accessed July 6, 2011).

———. 1964d. "Remarks to the Legislative Conference of the Building and Construction Trades Department, AFL-CIO." March 24. http://www.presidency. ucsb.edu/ws/index.php?pid=26127&st=&st1=#axzz1OVMNlaWR (accessed June 6, 2011).

———. 1964e. "Remarks to Members of the Southern Baptist Christian Leadership Seminar." March 25. http://www.presidency.ucsb.edu/ws/index.php?pid= 26130&st=&st1=#axzz1RElDmiff (accessed July 6, 2011).

———. 1964f. "Remarks to New Participants in 'Plans for Progress' Equal Opportunity Agreements." April 9. http://www.presidency.ucsb.edu/ws/index.php?pid= 26144&st=&st1=#axzz1RElDmiff (accessed July 5, 2011).

———. 1964g. "Remarks at a Reception for Members of the American Society of Newspaper Editors." April 17. http://www.presidency.ucsb.edu/ws/index.php?pid= 26166&st=&st1=#axzz1RElDmiff (accessed July 6, 2011).

———. 1964h. "Remarks to a Group of Editors and Broadcasters Attending a National Conference on Foreign Policy." April 21. http://www.presidency.ucsb. edu/ws/index.php?pid=26177&st=&st1=#axzz1OVMNlaWR (accessed June 6, 2011).

———. 1964i. "The President's News Conference." April 23. http://www.presidency. ucsb.edu/ws/index.php?pid=26182&st=&st1=#axzz1RElDmiff (accessed July 6, 2011).

———. 1964j. "Remarks in Pittsburgh at the Steelworkers Union Hall." April 24. http://www.presidency.ucsb.edu/ws/index.php?pid=26188&st=&st1=#axzz-1RElDmiff (accessed July 5, 2011).

———. 1964k. "Remarks to a Group of Civil Rights Leaders." April 29. http://www. presidency.ucsb.edu/ws/index.php?pid=26201&st=&st1=#axzz1RElDmiff (accessed July 6, 2011).

———. 1964l. "Remarks at the 20th Washington Conference of the Advertising Council." May 6. http://www.presidency.ucsb.edu/ws/index.php?pid= 26215&st=&st1=#axzz1RElDmiff (accessed July 5, 2011).

———. 1964m. "Remarks at the Coliseum, Knoxville, Tennessee." May 7. http:// www.presidency.ucsb.edu/ws/index.php?pid=26227&st=&st1=#axzz1OVMN-laWR (accessed June 6, 2011).

———. 1964n. "Remarks in Atlanta at a Breakfast of the Georgia Legislature." May 8. http://www.presidency.ucsb.edu/ws/index.php?pid=26233&st=&st1=#axzz-1RElDmiff (accessed July 6, 2011).

———. 1964o. "Remarks in Atlantic City at a Dinner of the New Jersey State Democratic Committee." May 10. http://www.presidency.ucsb.edu/ws/ index.php?pid=26241&st=&st1=#axzz1OVMNlaWR (accessed June 6, 2011).

———. 1964p. "Remarks in Tribute to President Kennedy at a Joint Meeting of the Cabinet and the National Security Council." May 28. http://www.presidency. ucsb.edu/ws/index.php?pid=26277&st=&st1=#axzz1QftZt1Rz (accessed June 29, 2011).

———. 1964q. "Remarks in Madison Square Garden at a New York Democratic Gala." May 28. http://www.presidency.ucsb.edu/ws/index.php?pid=26280&st= martyr&st1=#axzz1QftZt1Rz (accessed June 29, 2011).

———. 1964r. "Remarks at a Fundraising Dinner in Minneapolis." June 27. http:// www.presidency.ucsb.edu/ws/index.php?pid=26348&st=&st1=#axzz1RElD-miff (accessed July 5, 2011).

———. 1964s. "Radio and Television Remarks upon Signing the Civil Rights Bill." July 2. http://www.presidency.ucsb.edu/ws/index.php?pid=26361&st=&st1=#axzz1VP2mCOza (accessed August 18, 2011).

———. 1964t. "Remarks in the Cabinet Room at the Unveiling of a Bust of John F. Kennedy." November 19. http://www.presidency.ucsb.edu/ws/index.php?pid=26724&st=martyr&st1=#axzz1QftZt1Rz (accessed June 29, 2011).

———. 1965a. "Remarks at the White House Conference on Equal Employment Opportunities." August 20. http://www.presidency.ucsb.edu/ws/index.php?pid=27170&st=isaiah&st1=#axzz1OVMNlaWR (accessed June 6, 2011).

———. 1965b. "Remarks at the Signing of the Highway Beautification Act of 1965." October 22. http://www.presidency.ucsb.edu/ws/index.php?pid=27325&st=&st1=#axzz1OVMNlaWR (accessed June 6, 2011).

———. 1966. "Remarks in Baltimore at the Celebration of the Bicentennial of American Methodism." April 22. http://www.presidency.ucsb.edu/ws/index.php?pid=27558&st=&st1=#axzz1OVMNlaWR (accessed June 6, 2011).

———. 1967. "Remarks at a President's Club Dinner in Los Angeles." June 23. http://www.presidency.ucsb.edu/ws/index.php?pid=28318&st=isaiah&st1=#axzz1OVMNlaWR (accessed June 6, 2011).

Jones, Charles. 1988. *The Trusteeship Presidency: Jimmy Carter and the United States Congress*. Baton Rouge, LA: Louisiana State University Press.

Kagan, Robert. 2006. *Dangerous Nation: America's Foreign Policy from Its Earliest Days to the Dawn of the Twentieth Century*. New York: Knopf.

Kahn, Kim Fridkin, and Patrick J. Kenney. 2002. "The Slant of the News: How Editorial Endorsements Influence Campaign Coverage and Citizen's Views of Candidates." *The American Political Science Review* 96 (June): 381–94.

Kam, Cindy D., Jennifer R. Wilking, and Elizabeth J. Zechmeister. 2007. "Beyond the 'Narrow Data Base': Another Convenience Sample for Experimental Research." *Political Behavior* 29 (December): 415–40.

Kass, John. 1998. "Time for Clinton to Look for Work – And That's No Lie." *Chicago Tribune*, September 14, 3.

Katz, James Everett. 1984. *Congress and National Energy Policy*. New Brunswick, NJ: Transaction Books.

Kaufman, Burton I. 1982. *Trade and Aid: Eisenhower's Foreign Economic Policy, 1953–1961*. Baltimore, MD: Johns Hopkins University Press.

———. 1993. *The Presidency of James Earl Carter, Jr*. Lawrence, KN: University Press of Kansas.

Kearns, Doris. 1976. *Lyndon Johnson and the American Dream*. New York: Harper & Row, Publishers

Keener, Craig S. 1999. *A Commentary on the Gospel of Matthew*. Grand Rapids, MI: William B. Eerdmans Publishing Company.

Kellner, Douglas. 2007. "Bushspeak and the Politics of Lying: Presidential Rhetoric in the 'War on Terror.'" *Presidential Studies Quarterly* 37 (December): 622–45.

Kennedy, John F. 1960. "Speech of Senator John F. Kennedy, Greater Houston Ministerial Association, Rice Hotel, Houston, TX." September 12. http://www.presidency.ucsb.edu/ws/index.php?pid=25773#axzz1USQ66vAo (accessed August 8, 2011).

———. 1961a. "Address in Chicago at a Dinner of the Democratic Party of Cook County." April 28. http://www.presidency.ucsb.edu/ws/index.php?pid=8095&st=&st1=#axzz1USQ66vAo (accessed August 8, 2011).

————. 1961b. "Remarks upon Signing the Housing Act." June 30. http://www.presidency.ucsb.edu/ws/index.php?pid=8216&st=&st1=#axzz1USQ66vAo (accessed August 8, 2011).

————. 1961c. "Address in New York City Before the General Assembly of the United Nations." September 25. http://www.presidency.ucsb.edu/ws/index.php?pid=8352&st=&st1=#axzz1USQ66vAo (accessed August 8, 2011).

————. 1963a. "The President's News Conference." May 8. http://www.presidency.ucsb.edu/ws/index.php?pid=9192&st=&st1=#axzz1USQ66vAo (accessed August 9, 2011).

————. 1963b. "Address in Honolulu before the United States Conference of Mayors." June 9. http://www.presidency.ucsb.edu/ws/index.php?pid=9264&st=&st1=#axzz1USQ66vAo (accessed August 9, 2011).

————. 1963c. "Commencement Address at American University in Washington." June 10. http://www.presidency.ucsb.edu/ws/index.php?pid=9266&st=&st1=#axzz1USQ66vAo (accessed August 9, 2011).

————. 1963d. "Radio and Television Report to the American People on Civil Rights." June 11. http://www.presidency.ucsb.edu/ws/index.php?pid=9271&st=&st1=#axzz1USQ66vAo (accessed August 9, 2011).

————. 1963e. "Special Message to the Congress on Civil Rights and Job Opportunities." June 19. http://www.presidency.ucsb.edu/ws/index.php?pid=9283&st=&st1=#axzz1UdEwHFXo (accessed August 10, 2011).

————. 1963f. "Remarks at a Dinner Given in His Honor by President Segni." July 1. http://www.presidency.ucsb.edu/ws/index.php?pid=9331&st=&st1=#axzz1UdEwHFXo (accessed August 10, 2011).

————. 1963g. "Radio and Television Address to the American People on the Nuclear Test Ban Treaty." July 26. http://www.presidency.ucsb.edu/ws/index.php?pid=9360&st=&st1=#axzz1USQ66vAo (accessed August 8, 2011).

————. 1963h. "Proclamation 3559 – National Day of Prayer, 1963." October 8. http://www.presidency.ucsb.edu/ws/index.php?pid=24120&st=&st1=#axzz1UdEwHFXo (accessed August 10, 2011).

————. 1963i. "Remarks in Philadelphia at a Dinner Sponsored by the Democratic County Executive Committee." October 30. http://www.presidency.ucsb.edu/ws/index.php?pid=9504&st=Bible&st1=labor#axzz1I6ErWkU3 (accessed April 1, 2011).

Kernell, Samuel. 1997. *Going Public: New Strategies of Presidential Leadership.* 3rd ed. Washington, DC: CQ Press.

Key, V. O., and Milton Cummings. 1966. *The Responsible Electorate: Rationality in Presidential Voting, 1936–1960.* Cambridge, MA: Belknap Press of Harvard University Press.

Kierkegaard, Soren. 1964. *Repetition: An Essay in Experimental Psychology.* New York: Harper Torchbooks.

Kiewe, Amos, ed. 1994. *The Modern Presidency and Crisis Rhetoric.* Westport, CT: Praeger.

Kotz, Nick. 2005. *Judgment Days: Lyndon Baines Johnson, Martin Luther King Jr., and the Laws That Changed America.* Boston, MA: Houghton Mifflin Company.

Kraft, Joseph. 1979. "Carter: A Candidate Again." *Washington Post,* July 17, A17.

Krattenmaker, Tom. 2006. "Playing the 'God' Card." *USA Today,* January 29.

Kuhberger, Anton. 1998. "The Influence of Framing on Risky Decisions: A Meta-Analysis." *Organizational Behavior and Human Decision Processes* 75 (July): 23–55.

Kurien, Prema A. 2006. "Mr. President, Why Do You Exclude Us from Your Prayers?" In *A Nation of Religions: The Politics of Pluralism in Multireligious America*, ed. Stephen Prothero. Chapel Hill, NC: University of North Carolina Press.

Langston, Thomas S. 1993. "A Rumor of Sovereignty: The People, Their Presidents, and Civil Religion in the Age of Jackson." *Presidential Studies Quarterly* 23 (Fall): 669–82.

Lawson, Steven F. 1981. "Civil Rights." In *Exploring the Johnson Years*, ed. Robert A. Divine. Austin, TX: University of Texas Press.

Lazarsfeld, Paul, Bernard Berelson, and Hazel Gaudet. 1944. *The People's Choice: How the Voter Makes Up His Mind in a Presidential Campaign.* New York: Duell, Sloan, and Pearce.

Leahy, Patrick J. 1982. "Reality – Or a Caricature?" *Washington Post*, November 28, C8.

Lejon, Kjell O. 2009. "Religion and the Presidency of George H. W. Bush." In *Religion and the American Presidency*, ed. Gaston Espinosa. New York: Columbia University Press.

Lewis, Anthony. 1983. "Onward, Christian Soldiers." *New York Times*, March 10, A27.

———. 1998. "Muddying the Waters." *New York Times*, September 15, 27.

Lim, Elvin T. 2008. *The Anti-Intellectual Presidency: The Decline of Presidential Rhetoric from George Washington to George W. Bush.* New York: Oxford University Press.

Lincoln, Abraham. 1865. "Second Inaugural Address." March 4. http://www.presidency.ucsb.edu/ws/index.php?pid=25819&st=&st1=#axzz1P5WGxsrr (accessed June 12, 2011).

Lopez, Steve. 2005. "Mothers Mourn as the Elite Party On." *Los Angeles Times*, January 21, B1.

Los Angeles Times. 1957. "The President Says He Needs It All." May 22, B4.

———. 1963a. "Warren Lays Assassination to Bigotry." November 23, 6.

———. 1963b. "The President and the Congress." November 29, A4.

———. 1974a. "The Pardoning of Nixon." September 9, D6.

———. 1974b. "President Ford's Pardon of Nixon." September 14, A4.

———. 1979a. "The Scramble Starts." July 17, C4.

———. 1979b. "It Gets Worse." July 20, D6.

———. 1982. "Tempting the Soviets." November 24, C4.

———. 1985. "Bible a Two-Edged Sword in Defense Fight." February 8, B6.

———. 2005. "No Country Left Behind." January 21, B10.

Louis Harris and Associates. 1974a. Survey conducted September 1–September 6. Retrieved from the iPOLL Databank, Roper Center for Public Opinion Research, University of Connecticut.

———. 1974b. Survey Conducted September 23–September 27. Retrieved from the iPOLL Databank, Roper Center for Public Opinion Research, University of Connecticut.

———. 1974c. Survey Conducted November 1–November 4. Retrieved from the iPOLL Databank, Roper Center for Public Opinion Research, University of Connecticut.

Mabley, Jack. 1974. "Too Many Using God's Name Lightly." *Chicago Tribune*, September 13, 4.

MacPherson, Myra. 1976. "Devout 'Minister.'" *Washington Post*, March 21, 1.

Madigan, Charles M. 1998. "About 30% of American Voters Long Disapproved of President Clinton No Matter What He Did. Now It Seems He Has Handed Them Exactly What They Wanted All Along." *Chicago Tribune*, September 13, 1.

———. 2005. "Dancing in the Dark." *Chicago Tribune*, January 23.

Malinowski, Bronislaw. 1948. *Magic, Science and Religion*. Garden City, NY: Doubleday Anchor Books.

Maltese, John Anthony. 2009. "Communications Strategies in the Bush White House." In *Assessing the George W. Bush Presidency: A Tale of Two Terms*, ed. Andrew Wroe and Jon Herbert. Edinburgh: Edinburgh University Press.

Marty, Martin E. 1974. "Ford's Talk of God: Do Religion and Politics Mix?" *Los Angeles Times*, September 15, J4.

———. 1989. *Religion and Republic: The American Circumstance*. Boston, MA: Beacon.

———. 1991. "In a World of Shifting Rationales, Can a War Be Just or Unjust?" *Los Angeles Times*, February 3.

Marty, Martin E., and Jonathan Moore. 2000. *Politics, Religion, and the Common Good: Advancing a Distinctly American Conversation about Religion's Role in Our Shared Life*. San Francisco, CA: Jossey-Bass Publishers.

Mathisen, James A. 1989. "Twenty Years After Bellah: Whatever Happened to American Civil Religion?" *Sociological Analysis* 50 (Summer): 129–46.

Mattingly, Terry. 2004. "Religious Rhetoric Nothing New, Bush Scribe Says." *News Sentinel*, December 18, E2.

Mattson, Kevin. 2009. *"What the Heck Are You Up To, Mr. President?": Jimmy Carter, America's "Malaise," and the Speech That Should Have Changed the Country*. New York: Bloomsbury.

Mayhew, David R. 1991. *Divided We Govern: Party Control, Lawmaking, and Investigations, 1946–1990*. New Haven, CT: Yale University Press.

Maynard, Christopher. 2008. *Out of the Shadow: George H. W. Bush and the End of the Cold War*. College Station, TX: Texas A&M University Press.

McAdams, Dan P. 2011. *George W. Bush and the Redemptive Dream: A Psychological Portrait*. New York: Oxford University Press.

McAuliffe, Terry. 2007. *What a Party! My Life among Democrats: Presidents, Candidates, Donors, Activists, Alligators and Other Wild Animals*. New York: Thomas Dunne Books.

McCarthy, Colman. 1985. "Flight into Biblical Fancy." *Washington Post*, February 16, A23.

———. 1991. "What the Children Understand." *Washington Post*, February 3, F2.

McClellan, Scott. 2008. *What Happened: Inside the Bush White House and Washington's Culture of Deception*. New York: Public Affairs.

McFadden, Robert D. 2001. "Many Listeners Are Reassured by Tough Talk." *New York Times*, September 21, A1.

McGrory, Mary. 2002. "Time to Talk." *Washington Post*, September 15, B7.

McLellan, David, ed. 1977. *Karl Marx: Selected Writings*. Oxford: Oxford University Press.

McPherson, James M. 2008. *Tried by War: Abraham Lincoln as Commander in Chief*. New York: Penguin Press.

Mead, George H. 1934. *Mind, Self and Society: From the Standpoint of a Social Behaviorist*. Chicago, IL: University of Chicago Press.

Means, Richard L. 1970. "Methodology for the Sociology of Religion: An Historical and Theoretical Overview." *Sociological Analysis* 31 (Winter): 180–96.

Medhurst, Martin J. 1993. *Dwight D. Eisenhower: Strategic Communicator*. Westport, CT: Greenwood Press.

———, ed. 2006. *The Rhetorical Presidency of George H. W. Bush*. College Station, TX: Texas A&M University Press.

Meese III, Edwin. 1992. *With Reagan: The Inside Story*. Washington, DC: Regnery Gateway.

Mervin, David. 1996. *George Bush and the Guardianship Presidency*. New York: St. Martin's Press.

Metzger, Bruce M., and Michael D. Coogan, eds. 1993. *The Oxford Companion to the Bible*. New York: Oxford University Press.

Mieczkowski, Yanek. 2005. *Gerald Ford and the Challenges of the 1970s*. Lexington, KY: The University Press of Kentucky.

Milloy, Courtland. 2005. "A Hunger for More than Rhetoric." *Washington Post*, January 23, C1.

Morel, Lucas E. 2000. *Lincoln's Sacred Effort: Defining Religion's Role in American Self-Government*. Lanham, MD: Lexington Books.

Morone, James A. 2003. *Hellfire Nation: The Politics of Sin in American History*. New Haven, CT: Yale University Press.

Morris, Kenneth E. 1996. *Jimmy Carter: American Moralist*. Athens, GA: University of Georgia Press.

———. 2009. "Religion and the Presidency of Jimmy Carter." In *Religion and the American Presidency*, ed. Gaston Espinosa. New York: Columbia University Press.

Mueller, John E. 1973. *War, Presidents and Public Opinion*. New York: John Wiley.

National Opinion Research Center. 1957. Survey Conducted throughout April. Retrieved from the iPOLL Databank, Roper Center for Public Opinion Research, University of Connecticut.

Neikirk, Bill. 1979. "Moral Equivalent of Waffling." *Chicago Tribune*, July 22, A6.

Nelson, Michael. 2010. "Speeches, Speechwriters, and the American Presidency." In *The President's Words: Speeches and Speechwriting in the Modern White House*, ed. Michael Nelson and Russell L. Riley. Lawrence, KN: University Press of Kansas.

Nelson, Thomas E., and Zoe M. Oxley. 1999. "Issue Framing Effects on Belief Importance and Opinion." *Journal of Politics* 61 (November): 1040–67.

Neuhaus, Richard John. 1984. *The Naked Public Square: Religion and Democracy in America*. Grand Rapids, MI: William B. Eerdmans Publishing Company.

Neustadt, Richard E. 1960. *Presidential Power: The Politics of Leadership*. New York: Wiley.

New York Times. 1963a. "Troops at Tuscaloosa." June 12, 42.

———. 1963b. "Racial Assassination." June 13, 30.

———. 1963c. "Civil Rights: 'The Fiery Trial.'" June 16, 148.

———. 1963d. "Equal Rights, Not Politics." June 18, 36.

———. 1963e. "A Day of Prayer Set by President." October 10, 34.

———. 1974a. "The Failure of Mr. Ford." September 9, 34.

———. 1974b. "Pardon for What?" September 10, 40.

———. 1979a. "Riding Casually to War." July 17, A16.

———. 1979b. "Carter Plans Journey on a Riverboat." August 10, A9.

———. 1998a. "The Gloom Around Bill Clinton." September 9, A24.

———. 1998b. "Shame at the White House." September 12, 18.

———. 2002. "The Iraq Test." September 13, A26.

Nieves, Evelyn. 1990. "Thousands March in 16 Cities to Protest U.S. Intervention in Gulf." *New York Times*, October 21, 14.

Nixon, Richard. 1969. "Inaugural Address." January 20. http://www.presidency.ucsb.edu/ws/index.php?pid=1941 (accessed January 20, 2014).

Noonan, Peggy. 2001. *When Character Was King: A Story of Ronald Reagan*. New York: Viking.

Norpoth, Helmut. 2001. "Primary Colors: A Mixed Blessing for Al Gore." *PS: Political Science and Politics* 34 (March): 45–48.

Novak, Michael. 1979. "From the Right: Statist Leaders Are the Problem." *Los Angeles Times*, July 22, F1.

NRSV Standard Bible. 2007. New York: Harper Bibles.

O'Brien, Michael. 2009. *Rethinking Kennedy: An Interpretive Biography*. Chicago, IL: Ivan R. Dee.

Orend, Brian. 2006. *The Morality of War*. Ontario, Canada: Broadview Press.

Pach, Chester J., Jr. 2003. "Sticking to His Guns: Reagan and National Security." In *The Reagan Presidency: Pragmatic Conservatism and Its Legacies*, ed. W. Elliot Brownlee and Hugh Davis Graham. Lawrence, KN: University Press of Kansas.

Pach, Chester, Jr., and Elmo Richardson. 1991. *The Presidency of Dwight D. Eisenhower*. Lawrence, KN: University Press of Kansas.

Page, Benjamin I. 1996. *Who Deliberates? Mass Media in Modern Democracy*. Chicago, IL: University of Chicago Press.

Page, Benjamin I., and Robert Y. Shapiro. 1992. *The Rational Public: Fifty Years of Trends in Americans' Policy Preferences*. Chicago, IL: University of Chicago Press.

Parker, Kathleen. 2001. "All Is Fair in This War Except for Insensitivity." *Chicago Tribune*, September 26, 2001.

Patterson, Orlando. 1998. "What Is Freedom without Privacy?" *New York Times*, September 15, 27.

Pemberton, William E. 1997. *Exit with Honor: The Life and Presidency of Ronald Reagan*. Armonk, NY: M. E. Sharpe.

Perret, Geoffrey. 1999. *Eisenhower*. New York: Random House.

Peters, Charles. 2010. *Lyndon B. Johnson*. New York: Times Books.

Petersen, Clarence. 1974. "Begging Your Pardon, Sir." *Chicago Tribune*, September 13, 12.

Peterson, Tarla Rai, ed. 2004. *Green Talk in the White House: The Rhetorical Presidency Encounters Ecology*. College Station, TX: Texas A&M University Press.

Pew Forum on Religion and Public Life. 2010. "U.S. Religious Knowledge Survey." http://pewforum.org/other-beliefs-and-practices/u-s-religious-knowledge-survey.aspx (accessed March 31, 2011).

———. 2012a. "'Little Voter Discomfort with Romney's Mormon Religion." http://www.pewforum.org/2012/07/26/2012-romney-mormonism-obamas-religion/ (accessed January 15, 2014).

———. 2012b. "'Nones' on the Rise." http://www.pewforum.org/2012/10/09/nones-on-the-rise/ (accessed August 29, 2013).

Pierard, Richard V. 1983. "Reagan and the Evangelicals: The Making of a Love Affair." *The Christian Century*, December 21–28, 1182–85.

Pinkerton, James P. 2002. "We Cried and Remembered Together; North Tower, South Tower, E-Ring, Shanksville Were Our Battlefields." *Los Angeles Times*, September 12, B15.

Pixley, Jorge. 2004. *Jeremiah*. St. Louis, MO: Chalice Press.

Plotkin, Sidney. 1985. "Corporate Power and Political Resistance: The Case of the Energy Mobilization Board." *Polity* 18 (Autumn): 115–37.

Porter, Jennifer E., and Darcee L. McLaren, eds. 1999. *Star Trek and Sacred Ground: Explorations of Star Trek, Religion and American Culture*. Albany, NY: State University of New York Press.

Powell, Colin L. 1995. *My American Journey*. New York: Random House.

Powell, Mark Allan, ed. 2011. *The HarperCollins Bible Dictionary*. New York: HarperOne.

Preston, Andrew. 2012. *Sword of the Spirit, Shield of Faith: Religion in American War and Diplomacy*. New York: Anchor Books.

Prothero, Stephen. 2007. *Religious Literacy: What Every American Needs to Know – And Doesn't*. New York: HarperCollins.

———. 2010. *God Is Not One: The Eight Rival Religions That Run the World – And Why Their Differences Matter*. New York: HarperCollins.

Public Religion Research Institute. 2010. Survey Conducted November 3–November 7. Retrieved from the iPOLL Databank, Roper Center for Public Opinion Research, University of Connecticut.

Putnam, Robert D., and David E. Campbell. 2010. *American Grace: How Religion Divides and Unites Us*. New York: Simon and Schuster.

Quindlen, Anna. 1991. "The Domestic Front." *New York Times*, January 31, A23.

Ragsdale, Lyn. 2009. *Vital Statistics on the Presidency: George Washington to George W. Bush*. 3rd ed. Washington, DC: CQ Press.

Raines, John, ed. 2002. *Marx on Religion*. Philadelphia, PA: Temple University Press.

Ray, James Lee. 1998. "Does Democracy Cause Peace?" *Annual Review of Political Science* 1 (June): 27–46.

Reagan, Ronald. 1981a. "The President's News Conference." January 29. http://www.presidency.ucsb.edu/ws/index.php?pid=44101&st=&st1=#axzz1c5FXSBOM (accessed October 28, 2011).

———. 1981b. "Excerpts from an Interview with Walter Cronkite of CBS News." March 3. http://www.presidency.ucsb.edu/ws/index.php?pid=43497&st=&st1=#axzz1c5FXSBOM (accessed October 28, 2011).

———. 1981c. "Remarks at the Conservative Political Action Conference Dinner." March 20. http://www.presidency.ucsb.edu/ws/index.php?pid=43580&st=&st1=#axzz1c5FXSBOM (accessed October 28, 2011).

———. 1982a. "Address Before a Joint Session of the Indiana State Legislature in Indianapolis." February 9. http://www.presidency.ucsb.edu/ws/index.php?pid=42099&st=defense&st1=#axzz1YJQtDprs (accessed September 19, 2011).

———. 1982b. "Remarks at a Conservative Political Action Conference Dinner." February 26. http://www.presidency.ucsb.edu/ws/index.php?pid=42213&st=&st1=#axzz1cBymMoh (accessed October 29, 2011).

———. 1982c. "Remarks at the National Legislative Conference of the Building and Construction Trades Department, AFL-CIO." April 5. http://www.presidency.ucsb.edu/ws/index.php?pid=42368&st=defense&st1=#axzz1YJQtDprs (accessed September 19, 2011).

———. 1982d. "Address to Members of the British Parliament." June 8. http://www.presidency.ucsb.edu/ws/index.php?pid=42614&st=crusade&st1=#axzz1cBymMohv (accessed October 29, 2011).

———. 1982e. "Address Before the Bundestag in Bonn, Federal Republic of Germany." June 9. http://www.presidency.ucsb.edu/ws/index.php?pid=42618&st=&st1=#axzz1d2FahySK (accessed November 7, 2011).

———. 1982f. "Remarks in Columbus to Members of Ohio Veterans Organizations." October 4. http://www.presidency.ucsb.edu/ws/index.php?pid=43088&st=&st1=#axzz1cBymMohv (accessed October 29, 2011).

———. 1982g. "Address to the Nation on Strategic Arms Reduction and Nuclear Deterrence." November 22. http://www.presidency.ucsb.edu/ws/index.php?pid=42030&st=&st1=#axzz1dms4AaKg (accessed November 15, 2011).

———. 1983a. "Radio Address to the Nation on Defense Spending." February 19. http://www.presidency.ucsb.edu/ws/index.php?pid=40950&st=&st1=#axzz1Y-WljcQN7 (accessed September 20, 2011).

———. 1983b. "Annual Convention of the National Association of Evangelicals in Orlando, Florida." March 8. http://www.presidency.ucsb.edu/ws/index.php?pid=41023&st=&st1=#axzz1ZAK924cS (accessed September 27, 2011).

———. 1983c. "Remarks at the Annual Members Banquet of the National Rifle Association in Phoenix, Arizona." May 6. http://www.presidency.ucsb.edu/ws/index.php?pid=41289&st=&st1=#axzz1YWljcQN7 (accessed September 20, 2011).

———. 1983d. "Remarks at a Cuban Independence Day Celebration in Miami, Florida." May 20. http://www.presidency.ucsb.edu/ws/index.php?pid=41355&st=&st1=#axzz1cBymMohv (accessed October 29, 2011).

———. 1983e. "Remarks at a Dinner Honoring Senator Jesse Helms of North Carolina." June 16. http://www.presidency.ucsb.edu/ws/index.php?pid=41488&st=&st1=#axzz1ZAK924cS (accessed September 27, 2011).

———. 1983f. "Remarks at a Ceremony Marking the Annual Observance of Captive Nations Week." July 19. http://www.presidency.ucsb.edu/ws/index.php?pid=41604&st=&st1=#axzz1cBymMohv (accessed October 29, 2011).

———. 1983g. "Interview with Garry Clifford and Patricia Ryan of People Magazine." December 6. http://www.presidency.ucsb.edu/ws/index.php?pid=40876&st=&st1=#axzz1YJQtDprs (accessed September 19, 2011).

———. 1984a. "Remarks at Eureka College in Eureka, Illinois." February 6. http://www.presidency.ucsb.edu/ws/index.php?pid=39377&st=&st1=#axzz1cBymMohv (accessed October 29, 2011).

———. 1984b. "Remarks at the Annual Convention of the National Association of Evangelicals in Columbus, Ohio." March 6. http://www.presidency.ucsb.edu/ws/index.php?pid=39602&st=&st1=#axzz1cBymMohv (accessed October 29, 2011).

———. 1984c. "Remarks at the Young Leadership Conference of the United Jewish Appeal." March 12. http://www.presidency.ucsb.edu/ws/index.php?pid=39627&st=&st1=#axzz1d2FahySK (accessed November 7, 2011).

———. 1985a. "Remarks to Business and Trade Representatives During a White House Briefing on the Fiscal Year 1986 Budget." February 4. http://www.presidency.ucsb.edu/ws/index.php?pid=37925&st=&st1=#axzz1d2FahySK (accessed November 7, 2011).

———. 1985b. "Remarks at the Annual Convention of the National Religious Broadcasters." February 4. http://www.presidency.ucsb.edu/ws/index.php?pid=37936&st=&st1=#axzz1d2FahySK (accessed November 7, 2011).

———. 1985c. "The President's News Conference." February 21. http://www.presidency.ucsb.edu/ws/index.php?pid=38249&st=&st1=#axzz1d2FahySK (accessed November 7, 2011).

———. 1985d. "Remarks to Private Sector Leaders During a White House Briefing on the MX Missile." March 6. http://www.presidency.ucsb.edu/ws/index.php?pid=38292&st=&st1=#axzz1ZAK924cS (accessed September 27, 2011).

———. 1985e. "Remarks at a Conference on Religious Liberty." April 16. http://www.presidency.ucsb.edu/ws/index.php?pid=38486&st=&st1=#axzz1cBymMohv (accessed October 29, 2011).

———. 1985f. "Radio Address to the Nation on the Strategic Defense Initiative." July 13. http://www.presidency.ucsb.edu/ws/index.php?pid=38882&st=&st1=#axzz1d2FahySK (accessed November 7, 2011).

———. 1986a. "Remarks at the Heritage Foundation Anniversary Dinner." April 22. http://www.presidency.ucsb.edu/ws/index.php?pid=37171&st=crusade&st1=#axzz1cBymMohv (accessed October 29, 2011).

———. 1986b. "Remarks to Marine Corps Basic Training Graduates in Parris Island, South Carolina." June 4. http://www.presidency.ucsb.edu/ws/index.php?pid=37401&st=&st1=#axzz1ZAK924cS (accessed September 27, 2011).

Renshon, Stanley A. 2002a. "'The Polls': The Public's Response to the Clinton Scandals, Part 1: Inconsistent Theories, Contradictory Evidence." *Presidential Studies Quarterly* 32 (March): 169–84.

———. 2002b. "'The Polls': The Public's Response to the Clinton Scandals, Part 2: Diverse Explanations, Clear Consequences." *Presidential Studies Quarterly* 32 (June): 412–27.

Reston, James. 1963. "A Time for Reflection and Vigilant Calm." *New York Times*, June 14, 36.

———. 1966. "What Was Killed Was Not Only the President But the Promise." In *John F. Kennedy and the New Frontier*, ed. Aida DiPace Donald. New York: Hill and Wang.

Ribuffo, Leo P. 1989. "God and Jimmy Carter." In *Transforming Faith: The Sacred and Secular in Modern American History*, ed. M. L. Bradbury and James B. Gilbert. Westport, CT: Greenwood Press.

Rich, Frank. 2002. "Never Forget What?" *New York Times*, September 14, A15.

Rich, Spencer, and Mary Russell. 1974. "Congress Reacts Angrily." *Washington Post*, September 11, A1.

Ricklefs, Roger. 1979. "The Nation's 'Soul.'" *Washington Post*, July 18, A19.

Riker, William. 1962. *The Theory of Political Coalitions*. New Haven, CT: Yale University Press.

Riswold, Caryn D. 2004. "A Religious Response Veiled in a Presidential Address: A Theological Study of Bush's Speech on 20 September 2001." *Political Theology* 5 (January): 39–46.

Ritsch, Frtiz. 2003. "Of God, and Man, in the Oval Office." *Washington Post,* March 2, B3.

Roiphe, Katie. 1998. "Monica Lewinsky, Career Woman." *New York Times,* September 15, 27.

Roof, Wade Clark. 1993. *A Generation of Seekers: The Spiritual Journeys of the Baby Boom Generation.* San Francisco, CA: HarperSanFrancisco.

———. 2010. "From Ronald Reagan to George W. Bush: What Happened to American Civil Religion?" In *America and the Misshaping of a New World Order,* ed. Giles Gunn and Carl Gutierrez-Jones. Berkeley, CA: University of California Press.

Roper Organization. 1957. Survey Conducted throughout March. Retrieved from the iPOLL Databank, Roper Center for Public Opinion Research, University of Connecticut.

———. 1974. Survey Conducted September 27–October 5. Retrieved from the iPOLL Databank, Roper Center for Public Opinion Research, University of Connecticut

Rorabaugh, W. J. 2002. *Kennedy and the Promise of the Sixties.* New York: Cambridge University Press.

Rosenfeld, Megan. 1991. "The President's Preacher." *Washington Post,* January 18, C1.

Rosenthal, A. 1991. "Too Clever by Half." *New York Times,* February 1, A29.

Rosin, Hanna. 2005. "Taking Liberty to Revise Famous Speeches." *Washington Post,* January 25, C1.

Rossiter, Clinton. 1987. *The American Presidency; with a New Introduction by Michael Nelson.* Baltimore, MD: The Johns Hopkins University Press.

Rousseau, Jean-Jacques. 1893. *The Social Contract: Or, the Principles of Political Rights.* London: G. P. Putnam's Sons.

Rowen, Hobart. 1979. "A Hollow Ring." *Washington Post,* July 19, A19.

Royko, Mike. 1991. "Clock Is Running for America's Team." *Chicago Tribune,* February 1, 3.

Rozell, Mark J. 1993. "The Limits of White House Image Control." *Political Science Quarterly* 108 (Autumn): 453–80.

Ryken, Leland, James C. Wilhoit, and Tremper Longman III, eds. 1998. *Dictionary of Biblical Imagery.* Downers Grove, IL: Intervarsity Press.

Safire, William. 1991. "Don't Throw Away Victory." *New York Times,* January 31, A23.

———. 1998. "Starr's Unfinished Business." *New York Times,* September 14, 33.

———. 2005. "Bush's 'Freedom Speech.'" *New York Times,* January 21, A23.

Scheer, Robert. 2005. "1600 Pennsylvania Meets Madison Avenue." *Los Angeles Times,* January 25, B11.

Schieffer, Bob, and Gary Paul Gates. 1989. *The Acting President: Ronald Reagan and the Supporting Players Who Helped Him Create the Illusion That Held America Spellbound.* New York: E. P. Dutton.

Schier, Steven E. 2009. *Panorama of a Presidency: How George W. Bush Acquired and Spent His Political Capital.* Armonk, NY: M. E. Sharpe.

Schmertz, Eric, Natalie Datlof, and Alexej Ugrinsky, eds. 1997. *President Reagan and the World.* Westport, CT: Greenwood Press.

Schmich, Mary. 1998. "Starr Report Goes against Alien Ideals." *Chicago Tribune,* September 13.

Scott, Janny. 1996. "Alger Hiss, Divisive Icon of Cold War, Dies at 92." *New York Times*, November 16, 1.

Sears, David O. 1986. "College Sophomores in the Laboratory: Influences of a Narrow Data Base on Social Psychology's View of Human Nature." *Journal of Personality and Social Psychology* 51: 515–30.

Seelye, Katharine Q. 1998. "Embraced by Forgiving, Clinton Talks of Forgiveness." *New York Times*, August 29, A1.

Shaw, Annick, Stephen Joseph, and P. Alex Linley. 2005. "Religion, Spirituality, and Posttraumatic Growth: A Systematic Review." *Mental Health, Religion and Culture* 8 (March): 1–11.

Shogan, Colleen J. 2006. *The Moral Rhetoric of American Presidents*. College Station, TX: Texas A&M University Press.

Sidel, Victor W., and H. Jack Geiger. 1991. "Trip Wire of Armageddon." *New York Times*, February 5, A23.

Small, Melvin. 1999. *The Presidency of Richard Nixon*. Lawrence, KN: University Press of Kansas.

Smith, Craig Allen, and Kathy B. Smith. 1994a. *The White House Speaks: Presidential Leadership as Persuasion*. Westport, CT: Praeger.

———. 1994b. "The Coalitional Crisis of the Ford Presidency: The Pardons Reconsidered." In *The Modern Presidency and Crisis Rhetoric*, ed. Amos Kiewe. Westport, CT: Praeger.

Smith, Gary Scott. 2006. *Faith and the Presidency: From George Washington to George W. Bush*. New York: Oxford University Press.

Smith, Hedrick. 1964. "Johnson Pleads for Civil Rights at a Reception for U.S. Editors." *New York Times*, April 18, 14.

———. 1979. "Carter, Conscious of Risks, Seeks Wider Audience." *New York Times*, July 14, 1.

———. 1983. "Reagan's Jab at Russians." *New York Times*, March 10, A11.

Smith, Rogers M. 2008. "Religious Rhetoric and the Ethics of Public Discourse: The Case of George W. Bush." *Political Theory* 36 (April): 272–300.

Smith, Timothy B., Michael E. McCullough, and Justin Poll. 2003. "Religiousness and Depression: Evidence for a Main Effect and the Moderating Influence of Stressful Life Events." *Psychological Bulletin* 129 (July): 614–36.

Sonner, Molly W., and Clyde Wilcox. 1999. "Forgiving and Forgetting: Public Support for Bill Clinton During the Lewinsky Scandal." *PS: Political Science and Politics* 32 (September): 554–57.

Spalding, Matthew. 1999. "Making Citizens: George Washington and the American Character." In *Patriot Sage: George Washington and the American Political Tradition*, ed. Gary L. Gregg II and Matthew Spalding. Wilmington, DE: ISI Books.

Stam, Juan. 2003. "Bush's Religious Language." *The Nation*, December 22, 27.

Stanley, Harold W., and Richard G. Niemi, eds. 2011. *Vital Statistics on American Politics 2011–2012*. Washington, DC: CQ Press.

Stephanson, Anders. 1996. *Manifest Destiny: American Expansion and the Empire of Right*. New York: Hill and Wang.

Stepp, Laura Sessions. 1991. "Bush and Saddam's Holy War of Words." *Washington Post*, February 3, A22.

Stern, Mark. 1991. "Lyndon Johnson and Richard Russell: Institutions, Ambitions and Civil Rights." *Presidential Studies Quarterly* 21 (Fall): 687–704.

309

Stevens, Daniel. 2002. "Public Opinion and Public Policy: The Case of Kennedy and Civil Rights." *Presidential Studies Quarterly* 32 (March): 111–36.

Stevenson, Kenneth W. 2004. *The Lord's Prayer: A Text in Translation.* Minneapolis, MN: Fortress Press.

Stout, David, and Jeff Zeleny. 2006. "After Death of a President, Tributes Are Set for Capital." *New York Times,* December 28, 1.

Strober, Deborah Hart, and Gerald S. Strober. 2003a. *The Kennedy Presidency: An Oral History of the Era.* Washington, DC: Brassey's Inc.

———. 2003b. *The Reagan Presidency: An Oral History of the Era.* Washington, DC: Brassey's Inc.

Stuckey, Mary E., ed. 1996. *The Theory and Practice of Political Communication Research.* Albany, NY: State University of New York Press.

———. 2004. *Defining Americans: The Presidency and National Identity.* Lawrence, KN: University Press of Kansas.

Tackach, James. 2002. *Lincoln's Moral Vision : The Second Inaugural Address.* Jackson, MS: University Press of Mississippi.

Taylor, Charles. 2007. *A Secular Age.* Cambridge, MA: Belknap Press of Harvard University Press.

Terrien, Samuel. 2003. *The Psalms: Strophic Structure and Theological Commentary.* Grand Rapids, MI: William B. Eerdmans Publishing Company.

Thimmesch, Nick. 1979. "Mr. Carter on Energy: Sermon Better Than the Program." *Chicago Tribune,* July 20, B2.

Thomas, Michael C., and Charles C. Flippen. 1972. "American Civil Religion: An Empirical Study." *Social Forces* 51 (December): 218–25.

Till, Rupert. 2010. "The Personality Cult of Prince: Purple Rain, Sex and the Sacred, and the Implicit Religion Surrounding a Popular Icon." *Implicit Religion* 13 (August): 141–59.

de Tocqueville, Alexis. 1990. *Democracy in America.* New York: Vintage Classics.

Transcript. Billy Graham Oral History Interview, Special Interview, 10/12/83, by Monroe Billington, Internet Copy, LBJ Library. http://www.lbjlib.utexas.edu/johnson/archives.hom/oralhistory.hom/Graham-B/GrahamB.asp (accessed June 6, 2011).

Tulis, Jeffrey K. 1987. *The Rhetorical Presidency.* Princeton, NJ: Princeton University Press.

Tuveson, Ernest Lee. 1968. *Redeemer Nation: The Idea of America's Millennial Role.* Chicago: University of Chicago Press.

Unger, Irwin, and Debi Unger. 1999. *LBJ: A Life.* New York: John Wiley & Sons, Inc.

Vaughn, Stephen. 1995. "The Moral Inheritance of a President: Reagan and the Dixon Disciples of Christ." *Presidential Studies Quarterly* 25 (Winter): 109–27.

Viorst, Milton. 2002. "The Wisdom of Imaging the Worst-Case Scenario." *New York Times,* September 12, A27.

Wald, Kenneth D., and Allison Calhoun-Brown. 2011. *Religion and Politics in the United States.* 6th ed. Lanham, MD: Rowman and Littlefield Publishers, Inc.

Washington, George. 1789. "Inaugural Address." April 30. http://www.presidency.ucsb.edu/ws/index.php?pid=25800#axzz1Oz7PLcQb (accessed June 11, 2011).

———. 1796. "Farewell Address." September 19. http://www.presidency.ucsb.edu/ws/index.php?pid=65539&st=&st1=#axzz1Oz7PLcQb (accessed June 11, 2011).

Washington Post. 1959. "Image of America." December 4, A16.

———. 1974. "The Presidential Pardon." September 10, A20.

———. 1979. "Carter's Rating Rose Nine Percent after Speech." July 17, A15.

———. 1985. "Letters to the Editor." February 9, A18.

———. 1991. "Philosophers Agree on Criteria for Justifiable War." February 2, G1.

———. 2001. "The Money Trail." September 22, A28.

Watson, W. Marvin. 2004. *Chief of Staff: Lyndon Johnson and His Presidency.* New York: Thomas Dunne Books.

Weaver, Darlene Fozard. 2003. "Taking Sin Seriously." *The Journal of Religious Ethics* 31 (Spring): 45–74.

Weaver, Richard M. 1953. *The Ethics of Rhetoric.* Chicago, IL: Henry Regnery Company.

Weisskopf, Michael. 1990. "Democrats Criticize Gulf Policy." *Washington Post,* November 12, A1.

Werth, Barry. 2006. *31 Days: The Crisis That Gave Us the Government We Have Today.* New York: Nan A. Talese.

White, Ronald C., Jr. 2002. *Lincoln's Greatest Speech: The Second Inaugural.* New York: Simon and Schuster.

Wiedrich, Bob. 1974. "Did Ford Foresee the Pardon Furor?" *Chicago Tribune,* September 12, 22.

———. 1979. "A President's Defeatist Message." *Chicago Tribune,* July 18, A4.

Wilson, Bryan. 1982. *Religion in Sociological Perspective.* New York: Oxford University Press.

Wilcox, Clyde. 1996. *Onward Christian Soldiers?: The Religious Right in American Politics.* Boulder, CO: Westview Press.

Wilcox, Clyde, and Carin Larson. 2006. *Onward Christian Soldiers?: The Religious Right in American Politics.* 3rd ed. Boulder, CO: Westview Press.

Wilcox, Clyde, and Carin Robinson. 2011. *Onward Christian Soldiers? The Religious Right in American Politics.* 4th ed. Boulder, CO: Westview Press.

Wildavsky, Aaron. 1966. "The Two Presidencies." *Trans-Action* 4 (December): 7–14.

Wilentz, Sean. 2008. *The Age of Reagan: A History, 1974–2008.* New York: HarperCollins.

Will, George. 1991a. "Hard Work Avoided." *Washington Post,* January 31, A19.

———. 1991b. "Selective Morality." *Washington Post,* February 3, C7.

Williams, Daniel K. 2008. "Reagan's Religious Right: The Unlikely Alliance Between Southern Evangelicals and a California Conservative." In *Ronald Reagan and the 1980s: Perceptions, Policies, Legacies,* ed. Cheryl Hudson and Gareth Davies. New York: Palgrave Macmillan.

———. 2010. *God's Own Party: The Making of the Christian Right.* New York: Oxford University Press.

Wills, Garry. 1985. "A Way with Words." *The Baltimore Sun,* February 7, 19A.

———. 1990. *Under God: Religion and American Politics.* New York: Touchstone.

Witcover, Jules. 1976. "'Profound' Event." *Washington Post,* March 21, 1.

Wood, B. Dan. 2009. *The Myth of Presidential Representation.* New York: Cambridge University Press.

Woods, Randall B. 2006. *LBJ: Architect of American Ambition.* New York: Free Press.

Woodward, Bob. 1991. *The Commanders.* New York: Simon and Schuster.

———. 2002. *Bush at War.* New York: Simon and Schuster.

Woodward, Kenneth L. 2003. "The White House: Gospel on the Potomac." *Newsweek*, March 10, 29.

Zakheim, Dov S. 1997. "The Military Buildup." In *President Reagan and the World*, ed. Eric J. Schmertz, Natalie Datlof, and Alexej Ugrinsky. Westport, CT: Greenwood Press.

Zaller, John R. 1992. *The Nature and Origins of Mass Opinion*. New York: Cambridge University Press.

———. 1998. "Monica Lewinsky's Contribution to Political Science." *PS: Political Science and Politics* 31 (June): 182–89.

Index